Library

Patrons

With

Disabilities

By

Ray Turner, Ed.D.

ii

Library of Congress Card Catalog Number 96-60755 ISBN Number 0-9653037-0-5

Front Cover Graphic: Courtesy Indiana University.
Back Cover Graphic: Courtesy National Transportation and Safety Board and the American Library Association.

Dedicated To:

Russ Turner,
Professional Musician Who Conquered Barriers
To Information Access and Learned to Love Knowledge.

Michele Turner-Porter, Professional Mom Who Conquered
Fear To Speak the Truth and to Love.

Cynthia Turner, Special Educator, Mother, Wife
Who Learned to Live With and to Love This Author.

Library Patrons With Disabilities

Table of Contents

Library Patrons With Disabilities

Library Patrons With Disabilities

Library Patrons With Disabilities

Library Patrons With Disabilities

Library Patrons With Disabilities

Library Patrons With Disabilities

Library Patrons With Disabilities

x

Library Patrons With Disabilities

Library Patrons With Disabilities

The People's Information Bill of Rights:

All people are entitled to the information and services offered by libraries, clearinghouses, and information centers.

All people are entitled to obtain current and accurate information on any topic.

All people are entitled to courteous, efficient, and timely service.

All people are entitled to the right of confidentiality in all of their dealings with libraries, clearinghouses, information centers, and their staffs.

All people are entitled to full access and service from library and information networks on local, state, regional, and national levels.

All people are entitled to the use of a library facility or information center that is accessible, functional, and comfortable.

All people are entitled to be provided with a statement of the policies governing the use and services of the library, clearinghouse, or information center.

All people are entitled to library and information service that reflects the interest and needs of the community (Information 2000, 1991, page 57).

The guiding principles of these rights will be interpreted in the context of library accommodation for patrons with disabilities as defined by the American with Disabilities Act.

Library Patrons With Disabilities

Chapter One

Why Patrons
Enter
the Library

Patrons with Disabilities
and Their Reasons
for Entering Libraries

Librarians As Gatekeepers

Patrons with disabilities enter 8,000 public and 3,000 academic libraries each day. 88,000 elementary and secondary media centers also serve students with disabilities. More than 2,700 federal and 11,000 private libraries or special collections afford disabled patrons information access.[1] But do all public access libraries in America genuinely welcome patrons with physical or cognitive challenges or effectively meet their information needs each visit? Many libraries may reserve a different welcome to some special-needs patrons solely because of their disabilities.

Professional librarians are the physical and information gatekeepers for much of the information this nation can provide its people. Librarians control access to library information and are information gatekeepers to all who enter. Barriers to equal information access must be removed in the library for special-needs patrons. Librarians must provide reasonable accommodation to any patrons experiencing physical or information barriers.[2] Librarians either choose to provide reasonable accommodation or, at the other extreme, tend to ignore special-needs patrons. Some librarians serve patrons differently solely on their basis of their obvious disabilities. Professionals either facilitate equal information access and library barrier removal for the disabled or continue to maintain library constraints that limit equal information access. Library architectural barrier removal is also controlled by librarian gatekeepers. It is not just the library information that can be given or withheld. Librarians also control library access through tolerance or intolerance for the disabled. There are fundamental differences between library gatekeepers along the accommodation continuum. Let us reflect on what collection access and accommodation needs disabled information stakeholders have outisde and within their library.[3]

Patrons As Information Stakeholders

Patrons empower themselves as information stakeholders to meet personal information needs. Everyone who seeks access to public library information is an information stakeholder. But not everyone is a patron with disabilities who may be uniquely challenged to gain equal information access in the library like nondisabled patrons. Information stakeholders have a self-interest in, and a need for, information not personally owned but publicly available from the collection. Disabled information stakeholders are a diverse group with complex information and access needs often complicated by physical or cognitive challenges. Sometimes an individual's disabilities create a barrier to the library collection. At other times the disabled experience library barriers not yet removed. Equal information access, which may be already provided to those without disabilities, may not necessarily also be assured for individuals with disabilities.

Disabled information stakeholders are a diverse group with complex information and access needs often complicated by physical or cognitive challenges.

The Library Special-Needs Access Hierarchy

Maslow described a hierarchy of five major human needs as principle motivating factors for all human behavior. Do these needs also drive patron library behavior?[4] Maslow's theory is a virtual library information stakeholder definition schema.[5] The hierarchy includes physiological, safety, belonging and love, self-esteem and self-actualization needs. (See Figure 1-1).

Need to Self-Actualize

Need for Self-Esteem

Need for Belonging & Love

Safety Needs

Physiological Needs

Figure 1-1. Maslow's Hierarchy of Need.

Information stakeholders enter the library with these Maslow-defined needs or for other unspecified reasons. The needs hierarchy or schema cannot be exhaustive explaining all reasons patrons seek library information or why they choose to be information stakeholders. Some reasons for library entry are unknown. Others suggest stakeholders with disabilities display library behavior differs from their stated reasons for coming to the library. The United States Congress Office of Technology Assessment (OTA) (1990) suggested a relationship between Maslow's hierarchy of information stakeholder needs and patron reasons for entering the library:

> Communication and communication technologies are basic to all that an individual does. The following...examines the uses of technology in a whole range of activities that, together, might contribute to the individual's meeting all of the basic needs as defined by Maslow. The activities... include:
>
> ---education and self-improvement
> ---counseling and psychological support
> ---recreation and leisure, entertainment and self-expression
> ---social interaction
> ---economic participation
> ---personal business
> ---controlling and manipulating technology mediated interactions, and
> ---overcoming barriers to physical mobility (Office of Technology Assessment, 1990, page 216).

Proactive and Reactive Librarians

Librarian gatekeepers adjust to stakeholder needs for a diverse clientele. Librarians have their own hierarchy of professional needs met in part by the patrons they help. To the proactive librarian, patrons with disabilities are viewed as entering individuals with special needs. The existing library service system does not provide enough information that bears on how patron needs can be librarian-adapted. The disabled may be viewed by proactive librarians as absolutely worthy of being helped. Yet librarians may remain unclear as to what librarian-provided accommodation needs are relevant.

To the proactive librarian, patrons with disabilities are viewed as entering with individual special needs. For the reactive librarian, patrons with disabilities enter and bring problems either to be solved or ignored.

For the reactive librarian, patrons with disabilities enter and bring problems either to be quickly resolved or ignored. The reactive librarian views the disabled as a professional responsibility overload. The library is considered as already having services in place that meet disabled people's information needs. This professional considers providing conventional orientation and support will be enough and fully expects the disabled patron to get information independently or get out of the library. Differences between proactive and reactive librarians may be most obvious when considering how to provide effective library services for patrons with disabilities.[6]

Information Stakeholder Identifiers

From a proactive librarian viewpoint, information stakeholder identifiers may indicate why patrons enter the library and what their information needs are after entering:

Infoactualizers	**Self-Actualization Needs**
Infoproducers	**Self-Esteem at Work Needs**
Infosearchers	**Self-Esteem Using Information Needs**
Infosocializers	**Belonging and Love Needs**
Infosurvivors	**Safety and Physiological Needs**

Figure 1-2 New Terms for Special-Needs Library Patrons

Information stakeholders enter the library based on five major information need categories. Infosurvivors seek library information to meet overriding physiological and safety needs. They want information that provides safe refuge, solves personal safety issues and provides them temporary respite. Infosocializers want personalized, face-to-face, library-based social interaction from librarians and other patrons. Infosearchers gain personal library information contributing to self-esteem, self-improvement, recreation, leisure, entertainment, or self-expression but may lack specific information search strategies. Infoproducers develop products out of collection information for economic reasons, for personal business or self-directed education, viewing information as a commodity. Infoactualizers use the collection as a basis for information quests.[7] All information stakeholders exist within this framework except patrons who have no stated reason for entering or who exhibit random library behavior. Some who have no reason for library entry and no apparent survival, socialization, or work-related information are just "there." But if "just there," they typically do not stay long.

> **Infosurvivors require immediate information-- not from books, but from the librarian.**

Infosurvivors: Patrons Needing Immediate Library Response

Infosurvivors[8] require immediate information--not from books, but from the librarian. These information stakeholders are desperate. Abstract information fails when librarian gatekeepers face people entering only with physical or safety needs. Some patrons come off the streets and into the library in a panic. Reactive librarians ignore the needs of the homeless until they pass through the library portal. Their needs are so diverse that even proactive librarians become quickly discouraged and retreat from entering infosurvivors. When infosurvivors enter they become an immediate librarian responsibility and cannot be ignored.

Library Patrons With Disabilities

No Shirt, No Shoes, No Service

A family of unregistered aliens encamps at the rear of a public library building in a Texas border town in a shady, cool, wooded spot invisible from local police and the U.S. Border Patrol. A child is sent to the library foyer to sell family handmade weavings brought from Mexico. The foyer resembles a village marketplace but no one there is selling, trading, or bartering. Ignored by library traffic, the child begins to beg for food from the few who enter the library. The library administrator is informed about the begging child. This problem has happened before. The administrator calls the police. The reference librarian hears of the call and leaves her post for the foyer, subjecting herself to certain administrative disciplinary action. She speaks in fluent Spanish with the youngster. The child takes the librarian to the family encampment behind the library.

Police quickly arrive. The reference librarian translates the father's statements as he attempts to reconcile the situation. The police prevail. The family is moved to the local police station. Immigration and Naturalization Service (INS) agents take them into custody within the hour. Impounded in an INS facility for medical exams, they are inoculated and given minor health services. The mother is eight months pregnant. She wants her baby to be born in America. They are deported within three days on an INS bus back to the Federal Republic of Mexico. This confirms the head librarian's need in strict library policy for handling illegal aliens. The incident is reported in the reference librarian's personnel file for unspecified future disciplinary action. The library administrator considers the inexperienced reference librarian, a native Del Rio, Texas resident, as "newly trained, liberal, and misguided." The sign on the library door does not say WELCOME. It does not reveal in Spanish "SPANISH SPOKEN HERE." It says, "NO SHIRT, NO SHOES, NO SERVICE." The child in the foyer had no shoes.

Child and Adult Infosurviors

Children entering the library as infosurvivors include the homeless--there without parents, families, shelter, or food. Children need survival information from library gatekeepers and they need it immediately. Child welfare is the responsibility of all. We will not tolerate children not sheltered or safe.[9] Library gatekeepers must respond. Librarian proactivity or reactivity is simply irrelevant with children.

Adults entering the library have physiological needs to be met there, like everyone else. An adult infosurvivor's principal need is survival, not information. If the librarian's information deals directly with survival, the patron will be interested. Infosurvivor's needs are immediate and pressing.[10] They do not want the abstract information librarians often provide. Yet while entering the library to overcome physical barriers, they receive incidental librarian counseling and psychological support.[11] From some librarians, they receive outright rejection.

Infosurvivors are often street people, the homeless.[12] Their only need may be to drink at public library water fountains or use public restrooms or find temporary shelter from inclement weather. Some remain for extended periods, relocating from the street into the library until they offend by threatening others or becoming a "public nuisance." Some offend no one. A few may conflict with others, including other competing infosurvivors. Librarians call authorities to expel and exclude them from further library entry when "threatening others" or "exhibiting self-destructive behavior." Other librarians ask them to leave only when the library must close.

Infosurvivors are often street people, the homeless. Some remain for extended periods, relocating from the street into the library until they offend by threatening others or becoming a "public nuisance."

Adult infosurvivors entering the library have unresolved safety or shelter needs. Adults may be mentally threatened, perceiving themselves without shelter or protection. Disoriented infosurvivors do not know how to safely return to supervised living settings, group homes or residential treatment centers. The elderly become lost or disoriented during library visits. Initial library searches are forgotten, leaving the elderly in a panic to recall their location and reason for being in the library. Nursing home residents remember the library building but cannot recall how to return home. Some may be recently deinstitutionalized library patrons not oriented to the community:

> People in group homes or independent living programs frequently have been removed from large, highly structured, isolated institutional settings. They may be severely disabled people who need an attendant or skilled nursing care on a permanent basis or they may be individuals moving toward independent living who are using the group facility to receive support and counseling while in transition. A third category includes people who prefer to, or who are advised to, remain in a sheltered environment while still participating in noninstitutional activities...they have two things in common: First, they are people who have been, or would be in other times, out of sight and locked up for most or all of their lives; second, they are people we as librarians are not accustomed to dealing with. In all other ways they are individuals with distinct personalities and requirements. They may be friendly or mistrustful; patient or impatient; angry or good humored; likeable or irritating; perceptive or insensitive; self-aware or oblivious; arrogant or humble; socialized or awkward; verbal or silent...The disabled are very much like the rest of us, although they may need special response based on their individual disabilities (Zipokowitz, 1990, page 56).

Patrons with severe mental retardation and the mentally ill are infosurvivors with many reasons for frequenting the library. The physically threatened enter the library to escape real or imaginary threats or to avoid loneliness. Adult infosurvivor social interaction varies from being disruptive, assaultive, or threatening to withdrawn, fearful and threatened. At best, infosurvivors enter the library using media to relax, relieve tension or fatigue, to kill time, to avoid boredom and lonelinesss, or to evade social conflict or psychological problems.[13] At worst, they loiter in the library until physically expelled. Adult infosurvivors come to the library primarily for counseling and psychological support. They misjudge librarians for counselors rather than information facilitators. Facing safety and shelter challenges, infosurvivors seek public-access libraries and personnel for human interaction and personally interpreted information. But they are desperate. And that desperation breeds contempt. Personal information is perceived to resolve shelter, safety and survival needs even if asked in quiet desperation. Answers must come from librarians immediately:

Adult infosurvivors come to the library primarily for counseling and psychological support.

> A 1983 Harris Poll found that three out of five adults say they feel under great stress at least once a week. Problems with marriage or intimate relationships are the most frequent reason people seek help, followed by depression; relationships with co-workers, parents or children; lack of self-esteem or feelings of insecurity; substance abuse, personality or character disorders; and sexual problems (Office of Technology Assessment, 1990, page 218).

Infosurvivors overcome physical mobility barriers to survive using public access library resources. After gaining library access they are often not welcomed. Reactive librarians call the police. Proactive librarians leave their desks and go outside to determine what, if any, resources the library can bring to bear.[14]

Library Patrons With Disabilities

Gatekeepers and the Community Support Network

Librarians as gatekeepers are a part of a community support network. Network knowledge is life-saving, life-protecting infosurvivor information. Networked community support links people and services to infosurvivors. Public or private network members are ready, willing and able to help. Referral by librarian gatekeepers and the linkage with community support systems result in shared responsibility and resources provided to meet infosurvivor needs.

Help comes from churches and private agencies. Infosurvivors are assisted quietly without public fanfare. Publicity can be damaging to homeless families and children. Press recognition and emotional appeals for public help provide no sustained assistance after community sympathy has been temporarily aroused. Librarians know the community and the sustained adjustments provided beyond library mission statements and scarce library resources. Some librarians care and do help. Others insulate themselves from further intervention, effort and networking. Comprehensive infosurvivor needs can be overwhelming. It is understandable that some librarians avoid the infosurvivors. Infosurvivors do not fit the traditional "library patron" role.

Infosurvivor First Aid

Sometimes infosurvivors enter the library needing first aid. Hypothermia, heat exhaustion or heat prostration may combine with malnutrition, dehydration and disorientation for anyone under severe weather conditions. The homeless are particularly vulnerable to these immediate health-threatening conditions. First aid for entering infosurvivors is linked to other community emergency services. Certification in first aid is a standard service for all public workers and is an immediate appropriate librarian response to patron need. Patrons given first aid are removed from the library in emergency vehicles or by the police. As a public service facility, the library also is expected to respond similarly to personal mental health crises. Reporting child abuse or neglect is a librarian responsibility. Children who are hungry, sick, tired, lost or separated from parents require immediate assistance.

Public Library Infosurvivors

Public libraries in urban, suburban, and rural or sparsely populated settings receive a diverse walk-in clientele. Some walk-ins are infosurvivors. Adult infosurvivors are usually pedestrians or public transit users. Infosurvivors enter libraries for personalized information from librarians, not from books. How librarians provide this information and how they deal with adult infosurvivors and their conflicts with others may be significantly different, based on library setting, community expectations and infosurvivior tolerance. There is a difference in tolerance among librarians for patrons who do not fit the traditional library patron role. Library tolerance for infosurvivors is also based on whether librarians assume a reactive or proactive approach.[15]

Referral by librarian gatekeepers and the linkage with community support systems result in shared responsibility and resources provided to meet infosurvivor needs.

There is a difference in tolerance among librarians for patrons who do not fit the traditional library patron role.

Library Infosurvivor Tolerance

Differences in library infosurvivor response are based on library setting, community expectations and library tolerance for patrons seeking physical, mental or emotional shelter.[16] Walk-ins to public libraries in urban, suburban, and rural settings enter with diverse human needs and library use purposes. Library building location or characteristics give infosurvivors a reason to enter. Infosurvivors within walking distance use the library as any other public building to meet shelter or safety needs. Their contact with librarians may be minimal since many use public facilities and do not seek specific shelter or safety information.

No Solicitors

A small, rural Southwestern Oklahoma village uses a National History Site Registery home, donated to the community, as a public library. The rural librarian knows all of 3,000+ villagers and their extended families who have moved to larger communities over the past thirty years. Rural America is in major transition. Most library patrons are surrounding farm dwellers or "gentleman farmers" remaining in the village. Other residents commute many miles to work in a regional city where nonagricultural work can be found. An elderly stranger enters the village library attempting the sale of "old, rare books." He is persistent, adamant that the librarian examine his texts. He will not leave after being repeatedly and courteously refused. The librarian finally relents. After examining the collection, one first edition copy reveals a dedication to a local farm family written in the frontispiece. Rejecting purchase, and seeing no way to cause the elderly man to leave, the librarian demands that the stranger depart and threatens to summon the police. She blurts out "WE RESERVE THE RIGHT TO REFUSE SERVICE TO ANYONE!"

The deputy sheriff assigned to the village district is summoned by the librarian as the elderly man walks quickly for the main highway. He runs when the patrol car nears with lights flashing. The deputy picks up the "vagrant" who could not produce a driver's license or identification. Return to the village in the police car, the elderly man becomes highly agitated. The deputy knows the village has no jail. So he takes his "suspect" to the local nursing home, where he requests the home administrator to "restrain, perhaps sedate" the man even though procedures call for a physician to authorize any sedation. Many nursing home residents dress in street clothes and "wander into the library from the nursing home." This is the deputy's statement to the nursing home administrator, reflecting a prejudice against nursing home residents who wore institutional dress in earlier years.

All nursing home residents were not personally known by the deputy. The deputy viewed the "suspect" as a transient and a village troublemaker to be temporarily detained. The nursing home is the major industry for the town, serving many area residents and employing most of the village adults. The deputy telephones the farm family named in the first edition text proffered to the librarian while the nursing home director calms the gentleman without restraint and without sedation.

Differences in library infosurvivor response are based on library setting, community expectations and library tolerance for patrons seeking physical, mental or emotional shelter.

The call to the family listed in the book frontispiece reveals they were recently visited by a retired university history professor whose habits, while eccentric, were entirely legal. He had purchased several first edition books from them and had conducted an extensive interview with the locally prominent family. The deputy releases the professor "on his own recognizance" once he had become more calm. The librarian, now off duty, apologizes at the nursing home to the gentleman and, determining him to be harmless, drives the man home to the city. Shallow driving and passenger conversation followed their route to his urban address at first. But the librarian, in the process, came up with a win-win idea. The professor emeritus' attempt to "sell old, rare books" was actually a ploy to interview the librarian about local history, the real reason for his visit. During the drive home, he eventually apologized for his first edition sales approach without thinking to discuss local history with the librarian. The librarian later proved to be a rich source of local history information to meet his needs. The rural librarian's response to patron information needs had been the critical factor that kept the professor from moving to the local history discussion. The librarian did not have the "time to talk" with her busy schedule. Yet he was the sole patron in the library at the time. And she did not make "time" to carefully listen during the drive. The professor was visually impaired and never able to drive, so he had no license. He regularly hitchhiked to area towns for historical interviews and to purchase or trade first editions with the "locals." In retirement his lifetime professional skill were maintained as an avocation and deep interest in local history.

After reflection, the librarian implemented her information plan. Within three months, the professor was picked up again by the same deputy who had first detained him. This time the entire village held a day-long picnic in his honor. The professor, with portable cassette recorder, secured several valued local family interviews. The picnic/book sale brought other first edition dealers to the historically-rich community. Book sale proceeds were contributed toward the professor's retirement fund. Any books not purchased were donated to the village library. The professor now has a lifetime local library pass and village historical information access. He has been repeatedly invited to lecture at the rural community school concerning local history, people and events. The same people come to hear all about themselves as an ongoing community event. Regularly an honored guest at family gatherings, the professor is served dinner along with equally generous portions of local history. And he gives back to his audiences what he has received in "local color." Each of the listeners can identify with his presentation and take pride in their village history. This proactive process began when the librarian changed her mind about being too busy to talk to a patron, left her station after shift, took a personal risk, and helped a elderly stranger.

Supercrips

Jerry was an active and militant member of a wheelchair rights group whose activities included staging "wheel-ins" or "sit-ins" at various public facilities in a Western state metropolitan area. They privately called themselves the "Supercrips." They regarded themselves as a "militant group with disabilities." Several other wheelchair users joined Jerry in entering a regional public library to assess its accessibility from the wheelchair users' perspective. They

This proactive process began when the librarian changed her mind about being too busy to talk to a patron, left her station after shift, took a personal risk, and helped a elderly stranger.

The library director refused to respond to television interviewers' questions about library architectural barriers or compliance with the recently enacted Americans with Disabilities Act.

did not like what they found. Restrooms for both sexes on the library main floor lacked accessible stalls, roll-under access washbasins, towel dispensers to be reached from a sitting position and other architectural barriers. A host of other architectural and procedural barriers were quickly identified and obvious to people from a seated position. The Supercrips did not discuss or point out architectural barriers or other negative findings with any librarian at any time. Nor did they seek redress of grievances with the library director. Instead, they returned to the library main entrance and blocked doors by positioning electric wheelchairs, switches off, brakes set, at all entryways. Several hours of negotiation followed with the library administrator. Each Supercrip remained in place, refusing to move. Normal library traffic flow was completely disrupted; no one could enter or leave by publicly accessible doorways.

A local television crew had been invited to the preplanned Supercrip event and videotaped the incident, interviewing Jerry and fellow wheelchair users where library barriers were reported, with media attention, in detail and substance. The library director refused to respond to television interviewers' questions about library architectural barriers or compliance with the recently enacted Americans with Disabilities Act. Police were summoned to the library doorways. All Supercrips were arrested. Other patrons had been forced to enter through nonpublic access loading docks, thereby "disrupting the general public from use of the library," according to the stated complaint made by the library director to the police. Each Supercrip was bodily lifted, in wheelchair, and placed in conventionally-equipped police vans in full camcorder view. Their trip to the police station showed significant architectural barriers existed for special-needs detainees even in the public detention area. Because no barrier-free detention facilities were available in the city, arraignment was immediate after transport to the county court room. Each Supercrip was provided immediate release "on a personal recognizance bond." Audible derisive statements made before the judge by several Supercrip defendants were ignored. With court hearing dates set, each Supercrip was met by private or public accessible van and returned to his home at court expense. Courthouse restrooms and drinking fountains were inaccessible. The courtroom used for the hearing was moved to the main floor since other courtrooms on upper floors were wheelchair-inaccessible.

Before departure some Supercrips discussed meeting later for a "wheel-in" at the courthouse steps. This staged event, initiated by the Supercrips and covered by television and newspaper media, was broadcast on the local evening news. Reporters were publicly in sympathy with Jerry and his Supercrip colleagues. The library administrator was not interviewed then or subsequently by any television or newspaper reporter. No police, court or library interviews were permitted by the television station manager since Supercrips, as defendants, and the library, as the complaining party, were "in litigation."

Academic Library Infosurvivors

At academic libraries, security and walk-in clientele-access to public restrooms, telephones, water fountains and elevators are in the context of a larger campus environment. Academic libraries have closed or open policies for nonstudents, even nonstudents with disabilities; limited building access hours; and campus police or security to monitor library occupants. Faculty and students have privileged access to library collections. Secondary access is provided to the general public. Members of the general public with disabilities have no exclusive right to access academic collections over the rights of other general public members. The academic community holds unique expectations and standards regarding visitor, patron and student library behavior. General public library patrons with disabilities are expected to comply. Only disabled academic students are given the highest library service priority.

Academic libraries provide an institutionally-defined public service tolerating users, not library abusers.

Academic libraries provide an institutionally-defined public service tolerating users, not library abusers.[17] Intolerance in academic libraries leads to infosurvivors being designated as vagrants or as a public nuisance, and ultimate removal for patrons who do not fit the traditional library patron role. Academic police or security guards monitor library occupants, reducing infosurvivor walk-ins. Access to public restrooms, telephones, and water fountains is limited and inherently conditional on institutionally defined "appropriate library behavior." Patrons are moved out when loitering or disturbing others. Closed- or open-campuses limit library building access hours for all, reducing infosurvivor library time. The few adult infosurvivors entering academic libraries are removed and escorted off campus, where they are remanded to community law enforcement authorities. Colleges and universities are themselves small communities with subcultural expectations, holding community standards for visitor, patron or student behavior. Urban academic libraries may have a larger infosurvivor clientele. But some infosurvivors do not fit the traditional role even with disabilities.

Infosurvivors come to academic or postsecondary libraries for information about, or as a direct means to obtain, safety and shelter. Some infosurvivors come with disabilities that affect their library stay or reason for gaining personally-relevant information. Academics may be very infosurvivor-tolerant based on previous experience serving the diverse needs of the general public as a secondary goal to serving academic community needs. Serving patrons with special needs is a secondary library goal to serving the needs of the academic community. Guests or visitors are allowed to use campus libraries to meet personal safety and shelter needs. Some nonstudents have recognizable disabilities. Campus shelter is provided for students and faculty but not for adult infosurvivors, with or without apparent disabilities. Unauthorized campus visitors are a major concern. They may be perceived by the academic community and by campus security as a safety threat to students and employees. Disabled people can be just as threatening to students and employees as unauthorized threatening visitors without disabilities. Infosurvivor threatening behavior on campus is the issue, not patron disabilities.

Some infosurvivors receive counseling or support group services provided by academic or community agencies using campus facilities. These infosurvivors may have invisible disabilities and no apparent reason for nontraditional behavior exhibited on campus. If their client status is known by academics, their behavior can be better tolerated by campus security. But their status as clients requires anonymity and privacy between therapist and client, reducing campus security information to only the patron-observed campus behavior. As academic counseling clients, often used as subjects for counselors in training, they have a legitimate reason to be on campus during group services, but no reason to remain. Infosurvivors on campus for counseling services are tolerated, but their after-hour on-campus presence will not be tolerated when status changes from visitor to vagrant. No special status is provided after-hour visitors with disabilities. After-hour on-campus disabled guest presence must also be authorized by the academic community.x

Service Animals in the Library

Harold, a blinded Vietnam veteran, lived in a Veterans Administration community sheltered home. Part of his weekly activities included, through community outreach, his attendance at a local public college Post-Traumatic Stress Disorder (PTSD) support group, offered by the University Student Veterans Group. The service was not restricted to University student veterans but was extended to include area nonstudent veterans. The PTSD student group met at the college library on Monday evenings in a meeting room that opened to the outdoor library commons after-hours or into the library during library hours. Library workers could secure collection gates without disturbing anyone when the meetings extended beyond the library closing time. An open-air library commons area linked meeting rooms with doorways to the outside world.

Happy, a service animal, always accompanied Harold to PTSD meetings. He sat next to Harold and regularly barked through the meeting room window at passersby visible in the library commons. Support group conductors found that closing the meeting room door reduced Happy's response to canine-defined "intruders" visible through meeting room windows or transparent safety glass doorways. Drapes were also drawn during meetings to reduce Happy's barking. Happy was nonetheless frequently distracted by anyone outside or within the meeting.

At meeting breaks, Harold would take Happy to the outside parking area to meet the dog's personal needs, but not always on a regular or timely basis. Several incidents occurred when the animal could not refrain from soiling the meeting room carpet. Happy, an elderly dog, sometimes left a trail from meeting room door into the outdoor library commons. Harold seemed unaware of his animal's health status or Happy's propensity to incontinence. When accompanying Happy to the library commons, his master would not allow the animal to move onto grass to relieve himself. Instead, he kept Happy close by on the sidewalk. Happy would use every opportunity to relieve himself in the library commons area where NO PETS ALLOWED and KEEP OFF THE GRASS signage could be read by everyone but dog and master.

Harold's mobility orientation skill and training as a legally blind person was provided by the Veteran's Administration. Orientation did not reduce his discomfort and anxiety when negotiating grassy areas with the dog. He limited movements to library walkways. Overhead dangers such as tree limbs along the walkway, library signage and an outdoor kiosk for community event messages were significant commons barriers unless Harold stayed to the walkway.

Harold, a chain smoker, was not aware of the NO SMOKING signage in library meeting rooms. No tactile library signage was provided in public meeting rooms but was prominently posted elsewhere in the library and at all doorway entrances. Braille signage was provided only in public meeting room doorways within the library. Harold could not read Braille, like many other patrons with low vision developing legal blindness after war injury. The outdoor library commons was the only de facto designated NO SMOKING AREA in or near the building. No interior library DESIGNATED SMOKING AREA was available for smokers. No PTSD group member chided Harold for smoking or indicated NO SMOKING signage to him. Library staff ignored PTSD meeting events in general, considering the need for privacy in counseling to be paramount, compared to PTSD member compliance with library smoking rules--particularly in a public meeting area.

Weekly PTSD meetings were emotionally intense. Encounters between support group members were planned, even encouraged. Happy became more aggressive toward others during those encounters even after leaving the meeting area and leading his master into the outside library commons. In two incidents, college students were bitten by Happy as they walked past Harold on their way into the library commons area. Harold, unable or unwilling to control Happy's aggressive behavior, could only move the dog away from unseen pedestrians after they were bitten.

Several students did not report close encounters with the service animal, preferring to allow Harold and Happy to go their way as a "blind person and seeing-eye dog."

Student complaints went unresolved by library administrators. Several students did not report close encounters with the service animal, preferring to allow Harold and Happy to go their way as a "blind person and seeing-eye dog." Others regarded themselves somehow "prejudiced toward the disabled" or "not politically correct" if they chose to complain to library authorities. Following stressful meetings for both man and dog and occasional encounters with university students, Harold would carefully make his way back to his sheltered home with Happy, unaware of any serious canine misdeed, while proudly demonstrating his personal "community mobility for the blind."

During meeting breaks and before library closing, Harold and Happy would "tour" the library, loudly complaining to the attentive, almost over-solicitous, on-duty reference librarian about the limited talking book special collection. Harold's forays into the library from the public meeting rooms and complaints concerning the paucity of talking books were recorded by each librarian on duty, according to ADA-specified library policy. Library administration allocated additional funds for the next fiscal year to purchase talking book titles and services, as a direct response to Harold's noted demands. Harold was invited to suggest specific titles for the special collection. He ignored these requests, perhaps gaining more satisfaction from complaining than by resolving the basis for his complaints. He seemed most comfortable complaining to the librarian on duty. In Harold's world, negative social interaction with attentive librarians was better than no verbal interaction at all with library workers, his "personal public servants." Having fully exhausted the local talking book collection, he expected new titles to be available each week in conjunction with PTSD meetings. No new talking books was the basis for Harold to continue his vociferous complaints. Librarians were hesitant to confront Harold about Happy's behavior and considered Harold's behavior in not complying with library commons rules to be within "tolerable limits." No action was ever taken against Harold, support group members or Happy. The library administration's apparent decision was to ignore the incidents with students in the library commons. Student problems with Happy were never officially logged as "incident reports" by overly tolerant library staff. Happy eventually died of natural causes, leaving Harold unable to attend further PTSD meetings. The Veteran's Administration arranged for another service animal and scheduled a two-week stay for Harold in New England to secure and train on-site with another dog. The evening before plane departure, Harold committed suicide.

Public School Media Center Infosurvivors

School media centers, as public entities, must comply with the ADA in all services, programs or activities, including services open to parents and the public with disabilities.[18] Media centers may provide separate, readily-accessible outside entrances during after-school hours and over school vacation periods. Public access must always minimize risk to students, faculty and staff.[19] Exhibit spaces and meeting rooms are publicly available on an equitable basis, including disabled guests and community disability groups.[20]

Yet some people may be unwelcome in the school library or media center. School authorities may not tolerate unauthorized adult presence or media center use during regular school hours while permitting adult after-hour library use. In this instance, disability status of adults is irrelevant to policy decisions for library access.

School board policy usually reflects community infosurvivor tolerance. Some infosurvivors may check out books and sell them for street value. Others return them faithfully. Some treasure books, returning titles faithfully even when information they contain assists with personal survival and may be continuously needed. But the primary purpose for school media centers and children who are infosurvivors suggests:

> Society has a duty to protect children from abuse and abandonment. The first approach, we believe, must always be to help families help themselves. Often this means temporary help in managing their daily lives: money to buy groceries or pay the rent, or a temporary homemaker to offer respite care while a parent recovers from an illness or looks for a job. Sometimes, families require more structured support and services, such as counseling, substance abuse treatment, and emergency assistance. But when these forms of help are insufficient to enable parents to manage their lives and care for their children, society must ensure that children are protected...Accordingly, society must take every precaution to ensure that parental abuse and neglect do not become an excuse for community abuse and neglect. (National Commission on Children, 1991, page 72).

Students with Disabilities Physical Well-Being

A mixed child infosurvivor group can be observed in the media center. Childhood hunger is partially offset by federally-supported school breakfasts and lunches.[21] Qualified students receive meals at reduced or no cost. School lunch eligibility is based on family size and income criteria. Some children eat only what they bring to school. Others eat only at school. Child infosurvivors may be part of families receiving Aid to Families with Dependent Children (AFDC) or Women, Infants and Children Food Supplements (WIC). Bringing no lunch to school leads some to extort other students' lunch tickets, boxes or money. Media center librarians witness this extortion process between student "haves" and have-nots." Librarians must intervene. Child infosurvivors are required by law to attend school. Their school media center reading interests may be limited to cookbooks, food illustrations and "happy family" themes. Children who are not fed at home eat their only daily meal at school. Hungry children are not effective learners. Food information requests are a child infosurvivor indicator and present librarians the opportunity to informally interview students. These children wistfully observe library food displays or food group bulletin boards, quietly refusing to interact. "Latchkey" students remain well past school hours to "read," with no supervision at home and the librarian serving as an after-school caretaker.[22] The librarian is left doubtful about the family situation. The child feels self-blame and recrimination. Librarians feel guilty even observing such students, though few would willfully ignore children in need.[23] The children often weaken or starve over summer, Christmas, and other school breaks. For some, school breaks are not respite but a time to endure. There seems to be no satisfactory answer to these conditions within reach of school librarians.

> **Infosurvivors are generally not welcome who come to the corporate library not for information but to meet personal safety and shelter needs.**

Private Library Infosurvivors

Infosurvivors are generally not welcome who come to the corporate library not for information but to meet personal safety and shelter needs. The few adult infosurvivors who enter a private collection usually find library gatekeepers there quickly to remove them. Under ADA, private libraries are not responsible for providing personal adjustments to infosurvivors. Inappropriate librarian reactions to patrons with disabilities can be alleviated or avoided by a common-sense and courteous approach:

> 1. Be aware of body language or nonverbal cues, especially with communicative disorders; (2) Focus on the person, not the disability; (3) Approach the patron with respect, acceptance, and warmth as opposed to disapproval or reserve: (4) Avoid pity; (5) Offer assistance as one would to any other patron displaying some difficulty using the library; (6) Know the library's collections and services in terms of the special needs of disabled patrons; ...Reference librarians need to make a conscious effort to offer assistance early during the contact...and be prepared to gracefully accept either a polite or resentful declination (Allegri, 1984, 69).

Private libraries are small communities with visitor, patron and employee behavioral expectations and standards. Private collection gatekeepers may not be tolerant of infosurvivor patrons or allow them to be infosurvivor tolerant. In many corporate libraries, patrons may use collection information but not charge titles. Over 11,000 private, special or corporate libraries offer restricted public access, limited hours and building security. When private libraries provide public accommodation, they also must comply with ADA

tribal libraries are fully supported by federal information-access policy.[26] Passage of the Americans with Disabilities Act in 1990 significantly changed policies applying to private libraries and patrons with disabilities who visit there for information about shelter and personal safety needs.[27] Corporations affording public access to private collections have open or closed buildings, limited access hours, and security to monitor library occupants. Library security, and access for walk-in clientele to public restrooms, telephones, and water fountains is defined by corporate policy. Corporate policy is based on liability insurance coverage which distinguishes between employees and the general public. Employees with disabilities have separate rights, under the Americans with Disabilities Act, from those guaranteed to the general public patrons with disabilities.[28]

Private, religious, or corporate library sponsors have clearly defined behavioral expectations and standards for those who wish to access their collections. General public infosurvivors may not understand or demonstrate appropriate behavior, violating private library standards. They may not fit the traditional private library patron role. Private library behavioral rules or standards may often be implied but not clearly stated. Behavioral rules may be assumed by the librarian and only voiced to noncomplying patrons when they are asked or told to leave. By then, knowing the library rules is "too little, too late." Infosurvivors may not be tolerated, based on corporate culture, public relations policy or public access restrictions. Public access restrictions and walk-in clientele dress and behavioral standards are enforced by library security officials, who control access to elevators, restrooms, telephones, and water fountains. Public relations policies for private collections require accessible public facilities but dissuade suspicious or nonconforming persons from entering.

Infosurvivors may not be tolerated, based on corporate culture, public relations policy or public access restrictions.

Quiet in the Library, Please!

Paul, a 56-year-old adult schizophrenic, was moved from a Southwestern mental health facility to a group home within walking distance of a major state university. Near the university campus, the private Collection of Southwestern Photography (CSP) library provided fee-based public collection access. As a community service CSP provided reduced fees to university students and to persons over 50 years of age. Age was the basis on which Paul was eligible to access the collection. As a percentage of usable income, Paul paid a higher proportionate than anyone entering the private library. But he paid without complaint and spent many happy hours without incident in the CSP collection. He was well known by CSP librarians and posed many carefully thought-out questions. Through the library he had several times contacted notable regional photographers and had accompanied them on photo opportunities. Paul's therapist had encouraged desert flora photography as a hobby since Paul's low self-esteem and behavior problems were associated only with distant family members. Paul's photography interests and behavior at CSP were considered part of his therapeutic milieu. His nearby community-based group home was required to periodically reevaluate resident medications to maintain state and federal Medicaid reimbursement. Reviewing Paul's medications, it was necessary to stop his prescriptions for two weeks while noting any behavioral changes in his "milieu." That included CSP attendance without notice given to any CSP librarian. If no behavioral degradation occurred without medication, then each client, like Paul, was no longer eligible for continuing prescriptions. As a cost reduction measure, Medicaid required the prescription withdrawal interval for all clients. The nationwide policy proved to be misguided for many people requiring medication who, like Paul, had to be taken off their drug regimen. They had to endure, to survive.

Why Patrons Enter the Library

Librarians at CSP noted Paul's immediate behavioral changes from noticeable mild irritability on the first day to extreme auditory hallucination episodes in the days following. Paul no longer asked questions, became confused, could not remember or negotiate his way through the CSP collection. He began asking library staff sexually offensive questions. A week after regular, almost uneventful attendance for more than two years, Paul exhibited intolerable levels of private library behavior. Several continuing and repeated episodes during that next week resulted in Paul being forcibly removed from CSP and escorted back to the group home by the police. There were many other distraught clients at the same group home during that time besides Paul. And no one at CSP understood the reasons for such dramatic behavioral change in Paul.

Established CSP library policy for discount passes for retired patrons accepted post office box numbers and did not require telephone numbers, since many elderly CSP patrons lived at nursing homes, or were retired and living at homes without telephone service. The character of many discount pass holders had changed over the years, placing people like Paul in a private library policy grey area. CSP librarians had latitude to approve or reject discount passes based on their professional judgment. The policy was considered an example of "enlightened service to at-risk patrons." Concerned CSP librarians then had only a post office box address for Paul, which made contact at his residence difficult. They tracked down Paul's group home supervisor and telephoned, only after interviewing the police shift captain and gaining authorized access to the police CSP incident report as the complaining party. No charges were filed against Paul by CSP board of director decree, based on CSP librarian recommendations. Board and librarian strategy for Paul was to "wait and see" on his return to CSP after resuming his medication. Once Paul resumed medication he also resumed daily CSP library visits without incident. He still visits the library regularly to pursue his love of desert flora photography. He has taken several photo trips with local experts and advanced hobbyists. He is well-liked by others even though his dress and personal hygiene on outings and at library-sponsored meetings are tolerable but substandard. Paul's dream is to have his photographs displayed at CSP. CSP librarians are working on a private exhibit of his work.

Librarian Training For Patrons At-Risk

Schools of Information and Library Science may not train professionals to acclimate patrons in distress such as providing for their safety and shelter needs. Librarian training lacks recognition of patron at-risk needs that do not fit the traditional library patron role. Infosurvivors are, by definition, at-risk. Library patrons may be in distress and at-risk for many reasons. Librarians are not provided the counseling training or resources to support infosurvivor mental health issues. Professional librarians-in-training experience first-hand failure to meet infosurvivor needs. It may be considered in professional library circles as a legitimate "training experience" to fail with a number of patrons at-risk. Most librarians remember their early failures better than their early successes, particularly when remembering patrons with disabilities who are at-risk, who do not fit the traditional patron role. Professionals have found many patron at-risk needs to be beyond library resources. Librarians have subsequently defined library mission statements to exclude patron at-risk support services. But many of the infosurvivors at-risk may also be disabled patrons whose needs must be addressed in formal library mission statements, goals and objectives. Mission statements are ADA-driven, not librarian tolerance-driven.

A week after regular, almost uneventful attendance for more than two years, Paul exhibited intolerable levels of private library behavior.

Library Patrons With Disabilities

Patrons cannot be excluded from library services solely on the basis of their disabilities.[29] Yet librarians can meet patron personal safety and shelter information needs, even those of disabled infosurvivors. Federal library policy guidelines recommend specific approaches to enhance library and information services for the disadvantaged, including proactive information service outreach and training initiatives for the traditionally under-served.[30] The right to access public libraries has been clearly established for patrons with mental or physical challenges.[31] It is important that librarians recognize these patron rights and avoid excluding patrons who are not students or faculty and who have disabilities.

Infosurvivor Mental Health Issues

Patron mental health issues may be ignored by librarians or such patrons may be referred to community mental health agencies. Patrons who express mental health needs to librarians may be responded to in a variety of ways, many of them inappropriately. Yet professionals can direct the mentally ill to the library collection concerning independent living, personal health skills and self-care, money management, home management, consumer information and community mobility.[32] Deinstitutionalized patrons may simply require librarian directions to public transportation, bus schedules, recreation and leisure activities, library sponsored arts programs and similar information.[33] Infoshelters may require only a library bulletin board or signage interpretation or directions to library services. Surely these support services are within library means.

Library entry without clear information requests and librarians who ignore patron needs, may lead infosurvivors to remain when libraries close. They are quietly removed at closing, or turned over to community law enforcement authorities. The mentally ill in the library are considered to be at-risk patrons with disabilities:[34]

> Disabled patrons can have bad moods, be tired, unhelpful, or unpleasant just as easily as able-bodied patrons. Disabled persons recommend that librarians not accede to excessive and unnecessary demands and not let persons making such demands prejudice the librarian against other disabled persons (Allegri, 1984, page 66).

Infosocializers

Infosocializers are patrons in public-access libraries who come for recreation and leisure, entertainment and self-expression or library-based social interaction. They are social information stakeholders. Their "reading habit" may be accompanied by other library habits that are socially unacceptable to library gatekeepers. By abusing library rules or behavioral standards, they cause great concern to librarians who supervise them during self-reported, ostensibly "information-related" library visits.

Infosurvivors on campus for counseling services are tolerated, but their after-hour on-campus presence will not be tolerated when status changes from visitor to vagrant.

Infosocializers are patrons in public-access libraries who come for recreation and leisure, entertainment and self-expression or library-based social interaction.

Infosocializers seek verbal interaction with librarians and may not attempt or complete personal information searches. Their verbal interaction may be restricted only to other library infosocializers. They under-use, occupy or limit library resource access to others without using the collection themselves. Some require intensive library supervision while others pose no behavior management challenges. Infosocializers clearly focus conflicts between library stakeholders and gatekeepers, between information seekers and information providers.

When infosocializers seek information they usually access library mass media print sources. The Office of Technology Assessment (OTA) suggested that patrons may be television viewers who find friendship and intimacy in mass communications systems by developing "relationships" with media personalities.[35] To the extent such media personalities are represented in library collections, infosocializers require public access to that information. Patron socialization alone is not a primary library mission, though many libraries recognize socialization as an important library use side-effect or by-product. The central question remains: "What is effective or ineffective patron use of libraries?"

Public Library Infosocializers

Public libraries form an integral part of community social life. Infosocializers attend community library social activities or use library areas to socialize. Art displays, public speakers, self-help groups and similar community library social events reflect public needs and interests and may be of primary interest to infosocializers with disabilities.[36] Many people have a valid reason to enter libraries without directly accessing the library collection. So do disabled infosocializers. How public librarians tolerate infosocializers and their conflicts with others depends on how they under-use or misuse library resources.

Mrs. Smith

Mrs. Smith recovered from a near-fatal vehicle accident that left her permanently disfigured from third-degree burns. Several fingers missing, neck and face disfigured, blind in one eye and now hearing-impaired, it was a struggle for her to "go public" again, even to return to regular library visits and resume a lifelong library reading habit. A college graduate and an avid reader before the accident, Mrs. Smith reentered the library by attending assembly or "all-purpose" room lectures. Public lectures implied that assembly would be conducted largely in the dark with projected films or slides, thus providing her with assumed anonymity. These lectures gave her an opportunity to visit the library without personal librarian contact, and to escape before lectures ended when house lights were raised. Because of her accident-imposed low vision, she required seating in the front row to focus on the speaker, the lectern and the projected views from slides or videos. The library had recently installed a high-technology closed-loop system for the hearing-impaired which Mrs. Smith used without interacting with librarians during each lecture, bringing her own personal assistive equipment. Wearing a scarf and dark glasses and an overcoat, she avoided removing outer garments. But to view the screen or the lectern area she had to remove the dark glasses, replacing them with special distant-viewing refraction lenses, serving her remaining functional vision. Her appearance was unsettling to many lecture audience members and even to the presenters. Several complained to professional librarians on duty following public meetings. A few presenters suggested the library screen guests more carefully so as not to disrupt the presentation.

Art displays, public speakers, self-help groups and similar community library social events reflect public needs and interests and may be of primary interest to infosocializers with disabilities.

Mrs. Smith fit the traditional role not as a library patron, but as a lecture-viewing guest with disabilities. As an exemplary guest at all presentations, she never asked questions of the presenter nor turned to hear questions from the audience since turning would reveal her disfigurement. The closed-loop system did not pick up audience questions but only lectern-area output. She was left with only the presenters' answers to questions from the floor. Mrs. Smith always replaced viewing glasses with other dark ones before rising and exiting, usually before the meeting ended. Many would quietly comment to librarians concerning Mrs. Smith's hallway appearances before and after presentations, using terms such as "hideous," "freak," "appalling." Others, more diplomatic at the surface, referred to her with "unfortunate," "tragic," or "disconcerting" epithets. Some no longer returned to presentations because of her disfigurement and informed the librarian accordingly. The library administrator and board of directors took no action against Mrs. Smith and ignored all subsequent audience and presenter complaints concerning her disconcerting appearance. There was no legal basis others to complain, and no misbehavior on her part ever warranted asking her to leave or not return. Mrs. Smith continues to attend library lectures regularly.

> **There was no legal basis others to complain, and no misbehavior on her part ever warranted asking her to leave or not return.**

Academic Library Infosocializers

Academic library buildings, collections and services as well as library-based social events form an important collegiate culture emphasizing faculty, staff and student socialization. Members of the public, including infosocializers not associated with higher education, are welcome to attend library social events. Because academic libraries are major community cultural centers, some infosocializers enter with entertainment and socialization expectations and avoid directly accessing the library collection. For some with disabilities, the library is a rich social environment. But many others with disabilities find themselves isolated from the academic library.[37]

Each college or university has a closed or an open campus, limited library access hours, and security that monitors campus occupants during library social events. Library social events on open campuses have limited hours and preplanned special events security. Campus safety is at all times an issue for faculty and students. During library social events, general public safety is also a concern. Infosocializers become entangled with campus security or library meeting gatekeepers only when campus or library rules are violated. During library social events, infosocializers are considered the general public and are library information stakeholders.[38] Some academic libraries provide patron after-hour escort service to parking or public transit loading zones.

> **Each college or university has a closed or an open campus, limited library access hours, and security that monitors campus occupants during library social events.**

Academic librarians are often infosocializer tolerant. Yet undergraduate or graduate infosocializers may not exhibit information skill or maturity when library resources are under-used, or misused, tying up equipment, services and personnel. Casual infosocializers come into conflict with more resolute information seekers who must access the collection and may need immediate library help. Professional librarians are wise to offer "first come, first served" attention to all patrons and to avoid designating some as infosocializers and others as more worthy of immediate library support. For acting out infosocializers, academic librarians offer the "first observed, first removed" behavioral constraint.

In academic libraries, infosocializers are not well liked by a student majority who, with limited time and academic deadlines, require quick service. They are known as "infobarriers" or "frivolous searchers" by others waiting for library help and are seen as "wasting" librarian time. These terms derive from patrons viewing other patron library motivations and do not necessarily reflect the views of librarians, who are there ostensibly to serve all.

ADA-Man

The largest single source of library service complaints ever generated during one academic year was by a university student in an electric wheelchair who was known informally among library staff as "ADA MAN." His habit and statement was to "demonstrate my right of priority access to all library facilities and services." His approach was to wait for heavy traffic times at any library service. For example, he rolled to the online public access catalog (OPAC) station showing the International Symbol for Accessibility. There he would demand immediate, priority access. Other nondisabled students were already waiting or using the library's single, wheelchair-accessible OPAC terminal. Even longer waits were occurring at other OPAC terminals not designated as wheelchair or "handicapped-accessible." Students in line for OPAC would usually move away and wait at other busy terminals in deference to ADA-man's loud priority access demands. The designated OPAC terminal showed the sign: PLEASE GIVE PRIORITY ACCESS TO THE DISABLED. If they did not move, he would insist that the library administrator "give me access here and now!" He would, after rolling up to the OPAC designated accessible terminal, not use OPAC. Instead, he would wait for 5 to 10 minutes. If no other student protested or complained to the librarian on duty while waiting for ADA-man, he would simply leave the library. Any complaints would keep him there indefinitely.

In all incidents when immediate access was not provided or another student did not defer, ADA-man would file a formal written complaint before leaving the library. He knew well the route to the library administrator's office where complaints were filed. The complaint was regarding his failure to "immediately access a _____ service that was designated by the International Symbol for Accessibility." ADA-man believed the accessibility symbol gave him first personal priority to library services and equipment over all other library patron needs.

At other times he would roll his wheelchair through all library stack aisles. When a book cart, step stool or aisle-sitting browser was encountered blocking "his way," he would loudly demand immediate object or student removal. If the student sitting in the aisle quickly moved away, ADA-man would silently patrol other aisles, waiting for the next wheelchair access blockage. ADA-man would file a written complaint whenever an aisle was blocked for any reason, citing wheelchair access issues. ADA-man viewed physical library access to be the highest priority for the disabled. The disabled were "different, special."

During the academic year there was no single instance where ADA-man ever checked out a book, used reserve collections, studied or read in the library, or used any library equipment. His only "library equipment use" was to regularly ride the accessible elevator. He found no irregularities or dissatisfaction with elevator service except in one instance, when the elevator emergency phone did not provide a dial tone. So he struck the elevator emergency button mid-floor, sounding the alarm throughout the library. But no emergency phone service could be made to the elevator car after ADA-man ripped out the phone from its compartment during that incident. University police, with librarian help, removed him safely from the elevator. The elevator emergency phone receiver was later found disconnected and reinserted in the compartment. The phone was replaced by opening hours the next day, with restored dial-tone service maintained thereafter.

The university Office of Disabled Students responded to each of ADA-man's written complaints by letter, following up with phone calls to him and to the specific university services about which he had complained. All complaints were reported directly to the Provost. No Provost action was taken against ADA-man, except to place him on academic probation when his grades warranted that action. He was notified of academic

Library Patrons With Disabilities

probation exactly as other students with the same status were notified. He elected to attend another university the following year.

We miss ADA-man. His forays, while irritating to many, revealed many legitimate university architectural and service barriers and service policies and procedures that could not be foreseen by anyone other than a person in a wheelchair or at seated level in the library. Separate university responses to each of his complaints and the resulting incident reports exceeded one hundred man-hours during that academic year. Response time estimates to correct identified barriers and service inaccessibility exceeded more than 300 man-hours across the university. Yet we are a better academic library and campus because of ADA-man.

School Media Center Infosocializers

School infosocializers relate to peers and librarians for print and nonprint information in a social context. Socialization is a side-effect or by-product that occurs while print and nonprint information is found. Infosocializers have an interpersonal library learning style, gaining information access through discussion, lectures with question-and-answer periods, film and television.[39] They are there ostensibly for study or homework but socialize without print or nonprint information gain. Many do not do well in accessing library print information. Socialization skill deficits reflect on library-use maturity. Willingness to seek library information, if only for social purposes, may be a primary library goal for younger patrons.

Professionals encourage patrons to begin a "library habit."[40] Library skills are taught by professional librarians, who use the media center as an effective classroom to meet diverse and complex information needs.[41] Media center attendance and the "library habit" may be required by instructor or librarian. Students resistant to required library visits may at other times voluntarily go to the library for infosocialization. Student attendance only for infosocialization in the embryonic stages of the library habit is better than no library attendance. Infosocializers are welcome in school libraries. But the more library-skilled and information-focused patrons conflict with the less-focused. In media center classes a majority may pursue social ends, not library print information. Infosocializers may lack infosearching skill or be unwilling to undergo systematic library searches. Socialization wins out over collection access. Infosocializers may have significant reading problems that preclude print access redirecting them to nonprint collections, or only to library socialization with others.

Jeb the Library Bully

Jeb had an invisible library-context disability. He effectively disguised it while in the school library. His disability was most apparent only when attempting to read. Classroom teachers knew of his severe reading difficulties. But his learning disability could not be observed anywhere else in the school. And the librarian was not informed by regular or special educators of his exceptional status. His deficits in reading comprehension, spelling, written expression and problem-solving were severe. Reading deficits were more apparent to his teachers until the librarian noticed that no reading was taking place during library visits. His social skill deficits were most apparent and very problematic for the school librarian. He sought library books with themes and content much more immature than his chronological age. Inconsistent in book choice, he sheepishly indicated that immaturity to the librarian by one day selecting a "baby book," as he termed it. Yet he chose a book far above his functional reading level during the next media center visit. There seemed to be no pattern to his book choices or areas of interest, emphasis, themes, subjects or authors. His charging was solely for print information. Nonprint information was ignored. This puzzled the librarian who thought that Jeb would prefer to browse through the audiovisual collection.

Jeb was more focused on others in the library than on any print or nonprint information. He would not "tune in" to other student conversations nearby until any subject with which he was familiar was introduced. Then he would dominate the conversation, disallowing others from presenting their views. Students resented his domineering approach and would not associate with him in the library or elsewhere. Jeb became known among students as the "library bully."

Always late to the library, Jeb gave quick verbal excuses for not being able to arrive before the bell without a pass. On rare occasions when a pass was issued for his late library arrival, the librarian noted that Jeb could not read and would not comment on pass content. Librarian pressure to read library signage or directions for equipment use resulted in his refusal to ask for that equipment ever again. Charging books, opening vertical files, even looking through maps would often cause Jeb to suddenly leave the library without a return pass. If he did not leave, he would sit and protest any adult request to search further for any library information. He also refused to be read-to aloud.

Specific title assignments were given to Jeb by his classroom teacher. But only the librarian could find these books for him lacking any cooperative searching efforts from him. Peer library helpers or his classmates were treated offensively. His rare on-task behavior came only in spurts when the librarian directly intervened with adult-selected print information. Jeb did not independently find print information without librarian adjustments.

As a severely learning disabled student, only a systematic effort between librarian, regular and special educators helped Jeb use the library effectively.

His only library on-task behavior was to slowly copy verbatim from reference sources when given a classroom writing assignment. He had very poor penmanship and could not read aloud or silently the notes he had copied. He often misused library computers. Jeb preferred to play performance game software and avoided any computer programs requiring reading. Programs requiring thoughtful keyboard responses received only input jibberish. As a severely learning disabled student, only a systematic effort between librarian, regular and special educators helped Jeb use the library effectively. His gradual library success began by checking out pre-selected videos. This was followed by next-day interviews with the librarian concerning content, story sequence, characters and significant events.

Jeb later learned to successfully use talking books. Special collection access was developed by rehearsing the route from classroom to talking book shelving. Jeb was unable to read library signage or operate equipment. He still does not read, but now uses the library more effectively for entertainment and life enrichment with librarian support.

The Library Mission

The library mission is to meet information needs of a diverse patron population including non-readers, persons with disabilities and others who may require extensive library accommodation.[42] Infosurvivors and infosocializers have special library adjustment or support needs and are entirely dependent on personalized library help to find information. They may not develop library research skills. With additional skill, clearly defined information needs, refined library research strategies, and library support, infosocializers evolve to infosearchers.

Library Patrons With Disabilities

Infosearchers

Infosearchers enter the library to find print and nonprint information by accessing the collection. They gain information contributing to self-esteem, self-improvement, recreation, leisure, entertainment, and self-expression.[43] They may need library support provided by professional librarians. Infosearchers with disabilities have diverse library needs. Useful library adjustments to meet specific personal information search requirements are requested by the patron.[44] They have specific reasons for their library visits. Among them may be a search for information that builds self-esteem.[45] Reading for pleasure or for specific information brings many to the library, there to demonstrate the "library habit."

Acquiring library-based information increases the self-esteem and self-worth of infosearchers as information managers.[46] Infosearch skills are the basis for empowering everyone in the Information Age.[47] Librarians provide education and self-improvement to help infosearchers control and manipulate technology-mediated interactions through which they gain information.[48] The library is a social environment, a potential job placement site, and the source of inexpensive, lifelong recreational, informational, and educational opportunities.[49] And infosearchers are there ready to take advantage of those library opportunities.

Stuart and Bill, the Video Nerds

Stuart was the public library's highest single videocassette borrower, checking out and returning the maximum number allowed. He returned titles on time and rewound. He never borrowed the same video twice. The circulation librarian informally asked how Stuart liked a particular video he had returned. The librarian expected an excited or even a critical video review. Stuart would not respond. He could not recall or recognize any of the videos recently borrowed. But the librarian pursued the conversation no further.

Bill, a best friend, often accompanied Stuart to the library video collection. Bill checked out many titles on his own, but not as many as Stuart. Bill returned several video titles late, and a library fine was assessed. Fine payment required that Bill show a valid ID to continue student videotape-borrowing privileges. Stuart's borrowing privileges as a student were never challenged since he never had a late return fine. Bill's ID indicated he was a a student at the junior college with a part-time work-study job as a film lab worker.

Both Stuart and Bill began to return borrowed videos after the due dates and in the outside book return where video returns were prohibited. Video returns to circulation followed by librarian visual inspection were required during regular library business hours. No home contact telephone number and only a community college address and number were provided. The library required video borrowers to provide an ID with a local phone number to establish financial responsibility. A daytime query at the college phone number provided for both Stuart and Bill connected the librarian directly to the film production lab where a professor employing both students answered. Stuart and Bill had intended that they would be the only ones to answer the phone during normal business hours to prevent their supervisor from answering.

The professor questioned both Stuart and Bill and received no specific response from them concerning their overdue videos. As a faculty member, and in good faith, he offered to pay his student workers' library fines since "they were destitute." His query and their lack of satisfactory answers made him suspicious. He checked for other missing videos---titles not delivered to the community college library from the lab, and ultimately, videos not returned to the college library. The film lab received all new titles from shipping, verified their quality and returned damaged videos before forwarding the rest to library cataloguers. This was part of Bill and Stuart's job at the college.

Bill and Stuart were found to have been late in returning videos to the college library and in forwarding new titles from the film lab. The professor walked in on them eventually while using the film laboratory after-hours to pirate videos. College film laboratory copy equipment included dual videocassette recorders with an illegal video stablizer connection brought in each evening. But they left it overnight one time before the lab opened allowing the professor to discover the stabilizer the next day. The video stabilizer was removed and impounded. They had copied entire videos checked out from the public and college libraries or received for processing through the college film lab. The professor presumed that titles not clearing the film lab and as yet not delivered to library cataloguers also may have been misappropriated by the two since there was a continuous discrepancy between library video purchase orders filled and videos received.

Stuart and Bill were not closely supervised by the professor, since college requests for video production services had been met regularly. As they had produced, edited and distributed several excellent projects. They were the college's entire video production staff. And both were "exemplary student workers" until this discovery. Since video pirating was a serious federal offense, and repeated illegal copying a felony, both the public library administrator and the community college dean of students sought legal advice. Attorneys for both libraries suggested that further legal work would be required if a search warrant was to be issued. Both suspects lived with their parents. Lawyers suggested documenting titles loaned from both libraries to Stuart and Bill over subsequent months until term end. Stuart and Bill's videotape borrowing patterns went to zero at both public and college libraries during intersession and summer term, when neither were work-study employed. Stuart and Bill were reassigned to other, separate work-study positions "without prejudice" the next term. They had no subsequent access to the college film production laboratory. Stuart no longer borrows videos from either library. Neither does Bill. Borrowing privileges at both libraries were withdrawn until overdue fines were paid. And those fines were substantial. No further action was taken by either the public library or the college administration. Missing college video titles were never recovered. But the VIDEO NERDS were out of business.

Infohitchhikers: Electronic Library Patrons

Infohitchhikers are another infosearcher variant who use electronic library-accessible information sources via telephone, computer modems, electronic bulletin boards, online public remote access catalogs and databases.[50] These infohitchhiker sources are telephone accessible during or after library public-use hours, outside the library building, and can be accessed relatively anonymously.[51] Since technology may assist in overcoming physical barriers to library information, there may be many infohitchhikers with disabilities. But knowing the disability of any infohitchhiker is almost impossible. Central to infohitchhiking is their sophisticated telephone access capability:

> Today, a telephone subscriber can have a touch-tone service, custom-calling services, measured service, wide-area calling, speed-dialing, cellular service, and any number of other features. A bibliographic search can be done in the card catalog--the old-fashioned way--or via one of several different computer databases, containing either citations only or full copy. A text message can be sent via paper mail, electronic mail, facsimile, or overnight courier. In short, the range of communications options is [now] much wider (Office of Technology Assessment, 1990, page 233).

Librarians may never personally meet infohitchhikers.[52] These electronic library patrons may also be infoproducers or infoactualizers if information products or quests are sought independently and electronically. Infohitchhikers logon to communicate with library personnel via telephone, facsimile (FAX), electronic mail (e-mail), voice mail, conferencing systems, conference calls, local or long distance calls. Infohitchhikers may be extensive telephone reference service users. And they may not be card-carrying library patrons. They may over-utilize or inappropriately use library services intended or reserved for local patrons. Infohitchhikers are often outside the local geographic service area, outside the community or region, even outside the state or nation. And they are invisible to the librarian at the other end of the telephone line. With some, this "patron invisibility" causes significant library problems.

Library Patrons With Disabilities

Infohackers: Electronic Library Saboteurs

Infohackers are the final infosearcher variant who electronically access, manipulate, and compromise library-based information without authorization. They intentionally or inadvertently install computer viruses. Some access authorized library-based information without paying or being eligible for those services.[53] Infohackers present librarians with high-technology security issues. Librarians may not be prepared to deal with their unauthorized collection access expertise.[54]

Access To George

Sam, a junior high student, was well known for his hacking abilities. No one was aware of the extent to which he could easily gain access to a variety of secure databases. With a valid library card and written parental permission, Sam accessed a metropolitan public library's community bulletin board service called "GEORGE" like several thousand others with library cards. As a minor, parental access permission to GEORGE was required. His parents had no concept of their son's evolving expertise, the access levels he was able gain or how responsibly he was using GEORGE. But they found out in a most disconcerting way.

Sam not only learned the inner workings of the library minicomputer-based community bulletin board service. He also found a "back door" to other passwords and personal access numbers. Among those numbers discovered were the bulletin board system operator passwords for GEORGE's daily operation. The GEORGE system operator was a city employee who as a part of his duties required access to other city employee files and passwords. The GEORGE minicomputer was linked to the city mainframe computer and operating with a common set of passwords across the entire municipal computer network, young Sam could get to everyone in city government. Through GEORGE, Sam accessed the mainframe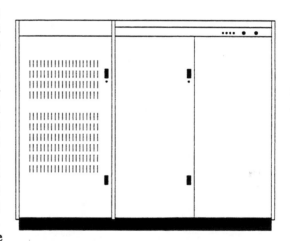

computer without system operator knowledge or permission. The mainframe considered Sam's keyboard entries as being from the GEORGE system operator and gave Sam access also to city budget and police files.

A State Bureau of Investigation (SBI) systems analyst was brought in after the security breach was discovered and following unauthorized access to city police files. The GEORGE system operator was the first investigated but after a month of observing the operator's routine access, he was no longer considered a suspect. Finding the real security breach was a much greater challenge. Who was accessing police files? Several thousand citizen members connecting to GEORGE daily were now under suspicion of infohacking. A volunteer systems analyst from a national computer distributor (the city mainframe provider and troubleshooter) was also called in. More than a dozen city employees and GEORGE password users set the trap. Their carefully orchestrated computer bulletin board interactions set the "bait," which consisted of a series of conversations (all supposedly private) openly discussing a change of city employee and account passwords. And Sam took the bait when he used the "new passwords" to access "bogus files" set up carefully to look real.

To identify Sam as the infohacker, to discover his multiple password system and to cancel out Sam's unauthorized entries took a total of six months and more than $50,000 of city funds. Sam's parents were informed of his infohacking. They could not understand what he had done. Sam's access to GEORGE was terminated and new passwords installed. The GEORGE minicomputer was no longer linked to the city mainframe as a security measure against future infohackers. Sam's service termination on GEORGE preceded federal and state laws concerning computer piracy done by minors. Sam has been profoundly deaf since the age of twelve due to complications of rubella. He was never prosecuted.

Infoproducers

Infoproducers develop library information products for economic reasons, for personal business or for self-directed education. Information is money to infoproducers. Their information access fulfills a critical need to enter the library. As articulate and proactive library information stakeholders librarian gatekeepers may find meeting infoproducer needs difficult and challenging. Infoproducers move quickly from one library to another searching regional, state, national or international collections. They regard librarians as information facilitators to generate personal information products from their searches. Advanced infosearchers as infoproducers are well represented among patrons with disabilities who cannot physically access the library building or make the library trek. Instead they access the collection by telephone and modem or through voice interactions with librarians. Infoproducers are the most likely to utilize library FAX as an alternate to physical library entry. Their onsite searches through library databases are often only done when databases cannot be accessed remotely. Infoproducers use online personal access catalog (OPAC) and CD-ROM database access more than others and have more advanced library research skills than infosearchers. They need and use library information in larger quantities than many other patrons. Some infoproducers avoid library entry by exhausting library collections and information databases remotely, electronically. Infoproducers complete the most comprehensive topical searches, have the most titles checked out at one time and the most interlibrary loans on order. At the same time, they have the greatest likelihood of generating the most library fines and end-user fees. Their support may be a cost- and time-intensive challenge to library resources and personnel demanding more library resources than any other patrons and expecting extensive routine library support. For infoproducers their information products are often time-intensive. Library adjustments must be quick and complete to meet their needs since they search with self-imposed information deadlines. The greatest conflicts come when other infoproducers compete for scarce library resources. Extensive information access requires equally extensive library equipment use. Infoproducers are the most likely to complain about equipment downtime, and can damage or accelerate library equipment repair schedules because of their unusually heavy use. Special library-use privileges are secured by infoproducers beyond those authorized for infosearchers or the general public when they seek "scholar" or "special user" status and access privileges. Library rules and regulations, policies and procedures are waived or modified when those special access privileges allow infoproducers special collection access and library accommodation. Infoproducers with disabilities have added justification for being helped.

Infoproducers complete the most comprehensive topical searches, have the most titles checked out at one time and the most interlibrary loans on order. At the same time, they have the greatest likelihood of generating the most library fines and end-user fees.

Telecommuters

Telecommuters infoproduce from offices as workplaces in their homes.[55] Telecommuters with disabilities may have restricted mobility outside and but can comfortably work at home as "legal" infohitchhikers to remotely access libraries and produce information from library collections. Working on individual schedules and at their own pace they maintain information production schedules as others would at conventional workplaces.[56] They access library information using the telephone, modem-equipped home computers, and FAX machines. Because individual schedules may not coincide with library service hours, they leave voice mail messages for librarians or FAX special requests to be met when the library opens. And librarians may find teleworker information needs very demanding. Many libraries have not yet evolved personnel policies and procedures to meet telecommuter informational needs.

Dr. X

As a sole proprietor and a home-based computer systems analyst, Dr. X gave the local public, university and regional libraries frequent information requests that could not be quickly or easily met. He earned the reputation of being a very difficult patron among area librarians working with (or as he considered, "for") him. Dr. X had the distinction of submitting the most Interlibrary Loan requests among all area library clientele. He frequently exhausted credit lines for computer online database searches. He lodged the most FAX-based library reference requests. He requested more microfilm and microfiche photocopies on record from two area libraries, both already accustomed to others high-demand requests. Dr. X was accustomed to librarian response in a matter of hours or minutes, instead of the days given conventional turn-around service to others. Overloaded librarians began to complain to their library administrators.

Voice phone, FAX and electronic mail contacts were made to Dr. X without response. A home visit by a library director was suggested during a regional library meeting. The library administrator found he was a home-bound paraplegic, caused by a spinal cord injury, and wheelchair mobility dependent. Area librarians were then not wheelchair accessible for the specialized onsite services Dr. X required. The visting library director concluded that he had no other options than to use remote library access. All subsequent library support requests were met, generally on his time frame, by area libraries.

Telecommuters with disabilities have restricted mobility outside and can comfortably work within their own homes as "legal" infohitchhikers who remotely access libraries and produce information from library collections.

Infonavigators

Some infoproducers use electronic mail to access remote library services more as a hobby than to produce work-related information. Like telecommuters, infonavigators do not ordinarily visit the library in person. Libraries are useful to them only if remote patron access is permitted to the MATRIX.[57]

> The MATRIX is a worldwide metanetwork of connected computer networks and conferencing systems that provides unique services that are like, yet unlike, those of telephones, post offices and libraries...The MATRIX affects the personal and social lives of millions of users...Research and subjective evidence indicates that those who use it tend to interact with many more people, not only by the new technology but also by telephone, paper mail, and physical travel (Quarterman, 1990, pg. xxiii).

Infonavigators often negotiate information access with librarian gatekeepers since the purpose of their information gain is not for work. Some librarians regard these demanding patrons as having lower priority information requests to be met than infoproducers who "work or produce with their information." And the MATRIX information base is incredibly large, perhaps global. Infonavigators often suffer from information overload.[58] Information overload brings infonavigators into contact with librarians to assist with information management, interpreting the meaning of information found, and applying it to their needs. Librarians become major information translators to infonavigators with information overload.

Infonavigators network with others without going through established library access channels or procedures.[59] Their support is minimal since many are virtually invisible to professional librarians. Without physical library entry and remote because of electronic library access, they are independent of librarians and are information self-directed. They shop for remote-accessible libraries and collections or databases like another customer might peruse clothing stores. These Information Age members are very sophisticated. As a hobby, they move across all available media print, nonprint, or electronic information formats, using advanced infosearching skills, to produce information. But infonavigators who get lost in the information world must have someone to talk to as they become reoriented. Enter the librarian as an information overload consultant to infonavigators.

Infonavigators expect library workers to have a similar orientation and level of remote infosearching expertise. They may frequently reject library recommendations as being "too unsophisticated," "too slow," or "irrelevant" in meeting their information needs. Some may display outright intolerance of other information-access competitors. Competition between other infonavigators may be invisible to library gatekeepers until access time and remote patron service equipment use overloads library resources. Library gatekeepers have much to plan for to meet infonavigator needs.

Infoactualizers

Maslow describes self-actualizing people as those who pursue a quest.[60] Infoactualizers use librarians and libraries to adapt to personal needs to transform information, generating new information forms and contexts. They are self-information gatekeepers and stakeholders. When information gatekeepers and stakeholders combine in the same person, the infoactualizer is the result. Self-actualizing people can also be patrons with disabilities. Infoactualizers with disabilities may experience challenges unrelated to their information quest. Or their information quest may directly involve overcoming personal disability.

Infoactualizers are sophisticated information users, producers and disseminators. As authors, researchers, and creative thinkers, they employ a broad array of library information sources. They use librarians very effectively. Librarians regard it a pleasure to support them while they pursue personal information quests, even though their support requirements may be complex and demanding. As voyagers in the information world, infoactualizers share no characteristics in common other than a quest for information by unusual means, by transformational means. In that pursuit, they may come into conflict with library gatekeepers and other patrons less internally guided for information gain and the need for self-actualization. Yet those conflicts can be resolved in mutually satisfactory ways. Infoactualizer contributions enrich all after they discover new ways to access information through complex mental maps, search strategies, and exotic information sources including the virtual library information community.

As voyagers in the information world, infoactualizers share no characteristics in common other than a quest for information by unusual means, by transformational means.

Sally, the Matrix Lady

Sally was not only a computer enthusiast but a self-labeled "science information addict." Through the assistance of her high school science and technology teachers, she joined COMPUSERVE,[61] THE SOURCE,[62] and BITNET[63] and globally connected to other science students. Her password to each of these networks was various forms of the term "MATRIX LADY." Sally was the first local student to join the NASA bulletin board, receiving slow-scan pictures of the Voyager fly-bys of Mars, Saturn, Uranus and Neptune on her home personal computer.[64] Connections to ARPANET[65] through her father, a military analyst, allowed another authorized access point to the global scientific community. MATRIX LADY now enjoys first-name access via INTERNET with leading scientists and other science enthusiasts throughout the world. As a futurist and a Mensa member she has served as a very young mentor to other, older science enthusiasts through INTERNET[66]. Avidly pursuing her quest for information by electronic, voice, facsimile (FAX) and digital means, she is an amateur radio operator with voice and single-sideband (SSB) license, communicating globally with scientists using direct, station-to-station data exchange. She has bounced signals off the Moon and listened to the reflected signal return. All this the MATRIX LADY did from a wheelchair, as a high school student with Duchenne muscular dystrophy.

Patron With Disabilities as Infosearchers

Some patrons with disabilities in the library context may have difficulty, on library entry, selecting search topics or strategies or using library resources effectively.[67] Unobtrusively observing patrons in difficulty and determining their support requirements changes with each person with disabilities and their unique reason(s) for library entry.[68] Patrons mental maps or information navigation skills are only apparent, however limited or faulty, to librarians who work closely with them.[69] Patron/librarian interactions define disabled patron support requirements. Some may need personalized librarian adjustments immediately on entry. Others may need substantial librarian support--from map, to directions, to direct information access.[70] Some may need help selecting quality titles to develop requested or directly implied informational needs. Patron-selected titles may not be appropriate from the librarian's viewpoint. Yet free title selection is an absolute right for information access.[71] Others will require accommodation in selecting materials that develop concepts in logical sequence, have no distracting parts and provide repetition to be understood. Patrons in difficulty may often require peer helper or continued and appropriate librarian supportive help during each library visit. Every visit may present new and different library adjustment challenges to both patron and librarian.

Accommodation does not include preemptive librarian judgments on library entry for patrons with disabilities information needs or library search skills.[72] Proactive librarians do not anticipate library support requirements but patiently wait and respond to specifically patron-requested help.[73] Librarians answer patron questions, think through search strategies with them, and direct them to requested information. Experienced librarians wait while patrons read and assist further only as requested.[74] No librarian can do the patron's thinking or supplement fundamental patron research skill beyond the patron's stated needs. Personal needs and access to information may be influenced by disabilities. Across all types of motivations for entering the library, some patrons have the complicating factor of disability, physical or cognitive challenges. In infosurvivors or infoshelters, disabling conditions complicate patron library support requirements. Disabilities in patrons may also make traditional librarian support strategies more complex.

Patron library-context behavior is the most significant factor in librarian response to known or stated patron needs. Infosocializers with disabilities demonstrate their most advanced information sophistication through library socialization. Infosocializers with disabilities who cannot read, write or who also have visual disability may still effectively use the library. Infosearchers, infoproducers and infoactualizers with disabilities have basic informational needs to be met with librarian support, each at their own level of information gain and for their own purposes.

Librarians may observe some library-context disabilities in patrons on entry, while other disabling conditions in patrons are not so apparent until later in their information search.[75] Unavoidably, the reference librarian will experience a situation where a person with an "invisible" disability seeks special accommodation.[76] For many patron with disabilities library accommodations are unexpected, unique and unpredictable events. Librarians must listen and serve to meet those needs. Patrons should always be given the opportunity to instruct their librarian on how to meet personal library support requirements.[77] On the other hand, librarians need to allow special-needs patrons to "take risks," to learn library skills rather than having library work done for them. If professionals are attentive, special-needs patrons will let the librarian know they are unable to undertake the task.[78] Patrons with disabilities may not fit the conventional library patron role, making their special-needs library support strategies unique to the librarian.

We may all experience library barriers and need library support. Yet we overcome those barriers to find information. Successful special-needs patrons receive librarian adjustments when they ask. Librarian help is provided to all who demonstrate need.

Some with disabilities find that their library performance is affected and need library support but may not ever consider themselves library-disabled.[79] Others have impairments that do not impact on library searches to the degree that constitutes a functional disability in the library. Patron impairment rises to the level of disability when single or multiple impairments in the same person substantially limit library infosearching.[80] A library disability is based on the functional infosearching effects of the patron impairment during library searches.[81]

Disability Accommodation Factors

1. **Patron statements or request for accommodation.** Patrons make statements to the librarian about their disability, or request library accommodation, or state their lack of infosearching skills which implies librarian accommodation.

2. **Observed patron library accommodation needs during patron visits to the library.** Patron dysfunctional library behaviors are observed by library personnel that require library accommodation without specific patron requests for help.

3. **Patron-specific disability definitions and terminology.** These include legal definitions and terminology to describe patrons with specific disability who enter the library.

4. **Patron reliance on library accommodation.** Patrons with specific library disability need library technology to obtain personal library information and they ask for library support to get that information.

5. **Patrons entering libraries with personal assistive or augmentive devices.** Patrons with disabilities who bring personal accommodation to the library are presumed to be patrons with disabilities.

Disabled Patron Statements

Librarians, as public servants, make adjustments to patron physical or mental limitations "resulting from the disability" only when those needs are made known on library entry.[82] The disabled in the library have the responsibility to make their needs known to librarians for appropriate help. Persons with disabilities not relevant to library activities are treated there as conventional library patrons, as the library general public. Librarians listen to every patron to understand how self-defined, library-relevant needs can be met in the library context.

Library Patrons With Disabilities

Disability self-help groups identify library needs, communicate those needs to librarians and monitor librarian help received by their members or peers.[83] Disability interest and self-help groups nationwide describe specific personal help needed by disabled peers. But no accommodation is more appropriate than that given to individuals requiring support because of their disability as they request library help.

Patron Accommodation Requests

Patrons may request library accommodation on entry and at any time throughout their library stay. Librarians may ask patrons with obvious disabilities whether they can meet needs unassisted or whether they need library support. Librarians, like other public servants, are required by Public Law 101-336 (Americans with Disabilities Act) to provide library patrons with disabilities the same consideration for library services that patrons without disabilities receive.[84] A patron otherwise qualified for library services cannot be denied services because of disabilities.[85] Disabling conditions in library patrons result from a variety of causes and can have a variety of information-access effects. The ADA also identifies disabilities in citizens in much broader terms than disability terms in conventional use.[86]

Observed Patron Library Support Needs

Failed Information Searches. Failure to find personal library information can occur at any time during any library visit. Physical and information barriers exist even in the best libraries.[87] Libraries have many information-access barriers in physical structure or in operational barriers to the collection through library service or policy. Alternative strategies with librarian support removes library barriers that apply to the individual with disabilities. If library barriers cannot be effectively removed, librarians work around barriers to avoid patron failures and adjust to their special needs. The Americans with Disabilities Act was designed to ensure that people are not discriminated against in the library because of a history of disability, personal library failure, or failure of the library to provide appropriate service.[88] Some disabled patrons fail to be information stakeholders, while others do not adequately represent their information needs to library workers. Librarians, as information gatekeepers, may also fail to meet their patrons' special information needs.

Partially Successful Information Searches. Gaining library-based personal information on library entry more often occurs with partial success than with outright failure. Disabilities in patrons does not necessarily imply library failure or partial infosearching success. That partial success includes moving to the library floor but not being able to move to all needed service areas, and difficulties with limited access to staff, collections and equipment. People partially succeed when they obtain some but not all personal information from library resources. They may settle for the wrong book--a single, incomplete, dated, inappropriate source--and draw faulty conclusions from their collection access. Some may be hasty and inclined to make inaccurate judgments based on the limited library information found. Some partially fail to be information stakeholders, to be information self-advocates, while others do not clearly or fully represent their special information needs to library workers. Librarians, as information gatekeepers, partially fail to meet some information needs. Librarians may not demonstrate good patron listening skills.

While many library patron characteristics for those who partially succeed can be described in the library context, some may clearly require support strategies corresponding to specific disabilities.[89] Many patrons experience partial success and exhibit some library disability. We all may be partially successful library searchers. Rarely are we completely successful during library infosearching. Some have specific library-context disabilities related to their library information quest. Others have invisible needs that limit library information gain.

Disability Definitions and Terminology

Professional librarians quickly and unobtrusively identify patrons with disabilities needs to be met in the library context.[90] Librarians serve all library patrons, including those with specific disability, the physically challenged, and the infosurvivors, infoshelters and infosocializers with disabilities. Patrons with disabilities in the library context may not lack infosearching skills. Nondisabled patrons may also significantly lack infosearching skills. Some patrons as disabled infoproducers are not limited by their disabilities and effectively gain library information to produce information products. Disabled infoactualizers pursue information quests independently or with library support, not based on disabilities, but on the basis of their information quest.

Some library impairments are disabling for particular individuals but not for others, depending on the stage of the disease or disorder, the presence of other impairments that combine to make the impairment disabling, or any number of other factors. Other disabilities in patrons may further increase their need for library support. Discussion of specific disabilities in library patron support strategies follows in later chapters.

Asking for library accommodation to meet personal library information needs places some patrons with disabilities in a dependency relationship with the librarian. In order to continue to obtain necessary library-based information, many disabled patrons come to rely on librarian accommodation. They come to expect it as their right. While librarians promote maximum infosearcher independence, some patrons are librarian-dependent for appropriate accommodation.

Patrons Bringing Personal Assistive Devices

Patrons with disabilities may enter the library bringing personal devices,[91] services and helpers.[92] Librarians may not <u>require</u> those patrons to bring personal assistive devices. Public library services are accessible to all. But personal assistive devices are accessible only to the owner bringing them to the library. Patrons are given the opportunity to choose among assistive devices provided by the library or the ones patron-provided.[93] No library obligation exists to provide personal assistive devices even though patrons are recognized to need those devices while in the library.[94] Only public access assistive devices are provided through library resources. Public access assistive devices may be identical to personal assistive devices brought in, but they are accessible to all patrons in the library who need them. The library is not a respository for patron personal assistive devices stored there until individually needed. Public access assistive devices resolve this information access problem for some special-needs patrons without their own personal assistive devices.

Summary

This chapter has established some of the primary differences, based on need, among patrons who enter the library. Maslow's hierarchy of needs was combined with the Office of Technology Assessment's interpretation of human communications to explain six major patron types with different information needs and different reasons for library entry. Each library patron is valuable and worth assisting, with or without the complications of disabilities. Concern for providing the best patron service requires library accommodation for disabled persons of all ages. Appropriate and timely library adjustments assure smoother, less problematic information gain by the disabled. If disabilities are observable in the library context, librarians can make rapid, unobtrusive adaptations to provide individualized service.

End Notes:

1. U.S. Congress, Office of Technology Assessment. (1990). <u>Critical Connections: Communication for the Future</u>. Washington, DC: U.S. Government Printing Office. Page 216.
2. Ibid, <u>Critical Connections</u>, 215.
3. U.S. Congress, Office of Technology Assessment. (1988). <u>Informing the Nation: Federal information dissemination in an electronic age</u>. Washington, DC: U.S. Government Printing Office. Page 130: "A library collection, regardless of format, reflects the information needs of its users, whether they be the local community, academic, research, special interest institution, State, or region."
4. Ibid, <u>Critical Connections</u>, 216: "Basic survival needs, such as food and shelter, come first, followed in order of importance by neds for safety; belonging and relatedness; ego, relating to one's position within a group; and self-actualization, autonomy, and creativity. Individuals seek fulfillment of higher-level needs only after satisfying lower, more basic needs. The full development of the individual, however, requires attention to those at the top of the hierarchy."
5. Maslow, Abraham. (1943). A theory of motivation. <u>Psychological Bulletin</u>, <u>50</u>, 370.
6. Lewis, Christopher. (1992). The Americans with Disabilities Act and Its Effect on Public Libraries. <u>Public Libraries</u>, <u>31</u>, 28: "Improving staff awareness of the needs of clientele with disabilities and planning ahead to fill those needs will be much more efficient and ethical than maintaining ignorance and waiting for the threat of a lawsuit to initiate change. Long before the ADA was passed, the goals of public library administration have included providing service and materials for all citizens, not just for those who were the least expensive to accommodate. Library administrators do not aim to serve all patron equally because there is a rule that says they hnave to; they do it because they have made a professional committment to do so."
7. The neologisms "Infosurvivor," "Infosocializer," "Infosearcher," "Infoproducer" and "Infoactualizer" were invented by this author to combine the importance of library information (info) with patron activities (surviving, sheltering, socializing, searching, producing and actualizing).
8. Infosurvivors, a neologism for patrons needing information for survival.
9. National Commission on Children. (1991). <u>Beyond rhetoric-a new American agenda for children and families: Final report of the National Comission on Children</u>. Washington, DC: U.S. Government Printing Office. Pages xvii-xviii.
10. Zipkowitz, Fay. (1990). "No one wants to see them: Meeting the reference needs of the deinstitutionalized." <u>The Reference Librarian</u>. New York: Hawthorn Press, 1991.
11. Salter, Charles A. & Salter, Jeffrey L. (1988). <u>On the front lines: Coping with the library's problem patrons</u>. Englewood, CO: Libraries Unlimited.
12. Ibid, Zipkowitz, 60.
13. Ibid, <u>Critical Connections</u>, 215.
14. Ibid, Zipkowitz, 64-65.
15. Ibid, Zipkowitz, 54-55.
16. Editor. (1983). California LSCA project to mainstream mentally impaired. <u>Library Journal</u>, <u>108</u>, 339-340.
17. Bekiares, Susan E. (1984). Technology for the Handicapped: Selection and evaluation of aids and devices for the visually impaired. <u>Library Hi Tech</u>, <u>5</u>(2), 60.
18. U.S. Department of Justice. (1991). <u>Americans with Disabilities Act Handbook</u>. Washington, DC: U.S. Government Printing Office. <u>ADA Handbook</u>, II-10.
19. American Library Association. (1988). <u>Information power: Guidelines for school library media programs</u>. Chicago: American Library Association. Pages 99-100.
20. Ibid, <u>Information Power</u>, 140.
21. Community Childhood Hunger Identification Project. (1991). <u>A survey of childhood hunger in the United States</u>. Washington, DC: Food Research and Action Center. Page 1.
22. U.S. Congress, House of Representatives, Select Committee on Children, Youth and Families. <u>No place to call home: Discarded children in America</u>. (1989). Washington, DC: U.S. Government Printing Office.

23. Ibid, National Commission on Children, 12.

24. Ibid, ADA Handbook, III-10-11 (Section 36.102) & III-27.

25. Ibid, ADA Handbook, I-24.

26. Information 2000: Library and Information Services for the 21st Century. A summary report of the 1991 White House Conference on Library and Information Services. (1991). Washington, DC: U.S. Government Printing Office. Pages 58-64.

27. Ibid, Information 2000, 34.

28. ADA Handbook, Title III.

29. Ibid, ADA Handbook, II-41 & 42.

30. Ibid, Information 2000, 10.

31. Ibid, ADA Handbook, II-89.

32. Cagle, R. Brantley. (1983). Reference service to the developmentally disabled: Normalization of access. Catholic Library World, 54, 267.

33. Ibid, Cagle 267: "...Among the rights denied him is the right to information about civil rights, travel and transportation, recreational opportunities, sexual information, adapted equipment, and other materials essential to daily living activities...[and the right to] choose his own reading material...Group home residents would be trained in the proper use of trains, buses, automobiles, airplanes and trolleys; identification and use of community parks, libraries, post offices, police and fire agencies, stores, restaurants, and cultural, historical, and entertainment sites, participation in community activities, such as conferences, public hearings, activities, political meetings and elections, consumer self-protection, self-representation and self-advocacy."

34. Ibid, ADA Handbook, II-18: "[Includes]...any mental or psychological disorder such as mental retardation, organic brain syndrome, emotional or mental illness, and specific learning disabilities."

35. Ibid, Critical Connections, 215.

36. Day, John Michael. (1992). Guidelines for library services to deaf people: Development and interpretation. IFLA Journal, 18, 33: "...libraries are often major cultural and social centers within their communities and offer a variety of programs which are interesting to the community."

37. Ibid, California LSCA project, 340: "Because of their social isolation, developmentally disabled adults tend to be unaware of the public library's resources...One problem with the training program, however, is scheduling: many clients are at work during the times (early morning and afternoons) that library staff are available. The alternatives are night programs or day programs that would require patrons to take time off from work...Another problem has been transportation: clients often do not know how to find the library on their own."

38. Ibid, Day, 34: "Libraries are often major cultural and social centers within their communities and offer a variety of programs which are interesting to the community."

39. Heinich, Robert, Molenda, Michael & Russell, James D. (1989). Instructional media and the new technologies of instruction: Third edition. New York: MacMillan. Page 398.

40. Ibid, Information 2000, 9.

41. Ibid, Information 2000, 5.

42. Ibid, Information 2000, 47.

43. Ibid, Office of Technology Assessment, 216.

44. Ibid, ADA Handbook, II-38.

45. Ibid, Information Power, 15.

46. Gengle, Dean. (1984). The netweaver's sourcebook: A guide to micro networking and communications. Menlo Park, CA: Addison Wesley. Pages 70-72.

47. Ibid, Gengle, 58.

48. Ibid, Gengle, 62-63.

49. Hoehne, Charles W. (1977). Service delivery systems for handicapped individuals. In, U.S. Government. (1977). White House Conference on Handicapped Individuals: Awareness Papers. Washington, DC: U.S. Government Printing Office. Page 391. See also, Gengle, 62-63.

50. Ibid, Critical Connections, 221-222.

Library Patrons With Disabilities

51. Quarterman, John S. (1990). The MATRIX: Computer networks and conferencing systems worldwide. Burlington, MA: Digital Press. Pages 30-31.

52. Ibid, Critical Connections, 222.

53. Ibid, Quarterman, 38-39.

54. Wright, Benjamin. (1990). Computer mediated communication and the law. In, Quarterman, John S. (1990). The MATRIX: Computer Networks and conferencing systems worldwide. Burlington, MA: Digital Press. Pages 637-655.

55. Ibid, Quarterman, 33. See also, McCormick, John A. (1994). Computers and the Americans with Disabilities Act: A Manager's Guide. New York: Windcrest/McGraw-Hill. Pages 216-235.

56. Ibid, Critical Connections, 223.

57. Ibid, Quarterman, Page xxviii: "The MATRIX is a worldwide metanetwork of connected computer networks and conferencing systems that provides unique services that are like, yet unlike, those of telephones, post offices, and libraries...The metanetwork of connected computer networks...is the prototype of a new communications infrastructure that will be as pervasive as the international telephone network."

58. Hiltz, S.R. & Turoff, M. (1985). Structuring computer-mediated communication systems to avoid information overload. Communications of the ACM, 28(7), 680-689. See also Gengle, 41-42; and Critical Connections, 235-236.

59. Ibid, Quarterman, 40.

60. Ibid, Maslow, 370.

61. CompuServe Information System, 5000 Arlington Center Blvd., P.O. Box 20212, Columbus, OH 43220. (614) 457-8650 or (800) 848-8990.

62. The Source P.O. Box 1305, McLean, VA 22102. (800) 336-3366.

63. Bitnet–EDUCOM Networking Activities, P.O. Box 364, Princeton, NJ 08540. (609) 734-1878.

64. NASA Science Network, c/o Marc Siegel (msielgel@ames.arc.nasa. gov.) NASA Ames Research Center, Moffett Field, CA 94035. (415) 694-6482.

65. Ibid, Quarterman, 143-146.

66. Braun, Eric. (1994). The INTERNET directory. New York: Ballantine Books.

67. Ibid, Information Power, 29.

68. Ibid, Information Power, 30.

69. Ibid, Critical Connections, 234-237.

70. Ibid, Information Power, 30.

71. Ibid, Information 2000, 57.

72. Ibid, ADA Handbook, 4.1.2(16)(b) & A4.33.7.

73. Ibid, ADA Handbook, 4.1.2(16)(b) & A4.33.7. See also Power, M.T., Rundlett, Carol & David, Myra. (1989). New challenges in helping students uncover information: The learning disabled student. The Bookmark, 47(11), 213-216.

74. Ibid, Power, 215.

75. Weingand, Darlene E. (1990). The invisible client: Meeting the needs of persons with learning disabilities. In The Reference Librarian. New York: Haworth Press. Page 78. See also, Dalton, Phyllis I. (1990). Productivity, not paternalism. Library Personnel News, 4(3), 43: "Many disabilities such as retardation and deafness are usually not visible, so the solutions may not be visible either."

76. Ibid, Day, 31: "With good reason, deafness has been called the "invisible handicap" because deaf people are not identifiable as deaf by casual observation and they tend to blend into the larger community...Additionally, people who are deaf from birth or who became deaf at an early age often have difficulty reading and have a tendency to not use libraries. Consequently, libraries and deaf people have been unaware of each other."

77. Ibid, ADA Handbook, II-38.

78. Allegri, Francesca. (1984). On the other side of the reference desk: The patron with a physical disability. Medical Reference Services Quarterly, 3(3), 71.

79. Freese, Michele & Cohen, Susan F. (1986). Awareness project for library service for the hearing impaired. Illinois Libraries, 68, 552.

80. Goltz, Eileen. (1991). The provision of services to students with special needs in Canadian academic libraries. Canadian Library Journal, 48(4), 264.

81. See related issues in ADA Handbook, II-39.

82. Ibid, ADA Handbook, I-13.

83. Ibid, ADA Handbook, I-3, I-12 (Section 1630.3).

84. Ibid, ADA Handbook, II-21 (Section 1630.1(a)) & III-46 & 47.

85. Ibid, ADA Handbook, II-21 (Section 1630.1(a)) & III-46 (Section 36.202(a)).

86. Ibid, ADA Handbook, II-16 to 24.

87. Ibid, ADA Handbook, II-30 (for library self-evaluation).

88. Ibid, ADA Handbook, II-22.

89. Ibid, ADA Handbook, II-15.

90. Ibid, Allegri, 68-69.

91. Ibid, ADA Handbook, II-26.

92. Ibid, ADA Handbook, II-28.

93. Ibid, Lewis, 26.

94. Ibid, ADA Handbook, II-53: "[ADA]...does not require a public entity to provide to individuals with disabilities personal devices, such as wheelchairs: individually prescribed devices, such as prescription eyeglasses or hearing aids; readers for personal use or study; or services of a personal nature including assistance in eating, toileting, or dressing."

Suggested Reading:

American Library Association. (1988). Information power: Guidelines for school library media programs. Chicago: American Library Association.

Lewis, Christopher. (1992). The Americans with Disabilities Act and Its Effect on Public Libraries. Public Libraries, 31, 25-28.

National Commission on Children. (1991). Beyond rhetoric-a new American agenda for children and families: Final report of the National Comission on Children. Washington, DC: U.S. Government Printing Office.

Quarterman, John S. (1990). The MATRIX: Computer networks and conferencing systems worldwide. Burlington, MA: Digital Press.

U.S. Congress, House of Representatives, Select Committee on Children, Youth and Families. No place to call home: Discarded children in America. (1989). Washington, D.C. U.S. Government Printing Office.

U.S. Congress, Office of Technology Assessment. (1990). Critical Connections: Communication for the Future. Washington, DC: U.S. Government Printing Office.

U.S. Congress, Office of Technology Assessment. (1988). Informing the Nation: Federal information dissemination in an electronic age. Washington, DC: U.S. Government Printing Office.

Zipkowitz, Fay. (1990). "No one wants to see them: Meeting the reference needs of the deinstitutionalized." The Reference Librarian. New York: Hawthorn Press. Pages 53-67.

Library Patrons With Disabilities

Chapter Two

Approach to the Library Door

From Parking Lot to the Library Entrance: Removing Outside Barriers

Librarians have previously regarded access issues outside the library not to be a part of their professional duties.[1] Physical barrier removal alone within libraries does not ensure patron with disabilities access.[2] Libraries remove architectural barriers outside just as librarians remove patron barriers to the collection.[3] Architectural and physical access barriers must be removed before disabled people can approach the library door.[4] Librarians, as public servants, and the library, as a public entity, must comply with the Americans with Disabilities Act (ADA).[5]

Library Architectural Service Barrier Removal

A fundamental paradigm shift among professional librarians is happening for the removal of external library barriers. Since passage of Section 504 of the Rehabilitation Act of 1973,[6] external barrier reduction has not worked effectively in many libraries receiving federal funds. The change, since 1990 and the passage of the Americans with Disabilities Act, increases responsibility for barrier removal to include librarians sharing with institutional or community leaders, boards of directors and disability groups.[7] Not receiving federal funds no longer waives ADA compliance requirements. Library ADA compliance plans now have become a matter of public record requiring easy access for all, including patrons with disabilities most affected.

A fundamental paradigm shift among professional librarians is happening for the removal of external library barriers.

Section 504 of the Vocational Rehabilitation Act of 1973 provided that all public facilities were to remove architectural barriers. Public entities were responsible for barrier removal if they received federal funds. Both public and private libraries serving the public, but not receiving federal aid, were exempt from barrier-removal requirements. Exempt libraries were not required to file five-year compliance and barrier-removal plans, as were nonexempt libraries. Five-year plans to remove architectural barriers could be appealed if substantial library compliance was proven. Over the past twenty years, many libraries resubmitted four minimally changed five-year plans to federal authorities without achieving significant architectural barrier removal. Other libraries may have registered buildings as National Historic Sites largely to avoid 504 compliance.[8] Patrons had to historically adapt outside the library without being helped from within.

Though Section 504 compliance plans were "matters of public record," some libraries or their administrators kept plans unchanged, while systematically resisting substantial noncompliance public review. Libraries with compliance or transition plans to serve the public were no longer under public review.[9] Individuals with disabilities had to initiate formal complaints or threaten civil suit against libraries to view compliance plans or to initiate grievance procedures.[10]

Library ADA Compliance

Another significant paradigm shift since 1990 has been the move from professional reactive to proactive library ADA-standards compliance. Evaluation-resistant librarians now promote ADA compliance evaluations and seek full ADA compliance in a highly visible public service context with community disability advisory council overview.[11] This has come even with limited resources and the necessity to prioritize library services.[12] This shift moves librarians beyond minimum ADA compliance to setting standards of safety and comfort for all coming to the library. Librarians join their administrators in establishing comfortable, daily external library-building access for all from parking lot to the collection.[13]

Library Patrons With Disabilities

External Library Conditions

Minimal library ADA standard compliance is simply not enough. The history of federal[14] and state accessibility laws[15] suggests that the ADA will promote more comprehensive barrier removal in public facilities than any previous standards.[16] Patron-stated needs combined with librarian sensitivity may assist information barrier removal more than library building architectural changes. Librarian knowledge of when and how to help the physically challenged may be as important as actual architectural barrier removal. But librarian sensitivity alone is not enough to eradicate external barriers. External and internal library architectural barriers have not been forgotten or ignored:

> The information assembled in the library will serve very little purpose if the disabled patron cannot access that information readily. The mobility impaired patron must be able to enter the building and move about in it; the hearing impaired patron must be able to communicate with the staff; and the vision impaired patron must have the means to use the printed word. These problems present a challenge in the library environment that can be resolved by evaluating the library building and instituting architectural changes, services, and policies that will aid the disabled user in using library resources (Kruger, 1984, page 9).

Sensitizing Librarians to Library Physical Challenges

The wheelchair is perhaps the most effective tool in sensitizing library workers to physically challenged patrons. Librarians experiencing a full-days "confinement" in a wheelchair, from the parking lot to the library building will begin to understand significant and practical differences between ADA-defined minimum architectural standards and the common remaining library barriers facing the physically challenged.[17] However, temporarily experiencing physical challenges from a wheelchair is not the same as understanding those challenges faced by permanently-disabled wheelchair users. That daily reality and perspective can only be effectively understood and communicated to librarians by the physically challenged themselves.

Comprehensive Library Barrier Analysis

Librarians assess patron mobility and physical access skills from curbside to the library entrance.[18] Numerous barriers are found and resolved through careful parking area and library building entrance evaluation. Foster & Lindell (1991) advise: "Evaluate the accessibility both inside and outside your [library] facility, noting placement of ramps/slopes for wheelchair users" (Page 59). Specific accessibility concerns for wheelchair users, expressed by wheelchair users themselves, are available.[19]

Other standards for library architectural barrier removal exist in addition to wheelchair access. Patrons who use walking aids, the blind, or persons with low vision, also need external architectural barrier removal. Patrons with disabilities are diverse. Some have conflicting external library access needs. Wheelchair measures are not enough for determining external barrier removal. Patrons with other disabilities must also receive reasonable accommodation.[20]

Patrons with disabilities are diverse. Some have conflicting external library access needs.

Disability Groups

Part of comprehensive library barrier analysis comes from disabled persons in the community where disability groups suggest additional service standards for libraries that meet or exceed ADA architectural standards.[21] Temsky (1982) suggests:

> Take a hard look at what your library has to offer...[to] go beyond a simplistic concern for physical accessibility to the overriding issue of...compatibility, which attempts to allow an individual to interact easily with the immediate environment. That environment may include a smiling face, a wheelchair for in-house use, a talking elevator, a sign language T-shirt worn by a staff member, or a public telephone with amplification. The message is clear: "We want you here." ...The advisory committee serves an important function, too, by informing the community of the library's efforts, so that new equipment does not go unused or special programs unattended (Page 5).

ADA Single Point of Service

Full library ADA compliance is beyond architectural minima. Adaptations for patrons with a mix of disabling conditions can be met with help from the library ADA coordinator. The ADA coordinator represents a single point of service as the responsible contact person for patrons with special library needs. Libraries serving the public are well-advised to appoint an ADA Coordinator, and an ADA advisory committee or accessibility task force:

> The ADA coordinator should be someone that is interested in providing library services to patrons with disabilities and should be conversant with the full text of the ADA, its rules, regulations, and guidelines, and other state or federal civil rights legislation, especially as related to providing services to people with disabilities (Pack & Foos, 1992, page 226).

ADA Advisory Committee

The ADA advisory committee conducts a library access forum among community members with disabilities. The committee also surveys the community to determine how best to meet patron library support needs:

> A consumer advisory committee can be helpful in planning the forum, designing the survey, and analyzing the information received. It can also assist in ensuring that needed changes are actually made and that improved programs and services do not lapse into inaccessibility. Fundamental to this process is the realization that you cannot meet the needs of people without actually asking them what they want (Gunde, 1991, Page 100).

Library Patrons With Disabilities

Removing barriers and meeting or exceeding ADA standard minima provides better library patron service. ADA standards alone do not represent final solutions to individual with disability access needs:

> Every decision about ADA compliance must be made on a case-by-case basis, taking into consideration the elements involved in the service or program and the needs of the library patron with a disability (Gunde, 1991, page 99).

Arriving Library Patrons with Disabilities

Librarians address collection access issues but may ignore exterior access problems. Exterior challenges are ordinarily beyond librarian view.[22] Patrons with disabilities out of librarian sight must not also be out of librarian mind. Before reasonable accommodation is assured within, safe approach to the library door must be resolved. The disabled attempt library entry by resolving exterior barriers for themselves. While in the library, they receive professional librarian support. Yet some disabled patrons visibly need help even to reach library entrances. The physically or cognitively challenged may not always arrive at the library as pedestrians, but may ride in accessible vehicles as passengers or drive specially equipped vehicles. When they arrive at the parking lot, however, they may be entering a high-risk library area.

High-Risk Library Areas

High-risk areas exist outside the library door. Librarians observe people distressed by events occurring before they can access the collection. This distress may be caused by risks associated with physical challenges met outside the library.[23] Many times library parking lots and building accessways are not safe.[24] Patrons are forced to park at considerable distance from the library building. Escort services are needed, but rarely provided, for incoming patrons with disabilities as well as outgoing ones.[25]

Parking lot crime is a significant concern for many coming to the library. More incidences of vandalism, assault and battery, theft, auto theft, and auto and pedestrian accidents occur in parking lots serving libraries than on many public streets. Well-illuminated, monitored, clean and accessible parking lots, walkways and building entrances greatly reduce accidents, injuries and crime risks for all. The physically challenged are particularly vulnerable. They are relatively easy marks for law offenders. Safe access to parking lot, walkway, entrance and building service routes must be assured.[26] Patrons are not soley responsible for their own safe arrival. Associated risks that architectural barriers impose, and the need for external library safety, cannot be ignored.

Physically challenged drivers must negotiate parking lots and find appropriate parking. Others, as passengers with physical challenges, disembark from accessible vehicles and contend with loading zone challenges before entering the library. All approach entrances unseen by librarians. Some face significant physical challenges before accessing the collection. Librarians cannot limit their professional concern only for patrons with disabilities only to barriers within the library. Passive street barriers; parking lot, loading zone, curbside, and walkway barriers combine with ramps, steps and other challenges to make a barrier-rich environment. All areas surrounding and within the library must be designed and constructed so that all can approach, enter, and exit the area safely from a barrier-free environment.[27]

All areas surrounding and within the library must be designed and constructed so that all can approach, enter, and exit the area safely from a barrier-free environment.

The National Center for a Barrier Free Environment recommends an exterior videocamera placed for parking lot oversight as well as at internal library security areas. Over time, use patterns emerge that are not noticeable during an initial parking lot inspection. Librarians discern unusual or inappropriate parking lot use patterns that clearly argue for increased monitoring--by librarians or by other designated officials--of parking lots, walkways and entrances. [28]

Adverse Parking Lot Conditions

Adverse parking lot conditions create barriers to users of walking aids or wheelchairs and to the mobility-limited.[29] Arrivals must find level parking spaces in a parking lot where vehicle parking and wheelchair access aisles are located.[30] Loading zone surfaces should be made level without grass, loose gravel or sand. Even poor paved surfacing makes forward progress dangerous for walking aid or wheelchair users. Parking lots blocked by poor drainage, standing water, ice or snow accumulation, or those with slippery walking surfaces impose significant problems for all.[31] The physically challenged have fewer mobility options than the physically capable.

Loading Zones

Off-street loading zones allow vehicles to pull into accessible parking spaces allowing the disabled to disembark. But disembarkation must not be into another danger zone. Loading zones allow the shortest accessible travel route from parking to library entrance.[32] Lengthy travel routes from accessible parking spaces make library access for the physically challenged unequal to more direct routes available to others not physically challenged. Off-street loading zones restrict traffic and reduce risks to all pedestrians. Without designated off-street loading zones, accessible vehicles, vans or buses require two adjacent restricted parking spaces. Lacking off-street loading space, they must park temporarily over several parking spaces in order to accommodate disabled passengers. This moves larger service vehicles out of parking lot lane traffic but also blocks multiple parking spaces. Loading zone and parking lot problems for the mobility-limited virtually define them as a high-risk group for library physical access.

On-street loading zones are also particularly dangerous for mobility-limited pedestrians. Potential street traffic hazards are avoided by off-street loading zones. Off-street loading zones restrict traffic and reduce risks to all pedestrians, particularly to the slower-moving mobility-limited.

Restricted Accessible Parking

Librarians are sensitive to restricted accessible parking and parking lot access. But librarian sensitivity is not enough. Accessible parking must be consistently reviewed on behalf of patrons with disabilities. Librarians cannot assume that patrons arrive at library entrances without parking problems. Through parking lot barrier accessibility review, all library patrons can be better served.

The National Center for a Barrier Free Environment recommends an exterior videocamera placed for parking lot oversight as well as at internal library security areas.

Library Patrons With Disabilities

Libraries comply with minimum ADA-specified numbers of restricted accessible parking spaces, based on overall parking space numbers.[33] Yet these minimum accessible parking spaces do not assure safe or effective parking for many disabled patrons. One out of every eight accessible parking spaces must be specifically van accessible, providing a minumum 96-inch-width (96″ or greater).[34] Yet how many library patrons use a van, or an automobile? Who are pedestrians and who take public transit are not known. These factors were previously considered irrelevant to effective library accommodation for the disabled. Yet parking spaces that meet vehicle and driver/pedestrian requirements are particularly relevant to the disabled who want also to use the library.

Parking space users who are disabled and who do not require side-mounted lift vans may park in smaller parallel, or diagonal restricted spaces, but are not required to do so. Exiting or reentering between vehicles in diagonal parking requires close-in patron repositioning when adjacent spaces are occupied. Studies show that lift/van/wheelchair users may require 204-inch-wide (204″) parking when lifts are fully-extended.[35] Few accessible library parking spaces provide these oversized dimensions. Thus 96-inch-wide (96″) disabled access parking does not allow access to a diverse group of other disabled parking permit-holders. Where will they park to access the library?

Some parking spaces are universal or oversized to accept large, specially equipped vans with side-mounted lifts.[36] Even with oversized spaces, drivers park over lines using two adjacent disabled parking spaces. Nonuniversal restricted parking requires vehicle overlap between adjacent parking spaces where common aisles are not provided.[37] Vehicles park at the extreme edge or over lines, extending lift equipment and reducing access to properly parked adjacent vehicles, or over spaces not providing aisles. Universal parking spaces, a minimum of 12 feet (12′) wide, limit these otherwise unavoidable parking space encroachments. Universal parking space provision or placement is not ADA-dictated. Restricted accessible parking accommodates vehicle side-operating wheelchair lifts. Passenger side-operating lifts are the safety standard for specially-equipped vehicles. Driver side-operating lifts would place patrons with disabilities into oncoming traffic. Lifts open, extend and move in vehicle pull-up spaces. Oversized parking spaces position restricted vehicles away from curbs on the side where the lift equipment will extend. Lifts fully extended or moving are a danger to other pedestrians both in parking lots or when encroaching on walkways.[38] Extended lifts may not be recognizable to patrons with visual disabilities, even with careful long cane use along a walkway barred by an extended lift. Lift encroachment into the walkway is more than a temporary convenience to the mobility-limited patron, but a real walkway hazard for other pedestrians.

Marked crossings or access aisles through the parking lot are recommended to provide the disabled and other users with clear and safe walkway areas.[39] Universal parking spaces provide restricted parking wide enough to allow vehicle side-door use 132 inches (132″) and a 60-inch (60″) access aisle surrounding the vehicle.[40] Oversized or universal restricted parking spaces designated for the disabled promote no competition between the disabled arriving in cars or vans since all universal spaces can accommodate either

Libraries comply with minimum ADA-specified numbers of restricted accessible parking spaces, based on overall parking space numbers. Yet these minimum accessible parking spaces do not assure safe or effective parking for many disabled patrons.

vehicle type.[41] Yet the ADA specifies only restricted parking spaces and does not specifically require oversized parking spaces. Further, the ADA does not require universal parking spaces to be placed at convenient locations. Inconvenient parking is easily overcome by physically able patrons who make the library trek. Can patrons with disabilities also make the library trek safely?

ADA-Specified Parking Signage

The ADA suggests that a sign be provided to alert van users to wider parking space aisles or spaces. But aisle or parking space use is not intended to be restricted only to accessible vans.[42] Designated accessible parking spaces can be used by anyone with disabilities authorized for special parking. Accessible parking spaces are marked with the International Symbol of Accessibility signage.[43] Parking lot location is specifically addressed in ADA Handbook:

> Accessible parking spaces serving a particular building shall be located on the shortest accessible route of travel from adjacent parking to an accessible entrance. In parking facilities that do not serve a particular building, accessible parking shall be located on the shortest accessible route of travel to an accessible pedestrian entrance of the parking facility. In buildings with multiple accessible entrances with adjacent parking, accessible parking spaces shall be dispersed and located closest to the accessible entrances (ADAAG 4.6.2).

Parking Barrier Awareness

People not disabled may not be barrier-aware. Others inadvertently or unknowingly reduce or eliminate physically challenged access.[44] Disabled parking signage is located so as not to be obscured by vehicles parked in that space.[45] Restricted parking is clearly visible to people with disabilities who attempt parking in designated spaces. Yet library restricted parking signage is often ignored.

Librarians do not know the parking preferences and needs of patrons with disabilities unless patrons inform them. Professionals must start asking, and listening, to identify specific patron parking needs. Patron answers generate specific parking solutions. Restricted parking is often located in parking lots to meet minimum numbers rather than addressing disabled parking convenience. There is often a failure to self-communicate special parking requirements to librarians or authorities who could provide effective library access.

Arriving drivers with disabilities find others using restricted parking without special use permits. The disabled do not support unauthorized parking any more than they would self-servingly condone their own inappropriate parking. Disability interest groups advocate ticketing and towing vehicles without restricted parking permits. This procedure, however, is applied inconsistently across the nation. How is disabled parking enforced outside your library? Competition exists among disabled users for restricted and accessible parking.[46] The ADA does not address the problem of restricted parking space numbers used by a diversity of disabled with widely different parking requirements.[47]

Library Patrons With Disabilities

The ADA simply establishes numbers of accessible parking spaces as a proportion of overall parking lot spaces available. Parking for the disabled is not predetermined by librarians since professionals have not accounted for general parking patterns, much less special-needs parking requirements. Some patrons with disabilities require universal parking spaces. Others can negotiate diagonal or parallel restricted parking spaces. Parking space needs are dictated by each patron's needs. And conflicts over limited accessible and restricted parking space are inevitable. For example, it may be the policy in postsecondary education to issue more permits than accessible or regular parking spaces, thereby creating excess competition among all patrons and even more intensely focused competition among restricted parking patrons.[48] Administrators reason that parking is not used continuously by the same person or vehicle throughout the day. Unused designated spaces limit institutional permit revenue.[49] Open and reserved parking areas may be adjusted according to this parking cost reduction policy. However, ADA-defined restricted parking space numbers may not meet local disabled patron needs. Where parking fees are assessed the public, individuals with disabilities must not be charged additional fees for designated accessible parking. But levying parking fees for disabled or restricted parking spaces already filled is another matter.

Restricted Parking Privileges

The disabled have limited parking options directly associated with their disabilities. Restricted parking spaces are not strictly or consistently enforced. Library workers, staff and faculty often view restricted parking as legitimate personal parking spaces. Other employees explain their professional duties as a rationale to park even temporarily in unauthorized restricted parking. Is it a valid assumption that nondisabled employees may use restricted parking permits intended specifically for the disabled? Institutional vehicles and delivery trucks are often the worst offenders. Parking in restricted spaces without restricted parking permits violates the law. Perhaps if librarians who mispark in designated accessible parking spaces do not regard themselves as law violators, it may instead be easier for them to regard themselves as imposers of service barriers on disabled individuals. Authorities avoid resolving the issue of citations for those disabled who mispark. Librarians avoid parking issues in deference to providing more clearly defined and manageable services to the disabled within the library. But for individuals with physical or cognitive challenges, restricted parking privileges alone do not resolve these library physical access problems. Authorities also respond inconsistently to disabled misparking. Are misparkers, even though disabled, legitimately ticketed even when they display restricted access permits? Since misparkers would be treated differently on the basis of disabilities, does the ADA suggest they be ticketed?[50] Parking citations are a legitimate, nondiscriminatory and justified penalty for the disabled who mispark. The librarian may be the first person to hear a legitimate complaint from a challenged patron about parking concerns. How will librarians and their supervisors deal with these legitimate parking complaints or patron grievances?[51] Centrally-located parking lots and spaces serving the library often are reserved for administration, faculty and staff.[52] Close-in parking is a perk not shared with library patrons with disabilities authorized to park in restricted spaces. Faculty not disabled are given de facto priority placement

Competition exists among disabled users for restricted and accessible parking. The ADA does not address the problem of restricted parking space numbers used by a diversity of disabled with widely different parking requirements.

to nearest curb cuts and walkways over disabled parking users. Unless librarians are themselves physically challenged, who require assigned parking spaces near library entrances, and who display restricted parking permits, those spaces should be designated as restricted for disabled patrons.[53] The ADA provides for redress of disparate treatment policies based on disabilities.[54] Questionable restricted parking privileges are based on faculty, staff or administrative status rather than on disability status. Community disability groups or advisory councils report this as one of their highest library access concerns. On this issue alone we may predict considerable litigation concerning separate but unequal parking access for individuals with disabilities. No clear line exists between disabled parking rights and privileges. Patrons needing specially equipped vehicles and having restricted parking permits abuse those parking privileges as do the nondisabled. Many law enforcement personnel are not trained for parking control that also directly affects the disabled. And some authorities privately acknowledge a de facto prohibition on issuing parking citations or enforcing fines on the disabled. Some do not ticket even when special designated parking permits have expired. A warning ticket or a note to renew expired accessible parking permits is a reasonable accommodation. A citation for continuously parking use with an invalid or expired permit is also a reasonable accommodation for others with disabilities who also need specialized parking and display their valid accessible parking permits. Are these non-issues for the professional librarian or do these issues directly affect patrons who are unable to enter the library because of outside parking problems?

Temporary restricted parking permits may not be obtained by drivers inexperienced because of temporarily imposed disabilities. Special challenges await the temporarily disabled person--who must obtain a special designation parking permit--while needing to park in restricted parking spaces before the permit is issued. Special events bringing temporary visitors with disabilities to the library provide restricted parking permit access. A patron catch-22 condition arises without prior temporary restricted parking permits.

Authorities may avoid citing disabled veterans or vehicles showing veteran status over other disabled who are not veterans. This builds resentment among disabled nonveterans who also have equal restricted parking authorization. This misguided practice may also have the effect of increasing conflicts between veteran and nonveteran disabled parking space users.

Reserved or designated parking spaces for the disabled are often occupied by unauthorized law enforcement vehicles not providing emergency service and not on official business. Even official business does not inherently provide special parking privileges over the needs of the disabled. For example, on college campuses, officers attend police training or criminal justice classes to obtain promotions or meet minimum job requirements through on-the-job coursework. Officers attending classes have student status, not police status, even though patrol cars are used and these students are in uniform. While officers can void their colleagues' tickets, or mispark without restricted parking permits, disabled respect for the police is not engendered. When officers require special parking they should obtain permits and not further compete with patrons with disabilities who also require

Reserved or designated parking spaces for the disabled are often occupied by unauthorized law enforcement vehicles not providing emergency service and not on official business.

Library Patrons With Disabilities

authorized, designated and restricted parking. Unfortunately, many times they are all competing for the same parking spaces. Librarians must consider who will win out-the officer or the disabled library patron. There are few officers, employees or other librarians who would not immediately correct their misparking, when quietyly reminded by a peer, another librarian or the library ADA coordinator when they recognize the problem of discrimination against the disabled.

Separate parking privileges for some and not others is inherently discriminatory assuming a legitimate reason to park is shared by all. The doctrine of separate but equal has been defeated in municipal, state and supreme courts with the Civil Rights Movement in the early 1960s. The ADA prohibits separate but equal disabled services.[55] Yet elsewhere the ADA specifies that separate disabled services, such as parking, may be appropriate:

> Nothing in this part prohibits a public entity from providing benefits, services, or advantages to individuals with disabilities, or to a particular class of individuals with disabilities beyond those required by this part (ADA Handbook, II-39).

Prejudice Between Disabled Parking Lot Users

There is a lack of clear accessible parking policy and regulation enforcement on behalf of the disabled. Professional librarians can no longer patronize patrons with disabilities by anticipating their needs. Librarians must be prepared to hear those needs clearly voiced by disabled patrons themselves, as self-advocates for specially designated library parking rights and privileges. When discrimination based on disability is asserted, the complaint must not be ignored. Librarians and other authorities have not yet determined if local patrons with disabilities themselves also hold myths, stereotypes and have paternalistic tendencies toward other disabled people. Professional concern for the nondisabled majority's misguided attitudes has left well-meaning librarians blind to negative attitudes the disabled minority hold for each other. Prejudice between individuals with disabilities may be a Pandora's box which many do not desire to openly discuss--much less resolve. Prejudice can be reduced when librarians and other authorities model nondiscriminatory attitudes and actions--even in their parking lot behavior. And an essential component of the library ADA coordinator may be to regularly go on "parking lot patrol."

Parking Access Priority

Litigation between disabled individuals or groups seem inevitable. How can the courts establish a viable priority ranking of services, needs or privileges for individuals based on disabilities who are so diverse? Needs of the disabled are diverse, individually identified and situationally resolved, one library patron at a time. Concerning specific parking policy for the disabled, some libraries have decided to abolish separate parking policies in the name of equality.[56] Where all disabled come to a facility parking lot, they come to designated accessible parking on a first-come, first-served basis.[57] But parking on a first-come, first-served basis for the disabled is only a partial solution when the disabled must further compete with limited numbers of accessible parking spaces. The larger solution seems to be increasing--above ADA minimums--the numbers and types of accessible parking spaces.

Disabled parking permits are issued to people with different parking needs, vehicles, mobility problems, and stamina.[58] Based on staminia alone, an individual with disabilities may request reasonable accommodation by being designated a reserved special parking permit holder for a space closest to the library.

Approach to the Library Door

The ADA does not recognize those with temporary disabilities who would otherwise be permitted restricted temporary parking permits. Temporary permits are not issued on the basis of individual parking need for patrons with disabilities. Parking policy lacks the precision to clarify to authorities issuing these permits how to determine individual parking needs between those with temporary, and others with more permanent, disabilities. Parking authorities must judge special temporary or permanent permit issuance when specific disability criteria have been met. Yet specific criteria or guidelines are lacking. Only with a physician's written statement documenting a patron's specific disabilities can most patrons secure special parking permits. With the absence of effective individual patron guidelines or sole reliance on patron special access needs statements, authorities must rely on medical judgment alone.

Authorities are not informed or equipped to determine actual individual parking needs. Permits do not specify special parking needs, only disabled-, reserved- or open-parking permit status. Permits designated specifically to support special parking needs generally do not exist. Special parking needs are as yet not effectively provided on an individual, patron-by-patron basis. The art of creating parking space accessibility for the disabled must evolve into the science of meeting individual parking needs just as it has evolved within the library to promote title, service area, library furniture and equipment accessibility for the disabled.

Parking Lot Meetings

Disabled community members or their representatives demonstrate parking lot problems using specialized vehicles and personal equipment. Disability support groups meet at parking lots, loading zones and along library walkways. Some form virtual parking lot patrols.[59] Without citation authority, some disabled groups elect to post private notices on offending vehicles. That often leads to dangerous interpersonal conflicts in parking lots. Parking lot meetings reveal needed parking changes and adjustments. Joining these groups should be local police or security who have parking citation authority. Citation policy and procedural changes allow local disabled users to meet local parking needs and help authorities provide equitable and compassionate parking lot control. Part of this community effort may be shared by the professional librarian since the implications so directly affect individual access to library information. From these parking lot meetings may come the need to designate accessible parking requirements on the patron's library pass to acknowledge the importance of parking access as a necessary component of library and information barrier-free access.

Pedestrian Movement in Parking Lots

When pedestrians with disabilities leave, enter or move between vehicles in library parking lots, other drivers may not view those movements. People move behind other vehicles when restricted parking spaces and immediate access to walkways off parking areas is not provided. Vehicle backing at restricted loading zones without drive-through capability reduces driver visibility for pedestrians.

Disability support groups meet at parking lots, loading zones and along library walkways. Some form virtual parking lot patrols.

Some disabled pedestrians cannot quickly avoid backing vehicles. Others cannot be effectively seen from driver rearview mirrors. Walking aid users tend to fall even under favorable mobility conditions. While recovering from falling, they are not visible to other drivers during parking lot backing or turning. Tragedy may not be averted in parking lots, even with the most careful drivers, or reduced by strictly enforced parking lot speed limits. In the parking lot, walking aid users are virtually slow-moving targets to vehicles not carefully driven.

The school bus industry is monitored by the National Transportation Safety Board in annual parking lot safety statistics concerning bus drivers and vehicles. Special equipment allowing driver front bumper viewing, wider side and exterior and interior rear viewing, has significantly reduced school parking lot injuries and fatalities. Small people are not easily seen, even by careful drivers with a long history of cautious driving. We may have unwisely assumed that being in harm's way was much less likely for adults in public parking lots than for children. Adults take full personal responsibility for their safety. Disabled adults also take full personal safety responsibility and face greater risks of injury nonetheless.

In the parking lot, walking aid users are virtually slow moving targets to moving vehicles not carefully driven.

Personal parking lot injuries occur that can be more damaging to already disabled people. Libraries are not responsible for parking lot safety, how their patrons use the lot, parking spaces or loading zones to make the library trek. But is the library trek as safe for patrons with disabilities as it is for others? Where and when does the professional librarian limit concern for patrons in their quest for library information? Where personal safety is the issue, that issue takes higher priority over direct access to library information.

Accessible Walkways to the Library

Free movement from parking lot or loading zone to library entrances must be possible for all. Parking lots and loading zones provide exterior accessible route linkage to library building walkways.[60] Without a smooth, continuous surface, many disabled cannot safely approach or enter the library. Walkways provide an important physical link to the library and all other buildings.[61] Accessible walkways are used both by pedestrians with disabilities and those less physically challenged:

At least one accessible route within the boundary of the [library] site shall be provided from public transportation stops, accessible parking, and accessible passenger loading zones, and public streets or sidewalks to the accessible building entrance they serve. The accessible route shall, to the maximum extent feasible, coincide with the route for the general public (ADA Handbook, 1990, ADAAG 4.3.2 (1)).

Curb Ramps at Walkways

Curb ramps are located or protected to prevent obstruction by parked vehicles.[62] Curb transitions from ramps to walks, gutters, or streets are flush and free of abrupt changes.[63] Abrupt changes reduce pedestrian falls or injuries and facilitate free movement to the library. When a patron falls, that person changes status from library patron to victim. Shall the library not consider accessible walkways to the library door as a professional librarian responsibility? In a personal sense, the next walkway fall could be yours rather than a another library patron's misfortune.

Clear, level or ramped walkways, without abrupt curb cuts and accessible to disabled people enable free movement from parking lot or loading zone to library entrances.[64] Curb cuts near restricted parking spaces enable safe movement between parking spaces and walkways. Whenever an accessible route to the library crosses a curb, curb cuts are provided.[65] As pedestrians, you can remember stumbling or unexpectedly stepping down jarring your gait, twisting your ankle or falling outright. For the disabled this relatively minor physical challenge may have more serious and long-lasting implications.

When a patron falls, that person changes status from library patron to victim. Shall the library not consider accessible walkways to the library door as a professional librarian responsibility?

To facilitate free walkway movement after disembarking, walkways leading to libraries must blend to a common level when crossing other walks, driveways, parking lot or loading zone surfaces.[66] Narrow library walkways or those interrupted by steps or abrupt level changes restrict disabled access. Raised islands at walkway crossings provide pedestrian cuts level with the street or parking lot.[67] Library walkways 60 inches (60") or wider permit dual wheelchair passing.[68] Gradual walkway grading avoids steep inclines that are difficult to negotiate in wheelchairs or that demand significant effort for the mobility-limited.[69] Walkway grading should be no greater than 5 percent (5%), or one foot rise to each 20 feet of run.[70] Remember that all walkways must blend to a common level to provide effective and safe library access.

Walkway Steps, Ramps and Surfacing

Walkways interrupted by steps, abrupt level changes or ramps make negotiation difficult and slow for mobility-limited patrons.[71] Library building steps or stairs are avoided by those who require ramps bypassing steps.[72] Ramped walkways have nonslip surfacing and are protected from bad weather surface problems.[73] Curbs, walls, railings or projecting surfaces prevent side-slipping off ramps.[74] Crutch or brace walkers tend to side-slip during forward movement on their way to gain library information. Handrails are available at library walkways, ramps or loading platforms.[75] But handrails are not always useful for crutch, walker or cane users since both arms are engaged in using the walking aid. Walkway barriers are silent library obstacles.

Library Patrons With Disabilities

Ramped walkways provide a five-foot-square landing at the library door for wheelchair repositioning before entry.[76] Wheelchair repositioning at ramped walkways is often required to initiate forward movement at the next ramp segment or where library ramps change direction at landings.[77] Ramped walkways also assist walker, crutch and cane users to reposition before attempting library entrance. When library walkway ramps with abrupt level changes are approached, wheelchair users must avoid tipping backward or bottoming out.[78] Manual wheelchair users with an attendant require larger walkway space during ramp use because of attendant-occupied space.[79] Turning space at walkway ramps is less for skilled manual wheelchair users who can tip back and move within wheel width. Powered wheelchair users use larger turning spaces.

Pedestrians are often blocked or delayed at library walkways by wheelchair users or other mobility-limited patrons.[80] Walking aid users make slow forward progress and require more time between parking space and arriving at the library door.[81] Mobile pedestrians can step off walkways safely onto level grass surfaces and pass by safely or wait and follow others' slow forward progress. Wider walkways permit safe passage for all unless heavily trafficked. Heavy-use walkways have a mix of pedestrians, some of whom must step off to make faster forward progress. Other pedestrians walk abreast, blocking others enroute. Observing walkway pedestrian traffic indicates a mix of walking patterns, walkway use and misuse. The librarian can informally evaluate these conditions by observing heavy pedestrian traffic and how pedestrians with disabilities interact with others before entering the library portal.

Heavy traffic on library walkways is a dangerous mix of fast and slow-moving pedestrian traffic.[82] Pedestrians may not follow the convention of walking to the right. Heavy traffic flow on external walkways with center or left-of-center moving patrons is always problematic. Crutch and cane users also have a wider stance during forward motion and may trip other pedestrians. Others are easily tripped during heavy walkway traffic and reduced cane-user visibility. Long cane users have walkway mobility limitations imposed by low or no vision. Wheel-equipped walkers have a tendency to drop or extend over the walkway edges unbalancing the user. The natural tendency of some pedestrians to yield the right-of-way to the mobility-limited often avoids collisions. Yet there is no standard beyond common walkway courtesy requiring anyone to move for anyone else. It inspires confidence in humanity to see pedestrians almost subconsciously resolve problems of forward movement in mixed traffic. But pedestrian traffic is at walking speed.

Other walkway problems make forward progress more complicated and dangerous when joggers, runners and cyclists share the path at faster speeds. One of the most common conditions outside libraries are multiple racks of bicycles at or near the entrance.Libraries should prohibit cyclists from pedestrian walkways or require them to walk their cycles in high-traffic areas.[83] Restricted bicycle paths parallel to heavy pedestrian walkways would limit traffic. Speeding cyclists at walkway-cycle path crossovers are traffic hazards for all. Colliding cyclists and pedestrians are both injured. Wheelchair

Heavy traffic on library walkways is a dangerous mix of fast and slow-moving pedestrian traffic. Other walkway problems make forward progress more complicated and dangerous when joggers, runners and cyclists share the path at faster speeds.

users have low relative-height visibility, compared to the cyclist. Librarians may only hear of these events as area incident reports emerge rather than understanding the direct connection between cyclists, pedestrians and library information access barriers. Walkway traffic mix is a significant library barrier to be overcome by patrons and removed by professional librarians.

Wheelchair users can see oncoming cyclist movement but are unable to move away or may move into the actual line of forward bicycle movement. At ramp curves, walkway landings or wheelchair rest areas, a speeding cyclist may not see mobility-limited pedestrians in time to avoid them. Cyclists must walk bicycles along pedestrian walkways or ride exclusively on cycle paths. Cyclists can then remount once pedestrian danger areas are passed. This pedestrian safety standard is a worthwhile one to be adopted by libraries.

External Library Building Ramps

Ramps provide another genuine concern for patron safety before library entry. Heavy walkway traffic at library exterior ramps require extra safety precautions. Ramps permitting building access for wheelchairs are negotiated with more care by wheelchair users than by pedestrians. Steep library ramps should be avoided. Ramps should rise no more than 1 foot for every 12 feet of run.[84]

Wheelchair and walking aid users experience traction or footing problems on library ramps.[85] Traction and footing are severely restricted when poor ramp surfacing is not quickly corrected. Ramp surfacing leading into the library must be resolved and kept free of ice, snow, sand, or rock salt and any other poor walking surface conditions.[86] Library ramps should have nonslip surfacing:

> People who have difficulty walking or maintaining balance or who use crutches, canes, or walkers, and those with restricted gaits are particularly sensitive to slipping and tripping hazards. For such people, a stable and regular surface is necessary for safe walking...Wheelchairs are propelled most easily on surfaces that are hard, stable, and regular. Soft loose surfaces such as...loose sand or gravel, wet clay, and irregular surfaces...can significantly impede wheelchair movement (ADA Handbook, 1990, A4.5.1).

Uncontrolled wheelchair rollback must be prevented. Losing balanced wheel grip or single-wheel traction abruptly causes uncontrolled wheelchair turns. Braking may not stop turns or rollback effectively. Rollbacks frequently spill the user.[87] This argues for an attendant to accompany wheelchair patrons. But many independent wheelchair users resent a suggestion for attendant help. Wheelchairs users have the right to choose.

Other pedestrians may not realize the danger of wheelchair user rollback on a library ramp. Wheelchairs rolling back collide with pedestrians. Rollback is difficult to control even for wheelchair users with prodigious upper-body strength:

> Wheelchair users with disabilities affecting their arms or with low stamina have serious difficulty using inclines. Most ambulatory people and most people who use wheelchairs can manage a slope of 1:16. Many people cannot manage a slope of 1:12 for 30 feet (ADA Handbook, 1990, A4.8.1).

Physically challenging library ramps without handrails that serve underground passageways, tunnels, overhead or open-area walkways place wheelchair users in immediate danger.[88] Parallel rails below handrail height are not required but avoid midramp roll-off. Dual or triple rails give the effect of closed railing and add a secure feeling for wheelchair users. Handrails on both sides of the walkway along walled ramps provide full security.

Library Patrons With Disabilities

Wheelchair users and other mobility-limited patrons become fatigued on library ramps and are slow movers.[89] Open handrails cause walkway disorientation for some with disabilities. The reader may have had a similar experience while walking over a bridge during heavy traffic flow beneath. Pedestrian forward movement is sensed but side-moving traffic disturbs balance. With the mobility-limited, this sense of unbalance may be increased. People compensate for this perceptual disturbance by purposefully looking ahead during forward movement and avoiding looking to the side. Walkway disorientation can also occur during heavy pedestrian traffic at walkway "cloverleafs."

Handrails at Library Walkway Ramps and Stairs

All must be able to safely and effectively use library walkway handrails if needed. Ramps with handrails on both sides enable independent wheelchair negotiation and help people overcome gravity effects during wheelchair movement, either to maintain a steady forward progress, or slow and control the downhill roll. Movement without traction loss, balance or forward progress at library ramps is difficult even for experienced wheelchair users.[90] Ramp handrail surfacing avoids user discomfort.[91] Ramp negotiation requires a six foot clear, level ramp base or landing, where wheelchair users begin or end ramp negotiation.[92] Library ramps should provide level rest areas at turns or on curves.[93] Handrails on both stair sides may not be effectively used by some walking aid users. They cannot reach library stairway handrails while maintaining balance.[94] Others use one handrail and cannot reach the opposite rail across the stair width. Handrails between 34 and 38 inches (38") above stair treads are within most stair user's reach.[95] Stair handrails should be positioned to extend a minimum of 18 inches (18") beyond top and bottom steps and have a minimum of 1 1/2 inch (1 1/2") wall clearance.[96] Without wall clearance, handrails provide balancing help but no gripping support for those patrons negotiating library stairs. Grip or balance loss by library stair users can be fatal. Handrails must be secure, grippable and well-maintained along the entire stair length.

Walkway Detectable Warnings and Hazards

Special detectable warnings on walking surfaces and curb ramps warn of walkway hazards using raised truncated domes.[97] Standardized surface features, built-in or applied to walkway surfaces, warn of walkway hazard approach.[98] High-contrast light-on-dark or dark-on-light walking surface features are felt by sound-on-cane contact.[99] Without meaningful long-cane contact or pedestrian tread, many library patrons with visual impairments become temporarily disoriented before they enter the library. Some can become "lost" on wide library walkways, ramps, entryways or in even in large parking lots. When disoriented, the approach of a sighted person may be welcome to reorient and reassure. Volunteering help to the blind must be done only if they appear disoriented. Offers of assistance may be accepted, or rejected either courteously or abruptly. Patrons must determine their own need for library approach help when offered.

Walkway hazards include pedestrian-barricaded open manholes and exterior library building or ground excavation areas. Underground utility steam vent warnings on walkways redirect people to safer walkway areas. External power panels or freestanding power transformers along library walkways should be pedestrian barricaded.

Where gratings are located in library walking surfaces, grating patterns are set perpendicular to the predominant direction of pedestrian traffic.[100] This prevents wheel-sink or wheel-locking between grating edges. Persons using wheelchairs may not have the strength to recover from a wheel-sink without assistance. Efforts to recover from a wheel-sink may unseat the user from the wheelchair. Unseated, many wheelchair users cannot recover chair seating without help.

Approach to the Library Door

Just as interior library remodeling requires warnings, exterior library walkways or ramps under repair or construction must also be pedestrian barricaded. Visual barricades may not be enough when pedestrians with low vision or the blind walk unaware through walkway tape barriers. Barriers must be more substantial for their safety. Temporary fencing helps pedestrians negotiate hazardous areas.

Lighting at Walkways and Ramps

Ramps and walkways should be well lighted for all pedestrians. Library entry and hazard warning signs should be readily visible to pedestrians outside the building along walkways. Yet under poor lighting or visibility conditions, the most accessible library area warning signs cannot be recognized. Low-hanging or protruding objects or signs over walkways or ramps should be avoided.[101] Lighting should also extend directly to the library entrance.

Exterior Library Stairways and Steps

The mobility-limited can negotiate library exterior steps and entrance stairs but may experience other access problems on the way. Both outdoor stairs and ramp walkway alternatives should be available at library entrances.[102] Library stairways connecting outdoor walkways are linked with accessible ramps.[103] Water, ice or snow accumulation on walking surfaces cannot always be avoided on outdoor stairways but must be consistently monitored by the professional librarian within.[104] Library stairways and steps present insurmountable barriers for those with severe mobility problems. Since few multifloor libraries present direct exterior elevator access, ramps may be the only clear alternative.[105] Some using walking aids find stair use more comfortable than ramps.[106] Walking aid users must maintain the shifting balance needed to negotiate stairs. Users with walking aids have a tendency to slip or trip on library walkway or stairway hazards.[107] Anyone with crutch experience knows the significant difference and physical challenge associated with going up, compared to going down, stairs. The librarian can better understand exterior library barriers by examining outside incident reports that happen to people with disabilities at library exterior stairways and steps. Outdoor library steps should have uniform riser heights and uniform tread widths.[108] Anyone experiencing sudden and unexpected step changes midstairs knows the jarring and unbalancing effect of nonuniform riser heights and tread widths. While they may not think in these architectural terms, their normal life can be instantly interrupted by these sudden and unexpected exterior library barrier events. Outdoor library steps covered with skid-free surfacing are preferable to avoid slips and to maintain good foot grip during step negotiation for all.

Patron Library Entrance Delays

Patron delays to library appointments are understandable during inclement weather. Librarians respect individuals with disabilities who labor diligently to keep up with the conventional pace of events in a regular day. For the disabled there is no library "regular day." Instead, a series of challenges must be met with poise, grace, and a consistently "good attitude." Professionals

The mobility-limited can negotiate library exterior steps and entrance stairs but may experience other access problems on the way. Both outdoor stairs and ramp walkway alternatives should be available at library entrances.

Library Patrons With Disabilities

should meet the disabled who have already struggled to enter the library, with an equally positive and supportive patron service attitude.

Libraries may be within a larger building or as a separate service building in a larger campus context. At least one library entrance nearest the loading zone should be wheelchair accessible.[109] Alternate library entrances for wheelchair or the mobility-limited can be used when other entrances, walkways or ramps are temporarily closed or blocked. Safe alternate entry must be assured for those who cannot gain access through the main library entryway. Some library entryways are not wheelchair-accessible. The main library entry is often inaccessible because of original building architecture, before retrofitting or adding an alternate ramp entry. Alternate access also must be provided when main library entrances are blocked.[110] Ramps at entryways circumventing stairs are the most common wheelchair access method. Other library entryways intended for private or service vehicles may not be publicly accessible.

Private entryways into libraries are not always clearly understood by pedestrians. People tend to assume that if a library worker is seen to use an entry, that entry is also open for their use. People with disabilities also tend to assume nonpublic library entryways provide patron safe entry. Nonpublic entry may not offer the same interior library signage guiding patrons to service areas along public entryways.

The mobility-limited sometimes use alternate library entryways at loading zones or ramps. Library loading zones or ramps for private or service vehicles are not always pedestrian safe. When loading zones or ramps are restricted to library service use only, entryway signage prevents unauthorized use. Signage redirects patrons to the main library entryway. Alternate library entryways may not be safe for the mobility-limited.

Library Entrance Identification

Library entrances must be clearly identifiable from the pedestrian viewpoint. Oversized entrance signage provides viewing at a distance or viewing from the parking lot. Distant building recognition precludes slow, laborious parking lot and walkway negotiation for patrons with disabilities before realizing the building approached is not the library. Library entranceways lacking accessible identification make building recognition difficult for the blind or visually impaired, even at close range.[111]

Mobility orientation for the blind, for example, requires a constantly updated "present location" mental map, knowing which building entrance is being approached and remembering subsequent entrance and exit orientation for future campus walkway or public street movement. Library patrons with low vision[112] or the blind are not forced to rely solely on mobility orientation but can gain information from entrance identification made accessible:

Each library building entrance and exit configuration presents unique problems for the physically challenged.

In building complexes where finding [library] locations independently on a routine basis may be a necessity, ...tactile maps or prerecorded instructions can be very helpful to visually impaired people. Several maps and auditory instructions have been developed and tested for specific applications. The type of map or instructions used must be based on the information to be communicated, which depends highly on the type of buildings or users (ADA Handbook, 1990, A4.30.1).

Raised or recessed letters or numbering on library signs at walkway level identify the building and specifically refer to cardinal direction building entrances. While cardinal direction (North, South, East, West, Southwest, etc.) entrance signage appears redundant and unnecessary for sighted pedestrians, libraries with multiple entrances disorient some patrons on entry or exit. You may better understand mobility disorientation by remembering the feeling when leaving a busy shopping mall and attempting to relocate your parked vehicle. Consistent identifiers placed on the wall adjacent to the latch side of the library door helps orient the patron. Identifiers placed on library walls at 60-inch (60") height, and at entrances or along raised walkways, are within tactile reading reach.[113] Service entry doors are easily confused with patron access doors and have signage, centered on doors at face level, indicating NO PUBLIC ACCESS.

On unauthorized entry, exterior library doors present a real danger to the blind or patrons with visual impairments. Door equipment controls should have tactile and Brailled markings. Tactile entryway warnings on doors leading to hazardous, off-limits or nonpublic use areas alert the visually impaired against entry to library equipment areas, loading platforms dropoffs, boiler rooms, exterior locked rooms, darkrooms, stages or low overhead passageways. Patrons approaching non-public access library doors are warned against entry by tactile door knobs, push bars or door-opening equipment. Tactile warnings include knurled or roughed door handles, knobs, pulls, or other pedestrian operating hardware. Well-planned main or secondary library entryways avoid dangers to entering patrons and do not require tactile warnings. Inaccessible library entrances have directional signage indicating the nearest accessible entrance walkway routes.[114] It is a conventional safety requirement that even non-public access library doors be usable for emergency exit. Non-public access library doors left ajar invite misuse and safety risks for patrons with disabilities.

Library door identifiers may not be recognized by a patron majority, yet they are critical to some patrons with disabilities. Library door signage typically includes EXIT, ENTER, or DO NOT ENTER messages. Clear library glass doors may not be visible to some patrons without large door frames, cross bars and some visual reference of door presence. Clear glass doors are equipped with visual identifiers at knee and face levels to help patrons avoid collisions or attempted library door walkthroughs. Graffiti, public announcements and all other related signage should be avoided on library service entry doors. Pedestrians must be able to see through the door to oncoming pedestrians who will be exiting.

Tactile entryway warnings on doors leading to hazardous, off-limits or nonpublic use areas alert the visually impaired against entry to library equipment areas, loading platforms dropoffs, boiler rooms, exterior locked rooms, darkrooms, stages or low overhead passageways.

Library Patrons With Disabilities

Library Entryways

When library entrances are within a host building, hallways or mezzanines provide immediate access to library service areas.[115] Entrances should be in close proximity to elevators for multifloor library access. Persons using library entryways should be visible to circulation librarians.

Entryways should avoid complex maneuvering challenges.[116] In well-planned libraries the circulation desk, card catalog area, online terminals, periodical and special collections, displays and equipment directions should be closely available on entry. Visitor conference or multipurpose areas near entrances should be immediately accessible for those not intending to use other library services. Multiple format library maps useful to all should first be presented at the entrance as an accessible public service.

Library Doors

Librarians must be sensitive to the presentation given to each patron as that person enters the library portal. Library doors operable by a single effort communicate far greater welcome to the physically challenged than a welcome mat. Even library welcome mats are physical barriers to the mobility limited when folded, misaligned or slippery. Access to the library must be provided more in architecture than in signage. Door handles, pulls, latches or locks requiring tight grasping, pinching or wrist twisting may not be operable by the disabled.[117] Doors inoperable or poorly operating in bad weather, windy conditions or unrepaired after weather damage, are barriers to all.[118] Fast-closing doors interfere with slow-moving patrons. Even experienced wheelchair users struggle to get the complex movements coordinated to provide smooth, independent door entry. Few novices in wheelchairs are successful without hand or finger injuries. Door-closing delay adjustments provide more time to manuever through doorways.[119]

Library door negotiation for the mobility limited is not easy. Wide, spacious library doors are more than architecturally or aesthetically pleasing features for many entering there. Wheelchair and walking aid users must reposition themselves before door opening in order to maintain balance. Then they move through and the library door closes behind them. Wider library doors are generally easier to negotiate from a wheelchair position, without interfering with other pedestrians.

Kickplates reduce glass door panel damage from wheelchair and walking aid users who must force open library doors with their equipment.[120] Forcing doors open with equipment and using the kickplate in this way may be a necessary step to regular wheelchair or walking aid user door entry. Door kickplates help us all. Patrons not physically challenged carrying books lean must against doors, get a partial grip on door handles, or use their feet at the kickplate to force doors open or hold them open while entering. Wheelchair or walking aid users cannot negotiate doors without kickplates since this would force them to lean heavily on doorglass. The mobility-limited cannot negotiate library doors while carrying objects or books that would restrict hand use. Thresholds and doorway surface height changes impose additional

Librarians must be sensitive to the presentation given to each patron as that person enters the library portal. Library doors operable by a single effort communicate far greater welcome to the physically challenged than a welcome mat.

Approach to the Library Door

library challenges. Wheelchair users do complex manuevering to get over library door-levelchanges while operating door controls.[121] For wider stance walking aid users, library double-leaf doors should provide 32 inches (32") or greater opening width.[122] Doors opening wider than a minimum of 32 inches (32") provide better wheelchair library access.[123] Entrances with two doors in a series should provide a minimum of 48 inches (48") of space between doors for easy wheelchair negotiation through the second series of doors.[124]

Independent library access for all means access to doorway entry without help from others. For many, library entry independence is impossible without power-assisted doors. Working and well-maintained power-assisted doors provide continuous independent library access for all and help protect dignity for the mobility limited. Power-assisted library doors operate with minimal opening effort.[125] Door opening resistance is reduced after activating a switch or when patrons maintain continually applied force to the library door.[126] When power-assisted door switches are activated, opening is full and immediate. Any less than full opening may not provide adequate space for wheelchair entry. Power-assisted doors should close within 30 seconds without patron effort. Doors taking more than 30 seconds to close waste building energy. But energy conservation measures are offset by fast-closing doors that are hazardous to the mobility- limited who become off-balance, fall or drop carried objects when doors close too quickly. When blocked, library doors should default to open, before closing, to prevent injury. Inoperative power-assisted doors make wheelchair and walking aid users dependent on others at library entryways. Automatic library doors equipped with power-operated mechanisms and controls open and close after user-signal activation or door touching. Patron approach switches are photoelectric devices, special floor mats, or touch pressure plates, mounted on library doors or on door handrails. Door touch plates or switches should be brightly colored with AUTOMATIC DOOR markings. Library door switches must be tactile and Braille- marked. Patrons with low vision or the blind require enhanced door switch visibility since background color or texture makes switch recognition difficult. Highly visible touch pressure plates for mobility-limited use should be positioned within easy wheelchair-user reach. Movement-sensing automatic library doors open when persons move into door range without direct door contact. Inoperable or delayed repairs to automatic door switches restrict library access.[127] Movement sensing has many operational problems including sensing blowing objects (newspapers, leaves) that signal door opening filling library entryways with debris. Dogs, cats and birds open sensor doors permitting unauthorized library entry when movement sensors cannot be readjusted or aligned for pedestrian traffic.

Windy days with blowing debris cause library sensor doors to overwork. Door blowback damages door operation. Disabling sensor door equipment renders manual library door operation difficult. Overworked doors are expensive to repair. Inoperable automatic doors restrict library access. Automatic door manual operation is typically more difficult than conventional library door operation. Automatic doors may be regularly hand-blocked to prevent blowing debris, snow or rain from entering the library. While reducing surface wetness and making floors less slippery, door blockage stops people who need to use

Independent library access for all means access to doorway entry without help from others. For many, library entry independence is impossible without power-assisted doors.

Library Patrons With Disabilities

automatic library doors. As with many library barriers, careful evaluation is needed in both favorable and inclement weather to understand operational problems and barrier events. Good weather requires different solutions than those that work best in inclement weather. Are librarians responsible for door operation and effective library patron access in all weather? Or is this a problem only for maintenance personnel? Who is responsible for patron-safe library entry?

Revolving Doors and Turnstiles

Revolving doors or turnstiles are effective library barriers to many mobility-limited patrons, presenting multiple entry problems for patrons using walking aids or wheelchairs. Pressure sensitive revolving doors and turnstiles are alternative ways to enter the library but must not be the only means of accessible entrance.[128] And turnstiles are another matter for patrons with disabilities. Accessible gates or alternate doors near turnstiles or revolving doors facilitate patron library entry. But heavy library traffic makes entering or leaving revolving doors dangerous for many people with disabilities. Quickly stepping in, walking forward, and stepping out will clear the revolving door. Turnstiles present similar physical challenges. Most mobility-limited patrons must avoid revolving doors and turnstiles and use an alternate library entry.

Revolving doors may present a situation where patrons with disabilities lose dignity when having to be assisted by others to enter their own library. Library doorway accommodation, when obviously needed, is provided immediately. Silent and respectful librarian help given at doorways and without further discussion or comment helps maintain personal dignity. Immediate help without request must be provided for anyone who gets caught in revolving library doors or turnstiles. Others at revolving doors help anyone who lose footing or balance. Gender-specific help is not the issue at the library portal. Help should be provided to all without gender bias. Librarians accommodate all patrons needing entry assistance. Is there any person needing help at the library doorway that a librarian would not assist? Is independent library entry only a patron responsibility? Or is it shared with the librarian within and others nearby when help is obviously needed?

Library Hallways

Libraries within host buildings have hallways leading to the library entrance. Interior hallway floors have a common level from outside walkways, ramps or steps connecting the library entrance with the larger interior building and ultimately to the outside world.[129] Without common-level entrance interconnections and hallways in larger buildings, the disabled cannot safely approach the library door. Hallway floors should be non-slip surfaced for safe use by the mobility limited. Librarians should caution janitorial staff to avoid heavy coatings of wax or polish which present a slippery walking surface. Polished hallway floors are attractive but provide surfaces difficult to negotiate for many who are mobility limited. Rubberized, non-skid flooring prevents slips and falls on smooth library hallways for wheelchair or walking aid users.[130] Yet wheeled equipment tends to slip even on nonpolished floors. Wheelchair users have more hallway surface stability than pedestrians with mobility aids or pedestrians without walking aids.

Revolving doors may present a situation where patrons with disabilities lose dignity when having to be assisted by others to enter their own library.

Approach to the Library Door

59

Wheel tracking and moisture on library hallway floors is regularly controlled by building janitorial services. Close attention to hallway surfaces is required. Floor mats and similar precautions do not remove all water from library walkway surfaces. Occupational Health and Safety Administration (OSHA) requirements to post cautionary signage in library hallways about wet surfacing does not stop the mobility limited from falling.

External library hallway access to the collection provides safe pathways for all. For example, exterior door closing equipment does not protrude into library walkways, causing head injuries common to patrons with visual impairments:

> ...most people with severe impairments of vision use the long cane as an aid to mobility. The two principal cane techniques are the touch technique, where the cane arcs from side to side and touchs points outside both shoulders; and the diagonal technique, where the cane is held in a stationary position diagonally across the body with the cane tip touching or just above the ground at a point outside one shoulder and the handle or grip extending to a point outside the other shoulder. The touch technique is used primarily in uncontrolled areas, while the diagonal technique is used primarily in certain limited, controlled, and familiar environments...Potential hazardous [walkway] objects are noticed only if they fall within the detection range of canes...When walking alongside protruding objects, they cannot detect overhangs (ADA Handbook, ADAAG-A4.4.1).

External Library Displays

Effective outside displays promote prolonged viewing and reading and are a related service outside the library building or in a mezzanine or commons area. Yet external displays are beyond librarian view and require constant monitoring. Displays outside the library collection permit general public viewing without creating traffic problems. External traffic problems are an unanticipated side-effect of highly effective library displays. External displays interconnect with accessible library entrances and services.[131] Disabled viewers enjoy external displays when viewing is not hampered by architectural barriers or hazards, even the hazards for some with disabilities of crowds viewing displays. External displays must provide adequate passing space along library service routes mixing display viewers and passing pedestrians.[132] Display placement at wide corridor intersections or spacious central library walkway hubs permits mixed-user passing space without walkway conflicts.

Stairway library traffic and display viewers are an incompatible pedestrian mix. Displays at stair tops, along stair runs or within stair landings are dangerous. Stairs interrupt library accessible service routes without providing elevator, ramp or other accessible means of vertical access.[133] Displays along stair walls distract from safe stair tread and riser negotiation.

Disabled viewers enjoy external displays when viewing is not hampered by architectural barriers or hazards, even the hazards for some with disabilities of crowds viewing displays.

Library Patrons With Disabilities

People assume different body posture for different tasks. Library display viewing body posture is different than walking body posture. Patrons with disabilities may have to consciously assume a particular body posture and consciously change it for different display viewing angles. Appropriate body posture for viewing external displays may overchallenge some physically or mentally challenged patrons. Display area floor surfaces should be stable, firm, and slip-resistant to permit viewer reading and enjoyment.[134] Pedestrians stopping midstairs to view exhibits create a library traffic hazard for other stair users. Stair landing displays encourage dangerous viewer wheelchair rolloff possibilities.[135]

Public Restrooms

Publicly accessible restrooms are required in host public buildings if not provided within the library itself. Patrons must not be required to utilize a public restroom by having to enter the library without the need to enter there for other purposes. Patrons approaching library collections may first use the restrooms in the host building or within the library. Public restrooms accessible within the library building are commonly provided during open library hours but closed after hours. Public restrooms must be barrier free. At least one accessible toilet is required for each sex per library floor located along accessible routes in the host building or within the library.[136] Wheelchair users must be able to enter each accessible host building or library area restroom without the need for personal assistance. A left- or right-handed approach to restroom facilities should be provided.[137]

Restroom arrangement provides clear floor space for wheelchair negotiation.[138] Each restroom must have at least one accessible stall.[139] Wet floor surfaces in restrooms are a frequent problem. Our culture has adopted a de facto different standard for cleanliness in womens restrooms than in mens. The mens restroom must be equally clean and safe for the benefit of all who enter, and particularly for the disabled. Each nonskid restroom floors should have regular janitorial service to prevent slippery, wet surfaces. Accessible stalls must have outward swinging, self-closing doors minimally 36 inches (36″) wide[140] to ensure adequate space for people using crutches, canes or walkers.[141] Stalls must be grab bar equipped, enabling persons in wheelchairs to perform a side or diagonal transfer between wheelchair and commode.[142] Stalls must show signage indicating restricted access for the disabled. Washbasins provide 34-inch-high (34″) top-level user surfaces[143] with at least 27-inch (27″) roll-under clearance.[144] Covered and insulated restroom drains and hot water pipes prevent contact with dangerous surfaces.[145] Mirrors no higher than 40 inches (40″) above restroom floor level assure seated wheelchair user viewing.[146] Towel racks and towel dispensers are no higher than 40 inches (40″) for effective wheelchair user forward- or sidereach.[147] The personal dignity of library patron restroom use must not be challenging to each and cannot be ignored by professional librarians who use the same facilities as their patrons.

Public restrooms must be barrier free. At least one accessible toilet is required for each sex per library floor located along accessible routes in the host building or within the library.

Water Fountains

People require publicly accessible water fountains in library areas, in a host building, if not within the library itself. One water fountain per host building or library floor must be available along accessible routes.[148] Wheelchair users can roll up to fountains while others, with difficulty, can bend to drink.[149] Front spouts and fountain controls should be operable with one hand and should not require tight grasping, pinching or wrist twisting.[150] Wall-mounted accessible water fountains with hand-operated spouts must be no higher than 36 inches (36").[151] Floor surfaces cause slippery footing.

Library Area Public Elevators

Elevators should be positioned along accessible service routes from accessible parking lots serving the library.[152] Libraries without public elevators provide elevator access elsewhere if within multifloor host buildings. Elevators must be located on the same floor as the library entrance.[153] If this were not the case, many would be prevented from entering libraries. Interior elevators provide access to multilevel collections. Within-library elevator service opens to library interior patron service routes.

Public elevators must have self-leveling doorways[154] with a minimum of 32 inches (32") clear opening width and provide no more than 1/2-inch (1/2") floor gap between building and elevator floor.[155] Non-self leveling elevators prevent effective library entry or exit by persons using wheelchairs and constitutes the equivalent of a door threshold barrier. Elevator hall call buttons should be no higher than 42 inches (42") above the floor.[156] Car controls should be raised, indented and/or Brailled.[157] Controls should be touch sensitive or easy to operate. Wheelchair users facing rearward should be able to see floor indicators through wall-positioned mirrors, or floors announced by recorded messages.[158] Elevators requiring roll-in wheelchair access also mean the patron must roll backward to exit. Rollback exit is not a desirable elevator service feature. This is avoided when interior elevator space allows wheelchair repositioning for forward exit.

Emergency elevator telephones are operable and monitored by librarians for quick response.[159] Elevator doors should automatically remain open for 20 seconds when doorways remain obstructed.[160] Since the physically challenged may obstruct doors during elevator use, this is a particularly important library elevator service.

Outside Title Returns

Pedestrian outside title returns are often positioned at library entryways, in door or wall slots, along outside ramps or as portable units. Drivers in vehicles return titles after accessing library parking lots, loading zones and drive-by return areas. No librarian interaction is needed for outside title returns.

Pedestrian outside title returns are often positioned at library entryways, in door or wall slots, along outside ramps or as portable units. Drivers in vehicles return titles after accessing library parking lots, loading zones and drive-by return areas.

All outside title returns post use restrictions, acceptance hours, and prohibit the drop of videotapes or other restricted media. Outside returns are locked during posted hours, requiring direct title return. Patrons directly access librarians to return titles during regular library hours. When titles are overdue, many patrons prefer a non-personal return, sometimes avoiding librarian interaction.

Outside return signage is not visible without proper lighting and safe after-hour access. All return areas should be well lighted, presenting highly visible patron return guides. Posted title return guides give a clear message readily understood by experienced users but not easily interpreted by novices. Outside return guides meet or exceed appropriate library signage requirements.[161] Alternative outside returns during regular hours are an effective library accommodation. Return deadlines should be waived to permit daytime drive-up book return for the disabled. Policy usually waives requirements for the disabled to return materials only to the circulation desk or other designated areas during regular business hours, without obligating the library to equally accommodate the nondisabled.[162] Addressing policy issues to deal with this problem is a significant library service to patrons with disabilities.

Drive-Up Title Returns

Drive-up title return service is an accommodation to the general public and motoring disabled. Drive-up returns account for variations in vehicle height. Driver flexibility, repositioning in vehicle seats and return side reach is assumed for all. Without driver flexibility, repositioning skill or effective side reach, drive-up returns cannot be used. This particularly limits drive-up return utility for drivers using wheelchairs while at the wheel. Some libraries have elected to provide dual passenger- and driver-side drive-up returns.

The disabled driving specially-equipped vans experience return difficulties in bad weather or when titles are dropped outside return slots. Many cannot safely leave the vehicle without lifts. Lifts require special zones and safe-use areas not ordinarily provided at drive-up returns. There may be other vehicles behind the disabled operator also waiting to use the drive-up. Lift use under these circumstances is slow, delaying others, and is not safe for the driver with disabilities. Lift use requires movement around the vehicle to the driver's side and presumably enough area to roll to the drive-up return slot.

Initial drive-up return attempts assume immediate success. But a drive-up return fails when titles drop outside the vehicle. Then the driver must leave the vehicle, recover the title and return it, as a pedestrian. Pedestrian return defeats the purpose of drive-up returns. Excessive title loss and damage occurs when disabled patrons leave without being able to safely exit vehicles to retrieve dropped titles. Titles dropped from the height of a vehicle is damaging to books returned in this way. This is not a viable option at heavy-use drive-up returns or under inclement weather conditions. The disabled driver-patron is forced to use other return options.

Return units are not disability-accessible for drivers who cannot also safely exit vehicles and return titles by hand. Disabled drivers may not effectively reposition vehicles at drive-up returns. Repeated title return attempts from a

Librarians hope that the frustrated patron with disabilities will report actual drive-up return difficulties to guide necessary changes in service that are needed by the few and not faced by the many.

vehicle are not possible or safe for wheelchair van users. They should drive on through and directly return titles later to the circulation desk. Librarians hope that the frustrated patron with disabilities will report actual drive-up return difficulties to guide necessary changes in service that are needed by the few and not faced by the many.

Drive-up returns permit vehicle backing to reposition for effective return reach and may include repositioning vehicles for effective return sidereach. Patrons with disabilities as seated drivers often have sidereach limitations. Driveways at returns should be wide enough to permit vehicle repositioning. Drive-up areas should be well lit, giving vehicle users maximum rear, side and frontal visibility. Narrow driveways discourage pedestrian passenger-side exits moving in front of, or behind parked vehicles, to return titles.

Portable Title Returns

Portable returns are wheeled-shelf systems allowing return in or outside library buildings. Portable returns are moved by librarians for later reshelving. The units can be easily vandalized, stolen or emptied, when placed outside. A full portable return may house several thousand dollars worth of replacement cost in books. Portables are more safely placed within library buildings, between vestibule doors or in mezzanines. Portables provide longer service hours than direct patron returns to available librarians during regular hours.

Door or Wall-Slot Title Returns

Door or wall-slot title returns after-hours may not accommodate all. Slot returns are required at accessible doors for wheelchair users who need door-slot sidereach access.[163] Sidereach unloading is a safer procedure since frontal slot return requires wheelchair patrons to lean forward with the weight of books. This weighted lean puts them off balance, tipping the chair.[164] Wheelchair or walking aid users may prefer sidereach slots when returning a single title.

Multiple titles at door or wall-slots require further special handling. Book bags attached to the rear of the wheelchair allow titles to be retrieved by reaching behind. Many in wheelchairs cannot effectively reach behind slots without attendant or librarian help so door or wall-slot return independence is replaced with reliance on others. Multiple titles carried on a wheelchair user's lap will fall during movement. Wheelchair users cannot often retrieve materials from ground level, nor can walking aid users. Multiple title return requires door or wall-slot use one title at a time, using the safer wheelchair sidereach.

Door or wall-slots returns are usually positioned at exterior accessible library service routes.[165] These returns provide safe temporary positioning for the disabled, avoiding slopes[166] and abrupt level changes.[167] Return slots on ramps circumventing stairs at library entryways are not wheelchair accessible. Slot returns placed between 9 inches (9") and 54 inches (54") are considered technically accessible for individuals assuming wheelchair sidereach.[168] Common placement within this range is at 36 inches (36") above floor surface.

Return openings, handles, return slots or slot covers should avoid patron hand or finger entanglements. Patrons with arm or finger weakness or incoordination are "caught" by fast-moving return slot covers. They should not be required to do hand twisting during slot operation or manipulaation that would require both hands.[169]

Posted library return restrictions often prohibit deposit of videotapes or other media formats. Posted return restrictions, possibily for talking books, are unreadable without Braille and tactile identifiers. Patrons sometimes ignore or do not understand return prohibitions. Special handling is required for Braille or audio recordings, precluding anything but direct return to the librarian.

Title Return Safety

Drive-up returns often share library parking or loading zones where pedestrians compete with patrons in vehicles for drive-up return access. Significant pedestrian dangers can be mimimized in well-lighted drive-up areas. Vandalism and materials theft is also reduced. But theft reduction using one-way return equipment may cause injury to the innocent when misused. Reflective markings and vehicle bumper guards aid in driver return negotiation at drive-ups. The technology used at drive-up banking service may be applicable to library return safety. Heavy mounting of the return box reduces book theft. Narrow return slots and oversized books sometimes block interior holding areas. Even with large interior compartments, heavy use leads to compartment overloading. Spring- loaded compartment floors expand volume with increased book return weight. Elevated baskets at door slot bookfalls work effectively until overfilled. Long bookfalls cause damage to the materials. Short bookfalls damage oversized books.

Returns that permit bad weather leakage should be avoided. Rain or snow melt damages books when moisture enters the return compartment. Return baskets enable library workers to transfer titles to portable trucks for further handling. Overloading cannot be effectively avoided when no library worker is on duty. Rescheduling library pickups can reduce return compartment overloading.

Library disabled patron diversity suggests that no single title return approach will work for all. Multiple return options provide universal return access. When return compliance is not possible or prohibited for the disabled, individual help is provided. People with mental or physical challenges should be given the benefit of the doubt during inappropriate returns.[170] Harsh telephone or overdue letter reminders to patrons with disabilities are counterproductive library policy. Librarian sensitivity to, and good communication with, every patron far outweighs the problem of late title returns. Nonphysically challenged library patrons deserve the same professional service standard.

Summary

Accommodation outside the library door has been discussed in conformance with ADA standards, which apply to libraries as public service entities. Reactive and proactive librarian responses were suggested as a basis for professional attitudes concerning patrons with disabilities. Arriving disabled library patrons can experience a variety of problems in the loading zone or parking lot. Accessible walkways must be provided along accessible library routes. Ramps, exterior steps or stairs are barriers to the library. Walkway detectable warnings assist with pedestrian movement. Power-assisted, automatic and manual operating doors were discussed requiring effective library building entrance identification. Revolving doors, turnstiles and security gates are potential library barriers. Alternate entry and warning systems for unauthorized library entry were discussed. There are many circumstances in which librarians are responsible for providing or assuring external library access in addition to collection access within the library.

Library disabled patron diversity suggests that no single title return approach will work for all. Multiple return options provide universal return access.

Approach to the Library Door

End Notes:

1.Information 2000: Library and Information Services for the 21st Century. A summary report of the 1991 White House Conference on Library and Information Services. (1991). Washington, DC: U.S. Government Printing Office. Page 57: "All people are entitled to the use of a library facility that is accessible, functional, and comfortable."

2. Powell, Faye. (1990). A library center for disabled students. College & Research Libraries News, 51, 420.

3. ADAAG. Appendix B. Americans with Disability Accessibility Guidelines. In, U.S. Department of Justice. (1991). Americans with Disabilities Act Handbook. Washington, DC: U.S. Government Printing Office. Section 4.3.2(2).

4. ADA Handbook. U.S. Department of Justice. (1991). Americans with Disabilities Act Handbook. Washington, DC: U.S. Government Printing Office. Page I-63.

5. Ibid, ADA Handbook, II-70 & II-89.

6. Public Law 93-112, 87 Stat. 394 (29 U.S.C. 794), as amended.

7. Ibid, ADA Handbook, II-89 to 92.

8. National Endowment for the Arts. (1992). The arts and 504: A handbook for accessible arts programming. Washington, DC: U.S. Government Printing Office. Page 20.

9. Ibid, The Arts and 504, 11-12.

10. Ibid, The Arts and 504, 14-16.

11. Ibid, The Arts and 504, 10.

12. Gunde, Michael. (1991). Working with the Americans with Disabilities Act. Library Journal, 116(21), 99-100.

13. Ibid, Information 2000, 57.

14. Raffa, M.F. (1985). Removing architectural barriers: The architectural barriers act of 1968. Mental and Physical Disability Law Reporter, 9(4), 304-308.

15. Hopf, P.S. & Raeber, J.A. (1984). Access for the handicapped: The barrier free regulations for design and construction in all 50 states. New York: Van Nostrand Reinhold.

16. Leung, P. (1990). Editor's comments. Journal of Rehabilitation, 56, 5.

17. Foster, Terry & Lindell, Linda. (1991). Libraries and the Americans with Disabilities Act. Texas Libraries, 52, 59-63.

18. Ibid, ADAAG 4.1.2(1) & 4.1.2(2).

19. Barry, A.M.O. & Priestly, L. B. (1980). Coping with inaccessibility: Assisting the wheelchair user. Washington: George Washington University Medical Rehabilitation Research and Training Center.

20. Ibid, ADA Handbook, I-63.

21. Cagle, R. Brantley. (1983). Reference service to the developmentally disabled: Normalization of access. Catholic Library World, 54, 266-270.

22. Laurie, Ty D. (1992). Libraries' duties to accomodate their patrons under the Americans with Disabilities Act. Library Administration & Management, 6, 204-205.

23. Mooney, Carolyn J. (1993). Cultured murmur of academe threatens to be lost in the roar over parking. Chronicle of Higher Education, 39(49), 15-16.

24. U. S. Congress. Student Right-to-Know and Campus Security Act of 1990. (Federal Register, October 22, 1993).

25. Lederman, Douglas. (1994). Crime on the campuses. Chronicle of Higher Education, XL(22), A31-41.

26. Ibid, ADA Handbook, II-65.

27. Ibid, ADA Handbook, III-149.

28. Fuller, H. (1981). Access information bulletin: Curb ramps, parking, passenger loading zones and bus stops. Washington: National Center for a Barrier Free Environment. For related video surveillance information, see Mooney, 1993, 15.

29. Ibid, ADAAG, A4.5.1.

30. Ibid, ADAAG, 4.6.3. & 4.6.6.

31. Ibid, ADAAG, 4.8.8. & A4.5.1.

32. Ibid, <u>ADAAG</u>, 4.6.2.
33. Ibid, <u>ADAAG</u>, 4.1.2(5).
34. Ibid, <u>ADAAG</u>, 4.1.2(5-b).
35. Ibid, <u>ADAAG</u>, A4.6.3.
36. Ibid, <u>ADAAG</u>, A4.6.3.
37. Ibid, <u>ADAAG</u>, 4.6.3 & A4.6.3.
38. Ibid, <u>ADAAG</u>, A4.5.1.
39. Ibid, <u>ADAAG</u>, 4.7.9.
40. Ibid, <u>ADAAG</u>, A4.6.3.
41. Ibid, <u>ADAAG</u>, A4.6.3.
42. Ibid, <u>ADAAG</u>, A4.6.3.
43. Ibid, <u>ADAAG</u>, A4.6.4.
44. Harkin, T. (1990). <u>Responses to issues raised about the Americans with Disabilities Act of 1990</u>. Washington, D.C.: United States Senate.
45. Ibid, <u>ADAAG</u>, 4.30.7.
46. Ibid, <u>ADAAG</u>, 4.6.4 & A4.6.4.
47. Ibid, <u>ADAAG</u>, A4.6.3.
48. Ibid, <u>ADAAG</u>, 4.1.2(5)(b): "Spaces required by the table (Total Parking in Lot/Required Minimum Number of Accessible Spaces) need not be provided in the particular lot. They may be provided in a different location if equivalent or greater accessibility, in terms of distance from an accesible entrance, cost and convenience is ensured."
49. Ibid, Mooney, 15.
50. Ibid, Mooney, 15.
51. Ibid, <u>ADA Handbook</u>, I-77: "Disparate treatment means...that an individual was treated differently on the basis of his or her disability...It may be a defense to a charge of disparate treatment brought under sections 1630.4 through 1630.8 and 1630.11 through 1630.12 that the challenged action is justified by a legitimate, nondiscriminatory reason."
52. Ibid, <u>The Arts and 504</u>, 14-16.
53. Ibid, Mooney, 15.
54. Ibid, <u>ADAAG</u>, 4.6.2.
55. Ibid, <u>ADA Handbook</u>, I-77.
56. Ibid, <u>ADA Handbook</u>, II-38.
57. Ibid, Mooney, 15.
58. Ibid, Mooney, 15.
59. Ibid, <u>ADAAG</u>, A4.3.1.
60. Ibid, Mooney, 15.
61. Ibid, <u>ADAAG</u>, 4.3.2(1).
62. Ibid, <u>ADAAG</u>, 4.1.2(2): "At least one accessible route complying with 4.3 shall connect accessible buildings, accessible facilities, accessible elements, and accessible spaces that are on the same site."
63. Ibid, <u>ADAAG</u>, 4.7.8.
64. Ibid, <u>ADAAG</u>, 4.7.2.
65. Ibid, <u>ADAAG</u>, 4.3.1.
66. Ibid, <u>ADAAG</u>, 4.7.1.
67. Ibid, <u>ADAAG</u>, 4.7.2.
68. Ibid, <u>ADAAG</u>, 4.7.11.
69. Ibid, <u>ADAAG</u>, 4.2.2 & A4.2.1(3).
70. Ibid, <u>ADAAG</u>, A4.3.1(2).
71. Ibid, <u>ADAAG</u>, 4.3.7 & A4.3.1(2).
72. Ibid, <u>ADAAG</u>, A4.3.1(1).
73. Ibid, <u>ADAAG</u>, 4.3.8.
74. Ibid, <u>ADAAG</u>, 4.8.8. & A4.5.1.

75. Ibid, <u>ADAAG</u>, 4.3.6 & 4.8.7.

76. Ibid, <u>ADAAG</u>, 4.8.5.

77. Ibid, <u>ADAAG</u>, 4.8.4(3).

78. Ibid, <u>ADAAG</u>, 4.8.4(3).

79. Ibid, <u>ADAAG</u>, A4.8.4.

80. Ibid, <u>ADAAG</u>, A4.2.1(1).

81. Ibid, <u>ADAAG</u>, A4.2.1(3).

82. Ibid, <u>ADAAG</u>, A4.3.1(1).

83. Editor. (1993). Berkeley bans bikes on campus pathways. <u>Chronicle of Higher Education</u>, <u>40</u>(7), A6.

84. Ibid, Berkeley, A6: "The University of California has banned daytime bicycle riding in most areas of its campus here after determining that pathways were too crowded for safe biking. The ban runs between 7:30 AM and 5:30 PM daily on all pathways not considered automobile roads. The ban was imposed because "the mix of bicycle and pedestrian traffic was becoming unsafe," said Lieut. William Foley of the university police department."

85. Ibid, <u>ADAAG</u>, 4.8.2.

86. Ibid, <u>ADAAG</u>, 4.5.1, 4.8.6 & A4.5.1.

87. Ibid, <u>ADAAG</u>, 4.8.8.

88. Ibid, <u>ADAAG</u>, A4.8.4.

89. Ibid, <u>ADAAG</u>, 4.4.1 & 4.4.2.

90. Ibid, <u>ADAAG</u>, A4.3.1.

91. Ibid, <u>ADAAG</u>, 4.9.4. & 4.2.6.

92. Ibid, <u>ADAAG</u>, 4.9.4(4).

93. Ibid, <u>ADAAG</u>, 4.8.4(3) & A4.8.4.

94. Ibid, <u>ADAAG</u>, A4.8.2.

95. Ibid, <u>ADAAG</u>, 4.9.4.

96. Ibid, <u>ADAAG</u>, 4.9.4(5).

97. Ibid, <u>ADAAG</u>, 4.9.4(3) & 4.4.1.

98. U.S. Architectural and Transportation Barriers Compliance Board. (1992). <u>Americans with Disabilities Act Accessibility Guidelines Checklist for Buildings and Facilities.</u> Washington, DC: U.S. Government Printing Office. Pages 4-2 and 4-3.

99. Ibid, <u>ADAAG</u>, 3.5.

100. Ibid, <u>ADAAG</u>, 4.29.2.

101. Ibid, <u>ADAAG</u>, 4.5.4.

102. Ibid, <u>ADAAG</u>, 4.4.1.

103. Ibid, <u>ADAAG</u>, A4.8.1.

104. Ibid, <u>ADAAG</u>, A4.9.1.

105. Ibid, <u>ADAAG</u>, 4.9.6.

106. Ibid, <u>ADAAG</u>, A4.9.1.

107. Couch, Robert H. (1992). Ramps not steps: A study of accessibility preferences. <u>Journal of Rehabilitation</u>, Winter, 65-69.

108. Ibid, <u>ADAAG</u>, A4.5.1.

109. Ibid, <u>ADAAG</u>, 4.9.2: "On any given flight of stairs, all steps shall have uniform riser heights and uniform tread widths...Open risers are not permitted."

110. Ibid, <u>ADAAG</u>, 4.14.1.

111. Ibid, <u>ADAAG</u>, 4.13.2.

112. Ibid, <u>ADAAG</u>, A4.30.1.

113. Lisson, Paul. (1987). Large print placebo. <u>Canadian Library Journal</u>, <u>44</u>, 5. "More than 80 percent of all people considered legally blind have usable vision. They are not blind; they have low vision."

114. Ibid, <u>ADAAG</u>, 4.30.6.

115. Ibid, <u>ADAAG</u>, 4.1.2(7b).

116. Ibid, <u>ADAAG</u>, 4.13.2.

117. Ibid, <u>ADAAG</u>, A4.13.8.
118. Ibid, <u>ADAAG</u>, 4.13.9.
119. Ibid, <u>ADAAG</u>, 4.13.10; A4.13.10. See also, <u>ADA Handbook</u>, II-51.
120. Ibid, <u>ADAAG</u>, A4.13.10.
121. Ibid, <u>ADAAG</u>, A4.13.9.
122. Ibid, <u>ADAAG</u>, 4.13.8 & A4.13.8.
123. Ibid, <u>ADAAG</u>, 4.13.4.
124. Ibid, <u>ADAAG</u>, 4.13.5.
125. Ibid, <u>ADAAG</u>, 4.13.7.
126. Ibid, <u>ADAAG</u>, 4.13.11 & A4.13.11.
127. Ibid, <u>ADAAG</u>, 4.13.12.
128. Ibid, <u>ADA Handbook</u>, II-51.
129. Ibid, <u>ADAAG</u>, 4.13.2.
130. Ibid, <u>ADAAG</u>, 4.7.11.
131. Ibid, <u>ADAAG</u>, 4.5.1.
132. Ibid, <u>ADAAG</u>, 4.3.2.(2).
133. Ibid, <u>ADAAG</u>, 4.3.4 & 4.3.2(3).
134. Ibid, <u>ADAAG</u>, A4.9.1.
135. Ibid, <u>ADAAG</u>, 4.5.1.
136. Ibid, <u>ADAAG</u>, A4.8.4.
137. Ibid, <u>ADAAG</u>, 4.17.1.
138. Ibid, <u>ADAAG</u>, 4.16.2.
139. Ibid, <u>ADAAG</u>, 4.16.2.
140. Ibid, <u>ADAAG</u>, 4.22.4.
141. Ibid, <u>ADAAG</u>, 4.23.4.
142. Ibid, <u>ADAAG</u>, A4.17.3.
143. Ibid, <u>ADAAG</u>, A4.17.3.
144. Ibid, <u>ADAAG</u>, 4.24.2.
145. Ibid, <u>ADAAG</u>, 4.24.3.
146. Ibid, <u>ADAAG</u>, 4.24.6.
147. Ibid, <u>ADAAG</u>, 4.19.6.
148. Ibid, <u>ADAAG</u>, 4.16.6.
149. Ibid, <u>ADAAG</u>, 4.17.1.
150. Ibid, <u>ADAAG</u>, A4.15.2.
151. Ibid, <u>ADAAG</u>, A4.27.4.
152. Ibid, <u>ADAAG</u>, 4.15.2.
153. Ibid, <u>ADAAG</u>, 4.3.2(1).
154. Ibid, <u>ADAAG</u>, 4.10.1.
155. Ibid, <u>ADAAG</u>, 4.10.2.
156. Ibid, <u>ADAAG</u>, 4.5.2.
157. Ibid, <u>ADAAG</u>, 4.10.3.
158. Ibid, <u>ADAAG</u>, 4.10.12.
159. Ibid, <u>ADAAG</u>, 4.10.13.
160. Ibid, <u>ADAAG</u>, 4.10.14.
161. Ibid, <u>ADAAG</u>, 4.10.6.
162. Ibid, <u>ADAAG</u>, 4.30.1.
163. Adapted from Miller, Richard T. (1992). The Americans with Disabilities Act: Library facility and program access under Titles II and III. <u>Ohio Libraries</u>, <u>5</u>, 9.
164. Ibid, <u>ADAAG</u>, 4.2.6.
165. Ibid, <u>ADAAG</u>, 4.2.5.
166. Ibid, <u>ADAAG</u>, 4.3.2(3).

167. Ibid, ADAAG, 4.3.7.
168. Ibid, ADAAG, 4.3.8.
169. Ibid, ADAAG, 4.2.6.
170. Ibid, ADAAG, A4.27.4.
171. Ibid, Miller, 9.

Suggested Reading:

ADA Handbook. U.S. Department of Justice. (1991). Americans with Disabilities Act Handbook. Washington, DC: U.S. Government Printing Office.

U.S. Architectural and Transportation Barriers Compliance Board. (1992). Americans with Disabilities Act Accessibility Guidelines Checklist for Buildings and Facilities. Washington, DC: U.S. Government Printing Office.

Library Patrons With Disabilities

Chapter Three

Adaptive Library Orientation

Orienting Patrons with Disabilities To Library Services

Successful infosearchers recognize and use librarians to find information. Coming to the library with a clear personal request, an information goal, and a mental map of the facility removes patron information barriers. Librarians orient those who do not know the library or don't understand available services. Assuring people with disabilities access to all library services often requires both adaptive and conventional library orientation.[1] Professionals using adaptive library orientation assume responsibility to provide equal access to information for the disabled as well as providing services to all others.[2] The patron with disabilities assumes responsibility to ask for and use adaptive library orientation.

Orientation for Families Impacted by Disabilities

Families become dysfunctional with the stress of a member becoming disabled.[3] Others are unwilling to recognize the extent of the family member's disabilities or the long-term implications of disabilities on family or personal life.[4] In the library, periods of emotional disorganization, even temporary mental illness, are sometimes observed in these family members.[5] Their need for effective library information is critical but they may be dysfunctional infosearchers. They may be unresponsive to conventional and instead require adaptive library orientation. Librarians provide both orientation types as and when needed for family member critical information gain.

Family members recover and in so doing progress from initial defensive retreat (avoiding information about disabilities, demanding responsibility for their behavior be assigned to or accommodated by the librarian, avoiding personal responsibility to infosearch, giving up life goals or objectives, radically changing information needs, interests, or reading habits) to incrementally more adaptive stages. Each adjustment stage requires particular library disability information appropriate to that individual. Each disability adjustment stage will also change how an individual patron will relate to, or react to, any librarian support. Over time and with adaptive library orientation and  the support of others, family members move to disability acknowledgement after self-accusation, self-pity, even self-hate.[6] And they can read about others' similar adjustment problems and solutions in the library. They can use the library as a focal point to find others to better understand how disabilities impact their lives.

Direct Patron Adaptive Library Orientation

Library patrons, after learning of their own disabilities onset, go through emotional stages from shock, anxiety, guilt, numbness, confusion, helplessness, and anger to disbelief, denial, and dispair.[7] Adaptive orientation alters conventional library orientation to meet their special library needs. There are three sources of this special orientation: group library tours for disabled patrons and their families; the individual's specific library orientation requests; and the history of librarians orienting each individual with disabilities.

Library Patrons With Disabilities

Group Library Tours

Group library tours orient patrons with disabilities together with other nondisabled patrons including members of their family. Orientation starts during library group tours when librarians consult with patrons about their specific service needs. Specific service needs change with the day, the information needed and group membership. Librarians and individual tour members together determine how those orientation needs or specific requests can be best accommodated. Services are explained and offered to patrons in all library service areas during the tour. Group library tours may not meet individual disabled patron orientation needs. Individual disabled patron tours and orientation are provided on request.[8] The disabled in the library context have equal opportunity to participate in and enjoy group library tour benefits and orientation. Orientation provided to groups is inherently less helpful than individual adaptive orientation when geared to specific individual needs. But the disabled may wish to remain anonymous in the group tour.

Individual Disabled Patron Orientation Requests

Professionals best orient one library patron at a time. All orientation is based on patron infosearching maturity. The cognitively-impaired, the low-functioning, and patrons with mental health problems can reasonably expect adaptive orientation geared to their needs. But even expert librarians are not specifically trained to meet all diverse disabled patron orientation requirements.[9] Librarians differ greatly in their ability to deliver adaptive library orientation to specific patrons, particularly to those with disabilities. Disabled patron orientation requirements must be stated to librarians before they can be met. Librarians sensitive to disabled patrons can unobtrusively anticipate what those orientation needs may be. Sensitivity to recognize, anticipate and then proactively meet special library patron need determines the success or failure of many professional services or how they are well or poorly received.[10]

Librarians informally assess patron attitude, mobility skill and accommodation needs from library entry to exit.[11] Well-planned services and equipment negate or overcome given library structural and architectural barriers. "Walk-throughs" by wheelchair or walking aid users reveal access problems not recognizable from the librarian's perspective. But walk-throughs are not enough, since only a tiny spectrum of patrons entering the library are wheelchair or walking aid users. There are many other patron-relevant disabilities in the library context that must also be accommodated. Procedural barriers are found through a careful library evaluation that addresses the special library needs of a diverse patron clientele.[12] But anticipated needs do not necessarily meet actual disabled patron specific orientation requirements to be provided by "their librarian." There may be a fundamental difference between disabled patron librarian-anticipated "needs" and actual patron orientation requirements from "their librarian." Alternative services are discussed below to help the library provide information access to all, based on patron anticipated library orientation needs but must be constantly contrasted with their actual library service orientation requests.[13]

> Librarians differ greatly in their ability to deliver adaptive library orientation to specific patrons, particularly to those with disabilities. Librarians informally assess patron attitude, mobility skill and accommodation needs from library entry to exit.

Adaptive Library Orientation

Perhaps the single most significant orientation barrier is a lack of trust between patron and librarian. When trusting librarian/patron relationships evolve, people working together successfully find library information. Patrons strive for infosearching independence based on trust, helpful and unobtrusive librarian orientation. Libraries plan to provide the same accommodation for the same disabled patron with the same staff whenever possible. It is by this standard of service that patrons with disabilities regard themselves as having genuinely personalized library orientation and service. They then have "their librarians." Patrons distinguish between other patrons and library workers for meeting their own information needs. Most patrons know who may be approached and who should be left alone. Some patrons know when to ask for help and some do not. Newcomers with special information access needs have much to quickly learn for library success. Getting help from someone need not be a challenge itself for patrons with disabilities. Librarians have no reason to assume that disabled patrons will intentionally avoid interacting with them and their orientation services.. Yet some do avoid interaction with them even though they judge themselves to need library orientation. The librarian determines patron willingness to obtain print or nonprint information independently or to ask for help. Face-to-face communication between librarian and patron is kept open. Future patron requests for help during the same, or the next, library visit are always librarian anticipated. Patrons with disabilities are not subtly communicated: "This is all the help you are going to be offered." Disabled patrons are self-advocates learning to take library risks.[14] Many want to become self-advocates in the Information Age. Adaptive patron orientation needs and requirements are reduced when patrons with disabilities who are novices in the library become familiar with library services.

Successful infosearchers are considerate of others. They enter quietly and proceed to information along service routes while respecting rights of others to equal information access.[15] Patrons ask directions from library workers, read signage and move to services. If patrons with disabilities require librarian help, they ask. The library is used during regular hours without abusing borrowing or other privileges. Not all--with or without disabilities--meet this ideal patron role.

Adaptive library orientation is both patron-specific and short-term, as well as situation-specific. That orientation is effective when caring librarians listen, help them when they ask, and accept the patron acceptance or refusal to be helped. Orientation is adaptive when help is accepted and meets the patron's personally-identified information needs. Some librarians may hold attitudes that interfere with infosearching by disabled patrons. Much of the librarian success with patrons with disabilities has to do with their professional orientation style. Librarians have individual accommodation styles that may be incompatible with their special library needs or requests. Or the new librarian may orient that patron in the same routine manner as the familiar librarian yet be ignored or rejected. Cognitively-impaired patrons may require reorientation with each new librarian on the scene. Other patrons anticipate and request specific librarians but often do not get them. They resist changing familiar librarians or services.

Much of the librarian success with patrons with disabilities has to do with their professional orientation style.

Patrons become disorganized when they cannot infosearch successfully. They may initiate infosearches without finding information being quickly diverted by other events or conditions. One of the greatest patron diversions that cause disorganized infosearches are new librarians. Personnel changes have significant patron behavioral implications. New or reassigned librarians unknowingly contribute to increasingly disorganized patron behavior. Familiar library services become alien when librarians are replaced. Patron attention may be diverted to the new librarian rather than orienting to new information

Library Patrons With Disabilities

content during group tours. The best patron adaptive orientation in the library is subtle.[16] Professionals are prepared to assist with infosearches when immature search behaviors are observed. Librarians regard even patron immature searches as legitimate steps toward infosearching skill development. This infosearching immaturity is still visible during group tours. Many who enter the library are patrons with special library needs based on information immaturity, not personal immaturity. Few who enter the library with visible disabilities have equally visible information support needs. They must be asked to determine their information needs.

History of Orienting Specific Patrons with Disabilities

Librarians establish a history of helping particular individuals with disabilities once they request adaptive library orientation. Patron additional requests during other librark treks further modify subsequent orientation content. If librarians fail to remember previous orientation strategies and how they fit, they may be sharply reminded by that patron. Impersonal orientation includes repeating sequences not needing that patrons review, over- or underestimating their skill during orientation, or not allowing for their day-to-day library skill variations. All have good days and bad days. Library skill variation is an individual characteristic for those with disabilities, as it is for everyone.

Librarians recognize regularly attending disabled patrons on entry. New patrons with disabilities are welcomed but usually do not immediately request adaptive orientation. New patrons needs are not initially known. Librarians observe from a distance and intervene as little as possible. They wait and watch to assess patron information barrier mastery. Professionals empower people with disabilities by maximizing their independence and minimizing their library accommodation.[17]Patrons are invited to identify themselves as individuals with disabilities and suggest their own specific library orientation at any time.[18] Even with careful observation library special patron orientation needs may not be immediately apparent. Much professional librarian effort is required to identify for the requesting patron what those special library information needs are and how each can be met. The librarian may help the disabled patron to make specific requests for their library orientation. But this is done only when observant librarians proactively interact with patrons. Librarians may be concerned that the patron orientation and service help offered may not be the help needed or wanted. How would librarians know if they don't listen to patrons with disabilities statements of need? Librarian fears of patrons rejecting help offered is well-founded when they do not listen and understand patron actual library orientation requests rather than listening for what is presumed to be their needs.

Even with careful observation library special patron orientation needs may not be immediately apparent. Much effort is required to identify for the requesting patron what those special library information needs are and how they can be met.

Barriers of Perspective

Librarians may fear their own ignorance of the disabled. Fear surfaces when librarians use negative stereotypes and paternalistic views about what is best for disabled individuals in the library context. Fear affects both librarians and patrons with disabilities. Only the individual patron knows what best library service is appropriate and required. It is the librarians duty to find what those special patron needs are and meet them without imposing any barriers of perspective. To do this, the librarian must listen to the patron. To be heard, the patron must communicate information and accommodation needs. The librarian must assume the disabled patron perspective, not the librarian's own perspective. And the patron must be helpful for successful infosearching.

Adaptive Library Orientation

As professionals, librarians are sensitive to hold no negative attitudes toward people based on their disabilities. All humans have prejudices and are at times insensitive to the needs of others. Librarians are offended by some patrons, not as a group, but as individuals, who enter the library for the "wrong reasons" from the librarian perspective. Professionals overcome personal preferences to work with all patrons, even offensive ones.

Librarian Attitudes

Librarians change their attitude toward each disabled patron when they have ample opportunities to interact with them and do not avoid them while in the library. Attitudinal barriers, fears or stereotypes held for people with cognitive or physical challenges do not help in meeting their information needs. These things should not be the basis for librarian attitude toward patrons with disabilities. Whatever contacts librarians have made with disabled individuals may have no bearing on what they need or request from librarians. Patience and listening skills will reveal their infosearching orientation and accommodation needs. Librarian attitudes that would cause professionals to respond to any patron with disabilities in an overly solicitous manner cancel their otherwise effective library accommodation. Professionals who hold a "blanket acceptance" attitude toward anyone with disabilities do not listen to patrons and will not help them infosearch appropriately. Overhelping is as destructive to patron infosearching independence as underhelping.

"Attitude contagion" becomes gradually diffused among library workers for disabled individuals. Librarians may forget that patron disabilities may have nothing to do with any functional disability outside the library. Disabilities in the library context are the basis for meeting special patron needs—not disabilities evident only outside the library portal. "Attitude contagion" is reduced by direct personal contact with disabled patrons as individuals, and not by avoiding interaction with them:

> Attitudinal barriers hinder library users just as much as architectural barriers. As more people with disabilities move into the public arena, others will begin to interact with them easily. Until that time, it may be necessary to make a special effort to learn and teach others to be aware of persons with disabilities and their needs (Foster & Lindell, 1991, page 59).

Librarian attitude contagion can also occur for specific individuals with disabilities as they enter the library. Negative attitudes toward specific disabled persons may enroach into the library and affect how librarians serve them during infosearching. Comments between library workers "forewarning" of a specific disabled patron arrival prejudice professionals and bias their orientation for that individual:

> No amount of information about the needs of disabled persons and the available resources for serving them will help if that information is heard by persons whose attitudes are negative. The critical factor...in educating librarians is to promote positive attitudes so that disabled persons come alive as individuals of ability. Pity, sympathy, and patronizing attitudes are not required; sensitivity to individual needs and willingness to work to eliminate the barriers which keep disabled persons from fully utilizing their abilities are. If positive attitudes exist, librarians will make the needed effort to learn and to put into practice what they have learned (Lucas, 1983, page 208).

Every entering patron deserves different attention, orientation and service from librarians. The entering patron may have special orientation needs that can be provided by librarians who do not hold stereotypic views concerning the disabled. Most librarians support this individualized service standard but some stereotypically suggest the disabled require "more attention" or after orientation are "at-risk" in the library. Patrons must continue to work with professionals who hold firmly to stereotypes associated with specific

Library Patrons With Disabilities

patron disabilities. Some librarians define people's needs by specific disability categories. Categorical thinking is incomplete thinking. It is a good start but not a good finish. Categorizing human beings may be descriptive but it may not necessarily apply to each individual. Disability categories or labels alone do not reveal individual library support needs. Categorizing patrons with disabilities can only be done, if at all, when patron requirements for library support are stated:

> ...[L]ike other professionals ...Classifying patron library services on the basis of disability alone does not determine individual capability in the absence of service determination on an individualized basis (Cagle, 1983).

Sometimes librarians call for formal test instruments or criteria to judge library behavior during individual library assessments and, following that, propose "formulamatic orientation" based on those assessments. Such formal assessment of the disabled sets them apart from the nondisabled, who are not formally assessed in the library. Formal assessment burdens the disabled with requirements not placed by the library on others without disabilities.[19] While formal criteria exist, and test instruments have been previously used, librarians must receive explicit patron permission to perform patron assessment. Formal assessment is often initiated by librarians--not by library patrons with disabilities. Librarians are not disability assessment experts. They are information science experts with their expertise applied to any patron who enters the library and specifically requests orientation based on their own infosearching expertise. Librarian-initiated formal orientation assessment is not needed. Any orientation for the disabled based on formal or informal assessment should be a patron's voluntary choice, not a library or librarian requirement.

Categorical thinking among librarians concerning orientation for disabled people usually changes with librarian experience with specific disabled patrons. Single or multiple disability categories do not describe or predict an individual's orientation or other service needs. Some disabled have diverse orientation and accommodation needs. They meet those needs independently in the library. While people may appear similar or have a disability in common, they have significantly different library orientation and accommodation needs. And each have specific, individual orientation and accommodation requests.

People with disabilities may choose not to avail themselves of orientation and service even if a particular accommodation has been library-selected on the basis of "their disabilities." The concept of "their disabilities" may be offensive to many patrons as though a librarian would know anything about the personal effect of disabilities on that individual. Patrons can request particular orientation and then decide not to use, accept or cooperate with it or with librarians. It is an individual patron choice. Each disabled patron has a history of accepting or rejecting library orientation. To the extent that professionals understand patron orientation histories, personalized service can be provided that will be readily accepted when needed and requested. Librarians may fail to provide disabled patron orientation when it is visibly needed.[20] These activities do not empower patrons with disabilities in the library. Professionals inform themselves about individual special orientation needs and requests, orient when asked, or only when the need for disabled patron orientation is clearly and unavoidably apparent. Some librarians consciously overlook fines, damages, or lost title orientation in order not to "upset the disabled patron," thereby condoning inappropriate behavior and discriminating in favor of disabled patrons solely because of their disabilities.[21]

Professionals inform themselves about individual special orientation needs and requests, orient when asked, or only when the need for disabled patron orientation is clearly and unavoidably apparent.

Adaptive Library Orientation

Library services are based on the present disabling condition and not on speculation about future patron with disabling conditions.[22] For disabled patrons, proactive librarians may paternalistically over-orient and over-help.[23] Reactive may librarians under-orient and under-help disabled patrons fostering their personal library information isolation.[24] Proactive librarians, though well-intentioned, can go too far. Skill assessment for any patron is a reactive librarian response to specific patron requests for help. When specific patron requests are made, the librarian responds by assessing the patron only to the extent that the requested orientation can be better understood and then implemented for that patron. Professionals deal with patron specific orientation requests one patron at a time.

Library Patron Diversity

Professionals think beyond disability categories to consider disabled individual differences. Expert librarians recognize individual patron behavior as library help indicators. If categories are to be used, then they should only directly address patron library accommodation. Categories should be relevant only in the library context when they provide effective adaptive library orientation. Categories should only be used when they specifically advance accommodation of individual patron requests. Categories have been proposed that described patron information need relevant to the library context. Suggestions have been provided on how librarians may react to those information needs. But descriptions of patrons must give a balance between anticipated or observed patron information need and their stated library service requests. Those stated requests are often found to be significantly different than any librarian anticipated categories of "information need." Librarians begin to understand patron diversity when they discover that individuals with the same type of disabilities have widely differing infosearching needs and interests. They may appear to the librarian as having something significantly important in common--a common disability--but working with them reveals another reality--that of personal infosearching diversity. Since patrons are so diverse, only library-relevant categories may begin to help librarians accommodate actual patrons with disabilities infosearching needs. Categories based on disabilities alone are not library-relevant. Categories do not assist the librarian to meet patron needs. Professional librarians, though well intentioned, may naively regard patrons in wheelchairs as having specific library barrier and collection access problems. Or professionals may think categorically across other types of obvious physical challenges in patrons. Each of these disability categories or physical challenges is descriptive but does not yield individually appropriate or library-relevant orientation strategies. Only library-relevant orientation can be determined by listening to disabled patrons stated library support requirements one patron at a time:

> Congress acknowledged that society's accumulated myths and fears about disability and diseases are as handicapping as are the physical limitations that flow from actual impairment (480 U.S. at 284).

Voluntary patron observations lead to specific librarian intervention strategies. Librarians observe patrons--largely after they have been asked to do so by those same patrons--and then help them when library skill development or their specific disabilities functionally limit information searches. Any librarian voluntary patron observation simply matches patron needs with library orientation (not disability labels, disability-specific library strategies or even thoughtful accommodations planned for persons having specific disabilities). When patron needs are voluntarily identified, then adaptive library orientation is provided.

Library Directories and Map Handouts

A fundamental part of adaptive library orientation is the use of patron accessible library directories and maps. Without immediate directions from accessible library directories, patrons with disabilities justifiably feel unwelcome entering their own libraries.[25] Directories are sometimes inaccessible to the disabled.[26] Reasonable accommodation is not provided by library directories alone. Maps to be taken with patrons should illustrate current library service areas, personnel and equipment, and show the best available access

Library Patrons With Disabilities

routes.[27] Map handouts are in multiple formats--immediately available at all entrances and near library directories.[28] Auditory, tactile and pictorial library maps orient everyone including patrons with disabilities. All library maps show exits and restricted areas[29] which people might not observe or understand without them. Map and directory information should be updated whenever library conditions change. Outdated handouts reduce library access.

Service Area Maps

Every library service area must be accessible if it is open to the public.[30] Service areas must be interconnected to provide continuous access to patrons with disabilities.[31] Maps of service areas should show that libraries furnish auxiliary services giving disabled individuals an equal opportunity to participate in and enjoy library service, program, or activity benefits. They also, over time, contribute to patron library mental maps. Service area map users should be shown adaptive floor plans and personally directed to reading areas.[32] Librarian accommodation for disabled patrons includes personal interpretation of directories and maps. This level of orientation is often provided during group library tours. Library service area maps should be detailed.[33] At a minimum they should show location and access routes to stacks, periodicals, the card catalog, the online catalog, to reference, circulation, where vertical files are located, audiovisual storage, displays, study and computer carrels, book returns, atlases and oversized book areas, reading tables, book trucks, group assembly locations, assembly seating and listening areas. Librarians help those reluctant to ask for help and those clearly observed to need help. Reading a directory or holding a map handout does not imply that the person understands directions, map content or can access library services.[34]

Every library service area must be accessible if it is open to the public.

Personnel Maps

Maps identifing the librarians regularly assigned to specific service areas link people with their helpers. Personnel maps allow visitors to self-orient, establish their current location, select service access routes, find the right people to help them and then find the right library information. Personnel maps direct patrons with disabilities to librarians for personalized help. When no appropriate or designated library worker is available, no adaptive library orientation can be provided. Being "on your own" in the library is an ineffective library accommodation even for patrons with disabilities who desire "library independence." "On your own" is an example of maximum insensitivity toward disabled patrons who fail to find the information they need without librarian help. Librarian help must come just in time, for the right person, and in just the right way to meet each disabled patrons needs. With personnel maps, all patrons can establish continuing relationships with particular librarians while doing infosearches. People gain in expertise and independence over time, through repeated contacts with specific personnel who are there to help. Personnel maps guide patrons to personalized adaptive library orientation.

Equipment Maps

Equipment maps should show equipment service locations on visually accessible floor maps, show floor map recordings, and indicate available Braille or tactile format library signs. Equipment not user accessible, or for library worker use only, should not be shown. Maps are specifically designed for patron use only since librarians already know equipment locations. Permanent, wall-displayed equipment maps are constantly updated as equipment locations and changing conditions dictate. Equipment map handouts are made available for patrons to take with them during their library trek and reflect current equipment status. Maps should show accessible service routes for patron equipment access.[35] Such maps orient patrons for library equipment locations but do not provide directions for operating the equipment. Operational guides should be mounted on each piece of patron-use library equipment explaining and illustrating appropriate use. Braille and tactile format maps at each entrance and at all service areas facilitate mobility to equipment for the visually challenged.[36] Wherever service guides or maps are used, they should be redundantly provided in Braille.[37] While the visually challenged may not use all library services, knowing equipment locations orients them to what can be used independently.[38] Operating directions in Braille should be located on each piece of equipment. Many visually challenged patrons cannot read Braille but can be helped to orient on equipment that displays tactile signage.

Recorded Library Maps

Assistive listening systems (ALS) at each service area provide the equivalent of recorded library floor maps.[39] Permanently installed ALS display the international access symbol for hearing loss and are used throughout the library.[40] ALS may include small radio transmitters giving users site-specific voice instruction or standard orientation as they approach.[41] Three specific ALS systems provide voice instruction including induction loop, FM, and Infrared technology.[42] At various library service sites, each ALS has patron-use advantages and disadvantages.[43] Like museum display headphones, portable ALS units are loaned at library entry and returned at departure. Base station transmitters link patron headphones, acting as receivers,[44] or earphones that plug into transmitter boxes to hear service site instructions or conventional orientation. ALS recorded adaptive orientation may not be fully understood without careful editing for disabled listeners. To be most effective, content must be library site-specific, referencing also specific local equipment, services, and personnel. Continuously updated content assures timely service and site-specific orientation. Without continuous ALS content updating, each service site becomes progressively less accessible over time. ALS earphone jacks with volume controls may not benefit hearing aid users.[45] Earphone jacks disallow hearing aid links. In libraries where patrons with disabilities can find service locations independently, prerecorded instructions can help both the sight- and hearing-impaired.[46] Carefully edited messages provide minimal orienting information to those not readily able to visualize library services. Recorded content directs patrons along accessible routes that are also integrated with other library service areas. Content addresses the most frequently asked orienting questions for the most commonly reoccuring infosearching demands. ALS equipment should not be placed in isolated sites, but in high-demand library service areas.

Auditory Walkways

Long cane users receive mobile library orientation without direct librarian help through "auditory walkways." Wiring under library service route carpeting or in flooring gives off beeps or vibrations picked up by a specially-designed long cane and audible to its user.[47] While this auditory walkway service provides effective service route access, it is not designed to provide specific service area orientation. Recorded library maps do provide specific service area orientation. ALS auditory walkway maps should also indicate areas of emergency rescue assistance.[48]

Maps-By-Touch

Maps-by-touch display orienting information specifically for patrons with visual impairment.[49] Tactile library floor plan maps show floor features, service areas and patron-accessible equipment using Brailled, raised or recessed lettering identifiable by touch.[50] Maps in this tactile format orient both the sighted and those with sight disabilities.[51] Library maps at the entrance and throughout all service and equipment areas should display raised or indented features to be understood by touch.[52] Tactile information must be located where it is easily accessible and presented throughout all library service areas in a predictable way to maximize patron use. Effective reading of tactile maps requires clear area floor space with safe pedestrian approach. Potted floor plants, displays or realia should be avoided in these tactile map areas.[53] Maps-by-touch provide

Library Patrons With Disabilities

service orientation for some on walls, door surfaces, and to the right of doorways, as do external library entrance identifiers or library signage using large print. Tactile maps also describe services or equipment operational procedures but must do so using oversimplified terms. Tactile maps necessarily contain reduced, or oversimplified, information. Tactile information alone fails to provide detailed and meaningful information without direct librarian accommodation and/or supplemental recordings.[54] Both tactile maps and librarian help, or tactile maps and recorded information, can assist patrons who need them. Reduced tactile map information at equipment is used more sparingly than are carefully edited equipment guides. Tactile maps are not Brailled, but provide lettered instructions orienting the visually limited. Raised borders around library signs that utilize raised characters are confusing to tactile readers unless the borders are set away from the characters:[55]

> To read a tactile map, start by finding its title, which is most often at the top of the map. Then, beginning at the upper left corner and proceeding in a clockwise direction around the map edges, check for any grid markings or geographical coordinates. Indicators may be notches or lines. The grid system helps to locate map features more quickly. Again, beginning at the upper left and this time scanning across the page from left to right and top to bottom, locate the key to symbols (legend), any notes, the north symbol, and the map scale. If there is no north symbol, assume that north is at the top of the map. Once the symbols become familiar to you, reading the map itself will be easier and more meaningful (National Library Service for the Blind, 1987, page vi) .

Pictogram Maps

Pictograms accompany library tactile maps. Directly below pictograms, or pictorial symbols, are equivalent verbal descriptors.[56] Interpretive library guides and audiotape devices may be more effective than pictograms in presenting orienting information, since pictograms and tactile maps must oversimplify the information. Many library services are more complex than that information contained in pictograms.[57] The more complex the pictogram content, the more difficult it is to understand what services are illustrated. Pictograms should be used only in conjunction with guides and audiotaped information.

Interior Library Walkway Awareness

Librarians must carefully consider the challenges imposed by interior library walkways on patrons with disabilities. Proactive librarians display a keen sense of walkway challenges throughout the library that may affect particular disabled patrons. The visually impaired are more library walkway-aware and better walkway-oriented than sighted pedestrians. The sighted unconsciously feel library walkway surfaces without registering walkway orienting information. Sound-on-cane techniques by long-cane users detect walking surface changes to show library walkway features.[58] From the entrance, each tactile library walkway is marked with both Braille and tactile identifiers to give them relatively safe library freedom of movement.

Mobility Trainers as Library Personal Attendants

Mobility trainers as personal attendants are highly skilled and specialized professionals who work with low vision patron mobility orientation in many settings. One of those important mobility settings for patrons with visual

Mobility trainers orient patrons with low vision or who are blind to assist in building a personalized library mental map.

impairments is the library. Mobility trainers orient patrons with low vision or who are blind to assist in building a personalized library mental map. Librarians, in turn, help by establishing policies and procedures to facilitate library use by visually impaired patrons. Responding to specific requests of library mobility training attendants while training patrons with visual impairment in the library is a necessary library accommodation and an important part of indirect patron orientation. Indirect patron orientation is provided by others, not the librarian personally.

Library Service Area Color Trails

Complex library buildings sometimes call for simple orientation strategies that all can follow to their preferred library service area. Being lost or confused in the library does not help orient patrons. For effective library orientation, accessible libraries present a visual color-coded trail to each service area. The color trail begins either from the library entrance or at the circulation desk. Color trails display high-contrast lines or walking surface markings. Each library service area is "color-coordinated" to match the color trail leading to that service area. No universal color-coding system has yet been adopted that provides uniform library service area designation. Universal color-coding systems would assist in orientation for patrons with disabilities. All trails lead back from each service area to direct patrons to circulation and library exit.

Circulation	Red
Card Catalog	White
Online Public Access Card Catalog	Yellow
Reserved Collection	Pink
Reference	Blue
Periodicals	Green
Library ADA Coordinator	Silver
Audiovisual Collection	Brown
Stacks	Gold
Vertical Files	Purple

Figure 3-1. Universal Library Service Area Color Codes

Patrons Reluctant To Ask For Library Maps

Some do not follow library service area maps well. Because of their library skill deficits, many have ongoing map orientation and service access problems. Those with disabilities in the library context may be reluctant to ask for map orientation.[60] Asking for a library map may translate to librarian dependency or imply a lack of personal library independence. Patrons have a choice among available adaptive library orientation methods including their personal library map use. But patrons using maps independently must orient themselves to library services limited to specific map information. Service area and equipment guide signage supplements basic library map information when the patron arrives in each service area.

Library Patrons With Disabilities

Library Safety Orientation

Under the rubric of library safety orientation many wrong impositions on disabled patrons have been done. Librarians have speculated as to what specific safety requirements are associated with what specific disabilities in patrons. Anticipating those anticipated safety risks, they have taken library measures that have been misguided--at worst ineffective, and at best, irrelevant. And librarians may have done so on the basis of anticipated, not actual, individual disabled patron safety risks. Library safety orientation for the disabled is based on actual risk and not on speculation, disability behavioral stereotypes or generalizations. Librarians cannot orient individuals based on any generalizations about people's library safety. Professionals must deal specifically with one disabled patron's library safety at a time. Effective library policy does not impose safety orientation burdens on the cognitively or physically challenged that are not placed on others, such as requiring them to be accompanied to the library by attendants. For example:

> Taken together, these [ADA] provisions are intended to prohibit exclusion and segregation of individuals with disabilities and the denial of equal opportunities enjoyed by others, based on, among other things, presumptions, patronizing attitudes, fears, and stereotypes about individuals with disabilities. ...[libraries] are required to ensure that their actions are based on facts applicable to individuals and not on presumptions as to what a class of individuals with disabilities can or cannot do (ADA Handbook, II-37).

Tactile Library Safety Warnings

Orientation includes tactile safety warnings as standardized library walkway surface features applied to, or built into, pedestrian floor surfaces. They are comparable to road surface warnings felt by drivers approaching turnpike gates.[61] Floor tactile warnings give pedestrians tread signals that can be felt orienting and alerting them to oncoming service area dangers.[62] Overhead dangers or abrupt walkway level changes along library service routes, stairs or other danger areas are indicated before they are encountered.[63] For patrons with visual disabilities, tactile maps provide additional library safety orientation. Tactile safety warnings are also provided on door handles to warn all of dangers behind that doorway. Yet the sighted may not register imminent danger like low-vision patrons. Tactile safety doors have knurled doorknobs on entries leading to restricted or dangerous equipment areas, loading platforms dropoffs, boiler rooms, locked rooms, darkrooms, or stages. ADA requirements and library orientation for low vision patrons help everyone gain library information by providing safety warnings for all. But all must recognize those safety warnings.

Professionals must deal specifically with one disabled patron's library safety at a time.

Library Overhead and Service Route Hazards

Orientation must include alerting patrons with visual impairments to library overhead hazards. Visually impaired pedestrians are particularly vulnerable to head injuries caused by library overhead barriers.[64] Protruding stack aisle objects, card catalog open shelving, portable book returns and similar equipment must be moved out of service routes and walkways or if these barriers cannot be removed, then tactile warnings should be installed to orient and forewarn. Such warnings alert all. Overhead hazards are particularly dangerous causing head, eye or shoulder injuries in the library.[65] Those hazards are easily recognized and avoided by the sighted but not by long cane users. Color contrast indicators or heat reflections off objects mislead long cane users to touch unprotected heat registers, radiators and other harmful library surfaces.

Adaptive Library Orientation

Equipment storage areas should have separate areas with closed doorways with this tactile warning system in place. Interior library doors leading to outside loading platforms must be knurled. Temporary hazardous areas include library equipment opened and under repair. Library equipment maintenance may also pose a hazard with equipment power units exposed and touchable by patrons. Library equipment maintenance agreements provide skilled workers who observe onsite pedestrian precautions that may not be also observed when librarians maintain equipment that exposes patrons to unnecessary risk. Library hazardous area signage should be positioned until maintenance or repairs are completed, the equipment closed and returned to operational status.

Designated Areas of Emergency Rescue Assistance

There may be nothing more frightening to a disabled person than being in a library without a way out during an emergency. Help can be found when patrons with disabilities go to designated areas of emergency rescue assistance. Tactile warnings located as needed on all Brailled maps indicate each library location danger as well as displaying areas of emergency rescue assistance.[66] In a library without designated emergency rescue assistance area orientation, no patron with visual disabilities is safe. Nor are many other disabled patrons including those using wheelchairs. Librarians assure orientation for safe wheelchair library entrance and exit. Emergency route and areas of emergency rescue assistance orientation increases personal confidence while using library resources. A library area of emergency rescue assistance is ADA-required. A working library plan for emergency support availability greatly increases patron with wheelchair safety and confidence. But that working library plan must be explained to each wheelchair user for the personal confidence and support it would generate.

In a library without designated emergency rescue assistance area orientation, no patron with visual disabilities is safe or others using wheelchairs.

Library fire prevention requires all service areas to post exits with clearly marked and highly visible evacuation plans or areas of rescue assistance for the disabled.[67] The assumption that all will evacuate the library with alarms sounding is not well-founded. Patrons with disabilities may react in unconventional ways, or cause unusual emergency exit problems for themselves and for others. Local fire codes require that emergency exit doors be crash-bar equipped, with doors releasing outward. And local fire code specifications have the highest and most pressing library priority.

Fire alarms can be patron-tripped without cause. Fire warning systems provide alarms for all library occupants, even if misused. A false alarm is better than a real fire without functioning alarms to warn building occupants. Since libraries may be occupied by slower moving people with disabilities, alarm access and response becomes a critical safety issue. There can be no compromise with this library fire safety requirement.

Audible and Visual Library Alarms

Audible and visual library alarms provide the visual or hearing limited more response time in emergency situations. Librarians hope that all, including patrons with disabilities have adequate response time in a real library emergency evacuation.[68] Fire department inspectors can recommend best extinguisher and alarm placement throughout the building. Inspectors test library warning systems, examine emergency evacuation signage, and verify fire prevention systems. Fire inspection recommendations should be immediately adopted and implemented as library policy.

Auxiliary emergency alarms are a "quiet" orientation strategy for all library patrons that is designed to particularly accommodate patrons with disabilities. Conventional and auxiliary alarms should provide both audible and visual emergency alarm systems in all library service areas, restrooms, meeting rooms, hallways, lobbies or common use areas.[69] Audible alarms alert all library occupants with an intensity and frequency designed to alert persons with partial hearing loss.[70] For the hearing impaired or deaf, alternative library-wide visual alarms display immediate and clearly understandable warning. Auxiliary emergency alarms spread both visual and auditory signals quickly and noticeably, raising overall light and alarm sound levels.[71]. Emergency library alarms are rarely visible or noticeable until used. These library adaptive alarms are critical for disabled patron safety.

Fire Extinguisher Access

Fire extinguisher access is provided to people when needed. Pictorial directions for fire extinguisher use enable anyone to quickly and appropriately extinguish small library fires. Fire alarms should be strategically positioned and accessible throughout the library building. Extinguishers are designated by appropriate local fire authority.[72]

Emergency Exit Doors

Crash-bar exit doors equipped with alarms have been traditionally placed at building exterior doors to set off alarms during unauthorized or emergency use.[73] Doors with crash-bars have alarm equipment at exterior building entrances to reduce pedestrian or patron danger. PUSH or PULL door signage display arrows to the right, or left, of door knobs, handles or crash bars indicate and redirect door-opening efforts. Few library glass doors are so-equipped at present. All should be.

Revolving Doors and Turnstiles

Pressure-sensitive revolving library doors or turnstiles provide alternative patron access, but must not be the only means of passage through an accessible exit.[74] Revolving doors or turnstiles are effective barriers for many mobility-limited patrons. Libraries adding accessible gates or doors adjacent to turnstiles or revolving doors facilitate exit for everyone. Facilitating safe and effective patron exit is equally as important as facilitating their safe and effective library entry. Librarians should help any patron needing exit assistance without qualification or reservation. Revolving doors present multiple exit problems for the mobility-limited using walking aids or wheelchairs.

Changing Patron Library Exit Conditions

It is not logical to assume that patrons with disabilities exit with the same ease, skill or barriers overcome as when they entered. There are many reasons for this. Disabled patrons become fatigued while in the library.[75] They may exit with additional titles not present on entry. Patrons may experience distress associated with conflicts with library workers, equipment, other patrons and with unsuccessful infosearching. And heavy traffic at revolving doors makes their use dangerous for many people with cognitive or physical challenges.

Facilitating safe and effective patron exit is equally as important as facilitating their safe and effective library entry It is not logical to assume that patrons with disabilities exit with the same ease, skill or barriers overcome as when they entered.

Alternate Library Exit

Librarians maximize safe library exit for all patrons using all available accessible portals. Alternate wheelchair accessible exits are provided when main accessible gates or doorways are blocked.[76] With library authorization some mobility-limited may need to use alternates to the main exit. It is extremely poor library planning when patrons using wheelchairs must enter only by the main entrance and exit only at an alternate portal. How can exit occur at alternate sites when those alternate exits are temporarily blocked, out of order or inaccessible to patrons with wheelchairs? Alternate library exit doors at vehicle loading ramps or mobile van service areas should be equipped with warning signals to prevent unauthorized use and redirect patron exit to safer, more accessible doors. Patrons may become disoriented when asked to use alternate exits as they leave the building to find the parking lot or loading zone. Library internal exit signage shows the exit but does not show access to the parking lot. It seems imbalanced when libraries are careful to provide orienting library signage to patrons on entry but not on exit. Some patrons attempt library exit even at unauthorized, alarm-equipped, well-marked exits cautioning users for claxon sounding.

Security Gate Exit

Main security gates equipped with warning signals limit unauthorized exit.[77] Library security gates within circulation view and control must provide easy and safe exit for the disabled. Alternative check-out aisles are provided in heavy-use libraries to accommodate patrons with disabilities.[78] Activating and deactivating security gate equipment is possible only when gate controls are within reach and doors are readily visible from circulation. A security gate out of circulation view and used by a wheelchair patron seeking unsuccessful exit cannot be supervised and does not accommodate patron exit. Marked buttons for disabled exit actuate a silent alarm (strobe or blinking light) at the circulation desk which brings immediate librarian response. Librarians then deactivate security gates and move to the exit to help. Librarians also may witness independent successful exit without further disabled patron exit problems.

Unauthorized Library Exit

The deaf or hearing-impaired attempting unauthorized exit may trigger high-intensity audible alarms disturbing everyone else in the library but themselves. Audible alarms at circulation triggered on unauthorized exit pose many other problems associated with library quality of life. Visual alarms are less intrusive, less disruptive to library exit, and equally effective.

Circulation Service Disruption

There is an immediate disruption of services to patrons at the circulation desk when exit alarms are tripped without real emergency conditions existing. Quickly resolved problems at the security gate exit reduce circulation service disruption while prolonged attention at the gate effectively stops circulation service. Providing for circulation backup by temporarily repositioning other library workers may be needed. Patrons crowded at circulation desks may all converge at the same time on library exits, doorways, stairways, ramps and walkways. This condition may be particularly true during library closing. Library doors are designed to allow individual use and tend to restrict multiple pedestrian departure. Library exit conditions should be well planned and when needed, reconfigured since exit conditions are different than entrance conditions.

Patrons crowded at circulation desks may all converge at the same time on library exits, doorways, stairways, ramps and walkways. This condition may be particularly true during library closing.

Library Patrons With Disabilities

Exit Ramp, Stairway or Walkway Barriers

Library exit ramps generally <u>decline</u> while entry ramps generally <u>incline</u> into the building. Patrons with limited mobility, who are fatigued from library work or are carrying extra books, face new physical challenges exiting <u>downward</u> on ramps than when entering ramps <u>upward</u> under different conditions. Stairways at library exits may be more difficult to negotiate when carrying books than stairway use at entry. Downtread stairway visibility is more limited than uptread visibility. Walkways leading downward and away from the library require caution for wheelchair users to avoid acceleration and roll-off when they are overloaded with library books. Ramp, stairway and walkway conditions may have worsened due to inclement weather not present at the time of library entry.

Departing Patrons With Disabilities

Just as libraries are responsible for ensuring safe patron library entry from the parking lot, so they are responsible to ensure safe library exit back to the parking space or to the patron vehicle. Patron entry conditions may not be present or may differ significantly on exit. Among these changes are library exit identification and orientation for appropriate exit use; exit ramp, stairway and walkway barriers returning to the parking lot; and heavy pedestrian traffic at library exits. Parking lot or loading zone conditions; the return to special designated parking spaces after locating the patron vehicle in a large or crowded parking lot; resolving unauthorized restricted parking citations or towing; dealing with restricted parking privilege abuse by others; and parking lot negotiation, are all relevant to library patron departure safety. Future library visits may be dictated by current successful or challenging library exit follow-up patron experiences and memories. When unsuccessful as infosearchers or overchallenged at library exit, patrons with disabilities may not return.

Parking Lot Changes On Exit

Assuming walkways were negotiated safely during library exit, the parking lot may have become crowded, reducing the ease by which personal vehicles can be identified and reached. When parking lot or walkway conditions are known to have deteriorated due to inclement weather, mobility-limited patrons must take additional safety precautions. Negotiating wet, ice, or snow-slickened walkways and parking lots challenges everyone, but it challenges the mobility-limited the most. Bad weather precautions are the responsibility of patrons with disabilities, but not all are bad-weather prepared. In addition to patron safety concerns at night, bad-weather conditions may require the patron to request library escort. Is library escort routinely available to all patrons on request?

Just as libraries are responsible for ensuring safe patron library entry from the parking lot, so they are responsible to ensure safe library exit back to the parking space or to the patron vehicle.

Finding and Reentering the Vehicle

Patrons may need to return to special designated parking spaces after locating their vehicle in large, crowded parking lots and must resolve unauthorized restricted parking citations or vehicle towing if they have misparked. For patrons with disabilities, towing is a significant mobility limitation requiring alternate transit. Others abuse restricted parking privileges or restrict access to specially-equipped vehicles. Parking lots sometimes must be negotiated under less-than-favorable circumstances while driving away and concluding the library trek.

Adaptive Library Orientation

Patrons Unable To Interpret Library Information

Orientation for patrons unable to interpret library information is a challenge to professional librarians. Some patrons with disabilities are unable to interpret information on entry and throughout the library stay.[79] Adaptive library orientation for these patrons must be individually provided on their request. No disabled patron is required to participate in adaptive library orientation. Their involvement is entirely voluntary. Without effective adaptive library orientation, disabled patrons have the right to continue being unable to interpret library information, as they choose. Yet most persons who enter the library want to be successful infosearchers and will probably avail themselves of appropriate and individualized adaptive orientation.

Orienting Patrons With Reading Disabilities

Initial new patron orientation may indicate some with severe reading disabilities. Patrons with severe reading disabilities or nonreaders have very limited access to library services and equipment without reading help. Those with specific learning disabilities may be functional nonreaders.[80] Signage without pictograms does not direct nonreaders to services.[81] Patron support does not exist until the librarian assists on request, or a personal reading attendant accompanies the nonreader.[82] Without patron requests for librarian reading accommodation, no special supportive reading service is provided.[83]

The nonreading patron must read independently, ask for reading accommodation or perform library workarounds independently.[84] Nonreaders have information read to them by reading attendants, family members or other companions. Patrons have a rich life-experience background, quality of thinking and vast information needs, even as nonreaders.[85] Nonreaders have personal information interests.[86] Some personal information interests are met by group viewing or listening without reading for understanding. Patrons who do not read may be passive, nonprint information receivers; dependent on librarians for print information. They may avoid asking for help for picture-intensive print or nonprint information.[87] These librarian dependents fail to secure print information without orientation. Yet many are motivated to enter the library and gain information without librarian help.

Patrons have a rich life-experience background, quality of thinking and vast information needs, even as nonreaders.

Nonreaders are sometimes confused with other patrons with disabilities.[88] Workers observe some demonstrating a "poor attitude" toward library skills.[89] Part of a disabled patron's library requirements may be to improve library skills and self-esteem even while being a nonreader. Patron reading deficits may require the patron to move from print to nonprint information choices to gain personal information. Library visits should be both enjoyable and informationally rich, productive experiences. Patrons do not enter the library with the specific intention to fail during infosearching. They want to succeed.

Librarians unable to surmise why help was declined may not recognize the patron with "invisible" disability." Nonreaders maintain personal dignity by not revealing to anyone in the library their reading accommodation needs. Many are skilled at having others read for them effectively manipulating others into helping without knowing they are helping a nonreader. Patrons who do not read are subtle and skilled at keeping their reading disabilities hidden. The immature claim they are unable to infosearch without extensive librarian help while never directly addressing their need for adaptive library orientation. Instead they regularly pursue and expect continuous librarian accommodation. The self-reliant have a right, on library entry, to fully circumvent or refuse orientation.[90] Some refuse to use library resources, voluntarily restricting access to nonreading information.[91]

Library Patrons With Disabilities

Many library services do not require reading including lectures, records, cassettes, compact discs, telephone reference, storytelling, reading groups, film or video presentations. Abundant library pictograms and richly illustrated collections reduce patron with reading disabilities demand for infosearching by reading. Nonreaders eagerly pursue interests with the librarian and library equipment support. Nonprint media access includes using portable cassette machines and earphones, talking books, talking dictionaries, encyclopedias, richly illustrated cookbooks, talking newspapers or magazines,[92] reel-to-reel recorders, assistance with coin- and card-operated photocopiers, even FAX machines. Related services at library equipment include using enclosed study carrels, listening rooms for taping or listening, volunteer readers, book talks, display posters featuring community events, oral presentations, storytelling, even library story-board displays. Nonreaders have a rich information environment in the library.

Information is eagerly pursued by nonreaders whose interests permit infosearching without having to read or without asking a librarian for help. Avoiding library help greatly restricts the nonreading patron's information window. Disorganized or cognitively impaired patrons may not consider requesting librarian orientation. They lack a working library mental map and are unable to find specific information locations or personnel from whom they can obtain information or directions.[93] Requesting adaptive librarian orientation reduces patron disorganization and helps them infosearch. It is a myth that nonreading patrons require minimal library equipment access and would be more likely to use group presentations or visit the library primarily for socialization. Nonreaders of all ability levels have their own information interests. Nonreaders access equipment more effectively when helped by librarians to select technology that works best for them. Orientation by the librarian does not contribute to the nonreader's feelings of inadequacy, information powerlessness, or an overall inability to be library information stakeholders. Professional librarians facilitate nonreading patron information empowerment.

Learning Disabled as Library Patrons Who Read

Three major types of specific learning disabilities (LD) exist in patrons: specific reading, math, or sensory-perceptual disabilities. Any LD patron can have one, two, or all three disability types. Further, each LD person can have mild, moderate, or severe levels of learning disabilities for each of the three types. Among patrons with LD, the largest group are persons with mild-to-moderate specific reading disabilities. Librarians may tend to generalize the term "LD" to only those patrons who have specific reading disabilities. The learning disabled, even with severe reading disabilities, can and do read. Learning disabled patrons represent a broad information interest spectrum and diverse learning styles, as do other library patrons.[94] They require a wide array of library equipment support.[95] High technology library equipment, such as CD-ROM, may be effective in providing patrons with learning disabilities reasonable accommodation.[96] Being learning disabled does not inhibit information needs but may limit effective searches without library equipment and orientation support.[97]

Patrons With Cognitive Disabilities

Some patrons may consistently demonstrate cognitive impairments in the library setting when they attempt to infosearch. There are many types of patron infosearching judgments that seem inappropriate by librarian standards. Behavior disorder overlays or cognitive impairments may be associated with patrons' reading or study skill deficits throughout the infosearching process and in every library service area. Possibly because of behavior disorder in the library context, some significantly misuse library resources.[98] For these

Three major types of specific learning disabilities (LD) exist in patrons: specific reading, math, or sensory-perceptual disabilities.

patrons, adaptive library orientation must be highly individualized. Librarians will often never know patrons' true cognitive disabilities infer cognitive problems from their library behavior. Some behaviors suggest specific librarian-generated adaptive orientation strategies. Other patron behaviors associated with their cognitive disabilities or behavioral disorders are unrelated to infosearching and do not suggest specific librarian strategies. Identification of cognitive disabilities in patrons does not categorically identify what help they need from librarians or how they can be helped to better infosearch. Patrons must specify their library infosearching orientation and accommodation needs. And the librarian must carefully listen to those who may not clearly articulate those orientation needs.

Library Orientation with Cognitive Assistance

Personalized or adaptive library orientation for individuals with cognitive disabilities will challenge the librarian to develop new strategies that may not apply to others with similar cognitive disabilities. But there are common infosearching challenges that can be augmented or supported through effective librarian orientation to begin patron infosearches and accommodation to complete the infosearching process. Among these newer developments are computer-based artifical intelligence (AI) systems to assist patrons to infosearch by making basic infosearching tasks easier, more transparent and intuitive. With these new AI systems placed at every major library service area and available with many library equipment types, all patrons will be helped, even those with cognitive disabilities. AI systems are patient, diagnostic and redundant for the patron in need. A unique AI service is required for each library equipment type and for every circulation or reference function that presents initial orientation or infosearching approach skills to new patrons or to those needing cognitive assistance.

Part of the library AI effort is to develop knowledge-engine equipped expert systems that contain procedures new users can follow to infosearch within the local library context. With this "intelligent assistant" to analyze and solve infosearching problems, certain infosearching challenges can be automated and standardized. Using a very simple question-and-answer approach and with simplified language content, one of the most valuable AI approaches using intelligent assistants is to prescreen infosearching problems before going to the librarian for more sophisticated, personal assistance. AI provides confidential tracking of patron infosearching efforts to assist each patron with each new library visit. They pick up the infosearch where they left off in a private, confidential setting.

Immature Infosearcher Orientation

Immaturity is more easily observable than a patron's disabilities--which may be neither visible nor easily observable in the library context. Yet for each age-grouping there are no normative library behavioral standards--only librarian assumptions or expectations about what is "library mature" or "library immature" patron behavior. Describing patrons as "library immature" is a flawed process. There are better alternatives. Assumptions about library maturity or immaturity are validated only after patron observation in several library situations over time. Once observed only in the library context, the librarian can better determine adaptive orientation when the patron returns. Librarian judgments alone do not help the immature patron to be more successful. Adaptive library orientation overcomes patron infosearching immaturity when it is responsive to patron infosearching skill levels, patron attitude and specific disabled patron accommodation requests. No method exists for professionals to judge immaturity without direct observation and patron contact. Immature infosearching problems are resolved by a library-based infosearch skills assessment and with full patron cooperation.[99] A functional library assessment provides specific steps to help patrons meet library challenges. Any assessment that attaches to patrons labels such as "library immature" or "immature infosearcher" are derogatory and meaningless without suggesting specific orientation and accommodation that librarians can provide for specific patrons. From another perspective, we are all library immature or immature infosearchers when faced with the size and complexity of information available even in a small library and within the global information technology reach of the Information Age.

Library Patrons With Disabilities

Orienting Patrons With Mental Retardation

Among library patrons with cognitive disabilities, some have mental retardation. In addition to other disabilities, and sometimes mistakenly called the "library immature," some library patrons have the complicating factor of mental retardation.[100] Conditions of disabilities in patrons such as low intelligence make patron library orientation and accommodation more complex.[101] Significantly low intelligence and concomitant social immaturity are not readily observable, but can be inferred, in the library context. Professionals may not notice retardation in patrons experiencing information barriers. They appear and act as any other patron having orientation difficulties in the library.

Even to specialists, patron orientation and infosearching immaturity due to mental retardation is not readily visible. Specific mental retardation characteristics in patrons may not be visually recognizable during orientation. Some with mental retardation are more readily identifiable when they exhibit significant adaptive behavior deficits or similar difficulties related to library use, rather than the immediate library orientation challenge.[102] Attributing or assuming mental retardation in patrons as an explanation for their observed library behavior or orientation needs reduces the dignity of individuals who are mentally retarded.

Even with effective library orientation, and their maximum personal effort, patrons with mental retardation may infosearch unsuccessfully. Librarians must assume that everyone entering the library intends to successfully infosearch there--not to fail. If patrons with mental retardation wish to be successful, librarians can provide adaptative orientation to do successful information searches. But librarians do not dictate what, to the patron with mental retardation, are their successful or unsuccessful infosearches. Each patron must define personal infosearching success criteria.

Patrons with mental retardation may have less severe learning impairments and still demonstrate library immaturity.[103] Being mentally retarded means that the patron has a younger mental age than chronological age with mental age established by a formal intelligence test. Mental retardation, however severe, does not automatically imply patron "library retardation" or "library immaturity." Confirming that a person is mentally retarded does not help the librarian know what that person needs or wants from the librarian or the collection. A valid mental retardation patron label does not indicate infosearching goals or objectives. It does not reveal their purpose for entering the library. They must be asked for their special orientation and information needs and carefully listened to for their often nonverbal responses.

The severely mentally retarded or developmentally disabled require minimal library equipment support because they are more likely to use group-supervised information access or visit the library primarily to socialize.[104] Patrons with disabilities of all ability and intellectual levels have personal information interests.[105] Some are met during library group viewing, individual passive viewing or listening without reading for understanding. Special collections have been suggested specifically for patrons with mental retardation to reflect their interests and information needs.[106] With the evolution of library and information science, librarians are beginning to recognize the critical need for the mentally retarded to be provided age-appropriate information.

Attributing or assuming mental retardation in patrons as an explanation for their observed library behavior or orientation needs reduces the dignity of individuals who are mentally retarded.

The mentally retarded have the right to access information about civil rights, travel and transportation, daily living activities and sexual information.[107] They need not be regarded by some librarians as "eternal children."[108] Disability-specific collections may not meet patron information needs in an integrated context. Specialized or disability-specific information is integrated with conventional library collections.

More than a social environment, the library is a source of inexpensive, lifelong recreational, informational, and educational opportunities, and accessible information on functional leisure, employment, and daily living skills.[109] While patrons with severe retardation may not read, their questions are significant and worthy of librarian attention and equipment accommodation. Lucas (1983) suggests:

> Pity, sympathy, and patronizing attitudes are not required; sensitivity to individual needs and willingness to work to eliminate the barriers which keep disabled persons from fully utilizing their abilities are. If positive attitudes exist, librarians will make the needed effort to learn and to put into practice what they have learned. It is easy enough to agree that attitude adjustment is required. It is less easy to bring about such attitudinal change (page 208).

Age-sensitive titles go beyond the high interest/low vocabulary collection to specifically include adult themes and format titles which place low reading demands on the mentally retarded library patron. Patrons with mental retardation eventually gain information to become effective library information stakeholders. They may evolve a narrow range of information interests and require periodic updating by the librarian to maintain and enhance those information interests. Professionals working with retarded individuals have as a therapeutic goal "client library independence." They evolve to library independence in stages by successful learning. As library independence develops, visits to the library for socialization through audience participation, during reading groups, for audiovisual displays or for exhibits increase. Middle library skill levels require orienting to library areas and services to check out titles of interest. Later library skill levels involve library equipment use to find other personally relevant information. Librarians often support patrons with developmental disabilities in every library service when they come with patron attendants, or the attendant gradually takes over patron support. A gradual phasing out of the librarian support, then the attendant, permits greater independent and successful library equipment use by patrons with developmental disabilities.

Orienting the Low Functioning

Some low-functioning patrons need immediate protection provided by librarians on entry without reference to library information. Librarians assist low-functioning patrons in every service area and for all their information needs. Librarians, however, are not required to provide for personal needs, toileting or lifting.[110] They may require extensive library accommodation.[111] To be effective infosearchers they must overcome what are for them significant library barriers. They may be multiply disabled with associated severe or profound mental retardation. The low-functioning demonstrate overall disabilities in the library context from entry throughout their library stay. As infosurvivors, they demonstrate in the library extreme social immaturity, delayed physical maturation, and significant deficits in adaptive behavior. These people have a greater need to socialize, not infosearch. Their information objective--and that of those who attend with them--may be for library socialization. When libraries provide public events, they attend for important entertainment and life enrichment which for them may be an otherwise sterile world.[112] Deinstitutionalization has placed persons with severe retardation in the community after residential institutions close.[113] They have the right to freely visit the library and use library equipment.[114]

Severely disabled who are also nonreaders do not select or interpret information as infosearchers. They may not know how to, or are not able to, ask for library help. Some are just beginning to gesture, sign or point to librarians for their personal information needs. Gestures alone do not help the librarian understand what

Library Patrons With Disabilities

information may be patron-needed. Signing may not be a skill that the librarian understands. Low-functioning signing may also be incorrect signing for librarians able to interpret American Sign Language. Low-functioning patrons as a normal course of events may have a very small functional signing vocabulary that does not include library- or information-relevant signs. Pointing without words does not always direct the librarian to desired information or accommodation. Personal attendants may interpret orientation or information needs for them. The librarian must listen to the attendant if patron-generated directions to information or library accommodation is not forthcoming. Low-functioning library patrons with severe disabilities may be disruptive to others or to themselves. Library disruptions are avoided or reduced when such patrons are accompanied by personal attendants. But libraries cannot require the low-functioning to bring with them personal attendants.[115] Librarians must inform themselves about specific severely disabled patron special library needs or be informed by others who support their special information requests.[116] Because of a personal attendant, other low-functioning patrons are library-independent. Many low functioning come with family members. They arrive in the library with skilled, personalized orientation or accommodation. Much can be learned by observant librarians from personal aides as family members. Observation over time yields a clearer picture of their special library orientation needs. Titles may be selected by the personal attendant to be later read to the low functioning patron who otherwise could not read themselves.

The Library Patron Disability Mix

Media stories often represent library patrons with multiple disabilities as persons requiring public sympathy, solicitous support and admiration for the slightest incremental information stakeholder achievement. The multiply disabled like the mentally retarded do not regard themselves as "eternal children" or the "eternally helpless," as media coverage might suggest. Nor are they helped by proactive librarian support without specifically requesting that help. Individuals with disability mix experience another, harsher daily reality for library orientation. When the media camera lights are off, they go back to being independent, capable infosearchers with quiet, unobtrusive and effective library support.[117] By definition, the multiply disabled experience a combination of any two or more disabilities that substantially limit one or more major life activity.[118] For them, this combination creates an infinitely wide diversity of library skills and information access needs.[119] There is an equal probability that they will have many library information access successes with or without librarian support. Being multiply disabled need not mean that the patron is librarian dependent or will require extensive supervision. Any library context disability combination in a patron is a "disability mix." Disability mix suggests librarians initially assume novice orientation for patron independent reading or equipment operation. But many with disability mix are already intermediate or expert library users. As patrons acquire library skills, their independent reading and library equipment use increases. When requested, the librarian accommodates them with comparable or alternative services. The most high technology or expensive library equipment support does not have to be provided. Only when libraries do not make reasonable accommodations can such patrons have legal ADA-based recourse.[120]

When the media camera lights are off, the multiply disabled go back to being independent, capable information stakeholders with quiet, unobtrusive and effective library support.

Personal Attendant Help

The challenge of patron disability mix and complex library services can be simplified when personal attendants arrive with the patron to the library. Multiply-disabled patrons are often accompanied by personal attendants, reducing direct patron librarian support. Personal attendants are professional helpers, family members, friends, siblings, or others. Most library accommodation is provided by personal attendants. But all attendant/patron or patron/family member groups must be librarian oriented on request, each for their own needs and according to their purposes for being in the library. Personal attendants or other family members may request specific accommodation on the patron's behalf. Librarians provide equipment support only to the extent that the attendant cannot obtain information without librarian help. Libraries cannot require personal attendants to accompany patrons with multiple disabilities.[121] Neither are libraries required to provide personal care associated with some patrons with disabilities. Professional library service emphasizes infosearching strategies, support and patron accomodation for infosearching needs rather than the personal support required by the patron during infosearching. When the patron does not bring personal support or a personal attendant, there is no requirement to provide accommodation beyond infosearching support.

Personal attendants or other family members accompanying the patron with disability may request specific accommodation on the patron's behalf.

Orienting Patrons With Mental Health Disabilities

Patrons come to the library who are depressed, aggressive, suicidal, anxious, delinquent, hyperactive, socially withdrawn, or extremely shy.[122] Sensitive librarians recognize these patron behaviors as library-help and guidance indicators for specific library orientation content. Library orientation assessments are based on librarian experience in helping individuals, and by handling requests for specific library support. Mental health categories or labels do not reveal personal information and support needs when patrons with mental health disabilities enter. Some with mental health disabilities are unrecognizable for their disabilities until library misbehavior occurs. Some patrons with mental health disabilities require more orientation support than others. Most can be oriented quickly and unobtrusively after determining what they individually need or after hearing their specific info-searching accommodation requests.[123] Orientation needs and potential risks to others are based on individual library behavior experience. Librarians sometimes mistake infosurvivor behavioral problems for infosearchers with a mental health overlay. Mental health problems may complicate other disabilities in library patrons. Patrons with disabilities don't come to the library with their mental health status marked on a library card. They come for personal librarian orientation and relevant library information.

Libraries As Stress-Free Environments

Mental health problems are sometimes masked by patron situational stress or even physical illness. Situational stress or life crises carry heavy stress loads that reflect in everything including why patrons need specific library information. Physical illness is known to have concomitant mental health impact on patrons who need specific library information. Libraries cannot be for all patrons stress-free environments but can reduce known stress sources during library orientation. Any easy, relaxed library atmosphere reduces everyones stress. And there is much information in the library about dealing with stress and about stress-free environments. Librarians link patrons with information and then stay out of their way. But librarians stay nearby to help the stressed infosearcher again if requested. Patron behavioral constraints and expectations are a part of every library culture and a challenge for every disabled patron. Librarians empower patrons with disabilities in the library context to maximize independence and minimize help or intervention within

Library Patrons With Disabilities

library behavioral standards. But patron independence and support must be in the context of acceptable library behavior. Disability tolerance for behavioral compliance in libraries varies widely. Librarian orientation for disabled patrons will necessarily reflect local library tolerance for their acting-out behavior. Acting-out behavior may not be directed at library staff but toward other patrons. The acting out patrons show a lack of consideration, failing to recognize others' rights to equal library information access. The ADA largely ignores the patron disability mix possible in all public-access libraries. Each disabled person may have the effect of restricting the rights of others who are also disabled. There is no specific ADA guidance on this.

Other patrons are disrupted while acting-out patrons move to service areas or wander the library avoiding orientation and not infosearching. A few patrons are influenced not to comply with library rules after viewing others who act out. One patrons acting out may have a "contagion effect" on other patrons behavior. Each library has a different "tolerance culture" for acting-out patrons during orientation and infosearching. Library tolerance or forbearance is based on collective librarian proactive or reactive approaches to acting-out patrons. One patrons acting out may be dealt with quite differently by one librarian than another librarian with the same type of patron behaviors or even the same patron. Tolerance or forbearance is an integral part of meeting patron special library needs. A tolerance culture is more workable when librarians are proactive and collectively tolerate acting-out patron behavior. When librarians are reactive, acting-out library patrons are often rejected and expelled before orientation, much less infosearching, can be completed.

Librarians recognize familiar patrons with mental health problems and begin to understand their "invisible orientation disability." The mentally ill may not break library rules, remaining well within acceptable library tolerance levels. No acting-out episodes may occur during many library stays well-after initial library orientation. But when acting-out does happen, professionals must respond for the safety of the patron, others, and library workers.

Professionals observe new patrons with disabilities from a distance and intervene subtly and minimally.[124] No mental health problems are assumed in new patrons until library behavioral episodes occur during or after orientation. Intervention criteria includes observing whether specific library episodes are disruptive to others than to the librarian. On balance, are behavioral episodes significant in the patron's overall library behavior? Is off-task library behavior a reasonable response to a stressful library-imposed situation during orientation? Are patrons reacting more strongly to library information, architectural or attitudinal barriers, disruptions and service inadequacies than others experiencing those same conditions? In this instance, patrons with disabilities may be "symptom bearers" for other patrons not being effectively served. Answers to each of these questions generate different library intervention strategies during orientation and infosearching. And other intervention criteria may apply. Librarians consider how long off-task behavior occurs and how disruptive it is to others. Does it significantly disrupt others or is the disabled patron experiencing a temporary orientation or infosearching difficulty? Are there also other library settings, or service areas, triggering off-task behavior?

Adaptive Library Orientation

These proactive questions help determine genuine disabled patron intervention strategies rather than a simpler reactive librarian response to ignore, exclude, then expell. A significant intervention for off-task library behavior is to leave patrons alone. During off-task episodes that engage others--and when other alternatives do not work--then patrons are removed from the library.

Consistent Library Rule Enforcement

Before library rules can be enforced they must be known or recognizable by patrons with disabilities. But what library posts rules of acceptable patron behavior strategically placed at each service area? This would be considered a legitimate example of "bad professional form" to post any such rules in the library. Instead, librarians unwisely assume that all patrons "know" the specific library rules for that library. Library rules are implied but not overtly stated. To comply with implied--but unstated--rules is an inherently complex and sophisticated social judgement expectation placed on the disabled. Library rules that do not have to be patron-implied are those guides and library signage intended to help all patrons successfully infosearch and/or operate library equipment. When those clearly stated operational infosearching or equipment guides or steps have been shown, the patron has been reminded and the patron continues not to comply with them, then that patron is considered a "rule breaker."

Rule-breaking patrons are responded to differently by each library's tolerance culture. Consequences for not following posted infosearching service area or equipment operation procedures are not explained and may not be consistently enforced in many libraries. Orientation content must clearly indicate library rules. Any library rule posted and already explained during orientation will be librarian enforced. Tolerance must not be provided only to the disabled since that would be reverse discrimination against others without disabilities. Tolerance need not be provided to the disabled beyond specific levels of reasonable accommodation. Maintaining consistent library rule enforcement, being patron facilitators and setting equitable limitations or penalties for all patrons is most important to limit patron acting out. Inconsistent rule enforcement invites those who are acting out to negotiate a new low in group library rule compliance for themselves. This may lead others to degrade their own library behavior, avoid infosearching and begin interfering with others who wish to infosearch.

> **Before library rules can be enforced they must be known or recognizable by patrons with disabilities. But what library posts rules of acceptable patron behavior strategically placed at each service area?**

Librarians wait and watch to assess rule compliance and often tolerate minor infractions. Librarians who do not tolerate minor library rule infractions are "rule enforcers." Rule enforcers generate many more acting out patron events over time than do librarians as "patron facilitators." Patron facilitators help the acting out patron to recover, save face and get back on task, or when unchallenged by others, to escape gracefully.

Infosocializers acting-out may reject librarian rule enforcement or librarian orientation outright. As acting-out patrons, infosocializers require constant supervision for library-based disruptive behaviors. These patrons demonstrate diverse inappropriate behaviors from initial entry and throughout their library stay. Conflicts with others reduce library orientation and accommodation options and increase the likelihood they will be asked to leave. Patrons with mental illness are oriented and accommodated like others when library help is requested and acting-out is avoided.

Library Patrons With Disabilities

The Library's Need to Know

No legal basis exists allowing librarians to secure "need-to-know" information from mental health agencies concerning library patrons with known mental illness. Agency contact may be helpful but information may be available only for general management guidelines. Information explaining specific patron library behavior or typical behavior exhibited in other social situations, or specific library intervention needs, may not be forthcoming. Mental health legislation, deinstitutionalization of many former psychiatric patients and other factors weigh against librarians getting adequate information without direct library observation and librarian personal orientation. When personal library orientation fails, direct librarian intervention is required.

Uninformed Librarians

Irrespective of librarian proactive or reactive inclinations, either type of uninformed librarian imposes barriers on acting-out patrons by helping when not needed or by anticipating potential acting-out events. Or librarians may fail to help, supervise or intervene when acting-out patrons visibly need assistance. Self-informed librarians provide help when asked or when patron need for intervention and help is apparent.[125] When librarian help is required, acting-out patrons may ask inappropriately. They may attempt library entry before or after regular hours. Abusing borrowing or other privileges, they lose those privileges like any other patron. Uninformed librarians cannot provide effective disabled patron orientation. Librarians may avoid helping aggressive patrons by not making reasonable accommodation or avoiding engagement or orientation with those who are acting out. They do not intervene until it is too late. Avoiding helping aggressive patrons provides a beginning point for that patron's off-task escalation. At the other extreme are other librarians that over-help aggressive patrons who do not request orientation or accommodation in an attempt to preempt library acting out. In this venue, professionals seek moderation in interventions for acting out patrons and with moderation can expect the most successful results.

Some patrons who are acting out require professional security measures for crisis control, rule enforcement and risk prevention.

Library Security

Some patrons who are acting out require professional security measures for crisis control, rule enforcement and risk prevention.[126] Libraries should review rule enforcement standards to maintain service delivery to other patrons and staff as an after-effect of acting out incidents during orientation or infosearching. All library patrons are subsequently further restricted in personal library independence after others act out. The library, following a patron acting out event, imposes tighter security measures on all.

Mental Illness and ADA Exclusions

Librarians consider some individuals within the rubric of "mental illness" but are not equally regarded as ADA-qualified individuals with disabilities:

> The term disability does not include: Tranvestism, transsexualism, pedophilia, exhibitionism, voyeurism, gender identity disorders not resulting from physical impairments, or other sexual behavior disorders; compulsive gambling, kleptomania, or pyromania; or psychoactive substance use disorders resulting from current illegal use of drugs. (ADA Handbook, I-50).

Adaptive Library Orientation

Expert librarians are assured that if the patron mental illness conditions listed above are demonstrated in the library, then those patrons are not ADA-qualified individuals with disabilities. Though they may have special needs to be accommodated during orientation, their behavior is dealt with in the same way as the general public, without specific ADA accommodation required. Disabled patron reasonable accommodation is based on functional library behavior, whether or not mental illness is suggested.

Behavioral Contracts

Behavioral contracts are part of the behaviorally disordered student's Individual Educational Program (IEP) and can be imposed in the library.[127] Specific appropriate library-based behaviors requiring patron, teacher, parent, administrative and librarian cooperation and communication are described in the plan. Library contingencies are applied when student behavior does not fulfill contract specifications. Students are made to know clearly what library behaviors are expected in what circumstances. They are informed of consequences for library acting out during orientation or infosearching.

Acting-out students may not distinguish between other patrons and staff, between who may be approached for help to meet their personal information needs and who should be left alone. They may not know enough specifics about personal information requirements to know when to ask for help. Others know how to use library equipment appropriately or when to get help for equipment use. No matter how skilled the librarian, acting-out student patrons may not get the help they need when they continue their significantly inappropriate behavior.

Orienting the Library Withdrawn

The withdrawn are persons with mental health problems whose special needs for orientation or infosearching are not apparent even to astute librarian observers. Their information skill disabilities and service needs in the library context are not observable and can only be inferred. Some withdrawn are the homeless seeking respite in the library, not information. A very few are patrons contemplating suicide. Others display clinical depression symptoms. Behavioral disability categories, mental health labels or labels such as "withdrawn" do not reveal their special library support needs. The withdrawn require help for appropriate library service. Some will need proactive librarian orientation to formulate infosearch strategies, help to clarify the reasons for needing library information or be directly assisted with infosearching. Personalized help includes selection of

Expert librarians are assured that if the patron mental illness conditions listed above are demonstrated in the library, then these patrons are not ADA-qualified individuals with disabilities.

Library Patrons With Disabilities

materials that develop concepts in logical sequence without distracting subjects, while avoiding titles containing life or situational crisis content or leading the reader to act on suicidal tendencies.[128] Titles selected should provide positive concept repetition and conflict resolution. Adaptive library orientation teaches the withdrawn to retrieve information using library sources when help is requested. Orientation content encourages withdrawn or extremely shy patrons to locate the reference desk, find reference librarians, state information needs, and follow recommendations to use appropriate resources. The librarian accompanies the withdrawn to services in support of information needs when requested.

Support for the withdrawn is complex from library entry to exit. No two withdrawn patrons need the same information, act in the same way, or require the same library orientation. Well-presented orientations are tailored to meet individual capabilities, the disability, personal interests and are patron-initiated.

Directions to library service areas, or identifying service locations, or referral to maps, does not assure information access. Library maps showing services are readily available and easily viewed at reference or circulation desks but may not be referred to or understood by the patron. Librarians interpret maps and translate abstract map symbols into directed patron movements on request. Some withdrawn need substantial followup, from map, to directions, to selecting specific titles. Help in selecting quality titles that develop stated or requested information in positive, supportive ways may be requested.[129] The withdrawn often require continued or repeated support to maintain self-selected appropriate reading during each library visit. Others do not clearly express special and personal library information needs. For some library withdrawn, resource selection, gaining information and obtaining answers to questions is a haphazard, unplanned or random process. Others seek desired information in inappropriate sources or locations even after orientation and librarian redirection. Some continue to randomly and unsuccessfully search inappropriate sources or locations without asking for help. They require reorientation and full accommodation, but they always they have the right to refuse it.

Support for the withdrawn is complex from library entry to exit. No two withdrawn patrons need the same information, act in the same way, or require the same library orientation.

Bibliotherapy may effectively assist the withdrawn through guided reading.[130] Many find great comfort through guided library reading. Patron-selected titles may not be appropriate from the librarian's viewpoint, but title selection is an absolute right for patron information access.

Orienting the Physically Challenged

Professionals subtly evaluate prosthetic or orthotic users to determine specific circulation, reference, card catalog, stack, periodical, and library equipment support needs in the context of their information request. In library service areas, and during infosearches, they experience a variety of physical challenges: walking, sustained standing, repeated bending or kneeling or pulling up from bending or kneeling, fine motor balance or carrying heavy or stacked objects while walking. Other patrons with the same prostheses, however, do not experience these infosearching challenges. Patron prostheses and library physical challenges do not necessarily match. It is not valid to assume that all with arm or leg prosthesis have the same library physical challenges or orientation needs. Descriptions in this section are intended only to suggest possible library orientation problems. Some prosthesis users have no library mobility orientation or infosearching problems.

Others have difficulties due to lack of prosthesis experience and skill. Depending upon the patron's lifestyle there may be many new challenges in the library not experienced at other locations in the community, at work, or at home. Many library equipment controls challenge first-time prosthesis users just as they may also be challenged during other major life activities and equipment use elsewhere. Prosthesis users gain in skill with added experience during infosearching using these personal accommodation devices. Leg brace users, for example, do not have difficulty caring for print or nonprint formats, finding service areas, locating periodicals or reference works. Patrons with artificial arm(s), hand or finger prostheses are highly visible on library entry. Recent developments in prostheses cosmetics make user recognition more difficult until arm use is required. These patrons adapt well to library-based infosearching. Those with both arms replaced have difficulty using doors, holding and manipulating objects in all media formats and operating library equipment or controls.[131] Large or heavy library door handles cause problems. Complex door opening mechanisms are difficult to operate.[132] Carrying several books at one time deters balance when walking. Librarians carry materials only when requested by patrons. Leg prostheses may not be visible on library entry although patron gait, balance or leg swing-through may be observably different. Artificial leg-using patrons have all or part of one or both legs amputated or missing since birth. Patrons using leg braces have nerve disabilities with existing limbs or weakened muscles causing toe dropping while walking. Leg braces elevate toes about 10 degrees while walking by mechanical spring action. Throughout the library, leg brace users are often physically challenged.

Walking aid users may not be patrons with library context disabilities. Patrons with significant mobility limitations are expected to use library equipment independently or be responsible for providing personal auxiliary aids or personal attendants. Libraries are not required to provide these personal auxiliary aids and services.[133] Librarians adapt for equipment or personnel brought with the patron during library equipment use. Part of librarian support is to orient both patrons with library context disabilities and their attendants for library equipment and service. Reasonable accommodation does not include directly assisting with patron library mobility.

Librarians should note that patrons with mobility problems are accustomed to slips and falls and to recover to walking status without help from anyone. If patrons ask for help during or after a mishap, the librarian would immediately provide it just as help would be provided to nonphysically challenged patrons who fall for any reason in the library. But helping patrons with mobility problems, and those with walking aids, is more complicated. Proper lifting

Physical challenges alone do not dictate patron special library orientation needs.

Library Patrons With Disabilities

and body management techniques are dictated by the physical therapist, the physician or, the nurse, but not by the librarian as a bystander. Most patrons with mobility disabilities can indicate to any bystander, including the librarian, how they can specifically be helped to recover according to their individual needs. In many instances, recovery is a frequently occurring problem and "really no big deal!" Patron training often includes recovery from falls with independence. To help when not needed is wrong. Neither should they be ignored when assistance is requested.

Dual or Single Cane Users

Patrons requiring single- or dual-cane mobility may enter the library with difficulty and there experience multiple barriers. Others enter gracefully, orient well and have no mobility problems throughout their library stay. Library mobility orientation is offered to patrons with canes only when requested or when observed mobility difficulties suggest library intervention. When observed patron problems suggest that the librarian can help, then help is offered. But it may be refused--with the patron electing to struggle on independently.

Infosearching skills are as diverse in cane users as they are in the general public. In the stacks, at vertical files, the card catalog or at other locations, cane users must try to avoid bending or kneeling when accessing or using media. While not directly associated with their physical limitations, some experience specific infosearching skill barriers. Patrons should be accommodated both for physical challenges in the library context and for their special library orientation needs. Cane users may have attitudinal problems adjusting to library mobility challenges. Librarian planned orientation for single- or dual-cane users is professional wasted time. Library mobility orientation should be provided only for those who ask. Stack accommodation is provided on patron request to retrieve, carry and handle titles when cane-using patrons must bend or kneel to reach shelves and cannot independently stand again. Carrying titles while walking may be difficult. Physical challenges alone do not dictate patron special library orientation needs. Many single- or dual-cane users will not request library orientation.

Crutch Users

Crutch users vary as widely in infosearching skills as do other library patrons without walking aids. Since using crutches are often associated with temporary physical challenges and the healing process, some are novices at crutch mobility but otherwise capable infosearchers. The temporarily disabled are not considered ADA-qualified individuals with disabilities.[134] Yet their physical challenges must be librarian accommodated on request. As with all patrons with special library information needs, orientation or infosearching requests must be faciliated. Single or dual crutch users typically need mobility orientation more for general library mobility and between library service areas than specifically to overcome library physical challenges for direct information gain. People with crutches are particularly sensitive to library slipping and tripping hazards, as they are on any walking surface.[135] The average crutch-using patron has a four-foot crutch swing, a three-foot standing crutch span and a three and one-half foot walking crutch swing. This makes access difficult to narrow stack- aisles.[136] Crutch use provides patrons more stability than cane use if there is a requirement to freely swing a leg through while walking. Patrons with crutches cannot hold or carry--without difficulty--items, books, papers or other media. To others in narrow library stack aisles or walkways, the crutch user is a walking or movement barrier.

Information access is an individual process to find library information. Some patrons, many with the same physical restrictions, may have learned to overcome library barriers to personal information.

Walker Users

Walker users are provided more movement stability than canes or crutches in the library. Those using walkers generally have weakness in both arms and legs and are limited to small, supported steps. Some are equipped with wheels in front, in the rear, or both. Walkers provide four posts with cross members for support midway up the structure, and a crossarm for user gripping. Posts have rubber grips for improved traction on walking surfaces and rubberized hand grips. To stand using a walker, the patron grasps a stable object in front of the seat and pulls forward and up. Library door opening is difficult for walker users. Door and equipment handles should be made graspable, manageable and at appropriate standing height reach throughout the library. Library doors should close slowly behind walker patrons to avoid collisions. Mobility orientation is provided during a carefully supervised individualized library tour, since for walking aid users, walking impairment is the most relevant problem in the library context. Help with media access, reach and use avoids patron bending or kneeling. Patron and librarian together determine where and when library help is needed. Adaptive library orientation includes showing patrons with walkers how to access and use stack information. Walker users require three and one-half feet of passageway width, making access in narrow stack aisles difficult. Walker equipment placed out of library walkways, but within user reach, is retrieved when needed while reading, writing, studying, keyboarding and equipment operation.

Manual or Electric Wheelchair Users

Information access is an individual process to find library information. Some patrons, many with the same physical restrictions, may have learned to overcome library barriers to personal information. Wheelchair users have special library information needs--not because they use wheelchairs--but because they request infosearching orientation and accommodation. For many infosearchers, wheelchair use is irrelevant to their information needs. Orientation may be only associated with initial library mobility challenges. Patrons are oriented or self-orient to wheelchair accessible water fountains,[137] restrooms[138] and public telephone locations.[139] Librarians are particularly sensitive to wheelchair entrance and exit access, emergency wheelchair evacuation routes or emergency assistance area orientation.

Wheelchair users experience minor difficulties using library services when they have arm control, can move themselves to service areas and have adequate reach and strength to carry various title formats. More physically challenged wheelchair users with limited arm use, poor reach and limited strength are unable to lift or carry titles and require additional library or personal attendant support. Some tire easily from the physical library challenge alone and may require personal attendants.[140] Those who do tire easily must provide personal library attendants themselves to successfully infosearch without the need for repeated rest periods, unnecessary infosearching delays and obvious frustration. Others have little difficulty directly gaining information but may request help with physical library service access. Some have difficulty caring for print and nonprint formats when titles are dropped or spilled from the seated wheelchair position. Access

Preemptive library help is not ADA-required or recommended. Preemptive help is disparate treatment for disabled patrons and should be avoided.

Library Patrons With Disabilities

to microforms from a wheelchair is difficult as is microform equipment use. Roll-up and roll-under access to all media formats, equipment operation for general direct information gain is better provided in a library without wheelchair-relevant barriers. Attendant help or library accommodation is needed for any who have difficulty controlling powered wheelchair movements during library furniture and equipment roll-up and roll-under.[141] People using powered wheelchairs themselves differ in their skill for movement in confined or heavy traffic areas. When wheelchair users become barriers to other patrons, librarians monitor and assist in restricted movement areas and stack aisles, and manage other traffic control problems. Personal attendants or librarians help wheelchair users in narrow library aisles.[142] But wheelchair attendant presence or attendant-augmented patron mobility cannot be dictated by librarians.[143] Wheelchair users and their personal attendants make larger traffic obstacles and impose movement barriers on other patrons in confined or narrow library walkways and service areas. Librarians may consider themselves insensitive to consider a wheelchair user and an attendant team as a "library barrier." Yet observing the physical space each team occupies, and during their movements between library service areas, an obvious physical barrier exists between the team and other patrons movements. This is not librarian insensitivity, but a library orientation reality.

Wheelchair users must avoid becoming barriers to other patrons whenever possible.

Wheelchair users must avoid becoming barriers to other patrons whenever possible. Librarians help during disabled patron movement in restricted movement areas, stack aisles and other traffic congested areas to resolve potential problems. Preemptive library help is not ADA-required or recommended. Preemptive help is disparate treatment for disabled patrons and should be avoided.[144] Personal attendants who help wheelchair users access the building, hallways, and enter and move safely within the library are a better solution. Working with patrons in wheelchairs teaches librarians to know when to intervene and when to leave them alone. Minimal help for patrons with disabilities, who are otherwise library independent, promotes their self-esteem and infosearching self-confidence. What better goal can librarians have for any library patron? Librarians learn when and how to help disabled patrons achieve the independence they desire. And no one can be sure that wheelchair use is necessarily a relevant disability in the library context. Expert librarians combine the science of personal observation with the art of personal diplomacy to provide appropriate patron service.

Orientation for the Blind

The blind or legally blind, otherwise known as the "print disabled,"[145] have disability-imposed complex information access restrictions that require librarian support.[146] Appropriate library equipment need not be complex but must provide information in usable formats for persons with print disability. Being blind restricts accessible library information and causes format dependency. The blind require library resources such as Braille print titles,[147] talking books, talking newspapers or magazines,[148] special format dictionaries,[149] and recorded information. Information access using these formats is not necessarily complex. Persons with "low vision" or the partially sighted also require individualized library equipment support,[150] including large-print typewriters.[151] An extensive library equipment mix exists to support the information needs of blind or low-vision patrons.[152] Orientation leading to independent use of equipment may not be a realistic librarian expectation for some visually impaired. Novice equipment orientation for the visually impaired is not significantly different from sighted equipment orientation. Novice equipment users, or those who cannot independently read guides and operate library equipment after orientation, may continue to require extensive equipment support. Reorientation on demand includes library-modified strategies based on individual equipment operational skills assessment and patron-indicated equipment support needs.

Brailled and/or tactile signage is the library orientation service standard for all visually limited patrons.[153] Professionals require orientation guidance from blind patrons and vision specialists to determine what will be for them effective library orientation and accommodation.[154] The blind, like the sighted, have speciallibrary information needs and requests. These cannot be met by group library tours. They must be met by personal library adaptive orientation. Libraries evolve the most realistic orientation guidelines one blind patron at a time.

Some disorientation occurs outside the library before entrance for the blind. Of major concern to blind patrons are improperly parked or mounted bicycles that must be prohibited from blocking outside walkway ramps. Other patrons may park their bicycles on walkway entrances--"It's only temporary." Entryway changes for library special events barr the door for some. Bicycle stands, wastebaskets, janitorial cleaning equipment and difficult-to-operate doors are constant library entryway barriers. What of the floor welcome mat that serves a dual purpose to wipe our feet--can this be rumpled and leave an unrecognizable walking barrier--until it is too late?

Relocated interior library furniture or equipment changes in commons areas, even patron traffic flow and crowded conditions all disrupt the blind patron's library mobility orientation. These external and internal library conditions or events disturb their constantly updated library mental maps. Moving from library entryway and between service areas may be difficult for blind patrons who rely on consistent interior library landmarks[155] and clues[156] that give direction of movement from their current position. Interior library changes such as moving equipment, furniture, and walkway arrangements deter their ability to orient for distances, move to service areas safely, and there access library information. Library interior room or service area numbering systems must be consistent and arranged in an intuitive way so that for the blind unmarked doors, several doors with the same numbers, service areas without numbers or with numbers out of logical sequence, and unmarked rooms such as study areas, alcoves or carrels will not be encountered.

The sighted are prohibited by library signage from sitting in entryways or using crutches, books, notebooks, bags and other property that block walkways to accommodate anyhone experiencing service route mobility challenges. But those precautions can be ignored by others who continue to block walkways and service routes. Walkthroughs with the librarian initially explaining the library room or area numbering system using a tactile map should include orienting the sight impaired patron to useful landmarks and clues. Each floor, service area and every piece of library equipment is integrated into their working mental map. From the intial walkthrough, the blind patron will evolve a personal system of orientation for library entry and exit, movement between service areas, and will reduce instances where soliciting aid from others will be needed. That patron must be able to retrace steps from any point in the library while using familiar library landmarks, clues such as sunlight from windows, the sound of equipment operating, the smell of a photocopier or of waterfountains. They can then expand their library mental map by self-familiarization during subsequent library treks.

Brailled and/or tactile signage is the library orientation service standard for all visually limited patrons.

Library Patrons With Disabilities

Pedestrian-safe libraries provide predictable service access routes allowing safe and independent library movement. Library mobility and independence for the blind require a clear and predictable travel path from entrances, between service areas, and back to library exits.[157] Clear library routes without overhead dangers and unblocked aisles reduce the likelihood of tripping, falling or colliding with objects or others to maintain their independent movement skills. Collisions with others are common experiences even skilled blind patrons often report. Independent library mobility may be the most significant patron special library orientation need and requested for accommodation. Pedestrian safe libraries are a signficant accommodation for all. The blind often benefit from safe library mobility more than other sighted patrons.

Common courtesy extended by the sighted permits the blind a wider movement area along library service routes. But others must quickly recognize blind patrons in order to extend that courtesy. The blind may be unaware of others' consideration. Library policy negates penalties when the blind unintentionally wander into nonpublic or restricted zones. The blind with a current library mental map and no distractions have no mobility orientation needs and do not encroach into restricted areas. Engaging the blind in conversation while they are moving in the library may be disorienting to their present location, route, direction and placement.

The best anticipatory library signage placement cannot foresee or forewarn the blind of temporary conditions without proactive librarian orientation. Permanent library walkway impediments must be removed. Proactive librarian walkway accommodation may be rejected by the blind, but their safety remains the library's primary responsibility. The librarian continues to intervene when patron library safety and mobility is directly threatened. The blind attempting independent and unguided library exploration without adaptive orientation demonstrate personal high-risk behavior. Personal aides or librarians as sighted guides must provide library mobility but also reduce, even temporarily, patron library independence.

Orienting Patrons With Low Vision

Low-vision patrons[158] can access information on entry without library help but may continue to have special library needs and service requests. Most low-vision patrons have residual vision allowing for library mobility but will continue to experience multiple library information barriers. Print information access may be their central concern. Based on residual vision and how library signage is viewed or read, patrons with low vision may request minimal signage orientation when they cannot independently read information from signs. But signage gives only directions to service areas and to library equipment. Signage does not provide direct patron access to library information. Augmented signage is required for everyone, even the sighted, to provide safe library mobility for all. Signage points the way--but librarians provide direct information access on patron request. The low-vision patron may also choose to ignore augmented signage seeking to be library-independent thereby further limiting direct information access and increasing personal risks.

Library mobility and independence for the blind require a clear and predictable travel path from entrances, between service areas, and back to library exits.

Library signage without enlarged print letters is difficult to read by patrons with low vision.[159] Libraries with large print, Brailled and tactile equipment controls that indicate directions and precautions find that adaptive library signage helps everyone, not just low-vision patrons, to see service area directions and find personal information. All public informational displays such as bulletin boards, easel signs and public service announcements should include high intensity colors, lighting and high contrast information easily read by all.[160] Low-vision patrons should be oriented for safe equipment use, as should all other patrons needing equipment access to gain valued print information. Temporary placards, floor signs (CAUTION-WET SURFACE) and other objects in service routes and along library walkways require librarian orientation.

Persons with low vision are often referred to as the "print disabled" who require print augmentation.[161] Being print disabled means that in the library every print source to be recognized and read must be augmented, enhanced, magnified, rotated, highly contrasted, well-illuminated, print color-ranges changed, and other print modifications made. The majority of library information is in print format. For the patron with low vision, nonaugmented print information is indeed a multiple library infosearching barrier. The library is filled with print information--hard for the sighted to access in some instances--and impossible for them to access without print augmentation. For these patrons, print access can be augmented in the library using a variety of strategies. Print surface glare or paper finish restricts visual engagement for us' all unless they can reposition the text. Control or repositioning for glare through exterior library windows requires patrons to move beyond conventional reading areas. Overhead lighting is designed for print reading but does not assist patrons to read print from library computer screens. Nonglare library monitor screens or monitors equipped with anti-glare visors and tilt-swivel bases assist them to read. Some with low vision are library independent. Patrons with low vision have the right to refuse library orientation.[162] Personal dignity and independence may be more important to them than any library information.

Long Cane Users

Long cane users include both the blind and some patrons with low vision who desire functionally independent movement to and within the library. Long cane users require help, on entry, in a variety of ways, to effectively use libraries in addition to their self-orienting efforts. External entranceway pavement must be firm (not gravel or grassed walkways) with a definite, consistent edge for long cane negotiation. Unpaved library entryways are difficult to negotiate not leaving a clear path indication to the library door. Tactile-marked library entryway step surfaces also require adequate railing supports. Well-lighted entryways provide safe entry for those relying on peripheral vision or with greatly reduced visual fields.[163] Entrance ramps should be identified and integrated with surrounding library pavement or floor surfacing. Entryway signage using tactile raised letters or Braille orients patrons to other tactile library signage, allowing long cane users to independently move within the library.[164] Grade changes or sharp floor or walkway declines within the library cause long cane user mobility problems.

Long cane users must rely partly on echoes to negotiate barriers and objects along library entrance and exit pathways and public use service routes. Sound-deadening library surfaces or low-noise entryways limit long cane user utility. They are a convenience to the general public by reducing library noise--but are a hazard to long cane users. Library sound-deadening is in direct conflict with long cane user mobility needs. Low-vision patron needs may be at odds with sighted library service preferences. Special-patron needs should have higher librarian accommodation priority than majority preferences.

Long cane users make a large moving object, blocking library entry walkways and traffic areas. For long cane users the possibility of tripping over others seated at or blocking library entryways is real. Careful cane storage and handling avoids nuisance touching, tripping or injuring others within the library.[165] Mobility mental maps are patron-built, maintained and continuously updated. The sighted can continuously refresh library mobility mental maps while long cane users rely on more limited updating information or librarian verbal orientation. Current library danger areas must be known to be avoided. Cane user preferences must

Library Patrons With Disabilities

be known during library orientation including accepting or refusing aid from a sighted guide.[166] The librarian may be requested to accompany the long cane user throughout library service areas during actual orientation as a sighted guide or to accompany the blind with another sighted guide. Long cane users have individual preferences when accompanied by sighted guides including the need to grasp the elbow or forearm of the librarian or personal attendant while negotiating library service routes.[167] The long cane is usually moved forward while both walk together or may be held close to the chest using the diagonal technique.[168] In some cases with long canes that telescope to full length may be compressed and put away during orientation. If these preferences are not known and respected library orientation content or effectiveness may be limited.

Service Animal Users

Libraries must permit service animals to enter accompanied by their visually impaired masters.[169] Patrons using service animals build, maintain and constantly update mental maps including danger areas, to effect the best and safest library mobility.[170] Many adults have service animals. But blind or low-vision adolescents do not typically use this mobility service:

> Service animal means any guide dog, signal dog, or other animal individually trained to
> do work or perform tasks for the benefit of an individual with a disability, including, but
> not limited to, guiding individuals with impaired vision, alerting individuals with impaired
> hearing to intruders or sounds, providing minimal protection or rescue work, pulling a
> wheelchair, or fetching dropped items (ADA Handbook, III-38).

Service animals are specially trained to protect their master with visual impairment from dangers such as street crossings, traffic and other conditions. They cannot alert the master to overhead dangers along walkways, service routes or in library service areas. Overhead stack obstructions, equipment storage or library public display areas cause significant problems since service animals have safe movement under them but their masters do not.[171] Librarians orient the patron, not the service animal. The service animal may fail to recognize the master's library commands and misdirect the patron.

Animal and blind or low-vision patron teams can block library walkways, entryways and traffic areas. Even when entryways and service areas are Brailled and display tactile signage, no library services are animal interpretable. Walkway ramps or entrance railings help service animal users avoid tripping, falling, stepping off library stairs, or losing secure footing. Railing containment provides safer library walkways. Surface grade changes, ramps, steps or curbs at library entrances cause patron problems when using service animal guidance. Prolonged library visits may lead to service animal incontinence. Extended library visits (two or more hours) should be avoided without animal respite. Patrons tend to keep valued dogs until they are elderly when they require more frequent trips outside. Sensitive librarians designate outside pet areas for the general public with service animal needs in mind.

Libraries must permit service animals to enter accompanied by their visually impaired masters.

All of the above situations presume that service animal users are patrons with low vision or are the blind. Yet service animals help the hearing impaired and other physically challenged. Most patrons with hearing impairment who use service animals do so in the home or work context, rather than in the library, to forewarn of intruders or unusual sounds. Could that service animal also alert the master for library alarms? Alarms cause some dogs to act erratically and would cancel any positive guidance provided to their master. They may require the librarian to intervene in an alarm situation to guide both to safety.

Adaptive Library Orientation   107

The physically challenged use service animals to retrieve dropped items or pull a wheelchair. These events also occur in the library. When they do, the librarian must sensitively observe service animal performance and intervene only when patron requested. And remember that service animals are also trained to protect their masters--even from well-intentioned librarian helpers. Librarians are cautioned not to distract service animals when "on the job" with their master. There is a special procedure for the blind to retrieve dropped objects that does not engage the service animal in the retrieval process.[172]

Patron Deposits and Library Fees

Libraries may require deposits for auxiliary aid use, such as assistive listening devices. Deposits must be completely refundable on return.[173] Charges should be based on actual, not projected, library costs, encompassing equipment and delivery, normal wear and tear, liability and insurance costs. Blind or low-vision patron auxiliary equipment use costs should be based not on one single patron user, but amortized over an entire library patron community. No library policy should reflect individually determined costs for patrons with disabilities requiring alternative site delivery. This would single out and discriminate against individual disabled patrons. No library policy should reflect determined costs for alternate site delivery based on any disability category. This would also discriminate against a whole class of individuals with disabilities. All patrons are considered potential alternate site users. When libraries refuse to participate in service integration they can be held liable for failure to make ADA-defined reasonable accommodation.[174]

Libraries may require deposits for auxiliary aid use, such as assistive listening devices. Deposits must be completely refundable on return.

The Speech or Language-Impaired

Speech or language-impaired patrons are characterized by significant language development delays, or by immature, faulty or no speech. Only when speaking skills are required will their speech or language disabilities become readily librarian observable. Included in speech impairment are articulation disorders (involving omissions, substitutions, additions, or distortions of certain speech sounds); visible cleft palate (oral and facial malformation); fluency disorders such as severe stuttering,[175] cluttering (cluttered or irrelevant speech),[176] delayed speech (using gestures, facial expressions, other physical movements and vocalizations such as grunts or squeals); tics or grimaces; and malocclusion (over- or underbite). The most common disorder associated with patrons with language impairment is cerebral palsy. This disorder affects the brain's speech center and is readily visible in the library context. But recognizing any cause of patron speech impairment does not specifically help the librarian to orient or accommodate. Speech impairments are irrelevant to successful infosearching unless patron success requires verbal interaction with the librarian. And patron verbal interaction with the librarian is the orientation or accommodation dilemma. Infosearching may not require patron speech output unless and until librarian help is required. If required, it may not be patron requested. Adaptive library orientation and infosearching support requires mutually understood accommodation strategies. How infosearching support is requested by the patron may vary widely, but information needs can be conveyed.

Patrons with "word blindness" may not command a spoken vocabulary related to infosearches. They are helped on request even though that request may be poorly articulated. The librarian anticipates the specific meaning of patron minimal spoken infosearching requests and then observes yes/no or pointing responses from them to further assist during infosearching walkthroughs. Yes/no gestural or nonverbal interaction from the patron is a very slow infosearching process. But it does work and can assist word blind patrons. They, like others with disabilities, have specific information interests in the library--even though they may not recall the right term to make a specific verbal request. Word blindness is a common disorder among stroke

Library Patrons With Disabilities

victims who may substitute unrelated or illogical words for the infosearching terms they need. Librarians must be cautious not to view the patron's accepting librarian help as a resolution of actual infosearching need. Many times patrons become discouraged or exhausted with the communication effort and accept librarian-selected titles as a compromise.

Orienting the Deaf

Delayed language development is an observable characteristic among many deaf infosearchers. Delayed language development is due largely to the time of the onset of deafness or whether that person was born deaf. Patrons who were born deaf have never heard human language and may have different thinking patterns developed without the benefit of hearing. Adventitiously deaf patrons were not born deaf, but acquired the disability after they lived in a hearing world and acquired some language development. Together, both deaf groups have a common characteristic--moderate to severe delay in language development. Language development delays directly affect how patrons think and how they infosearch. Their culture and information needs directly impact the kind of information they seek in the library. What would be of considerable interest to one deaf or patron with hearing impairment may be of no interest to a hearing patron. Yet all are served in the library.

Eight separate deaf communities have been recognized.[177] Each of these communities may have personal library orientation needs or special individual library information requests. Librarians who consider the deaf as a single group with common library infosearching needs because of their deafness are misguided. Infosearching goals are unique for every patron in the library.

> **Delayed language development is an observable characteristic among many deaf infosearchers. Their culture and information needs directly impact the kind of information they seek in the library.**

Support needs of the deaf or patrons with hearing impairment are almost invisible to professionals on library entry.[178] Among the few visible hearing-impairment indicators are hearing aids or related equipment, difficulty speaking with staff, speech reading (lip reading),[179] using writing pads to communicate with librarians, or using American Sign Language[180] or Finger Spelling.[181] These library events are not evident until the deaf person attempts to communicate. When patron interaction is attempted with the librarian, orientation for the deaf can be provided. Yet most deaf patrons do not interact with librarians, or with anyone else in the library, during their stay. By personal choice, and perhaps by inclination over years of experience, the deaf may elect to infosearch independently or never enter the library because of their self-imposed independent infosearching demands. It may for them be easier to infosearch elsewhere or not at all. Hearing impaired patrons also have a tendency not to use libraries.[182] Other deaf patrons take pride in personal library skill without indicating their hearing disabilities to librarians.

American Sign Language (ASL)[183] or finger spelling communication may be used in library service areas with the hearing impaired who may require it. Some librarians have voluntarily learned finger spelling or ASL to support the library context hearing impaired. Only three percent (3%) of the deaf community however, regularly use sign language anywhere, including the library context. Many deaf also do not have the "library reading habit." Professional librarians may not be part of the patron's deaf culture and may be ignored when signing during equipment orientation.[184] Librarians have been encouraged in the professional literature, to learn sign language as an important library support, but few deaf patrons will use signing during library visits. Unless the librarian is deaf, and shares the same deaf subculture, communication through signing may be problematic.

Adaptive Library Orientation

Library context signing for communication may be more predominant among deaf groups who together visit the library and jointly infosearch there. The librarian is left out of the signing group while attempting to provide effective library support. But being omitted is a positive indication for the librarian that the patrons with hearing impairment have gained library independence and autonomy. Interpreters can be used to provide orally delivered library materials.[185] For some hearing-impaired, sign language or Finger Spelling communication may be effectively used by librarians. No single librarian approach, specialized training, or communication skill will meet deaf patrons diverse communication needs. The richly diverse vocabulary and communication styles of deaf community members precludes any librarian specially skilled with one communication system to effectively work with all other deaf patrons who use a different communication system. Yet the librarian can find some common ground to communicate with each deaf patron regardless of individual communication styles, needs and requests. One deaf patron infosearching request at a time yields meaningful library orientation and accommodation guidelines.

Librarians have the responsibility of making sure that deaf people are library service aware. Patrons with hearing impairment deserve appropriate library orientation and accommodation.[186] Adaptive library orientation to serve the deaf or patrons with hearing impairment includes assisting them to find and personally useful compensating visually-oriented information.[112]

Library signage and clear, visual directions are especially important to those who can independently search, using library visual cues.[187] Libraries should post written announcements at entryway bulletin boards rather than rely on the deaf understanding library services soley by other means. Library visual cues are widely available, including HOW TO USE THIS FEATURE posters, bulletins or signage.[188] Readable and understandable brochures or handouts should be available and offered throughout the library, allowing more independent infosearching. Visual cues, guides and signage also help the deaf better use the library to infosearch. These strategies directly help all other patrons who also rely on infosearching visual cues. The deaf or hearing impaired primarily need communication support, rather than simple library equipment access to titles with visual content. Specially-trained library interpreters help the deaf or hearing-impaired operate library equipment.[189]

> **Library signage and clear, visual directions are especially important to those who can independently search, using library visual cues. Libraries should post written announcements at entryway bulletin boards rather than rely on the deaf understanding library services soley by other means.**

Speechreaders are helped by librarians who speak in a normal voice while presenting a full face and lip view. Librarians should repeat messages without discomfort or embarrassment. Even expert speechreaders typically miss a major portion of others spoken language. Meaning is extrapolated from the minimal lip reading information gained. Minimal speechreading information from the librarian must be supplemented by effective librarian gestures, nonverbal communication and directional mobility to library service areas. When the patron-preferred service area is reached, then infosearching can then slowly take place with librarian help.

> Look at the person as you speak. Don't put your hands in front of your mouth or speak with food or a cigarette in your mouth; Converse directly with a deaf person even when an interpreter is present. Look at the deaf person while you speak and while he or she replies; Don't overenunciate. A natural movement of the lips and tongue is preferable. Speak in short, simply constructed sentences. If a phrase or word is not understood, try

Library Patrons With Disabilities

repeating the idea using different words; Don't shout. If the person is profoundly deaf, it won't help a bit anyway. For a person who is wearing a hearing aid, a slightly louder voice may help, but shouting can actually hurt the person's ears and make it more difficult to understand what is being said. Don't be afraid to use gestures to help get your point across (National Endowment for the Arts. (1992). The arts and 504: A handbook for accessible arts programming. Washington, DC: U.S. Government Printing Office. Page 93).

Immature search strategies among deaf or patrons with hearing impairments are library orientation and accommodation indicators. Professionals aware that patrons with hearing impairments need orientation or accommodation do not provide either unless requested:

> It is very important that the library staff not feel discouraged they are not seeing large numbers of deaf and hard-of-hearing individuals after initiating services. It will take time for the deaf community to adjust to the idea that the library has services to offer them. Also remember you will never have the entire deaf community using the library, just as not the entire hearing community uses the library. But we should not be discouraged and we must continue to offer services which can be used by many segments of the entire community...Many deaf people are unaware of what is available for use in public libraries and therefore do not use their public libraries (Freese & Cohen, 1986, pages 552-553).

Orienting the Hearing Impaired

Hearing impaired patrons are disadvantaged unless they use their residual hearing in the library, or are oriented by the librarian to use listening area technology. Libraries offer other services for them including talking books, talking newspapers, assistive listening devices, sound boosters, telecommunications devices for the deaf (TDDs), and speech synthesizers. Other accommodation includes heavily illustrated reading materials in multiple formats that also help other hearing patrons who prefer to use illustrated information. Useful materials written specifically for patrons with hearing impairment include high interest/low vocabulary titles, literacy program materials and English as a second language [ESL] titles.[190]

Although some hearing impaired may not be able to "listen" while they communicate, as patrons they deserve the same level of library listening area services as the general public. Librarians are sensitive to listening area and library technology underuse and to their special library information needs and orientation requests. Listening area technology is carefully included in their orientation sessions. Some with limited or residual hearing experience difficulty infosearching when equipment, personnel or busy service traffic creates background noise. Background noise impairs those already marginally hearing, who rely both on verbal and visual information gain or require special auditory concentration to read. Background noise levels must be addressed during their orientation by the librarian and accommodation made whenever possible to meet their listening needs and requests.

People learn the need to respect the rights of others to listen and study during orientation. Patrons with hearing impairment perhaps more than the hearing model exemplary librarian behavior. They learn while being oriented to limit noise during visits, just as librarians do. By example, the librarians teach sound-level courtesy throughout the library, particularly in listening areas. This is an important orientation emphasis. The hearing impaired conserve any residual hearing through effective hearing aid use or assistive listening devices employed in designated library listening areas. Some library service areas provide accessible and noise-free or noise-limited patron listening. These designated listening areas are sound-controlled rooms, study or computer carrels with noise-reduction features, or equipment-use areas with supervised and controlled noise-levels. Like others, patrons with hearing impairment cannot be required to use designated listening areas when using library sound equipment unless the general public is required to do the same.

All patrons are free to elect not to use designated listening areas.[191] But they are not free to use noise-producing equipment in nondesignated library areas. All library noise producing equipment that can be taken with the patron should post use only in designated listening areas. The right to use designated listening areas and the responsibility to use noise-producing equipment only in those designated areas must be presented during librarian orientation.

Sound-producing equipment is librarian controlled to provide information in the playback mode. Use of earphones or headsets is supervised so that it does not disturb others. When sound-based equipment does not include earphones or headsets, or when group listening is required, listening area noise-containment measures are taken. Sound-containment for library equipment in playback mode includes film, sound filmstrip, audiocassette, reel-to-reel players, record players, and compact disk players. Patrons learn to use listening equipment safely, appropriately and independently while demonstrating care for recordings in various formats. Library adaptive orientation may include technical assistance for the disabled to teach use of recording playback equipment. ·

Patrons with disabilities may be unaware of, and therefore reluctant, to use listening area services open to the general public, due to limited or previously negative listening service experience. Designated listening areas are not created as "special rooms" to segregate any disabled person from otherwise integrated library services, settings or facilities.[192] It is an irony of library patrons with hearing impairment that many must have quiet to concentrate during infosearching. Yet these same hearing impaired may be obtrusively noisy for others in the library. Quiet library zones, reading rooms or reading areas are disrupted by hearing-impaired who are unaware of distracting others. Both the deaf and patrons with hearing impairment may create excessive library noise and distract other hearing patrons. But what librarian requires, expects or demands a quiet library? Emphasis during orientation to respect the rights of other hearing patrons must be subtly but clearly included for those with hearing impairment.

Library Displays

Library theme displays heighten interest and motivation for patrons with disabilities and others to read and also orient them to library information. Self-explanatory library displays do not require viewer orientation. Librarians orient viewers when they puzzle about displays or do not use interactive display content well or wish follow-up services from their librarian. Self-orienting displays assist and inform all who enter the library. Yet any objective for many library displays is to stir reader interest and heighten librarian followup requests. Display orientation is offered when viewers inquire. But making library displays self-orienting is a challenge requiring several strategies to be considered.

Well-designed visual displays provide for effective sightline viewing for wheelchairs users, other patrons with disabilities, and the general public.

Well-designed library displays provide for effective sightline viewing for wheelchairs users, other patrons with disabilities, and the general public. Accessible displays also meet ADA library standards.[193] Visual realia displays, library posters, or bulletin boards, include signage accompanying objects, emphasizing and repeating display characteristics. All visually-displayed library objects should include lettering, with characters sized or positioned for close viewing.[194] Seated viewers, such as patrons in wheelchairs, move to the front of the visual display, often through crowds. Nonglare finishes on display signage and on the objects displayed, where possible, permits more comfortable reading.[195] Demonstration displays or complex models should include large print, richly illustrated patron handouts.[196]

Permanent or long-term displays should utilize museum display technology that reflects planning for viewer safety and patron traffic control. Side-turned wheelchair display viewing along high-traffic service routes requires greater clearance widths to avoid competing with moving pedestrian traffic.[197] Crutch tips extending to a wide angle are for others an unseen display-viewing hazard.[198] Temporary displays should also accommodate expected nearby pedestrian library traffic. Realia, demonstrations, interactive models, posters, even conventional bulletin boards in high-traffic library common use areas cause noticeable traffic problems between viewers and nearby pedestrians. Popular displays should avoid temporarily blocking accessways or disrupting library traffic. Displays are positioned where multiple library traffic streams can cross without interruption.[199] Safety requires library barrier removal in display areas along accessible service routes.[200] Library displays should be avoided on stairways or ramps since all viewers there would constitute a significant walkway obstruction. Safe display placement assures maximum viewer access. Accessible and safe displays coincide with primary library routes. Barricaded or roped-off library displays are unsafe for viewers in wheelchairs, who may roll across or through ropes or barricades while viewing. The nearsighted require extreme close library display viewing and may damage displays not designed to be touchable.[201] Physically challenged viewers must not lean on window or glass-contained library displays. A recorded "DO NOT TOUCH" message can accommodate the visually impaired. Displays that are not touchable should be avoided in libraries where some patrons must ultimately touch to gain information.

Some library special-effects displays require viewers to stare for prolonged periods. They may be of interest to the general public but are perceptually distressing to some disabled patrons who may be unable to recognize these special effects even after prolonged viewing. Crowds gather at special-effects displays, blocking normal library traffic. Patrons may sit for prolonged periods in walkways to see them. The library must consider overall traffic impact when setting up special-effects visual displays. Auditory library displays provide both accessible listening and viewing, and comply with assembly area accessibility and assistive listening system (ALS) requirements. Display hearing or visual access requires close-in listener positioning. Recordings at auditory displays should address patrons with hearing impairment or others with disabilities who use ALS to augment auditory display signals. At auditory displays, ALS may provide signal feedback interference for hearing aid users while the visually impaired gain information by listening to display recordings.[202] Some multi-media displays incorporate computers and provide interactivity combining auditory, visual and tactile patron engagement. All computer equipment accessibility requirements must be met for the library display using this technology.

Displays can offer new library information by touch (tactile) or feel (kinesthetic) where patron involvement permits display interaction and manipulation. Visual and auditory library displays are sometimes combined with tactile features to make multiformat library information on raised or Brailled display signage accompanied by pictograms.[203] Touchable library displays should provide wheelchair roll-up and roll-under access.[204] All library kiosks should meet touchable library display criteria.

Special theme collection displays are temporarily removed from conventional shelf locations after being cataloged. Other titles are temporarily cataloged as reserved or noncirculating until removed from the display. Noncirculating or reserved display titles can be read after removal from the exhibit. It is unethical to display permanently noncirculating titles without careful notice posted that specific display titles will be noncirculating or on permanent reserve. Displays generate considerable reader interest. Using titles that cannot be patron-charged is equivalent to "false advertising." A promise given is a promise kept. Through temporarily noncirculating display titles, patrons with disabilities learn to use wait-listing. Among disabled patrons, better displays increase interest in title circulation.

Touchable library displays should provide wheelchair roll-up and roll-under access.

Adaptive Library Orientation

Assembly Areas and Meeting Rooms

Adaptive library orientation includes assembly area and meeting room use where first-time users with disabilities must either rely on library signage to find seating or be directed by library workers.[205] Librarians should orient disabled patrons to properly and safely use library meeting rooms or public assembly areas. Unsupervised library assembly for the disabled is inherently unsafe. Meeting rooms and assembly areas provide a common means of accessible library entry. Minimum wheelchair assembly seating capacity requirements range from one wheelchair location for every 4-25 seats to 6 or more wheelchair sites in assemblies of 500 or more seats. Wheelchair seating locations should be carefully planned to provide a variety of views or sightlines.[206] Wheelchair locations provide minimum clear ground and floor space from accessible assembly area travel paths. Ideally, wheelchair locations should be large enough for two wheelchaired people to orient and enjoy library assemblies or performances while sitting together. Attendants, friends and family sometimes want to sit with the patron using a wheelchair. Fixed assembly seating can be supplemented with portable seats that adjust to meet anticipated large or small group needs. Some guests with disabilities are accompanied by attendants who assist with assembly seating. No private group is exempt from meeting ADA-defined public access standards or discriminating against the disabled. No surcharge can be made over the public ticket price for designated wheelchair seating or other library assembly accommodations. When leasing or renting assembly or meeting rooms to private concerns, the library's public service role precludes allowing private group surcharges for wheelchair seating or accommodation. Seat availability is posted at assembly room entryways or wherever tickets are sold or distributed.

> **Librarians should orient disabled patrons to properly and safely use library meeting rooms or public assembly areas.**

Guest listening and viewing requirements must be considered in library assembly wheelchair and fixed seating plans. Viewing from a wheelchair precludes the occupant from moving easily to either side to improve the view. Wheelchair users may not have upper body or trunk strength to move from side-to-side when others block their direct sightline. Self-selected open wheelchair seating provides better visibility and allows for patron personal choice. Just as any patron would refuse or resist being seated with interrupted sightlines why would we expect patrons with disabilities and limited seating options to accept this disservice? Some libraries require use of designated wheelchair areas which are made to be integral parts of fixed assembly seating plans. Distances between seat rows, aisle widths and exits, and aisle arrangement, affect both wheelchair guests and the general public. Wider rows and aisles, providing emergency exit for all, are often dictated by local fire and safety codes. Designated assembly wheelchair seating requires library signage identifying wheelchair-only use restrictions. Assembly areas providing seating for wheelchairs should display the International Symbol for Accessibility signage so it is visible to wheelchair users.[207] Assembly guests should avoid overcrowding aisles and rows on entry or exit and clear aisles after obtaining appropriate seating. Wheelchair users should avoid blocking aisles and instead use designated wheelchair seating at row ends or at other locations. The mobility limited have extreme difficulty moving to accommodate those in fixed seating rows. People move along library assembly aisles and fixed seating rows to seating. Seated guests move or adjust when others pass. Ambulatory persons will twist to pass row-seated wheelchair, service animals, or walking aid users. Folded walkers, crutches, canes, or long canes occupy extra seating space near the user and block aisles or adjacent walkways. In reduced assembly lighting, walking aids carefully stored are not visible to those moving in fixed seating rows. At best, narrow fixed seating rows constitute a traffic hazard. They and their occupants restrict anyone using walking aids.

Library Patrons With Disabilities

For people who walk with difficulty, row spacing also increases mid-row seat access. If seated at end-rows, persons with disabilities must move for others desiring same-row seating or may courteously ask them to move to the opposite row-side or aisle and enter the row there. When patrons self-select end-row seats they must be prepared to accommodate others wishing to enter and sit in that row. Guests often resolve potential seating conflicts in a naturally courteous manner. Librarians should prevent crowd spillover into designated wheelchair seating areas when wheelchair-user occupied. Clear circulation paths and accessible assembly area routes assist the disabled to move within and between assembly areas and walks, hallways, courtyards, elevators, stairways and stair landings.

Without designated wheelchair assembly seating, users face the hazards of rolloff or overturning. Assembly safety precludes wheelchairs positioned in aisles. Regular chairs should be restricted to any locations not designated as wheelchair roll-up locations. Wheelchair roll-up areas should adjoin library accessible routes that provide immediate emergency exit to the lobby, interior hallways or building exits. Assembly wheelchair placement often adjoin accessible library service routes used also as emergency exit routes for the disabled.[208] Accessible restrooms, water fountains and public telephones are nearby when the disabled leave library assembly for personal needs. Assembly seating plans convey friendly public access to audience members including those with disabilities. Permanent seating in the upright position temporarily widens aisle clearance and aisle access for mobility-limited users. Movable library seating provides planning flexibility to accommodate diverse groups, including patrons with physical disabilities. Since library service includes assembly area or meeting room services, routes to those areas must be accessible and interconnect all other service areas.[209] Library emergency management plans should ensure safe, well-lit wheelchair or walking aid user evacuation from assembly areas.[210][211] Any assembly area without these safety precautions argues for not providing library assemblies as a public service since occupant safety may be compromised.

Library public address systems, intercoms or similar announcement systems may be inappropriate or ineffective since volume adjustments that might be appropriate for patrons with hearing impairment also disrupt other hearing patrons during infosearching. Yet earphones during public address system use is unlikely to be needed unless those same patrons are at library assembly. Patrons with hearing impairment require assistive listening devices at library assemblies.[212] Amplification for at least one public access telephone is provided during assemblies or group meetings. Coming to assemblies or group meetings may be the only reason many hearing impaired enter the library. Patrons with hearing impairment reposition to other seating to gain hearing that differs significantly from the hearing audience. Accessible viewing and listening necessitates that they cluster within comfortable hearing presentation range. Most library assembly areas have listening systems for use by anyone needing hearing assistance. Various assistive listening systems (ALS) augment standard public address systems by providing signals received directly by guests with special equipment or linked through hearing. Patrons with hearing impairment require preferential seating at the front of the assembly area even with ALS use. Repositioning during the program is required for hearing aid users who experience electronic feedback problems associated with public address systems.

Modified library policy for public assembly areas or meeting rooms permits service animal use by disabled individuals. Libraries accommodate service animals and ensure that users are not separated from animals at assemblies. Service animals have difficulties with loud assembly sounds, public address systems and electronic feedback, some of which is not audible to humans. None of these problems appear to risk others' safety or warrant excluding these animals from library assembly. Librarians are not required to manage service animals but must accommodate the patron with a service animal:

> ...the rule does not require a [library] to supervise or care for any service animal. If a service animal must be separated from the individual with a disability in order to avoid a fundamental alteration or a threat to safety, it is the responsibility of the individual with the disability to arrange for the care and supervision of the animal during the period of separation. (ADA Handbook, Title III-page 77.)

Adaptive Library Orientation

Summary

Adaptive librarian orientation helps people with disabilities in a variety of ways all based on their specific request for orientation. Librarians assess patron mobility and access skills and evaluate the library's physical layout for possible architectural barriers. Numerous orientation adaptations may be developed from a careful overall library assessment.

End Notes:

1. Lewis, Christopher. (1992). The Americans with Disabilities Act and Its Effect on Public Libraries. Public Libraries, 31, 27: "The ADA obviously has dozens of details that must be examined by librarians as they start to take steps to guarantee fair, nondiscriminatory access in their libraries. It is also apparent that compromises were made as the law was being written, so loopholes exist. However, it would be unconscionable for a library to use these loopholes as a license to avoid providing accomodations to an employee or a patron with a disability. It can be safely assumed that access to the services and programs of many public libraries will fall short of the ADA's requirements."

2. Pack, Nancy C. & Foos, Donald D. (1992). Planning for compliance with the Americans with Disabilities Act. Public Libraries, 31, 225-228.

3. Schell, G.C. (1981). The young handicapped child: A family perspective. Topics in Early Childhood Special Education, 1(3), 21-28.

4. Phinney, Eleanor. (1977). The librarian and the patient. Chicago, IL: American Library Association. Page 48.

5. Blacher, J. (1984). Sequential stages of parental adjustment to the birth of a child with handicaps: Fact or fiction? Mental Retardation, 22(2), 55l-68.

6. Hardman, Michael L., Drew, Clifford J., Egan, Winston & Wolf, Barbara. (1990). Human exceptionality. (3rd Ed.). Boston, MA: Allyn and Bacon. Page 461.

7. Ibid, Hardman, 460-461.

8. Hodges, Laura J. (1989). You've got what it takes: Public library services to persons who are mentally retarded. Reference Quarterly, 28(4), 466.

9. Wright, Kieth C. (1987). Educating librarians about service to special groups: The emergence of disabled persons into the mainstream. North Carolina Libraries, 45, 79-80.

10. Weingand, Darlene E. (1990). The invisible client: Meeting the needs of persons with learning disabilities. In The Reference Librarian. New York: Haworth Press. Page 85.

11. Foster, Terry & Lindell, Linda. (1991). Libraries and the Americans with Disabilities Act. Texas Libraries, 52, 61.

12. New York Library Association. (1992). Guidelines for serving persons with a hearing impairment. Library Trends, 41, 164-172.

13. Ibid, Hodges, 466.

14. Cagle, R. Brantley. (1983). Reference service to the developmentally disabled: Normalization of access. Catholic Library World, 54, 267.

15. ADAAG. Appendix B. Americans with Disability Accessibility Guidelines. In, U.S. Department of Justice. (1991). Americans with Disabilities Act Handbook. Washington, DC: U.S. Government Printing Office. Page 4.3.2(3).

16. Pinion, Catherine F. (1990). Audio services for the blind and partially sighted in public libraries. Audiovisual Librarian, 16, 27.

17. ADA Handbook. U.S. Department of Justice. (1991). Americans with Disabilities Act Handbook. Washington, DC: U.S. Government Printing Office. Page I-62(2).

18. Ibid, ADA Handbook, I-62(3).

19. Ibid, ADA Handbook, I-77.

20. Ibid, ADA Handbook, I-79. Section 1650. 15(d). Defense to Not Making Reasonable Accommodation.

21. Ibid, Hodges, 466.

22. Ibid, ADA Handbook, I-11.

23. Day, John Michael. (1992). Guidelines for library services to deaf people: Development and interpretation. IFLA Journal, 18, 35: "...it is the responsibility of libraries, themselves, to aggressively encourage deaf people to use their services."

24. Ibid, Day, 35: "...it is too easy to fall into the trap of thinking that since my deaf community does not use my library, I do not have to provide services."

25. Allegri, Francesca. (1984). On the other side of the reference desk: The patron with a physical disability. Medical Reference Services Quarterly, 3(3), 74: Librarians should look at their facilites in terms of creating a welcoming environment. With a minimum of expense or effort, certain obstacles can be removed which would improve access by all patrons, not just those with physical disabilities."

26. Sangster, Collette. (1986). Guidelines for library services to hearing-impaired persons. The Bookmark, 44, 106: "Because the process of locating information and materials in a library is confusing and complicated, the library should simplify and facilitate this process. Conspicuous directonal signs should be provided to encourage independent use."

27. ADAAG. Appendix B. Page 4.6.2.

28. Ibid, ADA Handbook, A4.30.4: "Interpretive guides, audio tape devices, or other methods may be more effective."

29. Ibid, ADAAG, 4.6.2.

30. Ibid, Pack & Foos, 225.

31. Ibid, ADAAG, 4.1.2(2): "At least one accessible route complying with 4.3 shall connect accessible buildings, accessible facilities, accessible elements, and accessible spaces that are on the same site."

32. Power, M.T., Rundlett, Carol & David, Myra. (1989). New challenges in helping students uncover information: The learning disabled student. The Bookmark, 47(11), 214: "Spatial disabilities may mean a [learning disabled] student needs much more than a walking tour of the library during freshman orientation. She or he may need an audiotape map or a textured [floor]map depending on his/her learning style."

33. Ibid, ADA Handbook, A4.30.4: "Accessible signage with descriptive materials about public buildings...may not provide sufficiently detailed and meaningful information."

34. Smale, Rebecca. (1992). Australian university library services for visually impaired students: Results of a survey. The Australian Library Journal, 41, 208.

35. Ibid, ADAAG, 4.3.2.(3).

36. Ibid, Power, 213.

37. Ibid, Smale, 208.

38. Ibid, Pinion, 28.

39. Ibid, ADAAG, 4.33.7: "Assistive listening systems (ALS) are intended to augment standard public address and audio systems by providing signals which can be received directly by persons with special receivers or their own hearing aids."

40. Ibid, ADAAG, 4.30.7(4); See also the International Symbol of Access for Hearing Loss Figure 43 at 4.30.7(4).

41. Freiser, W.F.E. (1983). New guidance system for the handicapped. Library Journal, 108(14), 1418.

42. Ibid, ADAAG, Table A2. Summary of Assistive Listening Devices.

43. O'Donnell, Ruth. (1992). Helping those with hearing loss. Library Journal, xxx, 55: "Making listening devices available at information, circulation, and reference desks allows people to effectively use the library. Library materials that have sound, e.g., videotapes, can be used with the aid of a listening device. Equipment that can meet these needs has a small microphone, receiver, and amplifier, it can be hard-wired (a wire connects the receiver to the sound source) or wireless."

44. No author. (1985). Hearing aid system for library programs. Library Journal, 110, 24.

45. Ibid, ADAAG, 4.33.7: "Earphone jacks with variable volume controls can benefit only people who have slight hearing loss and do not help people who use hearing aids."

46. Ibid, ADAAG, A4.30.1.

47. Ibid, Freiser, 1418.

48. Ibid, ADAAG, 4.3.11.5 & A4.3.10.

Adaptive Library Orientation

49. Ibid, Smale, 208: "The provision of tactile and large print maps and signs throughout the library can contribute to a visually impaired person's sense of independent and unintimidated movement."

50. Ibid, ADAAG, A4.30.1.

51. Liner, D.S. (Ed.). (1987). Tactile maps: A listing of maps in the National Library Service for the Blind and Physically Handicapped Collection. Washington, DC: The Library of Congress.

52. Ibid, ADAAG, 4.30.4.

53. Miller, Richard T. (1992). The Americans with Disabilities Act: Library facility and program access under Titles II and III. Ohio Libraries, 5, 10.

54. Ibid, ADAAG, A4.30.4.

55. Ibid, ADAAG, A4.30.4.

56. Ibid, ADAAG, 4.30.4 & A4.30.4.

57. Malinconico, S. Michael. (1989). Technologies and barriers to information access. In Effective access to information. Trezza, A.F. (Ed.). Boston: G.K. Hall. Page 124: "...it is insufficient to speak of barriers to access to a library's holdings, but rather we need to consider barriers to the satisfaction of a user's information needs, independent of the resources of any particular library. This at once expands the possibilities for satisfying a user's needs and makes the problems of gaining access to specific materials more complex."

58. Ibid, ADAAG, 4.29.4.

59. Ibid, ADAAG, 4.29.2. See also, Smale, 207.

60. Ibid, Allegri, 71.

61. Ibid, ADAAG, 4.29.2.

62. Ibid, Smale, 207.

63. Ibid, ADAAG, 4.4.1, 4.4.2 & A4.4.1.

64. Ibid, ADAAG, 4.4.2 & A4.4.1.

65. Ibid, ADA Handbook, I-15.

66. Ibid, ADAAG, 4.3.11.5 & A4.3.10.

67. Ibid, ADAAG, 4.3.11 & A4.3.10.

68. Ibid, ADAAG, A4.3.10.

69. Ibid, ADAAG, 4.28.1.

70. Ibid, ADAAG, A4.28.2.

71. Ibid, ADAAG, A4.28.2.

72. Ibid, ADAAG, 4.3.11(6).

73. Ibid, ADAAG, 4.29.3.

74. Ibid, ADAAG, 4.13.2.

75. Ibid, ADAAG, A4.3.1.

76. Ibid, ADAAG, 4.13.2.

77. Ibid, ADAAG, 8.3.

78. Ibid, ADA Handbook, III-75: "A [library] with check-out aisles shall ensure that an adequate number of accessible check-out aisles is kept open during [library] hours, or shall otherwise modify its policies and practices, in order to ensure tha an equivalent level of convenient service is provided to individuals with disabilities as is provided to others. If only one check-out aisle is accessible, and it is generally used for express service, one way of providing equivalent service is to allow persons with mobility impairments to make all [title charging] at that aisle."

79. Ibid, Power, 214.

80. Ibid, Power, 214.

81. Ibid, ADAAG, 4.30.4 & A4.30.4.

82. Ibid, Power, 215.

83. Ibid, ADA Handbook, I-61 & I-67.

84. Ibid, ADA Handbook, I-61 & 67.

85. Ibid, Cagle, 268.

86. Medrinos, Roxanne Baxter. (1992). CD-ROM and at-risk students. School Library Journal, 38, 30.

87. Ibid, ADA Handbook, II-39.

88. Hagemeyer, Alice. (1982). Library service and outreach programs for the deaf. Wyoming Library Roundup, 38(2), 15-21.

89. Ibid, Power, 214-215.

90. Ibid, ADA Handbook, II-39 & III-51.

91. Ibid, Power, 215.

92. Purdue, Bill. (1984). Talking newspapers and magazines. Audiovisual Librarian, 10, 82-85.

93. Ibid, Purdue.

94. Midkiff, Ruby B., Towery, Ron & Roark, Susan. (1991). Accomodating learning style needs of academically at-risk students in the library/media center. Ohio Media Spectrum, 43, 45-51.

95. Ibid, Power, 213-216.

96. Ibid, Medrinos, 29-31.

97. Ibid, Weingand, 77-88.

98. Ibid, Power, 214-215.

99. Ibid, ADA Handbook, I-63.

100. Ibid, Hodges, 463-469.

101. Ibid, ADA Handbook, I-63.

102. Ibid, Hodges, 466.

103. Lane, Elizabeth & Lane, James. (1982). Reference materials for the disabled. Reference Services Review, 10, 73.

104. Developmentally Disabled Assistance and Bill of Rights Act of 1975 (Public Law 94-103).

105. Ibid, Hodges, 466.

106. Editor. (1983). California LSCA project to mainstream mentally impaired. Library Journal, 108, 340.

107. Ibid, Cagle, 267.

108. Ibid, California LSCA project, 340.

109. Irwin, Marilyn. (1992). Library media specialist: Information specialist for students with disabilities. Indiana Media Journal, 14(1), 12.

110. Ibid, ADA Handbook, II-42.

111. Ibid, Hodges, 466.

112. Ibid, Day, 34: "...libraries are often major cultural and social centers within their communities and offer a variety of programs which are interesting to the community."

113. Homeward Bound V. The Hissom Memorial Center. 1988. See also, Goffman, E. (1975). Characteristics to total institutions. In S. Dinitz, R.R. Dynes & A. C. Clarke (Eds.), Deviance: Studies in definition, management, and treatment. New York: Oxford University Press.

114. Lucas, Linda. (1983). Education for work with disabled and institutionalized persons. Journal of Education for Librarianship, 23, 208. "The critical factor, then, in educating librarians is to promote positive attitudes so that disabled persons come alive as individuals of ability. Pity, sympathy, and patronizing attitudes are not required; sensitivity to individual needs and willingness to work to eliminate the barriers which keep disabled persons from fully utilizing their abilities are. If positive attitudes exist, librarians will make the needed effort to learn and to put into practice what they have learned." See also, Zipkowitz, Fay. (1990). "No one wants to see them: Meeting the reference needs of the deinstitutionalized." The Reference Librarian. New York: Hawthorn Press. Pages 53-67.

115. Ibid, ADA Handbook, II-42.

116. Temsky, R. Marlene. (1982). Some suggestions for public library service to disabled persons. Bay State Librarian, 71, 9: "The key to successful service to the disabled remains awareness: know who is out there; know what their needs might be; know what resources, human and material, are available. Keep cooperation between the library and the disabled community a lively process."

117. Jaschik, Scott. (1994). Colleges and the disabled. Chronicle of Higher Education, 90(33), A38-39.

118. Ibid, ADA Handbook, I-28. "Multiple impairments that combine to substantially limit one or more of an individual's major life activities also constitute a disability."

Adaptive Library Orientation

119. Ibid, <u>ADA Handbook</u>, I-28: "The ADA and this part, like the Rehabilitation Act of 1973, do not attempt a "laundry list" of impairments that are "disabilities."

120. Ibid, <u>ADA Handbook</u>, I-79.

121. Ibid, <u>ADA Handbook</u>, II-42.

122. Ibid, Hardman, 132.

123. Ibid, Pinion, 27.

124. Ibid, Pinion, 27.

125. Ibid, <u>ADA Handbook</u>, I-9: "[reasonable accomodation] adjustments must ensure that individuals with disabilities receive equal access to the benefits and privileges afforded to other[s]...but may not be able to ensure that the individuals receive the same results of those benefits and privileges or precisely the same benefits and privileges."

126. Ibid, <u>ADAAG</u>, 4.13.1 & 4.13.2.

127. The Individual Educational Plan (IEP) is an integral part of Public Laws 94-142 and 101-476 for students with disability.

128. Ibid, Phinney, 53.

129. <u>Information 2000: Library and Information Services for the 21st Century. A summary report of the 1991 White House Conference on Library and Information Services</u>. (1991). Washington, DC: U.S. Government Printing Office. Page 57.

130. Ibid, Weingand, 86.

131. Ibid, <u>ADAAG</u>, 4.27.4: "Controls and operating mechanisms shall be operable with one hand and shall not require tight grasping, pinching, or twisting of the wrist."

132. Ibid, <u>ADAAG</u>, 4.13.9.

133. Ibid, <u>ADA Handbook</u>, II-53.

134. Ibid, <u>ADA Handbook</u>, I-28: "...temporary, non-chronic impairments of short duration, with little or no long term or permanent impact, are usually not disabilities. Such impairments may include, but are not limited to, broken limbs, sprained joints, concussions, appendicitis, and influenza."

135. Ibid, <u>ADAAG</u>, A4.5.1.

136. Ibid, <u>ADAAG</u>, A4.2.1(2).

137. Ibid, <u>ADAAG</u>, A4.15.2.

138. Ibid, <u>ADAAG</u>, 4.16.2.

139. Ibid, <u>ADAAG</u>, 4.31.2.

140. Ibid, <u>ADAAG</u>, A4.3.1.

141. Ibid, <u>ADAAG</u>, 4.2.4.1.

142. Ibid, <u>ADAAG</u>, 8.5: "Minumum clear aisle width between stacks shall comply with 4.3 with a minimum clear aisle width of 42 in (1065 mm) preferred where possible."

143. Ibid, <u>ADA Handbook</u>, II-42 & III-71.

144. Ibid, <u>ADA Handbook</u>, I-77.

145. Roberts, Melissa Locke. (1985). Welcoming disabled readers to a new world of information. <u>Texas Libraries</u>, <u>46</u>, 55.

146. Ibid, Smale, 202: "These [survey] results describe an administrative insensibility to the supplementary requirements of visually impaired people as distinct from those of the general populace."

147. Ibid, <u>ADA Handbook</u>, II-13/14. "Qualified readers, taped texts, audio recordings, Brailled materials, large print materials, or other effective methods of making visually delivered materials available to individuals with visual impairments."

148. Ibid, Purdue, 82-85.

149. Ibid, Foster & Lindell, 62.

150. Lisson, Paul. (1987). Large print placebo. <u>Canadian Library Journal</u>, <u>44</u>, 5.

151. Ibid, Foster & Lindell, 62.

152. International Business Machines. National Support Center for Persons with Disabilities. (1991). <u>Resource Guide for persons with vision impairments</u>. Atlanta, GA: IBM.

153. Ibid, <u>ADAAG</u>, 4.30.4 & A4.30.4.

154. Goltz, Eileen. (1991). The provision of services to students with special needs in Canadian academic libraries. Canadian Library Journal, 48(4), 265.

155. Hill, Everett & Ponder, Purvis. (1976). Orientation and mobility techniques: A guide for the practitioner. New York: American Foundation for the Blind. "Landmarks: Any familiar object, sound, color, temperature or tactual clue that is easily recognized, is constant, and that has a known, permanent location in the environment" (Page 4).

156. Ibid, Hill: "Clues: A clue is any auditory (including object perception), olfactory, tactile (including temperature, kinesthetic, or visual (including color, brightness, and contrast) stimulus affecting the seses which can be readily converted to give the student information necessary to determine his position or a line of direction."

157. Ibid, ADA Handbook, II-65. See also, ADAAG, 4.3.2(3).

158. Ibid, Lisson, 5. "More than 80 percent of all people considered legally blind have usable vision. They are not blind; they have low vision."

159. Ibid, ADAAG, 4.30.4 & A4.30.4.

160. Ibid, ADAAG, A4.30.5.

161. Ibid, Roberts, 55.

162. Ibid, ADA Handbook, II-39 & III-51.

163. Ibid, ADA Handbook, I-21.

164. Ibid, ADAAG, 4.30.4 & A4.30.4.

165. Ibid, Hill, 42-43.

166. Ibid, Hill, 41-42.

167. Ibid, Hill, 36-40.

168. Ibid, Hill, 43-46.

169. Ibid, Miller, 8; See also, ADA Handbook, III-38 : "...[Libraries] as public accomodations, to modify policies, practices, and procedures to accomodate the use of service animals in places of public accomodation."

170. Ibid, ADA Handbook, III-38.

171. Ibid, ADAAG, 4.4.1, 4.4.2 & A4.4.1.

172. Ibid, Hill, 34-35.

173. Ibid, ADA Handbook, III-72.

174. Ibid, ADA Handbook, II-79.

175. Wood, K.S. (1971). Terminology and nomenclature. In L.E. Travis (Ed.), Handbook of speech pathology and audiology. New York: Appleton-Century-Crofts. Page 21: "...a disturbance of rhythm and fluency in speech by an intermittent blocking, a convulsive repitition, or prolongation of sounds, syllables, words, phrases, or posture of the speech organs."

176. Ibid, Hardman, 242: "Some people with a fluency disorder speak with what is known as cluttered speech, or cluttering. This type of fluency disorder is characterized by speech that is overly rapid (to the extreme), disorganized, and occasionally filled with unnecessary words-unrelated insertions that seem random."

177. Ibid, Hagemeyer, 15-21.

178. Kruger, Kathleen Joyce. (1984). Library service to disabled citizens: Guidelines to sources and issues. Technicalities, 4(9), 9.

179. Speech reading requires the user to view another's speech by watching lip movement, facial and body gestures to gain understanding and to communicate.

180. American Sign Language includes a vocabulary of approximately 6,000 signs. It is a Non-English language where signs represent concepts rather than single words.

181. Finger spelling is a signing system that incorporates each of the twenty-six letters of the alphabet allowing the user to spell each word on one hand.

182. Ibid, Day, 31-36.

183. Ibid, Day, 36.

184. Ibid, Hagemeyer, 20.

Adaptive Library Orientation

185. Ibid, Cagle, 268. See also, <u>Information 2000</u>, 19.
186. Ibid, <u>ADA Handbook</u>, I-39. See also Day, 33: "...it is imperative that the same level of service available to the general constituency of the library be equally available to clientele who are deaf."
187. Ibid, <u>ADAAG</u>, 4.30.1 & A4.30.1.
188. Ibid, <u>ADAAG</u>, 4.30.1 & A4.30.1.
189. Ibid, <u>ADA Handbook</u>, II-13.
190. Ibid, Day, 36.
191. Ibid, <u>ADA Handbook</u>, II-39 & III-51.
192. Ibid, <u>ADA Handbook</u>, I-77.
193. Ibid, <u>ADAAG</u>, 4.30.1 & A4.30.1.
194. Ibid, <u>ADAAG</u>, 4.30.6. See also, Lisson, 5.
195. Ibid, <u>ADAAG</u>, 4.30.5 & A4.30.5.
196. Ibid, <u>ADAAG</u>, 4.30.1 & A4.30.1.
197. Ibid, <u>ADAAG</u>, A4.2.1(1).
198. Ibid, <u>ADAAG</u>, A4.2.1(2).
199. Ibid, <u>ADAAG</u>, A4.2.1.(3).
200. Ibid, <u>ADAAG</u>, 4.3.2(3) & <u>ADA Handbook</u>, II-65.
201. Ibid, Lisson, 5.
202. Ibid, <u>ADAAG</u>, A4.33.7: "Some listening systems may be subject to interference from other equipment and feedback from hearing aids of people who are using the system. Such interference can be controlled by careful engineering design that anticipates feedback sources in the surrounding area."
203. Ibid, ADAAG, 4.30.4 & A4.30.4.
204. Ibid, <u>ADAAG</u>, 4.2.4.1.
205. Ibid, ADAAG, 4.30.1 & A4.30.1.
206. Ibid, The arts and 504, 67, 69 and 74.
207. Ibid, ADAAG, 4.30.6.
208. Ibid, ADAAG, 4.3.2(3) & 4.33.3.
209. Ibid, <u>ADAAG</u>, 4.3.2(3).
210. Ibid, ADAAG, 4.3.11.5 & A.4.3.10.
211. Ibid, <u>ADAAG</u>, A4.3.11.4.
212. Ibid, <u>ADAAG</u>, 4.33.7.

Suggested Reading:

Allegri, Francesca. (1984). On the other side of the reference desk: The patron with a physical disability. <u>Medical Reference Services Quarterly</u>, <u>3</u>(3), 65-76.

Day, John Michael. (1992). Guidelines for library services to deaf people: Development and interpretation. <u>IFLA Journal</u>, <u>18</u>, 31-36.

Hagemeyer, Alice. (1982). Library service and outreach programs for the deaf. <u>Wyoming Library Roundup</u>, <u>38</u>(2), 15-21.

Hill, Everett & Ponder, Purvis. (1976). <u>Orientation and mobility techniques: A guide for the practitioner</u>. New York: American Foundation for the Blind.

Hodges, Laura J. (1989). You've got what it takes: Public library services to persons who are mentally retarded. <u>Reference Quarterly</u>, <u>28</u>(4), 463-469.

Chapter Four

Library Service Areas

Overcoming Library Barriers To Equal Information Access

Finding the right library service area is not easy for some patrons with disabilities, just as it is difficult for others to select their own "right library information." Conventional library strategies are modified to reasonably assure disabled patrons library success. Library service areas can be transformed into barrier-free information access zones through adaptive library orientation. Just as barrier-free loading zones are provided for all outside the library, so can the library also arrange each service area to be a designated barrier-free information access zone.

Library service areas for patrons with disabilities are created with careful planning for patron service and attention to detail. Conventional library accommodation for nondisabled patrons is personalized service that, like adaptive library orientation, meets special patron library information needs. Conventional and adaptive library orientation occur together in library service areas. All library service areas must be barrier-free access zones to personal information. Without barrier-free access zones, libraries do not facilitate patrons with disabilities as information stakeholders.

All patrons select among print, nonprint or computer-based library information format options. Some specialized accessible format options are not offered in local collections. Specialized accessible library information format options include Braille, tactile, pictogram, microform with augmentation, talking book, augmented electronic information and library interface with personal assistive devices brought in by the patron.

Accessible library information format options may still not meet individual needs and will require further specific librarian orientation and accommodation. Some accommodation strategies involve library workarounds where physical barriers in library service areas are circumvented, or library procedures are changed to facilitate patron information gain. Library help begins as personal orientation provided by the librarian on request from the patron. Personalized or adaptive orientation, workarounds and direct personal accommodation are all provided in library service areas.

All library service areas must be barrier-free access zones to personal information.

The Card Catalog

> To use the standard card catalog, a reader must be able to go to the cabinet, read the labeling, reach for a drawer, grasp the handle, pull out the drawer, lift it onto another surface to view the entire file, hold the place in the file while recording the information on paper or card, and return the drawer to its proper place by both carrying it and inserting it into its open slot. These actions require adequate visibility, reach, strength, and coordination (Phinney, 1977, 230).

Card catalog personal management has not changed significantly since Phinney first described the personal access process. Personal orientation at the service area enables information access for all who use the card catalog system.[1] But during these intervening years many have not been successful at the card catalog. As Phinney (1977)[2] implied above, there are many patron- and library-imposed card catalog barriers. Aisles may not be ordinarily thought of as having hidden card catalog barriers by nondisabled persons until aisles are crowded. Walkway crowding at the card catalog is incidental to normal heavy use until patrons using wheelchairs, walking aids or patrons with low vision are part of the patron user mix there. When others pull and extend card catalog shelves, walkway barriers are presented for low-vision patron negotiation. Personal reading attendants must assist patrons with visual disabilities to effectively use card catalogs and maintain safe catalog aisle movement.[3] Help from others may be required in crowded card catalog aisles. No library can reasonably avoid crowded conditions in all service areas.

Library Patrons With Disabilities

Card catalog furniture is diverse in arrangement, height and accessibility in many libraries. While card catalog cabinets provide the same service in these libraries, they do so to a diversity of special-needs patrons with each card catalog configuration. When all card catalog infosearching needs combine, some patrons with disabilities are better served with one cabinet arrangement over another. There is no one best card catalog furniture configuration. Cabinet signage, guide content, note-taking surfaces, standing or seated access problems, even area walkways and aisle configuration can either be library barriers or can effectively facilitate infosearching. This must all be determined one patron at a time. Basic card catalog access is complex for many patrons with disabilities. Effective catalog users must read card guides. Card tabs are read in card trays, along with guide letters and words that direct patrons to the collection. Card catalog signage should consistently show high contrast light-on-dark or dark-on-light character sizes readable at normal viewing distance.[4] Signage at the card catalog in this way makes visual access easier for all patrons. Viewing card guides and locating card shelving may require extensive user orientation.[5] Reading catalog end-shelf and front-tray guides are important orientation components.

Professionals accommodate patrons with disabilities and consult with them to suggest card catalog research skills when asked.[6] People with reading disabilities and some learning disabled find using manual card catalogs difficult.[7] Another barrier-free library service area can be provided both through patron accommodation and effective card catalog setup. For a diverse patron clientele, professional skill when helping at the card catalog requires real card catalog expertise combined with the fine art of patron diplomacy.

Readers identify author, title and subject cards and discriminate print and nonprint source cards. Catalog users then locate specific shelf and title locations. Since cards cannot be removed, users make personal notes from card information or rely on detailed card content memory. Librarians review card catalog trays with patrons at adjacent study or reading areas. Librarians must pull the tray for some, move with the patron to a reading area, and review contents with the patron there.

Catalogs require reading to grasp and remember subject heading, author or title and related catalog information. Infosearching at the card catalog is a complex puzzle with each successful activity a piece fitted into place. Readers use card citations and locate specific sources by finding appropriate subject headings and descriptors. Patrons understand information sources by using cards to find specific titles and retrieve information. Information retrieval requires searching by call number or media code, author, title or subject. People read card content to obtain title information and go to appropriate shelf or title storage locations. For any patron, finding title information and then being able to obtain actual titles are distinctly different processes.

A quality standard for card catalog service is the ease by which patrons with disabilities can write notes from card catalog information. It is better to provide onsite note-taking support at the card catalog without moving trays elsewhere. Note-taking is supported at the card catalog when shelves pull out to hold trays at working surface levels. Writing surfaces may be built-in to the card catalog cabinet. Storage shelves, when pulled out, permit both tray holding and writing. When tray loads are removed or writing downward pressure ceases, an innovative hydraulic-controlled writing surface withdraws to the storage postion within the cabinet. Extended card trays and writing surfaces present dangerous walkway hazards without automatic shelf return. For multiple note-takers, card catalog furniture design otherwise provides angled writing surfaces (like the angle of a dictionary stand display) between banks of trays.

People find shelf print- or non-print information locations using the existing library classification system. Successful searches may require card catalog cross-reference infosearching through any logical author, subject and title strategies.[8] Personalized patron help makes card catalogs a library barrier-free search zone. For some disabled patrons, learning and using cross-referencing skills is a complicated librarian and patron task. Others cross-reference with ease and without library help.

Wheelchair User Card Catalog Services

Card catalog cabinet setup often provides inaccessibly narrow aisles for patrons using wheelchairs or walking aids. A 36-inch (36″) aisle width[9] at the catalog may not assure wheelchair or walking aid user access when card trays are pulled out, reading or writing surfaces protrude into the aisle or when multiple users are present. Successful catalog forward wheelchair reach requires a wider aisle for wheelchair repositioning and a maximum 48-inch-high (48″) upreach and a minimum 15-inch (15″) downreach above the floor.[10] When wheelchair or cane, crutch or walker users approach parallel to card catalog shelves, maximum high side-reach is 54 inches (54″) and low side-reach is no less than 9 inches (9″) above the floor.[11] Catalog shelf viewing and tray securement above wheelchair-user eye-level requires library adjustments.[12] High or low shelves present the mobility limited with poor tray and card visibility. Card catalog tray selection, reaching high or low card trays, finding cards, reading book number, subject, title and author notations are patron-requested librarian accommodations. Librarian help at card catalogs is frequently comprehensive for patrons with disabilities.

For some disabled patrons, learning and using cross-referencing skills is a complicated librarian and patron task.

Some electric wheelchair users with arm movement capability read file labels only from the seated position. Where possible, card catalogs are lowered to accommodate these patrons.[13] Separate ADA-dictated library policy to reshelve card files is not indicated or recommended for wheelchair users. Attendants or professionals help with card tray reshelving. Everyone who needs help at the card catalog should be provided that help when requested. Other patrons using wheelchairs or walking aids have very limited arm, hand or finger use in addition to limited or no walking ability. Movements for some may be restricted to single-switch toggle wheelchair controls and no related capability to reach or handle library titles, card trays, even cards. Electric wheelchair users may also be unable to take notes. They must rely on recording devices for verbal note-taking. Their catalog use without other related personal support is not recommended. Yet patrons with disabilities are free to refuse librarian offers of help.[14]

Prosthesis Users at the Card Catalog

Patrons using prosthetic legs or leg braces find card catalogs problematic when reaching for highly-placed, low or ground-level card trays. Paging through cards may be difficult and require help. Mid-level trays are more reachable. Moving card trays to a reading area is not difficult unless trays are heavy or more than one tray is removed and carried. Some library card trays do not permit patron removal. For many, a library requiring patrons to remove trays without nearby reading platforms is one imposing a significant infosearching barrier. Some card catalogs require prolonged patron standing while reading cards. Seating while reading cards is the preferred access mode. Seated card use is not a conventional service in many libraries. Seated card readers must remove trays from cabinets possibly beyond reach, and read in aisles while standing to hold trays thereby blocking others from card tray access. Paging through card trays may be difficult and require help for patrons with arm, hand or finger prosthesis. Physical barrier-free card catalog access is not always assured without librarian help. Even with librarian help, patrons may not link card information to actual title access.

Library Patrons With Disabilities

Low-Vision Patrons at the Card Catalog

Conventional card catalog setup discourages low-vision patron independent use without further significant accommodation.[15] Even sighted users find card manipulation difficult. The sighted librarian finds co-viewing for card reading difficult when low vision patrons require extreme magnification to read card content. Cards for low vision patrons cannot be recognized or read without hand magnifiers. Conventional cards are not accessible unless through magnification they also indicate a large talking book or large-print format collection. Card catalog pictograms are low-vision patron aids when equivalent verbal descriptions accompany each pictogram display.[16] Pictograms show safe and effective card catalog use.

Persons with low vision experience difficulty at catalog searching when overloaded card drawers make hand magnifier use difficult.[17] Overloaded card drawers are a barrier to everyone. Professionals give reasonable card catalog help on request.[18] Help can be subtle, respecting individual patron desire for library and reading independence.[19] Librarians must not refuse reasonable requests for help.[20] But patrons with low vision may refuse card catalog accommodation.[21]

Conventional card catalog setup discourages low-vision patron independent use without further accommodation.

Librarians may not require a reading attendant for patrons with low vision.[22] Having attendants with the low-vision patron at the card catalog is an entirely patron-elected personal service. It is a questionable assumption held by some librarians that low-vision patrons require access only to large print and not to conventional print library information.[23] With newer state-of-the-art library technologies, low-vision patrons readily access conventional print and large-print collections. While low-vision patrons may prefer conventional card catalog technology and expect to use magnification to gain access to limited special-format library information, technology now opens their access to conventional print information. Their card catalog access is no longer limited to Braille-based or recorded information when given access to the entire library print collection via state-of-the-art technology.

Libraries automating from manual to online public access catalog services may reduce card catalog and library signage Brailling efforts directing only to Brailled local collection titles. Library print card-to-Braille catalog conversion technology is available but not implemented except for some libraries with extensive Braille collections.[24] Conversion to Braille is expensive, requiring reconfiguring whole card catalog systems which usually serve a very small percent of the total patronage. Braille conversion technology requires Brailled paper cards with less information on each card because of the more widely spaced Braille lines and characters. Card numbers needed per title would be doubled with at least two cards serving one Brailled title.[25] Space and access considerations overrule Braille readers. Such Braille conversion technology is usually placed at other library locations rather than in the card catalog service area.

The Online Public Access Card Catalog Service

The online public access card catalog (OPAC) provides computer technology to electronically retrieve entire library collection information using author, title and subject keyword searching entered at the keyboard. Online users read citation information from computer monitors where specific titles are quickly located by keying-in OPAC database searches from onscreen menus shown on monitor displays using appropriate subject headings and descriptors. OPAC requires onscreen information reading skill to find subject headings, authors or titles. Reading important onscreen OPAC information may require further library orientation and accommodation as well as a careful review of the reading ease of screen information.

Library technology evolution closes card catalogs and virtually forces all patrons to the OPAC.[26] Libraries close their collections to make the immediate transition from card catalog to OPAC or patrons with disabilities face partial collection access on OPAC and the balance using card catalogs during the transition. Their infosearching labor to find the right title is doubled, compared to nondisabled patrons. And this doubling of patron infosearching effort is technology overload. There are many patrons afraid to use the new OPAC who hope to find the old, familiar card catalog still there. Orientation for the more exotic OPAC computer-based equipment also poses specific use problems for many disabled patrons.[27] Patrons may resist the move to OPAC and not return to the library. This may be the ultimate library technology barrier without OPAC onscreen help menus and an effective new user tutorial available.

OPAC novices with disabilities, like their nondisabled peers, have little more than fear of the unknown with which to contend when help screens and user tutorials are built-in. As patrons become more proficient with OPAC, some experience greater infosearching problems and an equally greater need for librarian accommodation. Intermediate-level OPAC users soon diverge into two groups: one with and one without OPAC technology overload. The nondisabled and each individual disabled patron experiences significantly different information barriers at OPAC. As OPAC use increases, technology overload occurs with some disabled patrons. When OPAC proficiency is gained most nondisabled infosearchers will be "experts" without technology overload having overcome any relevant OPAC barriers to obtain their information. But the disabled may struggle on for OPAC proficiency or expertise as continuing or recurring barriers or physical challenges are overcome daily. Why then would the patron choose to return to the card catalog, or use the library at all when only OPAC access now exists for infosearching--and that access is not barrier-free or user friendly? Card catalog use is the conventional patron information retrieval method. Library state-of-the-art technology provides the online public access catalog (OPAC) alternative. However, for many with disabilities, OPAC technology may not be the preferred search method over card catalog infosearching. The choice between conventional card catalog and OPAC use should be each disabled patron's right. In many libraries the choice between card catalog and OPAC has been preempted by library policy.

> **As patrons become more proficient with OPAC, some experience greater infosearching problems and an equally greater need for librarian accommodation.**

Oriented users begin with a working cursor at the OPAC main menu. Patrons recognize certain events at successive menu and submenu screen displays requiring further operator decisions. Decisions at keyboard entry are patron-echoed on OPAC screens as specific user keyboard responses are made among available menu options. Without onscreen keyboard response and "echoing" of patron input, many patrons get "lost" in the OPAC menu system. Well designed OPAC library software is "error trapped" to avoid locking up the system because of incorrect keyboard operator entries. New users have difficulty finding onscreen information and may repeat keyboard commands, becoming further "lost" in OPAC. They can even get "lost" onscreen with complex OPAC screen information displays. All patrons using OPAC are literally forced into developing an OPAC mental map. Some do not develop effective OPAC mental maps.

The best OPAC programs have a constant HELP SCREEN feature at any step in the program and ESCAPE TO MAIN MENU to correct or minimize OPAC user disorientation. OPAC user disorientation in this sense is a challenge to the patron's OPAC mental map. Error-trapping ignores all OPAC keyboard entries except appropriate keyed-in options displayed onscreen. When wrong keys are pressed, or when keys are held down or repeatedly pressed, the OPAC program patiently redirects the user to a more effective and positive response. OPAC informs all patrons midsearch of where they are now, how to retreat gracefully, or how to go further in the infosearch.

OPAC screens have used poor wording in operator commands such as: "Hit Return." Patrons have been known to literally hit the keyboard. A better OPAC operator onscreen injunction would be to "PRESS THE RETURN KEY." OPAC keyboard operations may be literally interpreted by some novice OPAC users. Poor OPAC software design provides cryptic responses to all users. Programs "hang up," resulting in patrons walking away and never returning to OPAC because of faulty software design and subsequent technology overload. Not only do they retreat from OPAC, they may retreat from the library altogether.[28] Thus an effective patron library barrier is maintained and barrier-free OPAC access avoided. Technology overload is the patron's problem. But faulty OPAC software design that contributes to patron technology overload is a library responsibility.

For some OPAC computer anxiety is a significant "hidden" or "invisible" barrier to information access, sometimes extending even to asking the librarian for help. Computer proficiency reasonably assures patron independence and success while using OPAC. Proficiency may require framing questions to librarians and receiving personal help during computer searches with librarian and disabled patron sitting side-by-side at the OPAC computer.[29] Librarians must be nearby or quickly accessible to anxious infosearchers. The computer industry describes this patron or customer anxiety-reducing process as "hand holding." Computers are underused by the disabled when they avoid orientation and attempt unsuccessfully to independently use OPAC. Computer orientation may not be forthcoming for patrons from some few librarians who continue to hold fears about individuals with disabilities as computer users.[30] Librarians may not have clearly designated orientation responsibilities to provide specific computer support services to disabled patrons.[31] They can learn to provide effective computer orientation to the disabled in addition to help screens and onboard OPAC user tutorials.[32] But the skilled librarian as a OPAC operator may not be equally skilled at orienting OPAC patrons with special needs.

Librarians may not have clearly designated orientation responsibilities to provide specific computer support services to disabled patrons.

Citation, abstract, or full-text collection access levels can be provided by OPAC. The majority of library OPACs today provide citation-only access with local libraries rarely providing full-text service. Abstract and full-text service is a technology that is now within reach of larger libraries or libraries networked with other OPAC libraries. Library core collections become smaller when shared across the network and are accessible to regional, statewide or national patron service areas. OPAC patron access may be linked to larger interlibrary networks without visible differences apparent to the patron operator:

> Traditional retrieval systems in book or card form are frequently supplemented with, and in some cases replaced by, microcomputers and online systems. These electronic catalogs make possible more convenient and extensive searching that widens the range of available resources...Supplemental data sources include online searching of electronically stored databases, union catalogs of other information agencies' holdings, networks that provide access to specialists in various fields, and interlibrary loan networks (American Library Association, 1988, page 31).

Since OPAC use is an application requiring patron general computer proficiency, computer-based information requires operators to first physically access the computer, keyboard, view the monitor comfortably before they can comprehend on-screen information. Invisible to the patron are a progression of database access "windows." Each window is an OPAC menu, submenu or text screen. We can envision

OPAC database window access as comparable to scanning frames of microform only at electronic speed and with no visible onscreen movement distortions. While microform frame scanning is analogous to OPAC database windows, it is far from a literal mental map built from actual OPAC programming and relational database logic.

User guides or library signage shows patron OPAC monitor orientation.[33] Library visual guides are readily viewed by seated- or standing-only OPAC users. Quality OPAC guides show consistent library signage with light-on-dark or dark-on-light user specified display selection for all to better read guides.[34] OPAC screen guides show contrast- and glare-control patron preference adjustments. Monitor controls are critical for low-vision patron access. Tilt and swivel-base OPAC monitor mounting provides flexible patron viewing, reducing screen glare and increasing screen reading ease. Terminals lacking screen controls and flexible viewing adjustments afford minimal service when patrons lack visual engagement and imposes another OPAC barrier to effective information access. Monitor screen users must read directions to recognize when and how each OPAC information screen or menu is keyboard-activated. When encountering blank OPAC screens, signage at the monitor should alert the user how to activate the monitor.[35] OPAC monitors automatically turn off after non-use intervals. For some users, a blank screen may indicate monitors are powered down or not working. When any key is touched, the monitor is activated displaying a fresh search screen.

OPAC users find on-screen information directing them to specific title locations. That screen-based information must be printed out, recorded by note-taking or remembered.[36] Many patrons forget paper and pencil while using OPAC. All patrons cannot be expected to remember OPAC information for prolonged periods to effectively find library information. A simple low-technology accommodation is to have note cards and pencils available near OPAC keyboards. Patrons bringing in their personal recording devices should be permitted at OPAC for note-taking support. For people with hand, finger or arm mobility limitations, missing arms, hands, or digits, note-taking is impossible or impractical without recourse to OPAC printouts. OPAC printouts also may be easier for deaf patrons than search notes and other written information during infosearches.[37] Yet few libraries currently provide this important OPAC accommodation, relying instead on the expectation that the patron can and will take notes from OPAC screens. Taking OPAC research notes on paper or note cards may require alternative library accommodation.[38] Dedicated OPAC terminals do not offer user-accessible word processing programs but manual or electric typewriter access at OPAC terminals is not realistic would be as reasonable accommodation. Libraries are not required to provide the most expensive or state-of-the-art reasonable accommodation for patrons with disabilities.[39] Low technology support may often be the preferred patron choice.

OPAC Terminal Overcrowding

At least one OPAC terminal should be made fully wheelchair accessible if several are available. If only one OPAC terminal is available then that terminal must be made accessible. Physical access to OPAC and keyboard for

Tilt and swivel-base OPAC monitor mounting provides flexible patron viewing, reducing screen glare and increasing screen reading ease. Terminals lacking screen controls and flexible viewing adjustments afford minimal service when patrons lack visual engagement.

Library Patrons With Disabilities

wheelchair, walking aid users and others with special needs must be assured.[40] Long waits often occur for patrons with disabilities, even at accessible OPAC terminals. OPAC terminal competition for wheelchair users is a real library barrier. Limited accessible terminal numbers also create a barrier to other patrons. The impact of limited but inaccessible OPAC terminals constitutes disparate disabled treatment and is prohibited by the ADA.[41]Limited wheelchair terminal access increases patron computer service competition. Accessible terminals are far more expensive than regular seated or standing-use terminals because of adaptive library furniture meeting roll-up or roll-under requirements and added specialized peripheral equipment to augment screen displays, give printouts or provide speech synthesis. With fewer expensive terminals it is more likely that each terminal will be occupied, even crowded. The heavier demand at terminals, the faster patrons must use OPAC and move on. With faster OPAC searching a more focused patron infosearch is then required. Rushed infosearches identify fewer sources and provide less satisfactory infosearching results. Patrons may not feel they have time to take notes before the next user demands access. At the OPAC terminal, and under heavy user demand, there is no time for infosearcher reflective or critical thinking. Wheelchair or walking aid users at high-demand OPAC accessible terminals, with others waiting for that terminal to be open, provide a conundrum. OPAC users with disabilities have no inherent right to use terminals for longer periods than the nondisabled. And so when they use OPAC for longer periods they come into conflict with others. There is clearly a need for OPAC library policy to impose time limits on heavy-demand terminals or at least during heavy-use periods and to enforce these policies equitably.

Wheelchair or Walking Aid User OPAC Access

OPAC service is typically provided on display tables where computer terminals are grouped in rows for multiple users. Clearances between fixed accessible tables should provide a fully accessible wheelchair or walking aid user route to OPAC, and clear table floor space.[42] OPAC use from roll-up accessible tables empowers the disabled by encouraging their infosearching independence.[43] Forward-[44] and side-reach requirements[45] for persons using wheelchairs are frequently not met at OPAC monitors or keyboards. At least five percent (5%) of the total OPAC units must be wheelchair useable[46] with proper knee clearance and reach ranges[47] and service locations situated along accessible library service routes.[48] Accessible OPAC terminals are more widely spaced and occupy more library floor space than regular OPAC terminal configurations. Realistic planning provides at least one fully accessible OPAC terminal at every library terminal site grouping. Where OPAC terminals are dispersed, each OPAC service area calls for a fully wheelchair accessible terminal.

Standing-only OPAC use was designed to quickly move people from OPAC searching into the local collection. The librarian assumption may be that standing OPAC users are less comfortable while searching and will move on more quickly than the seated. Less OPAC time per user provides more access per terminal during heavy-use periods for more users. Libraries experiencing heavy OPAC use consider standing-only access the preferable alternative. For those with disabilities who cannot stand for prolonged periods, a standing-only OPAC use requirement is a continuing barrier and is not patron-preferred.[49] For the disabled, standing-only OPAC use is disparate treatment, singling them out to their disadvantage.[50] Some libraries maintain that patron-seated OPAC access is unnecessary, without considering the implications for patrons with disabilities.[51] Some libraries offer high seats, requiring an almost standing-level OPAC keyboard reach. Seated OPAC monitor viewing and keyboarding by the physically challenged is the patron-preferred mode particularly for deeper searches. Libraries must consider patron accommodation preferences.[52] Seated- or standing-only use places others in direct competition with patrons with physical or cognitive challenges. Effective library planning includes a mix of seated- and standing-access OPAC terminals at each terminal grouping. Within these mixed groupings are seated-only wheelchair accessible OPAC terminals. Establishing five percent (5%) of accessible seated-only OPAC terminals in only one location, when all other OPAC terminals are standing-only and disbursed throughout the library, is not best practice.

Library Service Areas

Low-Vision Patrons At OPAC

Patrons with low vision are often called "the print disabled."[53] When OPAC screen viewing is problematic, patrons with low vision are also regarded as "screen disabled." Some require adaptations to optimally view or read computer monitor output.[54] OPAC access is more workable for those with low or limited peripheral vision who may need to view computer monitors at extreme close range.[55] Only high contrast black-and-white screen diplays with higher-than-normal contrast control settings can be read by many screen disabled. Only high resolution monitors can be effectively viewed at extreme close range without screen-imposed character distortions. Color monitors are attractive to the library general public but may impose significant viewing problems for patrons with low vision who may also be color-recognition disabled. For others with color blindness, color monitors are irrelevant to screen recognition and reading to gain library information. OPAC screen disabled users should be given an option to change screen displays from positive to negative for optimal contrast and increased reading comfort.[56] Search times are degraded and the search-path complicated for patrons with low vision.[57] Special OPAC access terminals are equipped with Brailled keyboards.[58] Some OPAC monitors provide magnified screen area viewing.

> **Patrons with low vision are often called "the print disabled." When OPAC screen viewing is problematic, patrons with low vision are also regarded as "screen disabled."**

OPAC Speech Synthesis Technology

Speech synthesis technology enables patrons with low vision, the blind, long cane or service animal users who were previously unable to accomplish total library searches now can search through entire collections. Many would otherwise be restricted to searching only for Braille titles, audio recordings or videocassettes.

Blind or visually impaired OPAC users require speech synthesizer-equipped terminals to use OPAC screens.[59] Synthesized speech on existing online computer catalogs offsets lack of visual engagement.[60] Enhanced speech synthesis technology on selected OPAC terminals reproduces speech from screen output. Screen output to synthesized speech is distracting to many patrons requiring this specialized OPAC service. Areas of information on the screen must be isolated for speech synthesized reproduction only leaving other screen areas not continually read aloud. But speech synthesis on library computers may be disconcerting, even to experienced special-needs users. Many OPAC screens have redundant information displayed that, if continuously speech synthesized, would greatly slow the OPAC infosearching process. Many existing OPAC systems do not include speech synthesis. OPAC without speech synthesis requires the use of personal readers or direct librarian help for the blind or visually impaired.[61] Independent OPAC use is not possible for many with low vision without speech synthesis or personal attendants to read OPAC monitor output.

The Learning Disabled At OPAC

Patrons with learning disabilities (LD) often require computer literacy skills assessment and specific help for successful OPAC use.[62] At OPAC terminals, the learning disabled are "patrons with invisible cognitive disabilities."[63] At OPAC or anywhere else in the library, professionals cannot recognize LD patrons only through simple observation, but must observe how they read print or screen information.[64] LD patrons must inform others of their OPAC accommodation needs.[65] But the learning disabled's refusal to accept OPAC reading help when offered is their ADA-defined right.[66] LD patrons, like many other patrons, may become confused during OPAC searches and have difficulty sorting out relevant screen information. They may be unable to take notes from OPAC information without librarian or personal attendant help.[67]

Prosthesis Users At OPAC

OPAC keyboarding is difficult, slow or impossible for patrons with arm, hand or finger prosthesis. Patrons using walking aids at OPAC require operation from a comfortably seated position. Many OPAC terminals offer barrier-free seated access. Patrons with leg prosthesis usually require OPAC keyboarding and monitor viewing from a comfortably seated position. Prolonged standing while keyboarding, or viewing monitor and OPAC information, is not recommended and may not be possible for some patrons using various prostheses. Policy requiring standing OPAC use to increase patron turnover creates unnecessary stress for many prosthesis users. This stress is evident when OPAC terminals are crowded, other patrons impatient, and conflicts begin between the disabled patron and others. A growing number of physically challenged patrons use personal computers or laptops at home, school, or the workplace who can easily overcome library OPAC terminal access challenges. Most physically challenged make the transition between library and other computer systems with ease.

OPAC User Safety

OPAC terminals are protected against accidental user disconnections. Some users with leg prostheses have involuntary leg movements that disrupt unsecured OPAC cabling or power connections.[68] Disconnections caused by leg protheses users can be avoided by securing OPAC cabling away from user reach, during seating or patron leg movements. OPAC users should be provided 27-inch (27") height, 30-inch (30") width and 19-inch (19") depth knee clearances.[69] OPAC equipment connection monitoring and maintenance is a librarian responsibility.

The Periodical Service Area

Adaptations for disabled patrons and others to use general and special subject periodicals, magazines, journals, or newspapers can be made on request. Highly visible and working library guides greatly facilitate access to periodicals. Orientation includes distinguishing magazine types, determining publication frequency, using tables of contents and finding specific articles. Readers identify periodical cover and article titles, dates, and page numbers. Special subject access requires patrons to further search using periodical indexes by locating and decoding index symbols and abbreviations. Periodical infosearching support ends when the right article in the right journal is accessible for each patron with disabilities. Any less standard of periodical support is incomplete accommodation. Periodical service support usually requires quick response when patrons who are novice library infosearchers request help.[70] People are uncertain of the value of periodical-based information and may quickly give up their search without immediate support. Periodicals may not be regularly or effectively supervised when no one is the designated periodical librarian. All librarians may be asked to help in periodicals or periodical service designated as a "floating position." Patrons with disabilities may have difficulty locating designated helpers. Library staff direct or accompany people to professionals who can and will help.

Policy requiring standing OPAC use to increase patron turnover creates unnecessary stress for many prostheses users. This stress is evident when OPAC terminals are crowded, other patrons impatient, and conflicts begin between patrons with disabilities and others.

An ADA-designated specialist helps when referred by other library workers.[71] Periodical worker photographs at the library entrance or in the periodical area indicate who patrons can approach for help.[72] Personnel photographs for patron recognition must be current and updated regularly. Some disabled patrons ask help from other patrons and are refused. Other patrons cannot be expected to provide professional library service. Attendants may accompany patrons to periodicals and throughout the library trek. Yet this makes the disabled patron dependent on others for periodical access. Some wish not to be dependent on anyone.

Periodical Browsing

Reading for pleasure is often done by periodical browsing. Browsing does not produce in-depth, subject matter searches. Browsing may be limited to currently shelved periodicals before a deeper shelf or collection search is initiated. Periodical browsing is less demanding than specific subject article searches. Browsing by the disabled is an excellent library experience for those unable to systematically subject search or who lack specific periodical reading interests. Yet systematic information searches quickly exhaust open-shelf periodical access and lead to deeper, more systematic searches. Patrons with disabilities must have access to the deepest periodical searches possible in every library. Browsing is easier with upright periodical display. Periodical stacks with flat shelves expedite infosearching but limit visibility from high- or low-shelf positions. Both angle or flat periodical displays impose physical challenges to many disabled patrons. Periodical issues not quickly accessed are regarded by most library patrons as nonexistent. Only with discipline, experience and infosearching expertise are patrons likely to search further than visibly shelved periodicals.

Periodical Shelving

Because shelf height in periodical stacks is unrestricted, help may be needed to see, select and reach periodicals at high- or low-shelf locations.[73] Periodicals are placed at middle-shelf levels to maximize patron reach. Adjustable and movable periodical shelving instead of built-in-place shelving offers service flexibility and improved reach. Total periodical shelf space interacts with periodical collection size to limit mid-level shelf display available. With minimal mid-level shelf display area libraries must then display periodicals at upper- and lower-shelf levels where issues are more difficult to see and to reach. Flat, upright, or angle shelf configurations affect disabled patron periodical reach. Flat shelves displaying most recent and back periodical issues require periodical viewing from an angle. Upright periodicals are more easily viewed but do not allow viewing or reaching behind for back issues. Periodicals with slippery covers shift off stacks, out of hand and fall. When titles fall some with disabilities may not be able to retrieve them from the floor. Angle periodical displays have a greater propensity to spill contents during patron use. Open shelving with backstops avoids periodicals sliding to the rear. Reshelving without shelf backdrops further spills and damages periodicals. Each library periodical configuration requires different librarian adaptations. Single-faced shelving units around outside walls give greater periodical floor space for wheelchair movement and general user traffic flow.[74]

Because shelf height in periodical stacks is unrestricted, help may be needed to see, select and reach periodicals at high- or low-shelf locations.

Library Patrons With Disabilities

Secured periodical shelves prevent the mobility limited from falling against shelves and spilling shelf contents particularly when patrons overextend the reach for periodicals. Spills, slips and falls are common daily events for some mobility limited who often learn through experience to recover from falls and go on with life activities otherwise uninterrupted. But spills, slips and falls are inexcusable if caused by unsecured periodical shelving.

Reshelving Periodicals

Many libraries direct periodical users not to reshelve periodicals. If this local library condition exists, periodical area signs indicate DO NOT RESHELVE PERIODICALS. This signage should be, like other library signage, readily visible with consistent high-contrast lettering with characters big enough to be read by anyone approaching each guide.[75] Patrons take unshelved periodicals beyond the periodical reading area. Periodical "drift" about the library may be unavoidable. Mishelving periodicals reduces access for the next reader until librarians reshelve. Only a comprehensive periodical shelf search will help library workers identify and realign mishelved or misplaced periodicals. Reshelving cycles are frequent and comprehensive throughout all periodical and reading areas and, as every librarian knows, is a very time-consuming and labor-intensive process.

Periodical Handling

Periodical handling requires reader physical skill and responsibility. When properly handled, periodicals need not be damaged or replaced for any reason other than for normal wear and tear. Poor handling includes folding page corners, or lifting periodicals by single pages, which loosens bindings or removes pages. Some patrons vandalize periodicals by removing periodical inserts or tearing out articles, drawings or pages. Tearing out issue inserts left by librarians is less offensive than tearing out periodical sections. Neither patron behavior should be librarian-condoned. Mishandlers fold back periodicals while reading and leave issues in disarray. Mishandling causes unintentional damage and accelerates periodical wear. There should be no faulty librarian assumption that patrons with disabilities will mishandle periodicals any more than others. Periodical misuse must be resolved by the library one patron misuser at a time. Disabled periodical mishandlers should receive the same consequences as all other library patrons. Prompt damaged issue replacement provides continued access to popular periodicals.

Disabled periodical mishandlers should receive the same consequences as all other library patrons.

Overall library environment and periodical use is greatly influenced for patrons with disabilities by professionals working there in a safe, professional and courteous manner.[76] What all librarians model is what patrons often do. Caring for print media requires librarian supervision or careful patron modeling of librarian periodical handling. Professionals are sensitive to the periodical uses their behavior establishes in patrons.

Libraries that use periodical covers or jackets minimize periodical damage. Yet covers frequently cause other disabled patron handling problems including: covers with a slippery finish making them hard to handle and easily dropped; covers that lose gloss finish and, over time, make issue covers difficult to recognize; cover bindings that reduce patron ability to place the periodical into the full-open reading position; and cover bindings that force issues shut when patrons remove their grasp. Periodicals mounted in protective covers are difficult to photocopy without page-edge distortion. Page-edge distorted copies remove the information format transfer technology many patrons require for print augmentation. Covers must not be removed during photocopying which when doing so may extensively damage issues. For patrons with physical or cognitive challenges, librarians must consider both the advantages and disadvantages of periodical covers for their disabled patronage. Consistent disabled patron expressed preferences should guide supportive library policy regarding periodical cover use.

Periodical Return Carts

Mobile return carts in the periodical reading area should be positioned to return more issues faster to their periodical shelf locations. Return carts also limit title spills and periodical damage. Carts simplify periodical handling by giving a place to return issues other than to mishelve. Carts provide a place to locate issues before reshelving. Return carts show designated periodical return signage.[77] Signage on return carts should meet high-contrast and lettering-size adaptive reading configuration requirements. Messages prohibit patrons from reshelving periodicals other than returning them to the cart.

Low-Vision Patrons in Periodicals

Specific periodical accommodation may be needed for low-vision patrons during their orientation to provide barrier-free reading zones.[78] Periodical guides should show high- contrast light-on-dark or dark-on-light lettering with characters big enough to be easily read when anyone approaches.[79] Pictograms simplify periodical guide messages.[80] But periodical guides--even those highly readable by patrons with low vision--do not give them access to specific periodical articles, illustrations and content.

Brailled periodicals are housed in periodicals or other special use locations.[81] Brailled or tactile periodical guides[82] or pictograms lead the visually limited or blind to specialized Brailled periodicals,[83] large print[84] or talking book collections.[85] Special reading or recording equipment orientation is needed. Maximum individual reading effort is required for low-vision patrons to read.[86]

Reserved Reading Rooms

Designated reading areas, reading rooms and reserved collection management limits periodical and other title movement to specific library locations. This carefully planned placement can decrease reshelving labor costs depending upon reading room location and distance from periodicals and the stacks. Reserved reading may be in separate library rooms where periodical collections surround patron readers. Surrounding patrons with the close-in periodical collection may be aesthetically pleasing to the majority of readers and librarians but visually distressing to low-vision patrons. Patrons with low vision generally require special lighting controls, a neutral or light background and the ability to reposition reading surfaces for close-in viewing. Each of these requirements reduces the utility of being surrounded by periodicals where individual lighting cannot be controlled or where complex or distracting visual background cannot be eliminated. This also suggests that any reading room, area or reserved collection also provide study carrel options to respect patron preferences and needs.

Brailled or tactile periodical guides or pictograms lead the visually limited or blind to specialized Brailled periodicals, large print or talking book collections.

Library Patrons With Disabilities

Restricting periodicals to the reading room minimizes issue loss or damage. So does reading area supervision when done by an observant librarian. Hand-carrying stacked periodicals to a reading area is difficult for people with mobility or upper body movement limitations. Constant librarian emphasis must be placed on the comfort of the physically challenged while infosearching and during their reading room use. Effective reading room furniture and arrangement consistently reduces patron frustration and the real possibility that the physically challenged will have a negative "library attitude." A negative library attitude by any patron directly increases their probability to "act out" in the library, refuse further librarian offers of help, to mishandle periodicals, or not return to the library--especially not use the reading room or area service.

These rooms or reserved areas disallow or severely limit some disabled patron access to photocopying services when photocopiers are not nearby. Photocopiers located in reading rooms or areas without adequate equipment ventilation, sound buffering or an alcove generate heat, noise and light effects that may disrupt patron reading. There is a constant tradeoff between the librarian's ability to monitor and control unauthorized photocopying and patron periodical photocopying service. Patron net information gain may be determined largely by photocoping more than titles charged, or read within the library and not charged.

Reading Tables and Seating

Library reading is more comfortably done over time while sitting. Prolonged standing while reading becomes uncomfortable for all--particularly for the mobility-limited.[87] Chairs and tables in periodical reading areas or library reading rooms are arranged to limit pedestrian distance between shelf and a comfortable place to sit and read. Reserved collections often do not provide immediate area reading chair or table access. Reading rooms without comfortable furniture for prolonged reading are a patron disservice and an unnecessary barrier to free periodical reading. Reading area seating, including designated accessible seating, provides a minimum of one fully wheelchair accessible fixed seating space at table or study carrel in the periodical area.[88] **Designated wheelchair accessible reading areas, reading rooms or reserved collections are situated along wheelchair accessible routes that interconnect with other library service areas.**[89] Minimum clear accessible route widths should be maintained throughout designated periodical reading areas to assure safe wheelchair passage and turning capability.[90] Reading-area furniture positioning should provide generous space between users beyond wheelchair minimum designated clear route widths.[91] Without extra turning space between reading tables, wheelchair users bump into surrounding objects or others in reading areas.[92] Doorways leading to reading rooms must also be wheelchair accessible. Study and reading areas should provide at least five percent (5%) fully wheelchair accessible fixed seating and tables.[93] Thirty-six inch (36") minimum clearance between reading tables permit wheelchair traffic--but wider clearances enable wheelchair movement in reading table areas.[94] Turning space in reading table areas should permit 180 degree (180^0 turns within 60 inches (60") for wheelchair positioning at the table.[95] Librarians observing wheelchair user needs at reading tables may effectively use access dimensions larger than the ADA-minima required.

Library Service Areas

137

Wheelchair users find positioning at fixed reading table seating difficult compared to movable seating. Reserved wheelchair seating table spaces should provide clear floor space, making roll-up and roll-under reading, study and writing easier.[96] Fixed or movable reading tables should have knee clearance 27 inches (27") high, 30 inches (30") wide and 19 inches (19") deep for wheelchair users.[97] Study or reading tables should provide clear knee space underneath for wheelchair users but not be too high for sustained comfortable reading. Table height is from 28 to 34 inches (28" to 34") above floor surfaces accommodates wheelchair users.[98] Reading tables are a part of the library's fixed seating plan.[99] A substandard library fixed seating plan provides more room for books than people. Patrons must stand to be served through that poorly planned library, thereby increasing patron numbers served but reducing each patron's library stay. Any infosearcher making the trek to the library has less satisfactory net information gain. Librarians may be satisfied through increased numbers of patrons "served" but patrons have underlying dissatisfaction with actual services "gained." Disabled patrons may choose to be silent with inadequate library accommodation, but that does not mean they are satisfied with library service.

Patrons with disabilities are likely to put all library seating to heavy use. Under normal conditions "...they may drop or fall heavily into the seat; lean far forward and put full weight on the front of the arms when rising; grasp the back of a chair as a brace when walking; fall to one side on sitting and rising; or shift weight frequently both while seated and on rising (Phinney, 1977, 235)." All of these physical challenges to reading table, seating and library furniture requires them to be "industrial strength" in construction and maintenance features to serve well a diverse library patronage. It should also be noted that sitting into a deep, comfortable library reading chair requires a different set of physical capabilities than rising up from such seating.

At reading tables other seated readers reduce wheelchair service route passage width with their extended limbs. Personal effects on the service route, in reading areas or on reading room floors limit physically challenged mobility. Others less challenged can step over. Some physically challenged cannot. Designated wheelchair accessible reading tables display the international accessibility symbol.[100] People using wheelchairs may not be able to move heavy reading chairs to reposition themselves to read. Chairs used by the ambulatory sometimes block reading table wheelchair use. The ambulatory tend to rest legs on repositioned chairs at reading tables, blocking others from full table use. Double-chair use is tolerated until wheelchair users or other physically challenged require that table area. Others often naturally defer during wheelchair approach, displaying sensitivity to their disabled peers. Prolonged reading in stack aisles is anticipated but can be minimized through subtle architectural design and reading table arrangement. Adequate stack lighting increases reader safety.[101] Preferential reading table lighting subtly moves readers from stacks to reading tables. Tables and seating near the stacks promote reading outside stack aisles, thereby reducing prolonged stack aisle occupancy.[102]

Disabled patrons may choose to be silent with inadequate library accommodation, but that does not mean they are satisfied with library service.

Library Patrons With Disabilities

Carrel Service Areas

Library carrels provide reading table, stack, periodical and vertical file aisle reading alternatives while limiting patron distractions in those busy library areas. Effective carrel study or reading habits can be taught and librarian modelled. Library carrels allow infosearching and reading in relative privacy.

Some may not prefer carrel use since this furniture is somewhat confining to patrons with physical challenges, such as those who use walking aids. But all patrons must have a library choice among study and reading site options. When librarians preempt the disabled from avoiding carrels, they isolate the disabled from others and discriminate against their right to freely choose reading, study, or viewing sites. Patrons with cognitive or physical challenges can read in public reading areas or in private library carrels. It is their right to choose where they read.

Librarians redirecting the disabled only to study or computer carrels in place of open reading tables subtly convey an "unwelcome in the library" or "don't mix with nondisabled others" or even an "avoid being rejected by others prejudiced against the disabled" message. When librarians redirect disabled patrons only to computer carrels, they suggest "don't operate computers in public because you are disabled." None of these harsh or discriminatory messages are librarian-intended, but sensitive patrons interpret librarian redirections to carrels in those terms. People with disabilities elect to use study carrels not designated specifically for disabled because of personal, not librarian, preferences.

Reserved Carrels

Some library carrels are provided on a reserved basis. Patrons must understand carrel reservation conditions. Reserved carrels designated for use by the disabled may be used by others until the disabled rightly demand and expect priority access. But disabled-patron demands for reserved carrel access increase patron conflicts and resentment. Each patron with disabilities must decide what potential conflicts with others will result when these personal demands are made.

Crowded seating and reading tables distract readers, limit collection searching and detract from quality reading time. Carrels alleviate reader crowding, increase individual reading opportunities and at the same time limit library noise while reducing visual distractions to help readers concentrate. Fully accessible and reserved carrels for patrons using wheelchairs, like reading tables, offer knee clearance and clear floor space, enabling prolonged reading, study or writing after easy roll-up, roll-under or repositioning. Study carrel reading and writing work surfaces may be too high for sustained wheelchair use without adaptations. Yet auxiliary aids and service users cannot be "confined" by library policy only to carrels unless all others with the same specific equipment brought to the library are also so restricted. Carrels provide controlled lighting by moving light direction and intensity beyond overhead or ambient light sources. Lighting controls should be accessible and placed no higher than 48 inches (48") to 54 inches (54") above floor level, enabling

Patrons with cognitive or physical challenges can read in public reading areas or in private library carrels. It is their right to choose where they read.

control forward or side reach from the wheelchair.[103] Some carrels provide a better environment for use of auxiliary aids and services. "Wet" carrels with electrical power outlets allow personal assistive listening device, taped text, and audio recording use. "Dry" carrels lack electrical outlets for specialized personal or library equipment use. Wet carrels may be used extensively for library computer equipment infosearching applications.

Computer Carrels

Librarians orient disabled patrons to select library equipment they need for information gain at computer carrels. Librarians observe and assist patrons with disabilities, on request, with the growing variety of library-provided or personal assistive devices. Complex patron decisions must be supported with library resources and with librarian expertise at a progressively wider array of complex equipment used in computer carrels. Carrels and equipment may present inherent access problems for some patrons with physical challenges. At orientation, it may take extra effort to help those patrons with disabilities understand specialized library equipment use conditions.[104] The disabled can confuse their right to access equipment with the special handling required of everyone for effective and appropriate computer equipment use. Computer carrel orientation should include specialized equipment and appropriate computer technology use. A minimal but real risk exists for damage to computers, keyboards, monitors, printers and other equipment while reading or improperly operating them. Due to limited library computer experience, some disabled patrons may be unaware or reluctant to use specialized computer carrels and the assistive equipment available there. Technology is relatively hidden in computer carrels and not be readily patron visible or accessible from service routes. Specialized carrels should be clearly shown on library maps.

People with physical or multiple disabilities may be limited to computer-equipped carrels that provide their only access to information gain while maintaining daily activities supplemented through library help:

> The PC can be the window to much of the world for the blind and others with vision problems. It offers new hope, as well, to the deaf, the voiceless, the slow learner, the mentally retarded, to people with brain injuries, and most dramatically, to those contending with severe mobility problems...Those with multiple disabilties need computers not only to learn and work, but also to communicate with their families and friends. For the blind or hearing impaired, the quadriplegic, and the victim of cerebral palsy, the computer is a ticket to personal accomplishment and economic independence, as well as freedom from the isolation that often accompanies disability...Unfortunately, the same technology that offers so much power is sometimes an effective barrier to access to information in the library (Edwards, 1989, page 22).

A fundamental library barrier is the competition between patrons for library services and collection information. Professionals may not consider patron competition when planning effective, barrier-free accommodation. Since library service competition is a barrier, the effects of competition must be carefully considered. Computers providing access to patrons with wheelchairs may be overused by others when others are present and waiting for extended periods. Computer access time limits are an excellent library policy for all patrons, with full consideration for those with disabilities. This situation is constantly librarian-monitored and adjustments made on an individual basis. Computer carrels are high-demand library sites compared to study carrels and should be carefully planned to permit user supervision in order to guarantee fair, nondiscriminatory access. Computer carrels positioning throughout the library should be monitored to assure full access for all. Providing accessible computers means at least one wheelchair accessible computer per library floor. Patrons with disabilities thereby join their nondisabled peers as computer technology "haves" rather than being library technology "have nots."

Patrons using reserved carrels avoid leaving personal belongings in carrels for prolonged periods and are careful to remove personal assistive devices, printouts and diskettes. Computer programs are returned to main menus and computers turned off. Patrons remount equipment dust covers and return library software. Libraries may not have evolved effective personal effects controls or policy. With increasing numbers, patrons bring their own technology that must interface with library technology. Libraries must carefully consider the implications of personal effects on library computers. Personal effects stickers control for library software and computer equipment "shrinkage." Special personal effects security use stickers may be attached to personal assistive devices and personal software at entry to permit equipment and software removal from computer carrels on library exit. The same security use stickers control unauthorized removal of library property.

Computer Carrel Lighting

Effective computer carrel lighting must meet both patron reading and screen viewing needs. Computer carrels are not lighted for work surface or lap-reading but for viewing monitors. Carrels block or control overhead lighting or other light sources reducing ambient light during computer use. Lighting may be appropriate to avoid monitor glare and facilitate keyboard use, but may not assure adequate reading illumination. White-panelled computer carrels maximize overall illumination generally without adding to monitor glare while assisting patron print reading at computer carrels. Print reading at computer carrels is at cross-purposes with monitor viewing. Monitors equipped with glare screens and swivel bases enable frontal, but not side viewing. Patrons must reposition for frontal viewing. When a monitor is moved to meet the needs of one user, the next user may need to reposition monitor, keyboard and other carrel equipment. Continuous repositioning and accelerated wear increases the likelihood of equipment damage. Yet this is an inherent requirement to meet the needs of the physically challenged and their diverse needs.

Appropriate Library Computer Technology

Overall computer use may be more effective and appropriate when patrons with disabilities indicate to librarians what library technology works best for them. And that personal "best fit" library technology may be reserved for computer carrel use only. A primary library objective is to provide patrons microcomputer and other appropriate technology that enables independent print and microform access.

Technology purchases without careful local studies validating computer user needs may leave library technology very much underused. Computer technology for the disabled may be significantly underused without proper orientation. Yet once patrons are oriented to technology, use will increase, along with increased demand for library technology access. This drives libraries to purchase more technology to meet higher patron demands.

Computer Carrel Work Surface Space

Prolonged study at computer carrels is counterproductive since carrels have very limited reading surface space. Unintentional keyboard entries are made while handling titles. Books stacked in computer carrels further limit work surface space. Keyboards can be mishandled by placing reading material on the keyboard surface. Keyboards interfere with face-on book reading. Lap-held books fall off and must be retrieved from the floor. Lap-held books interfere with keyboarding and viewing the monitor while at the same time keeping the reading place. Users frequently reposition themselves during prolonged computer use. Chairs at carrels must swivel to allow for repositioning to do different tasks. With each repositioning effort, movements are restricted to the computer carrel's relatively small floor, chair and work surface space. Repositioning away from the keyboard helps to read but then increases keyboarding reach. Repositioning for reading or for keyboarding or monitor viewing all impose physical demands that increase patron fatigue. When patron fatigue occurs infosearching is decreased and computer mistakes increase.

Library Service Areas

Reserved Computer Carrels for Wheelchair Users

Reserved computer carrels are fully accessible for wheelchair users who may otherwise find it difficult to use library computers without designated disabled reserved access. Wheelchairs require roll-up and roll-under seated access during reserved carrel computer use.[105] Carrel surfaces may be just right for print reading but too high for wheelchair user sustained keyboarding. The work surface must be lowered for keyboarding or provide dual working surfaces with a pull-out keyboard tray at a lower work-surface level. Computer controls are accessible when placed no higher than 48 inches (48") above floor level within easy wheelchair user reach.[106] Without roll-up access reserved computer carrels become effective library information barriers for patrons using wheelchairs. Accessible computer locations on library maps show equipment and also assure wheelchair accessible service routes.[107]

Librarians help patrons using wheelchairs checkout software from storage areas or placed on reserve. Spilled diskettes are not easily reached or recovered from the floor by a person in a wheelchair. They must turn to place the objects in rear-mounted backpacks or tote bags and recover them without spilling. Librarians help retrieve diskettes to computers when loose diskettes fall from containers or dust jackets.

Wheelchair accessible library computers show the international symbol for accessibility guide with priority access given to the disabled at all times.

Reserved wheelchair accessible computer carrels show the international symbol for accessibility[108] guide with priority access given to the disabled at all times. Reserved computers, monitors and printers should be only at wheelchair accessible carrels.[109] Wheelchair users may find it difficult to reach and extend forward from a sitting position to operate computer controls. Some reposition to the right or left and access computers from the side while maintaining torso balance during keyboard or mouse operation or use forward-[110] or side-reach for disk drive and software access.[111] Electric wheelchair users may have more difficulty operating computer equipment with arm, hand or finger movement limitations. Manual wheelchair users may also lack arm, hand and finger strength and coordination for keyboard or mouse operation. People using wheelchairs tire more quickly during computer monitor reading than reading from print media. Librarians help patrons using wheelchairs access library computers as needed and only on patron request.

The Visually Impaired At Reserved Computer Carrels

Low-vision readers choose reserved computer carrels and bring along personal magnification devices for vision augmentation.[112] Limited peripheral vision requires repositioning reading matter for extreme close-up viewing. Frequent keyboard- or monitor-repositioning is distracting to others unless done at a more private computer carrel.[113] Brailled or large print material reading from computer carrels may be the blind or visually-impaired patron preference. Low-vision readers find less auditory distractions at reserved carrels and fewer friendly interruptions by the curious or solicitous. Others may use high technology specialized equipment available only in designated carrels. While the nondisabled are free to use reserved carrels, the disabled still have priority access.

Enlarged Print Technology

Enlarged print technology is often based at reserved computer carrels for low-vision print access. Simple hand magnification devices may be used without recourse to more sophisticated magnification technology. Closed circuit television systems such as the APOLLO laser and VISUALTEK systems provide video

Library Patrons With Disabilities

camera, light source, magnifying lens and monitor to produce enlarged print at the monitor. Conventional library print sources can be placed on a reserved carrel-based movable table under a library camera that produces enlarged computer screen print displays on oversized library monitors.[114] Screen magnification software is also available to be displayed on large monitors.

Hard Copy Printout Enhancements

Hard copy printout enhancements suitable for low-vision users may be added in designated reserved computer carrels for personal hard copy Braille.[115] Library print material can be scanned, then read aloud via synthetic speech or translated to Grade II Braille and presented as hard copy Braille by an embosser. This technology mix may not be possible at home due to the prohibitive personal technology expense.[116] Other patron accommodation in the reserved carrel includes library-owned scanners and optical character recognition (OCR) scanner software converting text to synthesized speech and/or screen output with magnified images displayed.[117] Personal laptops with hand scanners brought by the patron give them access to print information at all library sites. Then patrons move scanned files to reserved computer carrels for display on larger library monitors. A standard of library service suggests increasing the number of oversized computer monitors, particularly at reserved and designated sites where other assistive technology will be used by the visually disabiled.

Computer Printers and Hard Copy Access

A computer-proficient patron is librarian-oriented to make a printout when hard copy is needed. Printouts are a more permanent source of information that are portable for patrons with disabilities. Printouts are library information take-outs without the need of a library charge card. Library computer and printer use requires computers or printers at accessible tables or study carrels. At least one printer-equipped terminal should be fully accessible to the seated physically challenged during printer operation. Printer stands should be no higher than 28 inches (28″) to 34 inches (34″) for ease of paper tearoff, manual paper feed and other printing operations.[118] Printouts are taken with the user. Accessible library printers require stand placement and cable connections near the computer. Library printer use requires table-mounted printer placement on wheelchair and walking aid accessible tables or study carrels.[119] At least one table-mounted printer should be fully wheelchair accessible among other available printers. Table-mounted printers are placed 28 inches (28″) to 34 inches (34″) above floor level for ease of paper tearoff, automatic paper or manual paper advance and other printing operations.[120] Printers should be located between computers on display tables with printer cabling that does not block wheelchair accessible service routes.[121]

Local area networked (LAN) computers can be dispersed throughout the library and may be distant from actual printout access. Patrons may be required to move from the computer terminal to other service areas to pickup printouts there. For some physically challenged, that distance between terminal and printout access is a significant library distance barrier. Automatic printer switching may be required. Improper printer switching, when library required, loses patron printouts by directing printouts to dysfunctional printers or to printers completing other print jobs. Patrons may not understand that print jobs are completed in the order entered into printer memory buffer. Local Area Network (LAN)

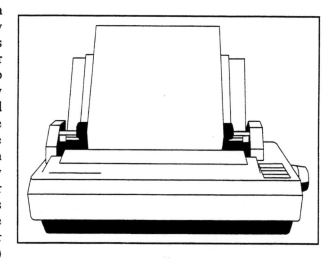

mounted printers avoid patron printer switching requirements and permit multiple library computer user access to the same printer. But some libraries have multiple printers on the LAN that allows printout misdirection. Multiple users may not select and take away their own printouts, but others.' This leads to major patron- and patron-librarian conflicts without clear printout site specification that is both patron-accessible and patron understandable.

Patrons need to know how to request librarian help when printer problems occur. The most frequent librarian printer intervention request is for paper replacement, followed by printer ribbon replacement. Laser printers require frequent paper tray reloading. Reloading trays is not a patron responsibility but does interrupt and delay information printouts. Printer adjustments, reloading paper feeds, changing ribbons or cartridges and other maintenance are librarian duties, not patron activities. Computer printers are high-maintenance equipment requiring continuous librarian support.

Plain paper stock handling may be more disabled library patron manageable than impact printers requiring fan-fold paper. Printouts are often difficult to read when impact printer ribbon changes are needed or when laser printer cartridge replacements are librarian deferred. Fan-fold plain white or greenbar paper often lacks a nonglare finish and high-contrast printout qualities needed for effective low-vision patron use.[122] Fan-fold printouts are less readable over time than laser-printed plain paper because of their tendency to fade. Plain-paper printouts are the preferred library service standard. Printers have paper storage feeding systems that function properly without fan-fold paper drift across the floor. Paper floor drift is a particular frustration for walking aid and wheelchair users who value their printouts but cannot access them it at floor level but destroy floor-positioned paper during their necessary mobility movements. Wastebaskets placed near the printer enable unneeded printouts and paper alignment tearoffs discard following normal printer use. But wastebasket height must not exceed 48 inches (48") for effective reach by wheelchair users. Laser technology provides consistent quality printouts generally more visible and readable than impact printers and at a faster pace. Laser printers may not need library noise containment systems required for other impact printers. Patrons often print to legal-size paper stock when desiring letter-size printouts. Earlier printouts may have been designated for legal-size without current patron knowledge. Patrons must request librarian plain paper reloading and not attempt it themselves.

Computer Carrels or Special-Use Equipment Rooms

Designated reserved computer carrels housing specialized equipment provide single-site access to highly specialized library technology such as Compact Disk-Read Only Memory (CD-ROM) technology, online catalogs, FAX machines, optical scanners, laser printers, reading machines, or closed-captioned video players. People with restricted hearing can operate telecommunication devices for the deaf (TDDs) at computer carrels or in specialized rooms. The library must determine what special equipment expense underlies disabled patron equipment access at the computer carrel or in the specialized room. And specialized rooms inherently separate the disabled from others.

Personal Laptop Computers and Multi-Media Output

CD-ROM-based multi-media is now disabled accessible using library computers or personal laptops crosslinked to library multi-media output devices. Libraries must plan for additional CD-ROM title special collection access for all patrons including those with disabilities. Libraries should also plan to accommodate patrons with disabilities who bring their own CD-ROM titles to the library by placing playback equipment in designated listening areas. The library must also establish guidelines for personal CD-ROM titles brought in that are consistent with other library policy regarding personal videos, audiotapes and other technology.

Patron Health and Safety At Library Computers

Prolonged monitor viewing has been shown to promote eye fatigue.[123] The visually impaired, for example, must practice vision conservation by avoiding prolonged monitor viewing. Workers report various stress factors and symptoms with prolonged computer use.[124] The library has no legal requirement to introduce stress reduction measures for patron computer users who are not also employees. Patrons are presumed to be short-term or incidental computer users during infosearching. This is a questionable presumption when actual computer use is compared between librarians and infosearching patrons. Patrons may spend more time at library computers than most library workers.

A worthy library service standard is to provide all accessible computers with wrist rest guards, static charge pads, monitor glare screen dampeners, and ultraviolet radiation screen protection to reduce potential computer-use stress for employees and patrons alike.[125]Static guards at keyboards, at the computer base, and underlying other equipment setups prevent static discharges when anyone first touches computer equipment. Battery-operated electric wheelchairs can initiate computer-damaging static discharges. A wheelchair user's body and the rubber-wheeled chair together act as a natural condensor when rolling over statically-charged library carpeting. Static discharges can instantly damage sensitive computer equipment causing greater damage than any other computer misuse event in the library. While not an intentional patron misuse problem, the solution remains with the library to establish and maintain preventative static discharge safety measures.

Protecting Library Computer-Based Information

Library computer system software on floppy diskettes or hard disks can be overwritten when program configurations do not limit patron direct data access options. Patron direct software access restrictions are imposed and only write-protected data disks are used that are patron accessible. Patron data overwrites to library data are sometimes self-correcting when patron software versions brought in do not match with library software versions. Librarians can intervene when software locks up the system to correct data version incompatability. But version imcompatability is not a library system-wide data access management solution. When these problems are systematically resolved by the librarian, both patron and library needs are better served and library data protected.

Patrons who bring in personal data disks may unknowingly import computer viruses if library computers are not equipped with automatic virus detection and removal software. Viruses introduced move on to other library computers without viral control software automatically screening all data disks. Virus onscreen protection alerts can be ignored or defeated by sophisticated patrons. Any further keyboard activity will cause eventual and total library computer system failure. Networked library computers must have network virus precautions to prevent total library computer system failure.

Static discharges can instantly damage sensitive computer equipment causing greater damage than any other computer misuse event in the library.

Librarians As Computer Maintenance Workers

Access to library computers is in part directly related to their being prepared by librarians. Disabled patron access to library computers does not include basic computer orientation for booting the computer, handling floppy disks, using software appropriately in disk drives, and formatting or copying files. These preparations are reserved for librarians setting up library computers for daily use before patron computer access. Librarians, in this sense, become computer maintenance workers. Nor does library computer service orientation include reviewing patron ability to boot computers, access disk drives or software. These functions are also already done by the librarian.

Initial librarian computer preparation for general public use throughout the day includes providing a working cursor or main menu access for patron keyboard responses. Midday or end-of-day powering-down computers,

parking hard disks, saving programs and other utility activities such as reshelving software media are librarian followup tasks. Saving daily work progress in software files is usually not necessary since patrons access library information without the need to save retrieved information in software format.

Newspaper Service Areas

People identify newspaper sections in the library to compare local, regional and national issue coverage, requiring skilled reading. Finding library newspaper information often means using newspaper indexes, determining publication frequency and reading specific newspaper issue dates. Newspaper readers may require librarian help to interpret information found or be assisted with personal reading.[126] Library newspaper subscriptions should far exceed personal patron subscriptions to provide a more extended news reading service than available at the disabled patron's home or workplace. There are many national disability group newspapers not routinely subscribed to by the library that may be of specific interest to, and extensively read by, disabled patrons.[127]

Newspapers should be positioned for comfortable personal reading distance. Pages must be folded or positioned without tearing them. Newspaper finish and contrast quality varies greatly per page. Page finish usually requires hand magnifier use by patrons with low vision[128] and special lighting controls.[129] The severely nearsighted move newspaper surfaces very close to read them effectively.[130] Copy quality is librarian-monitored and misprints rejected before newspapers are installed in holders or shelved. Large print newspapers are made available just as other newspapers are displayed.

Some patrons are disoriented when newspapers are in disarray. They may refuse to further search for needed newsprint information.

Holders are removed without tipping newspaper racks. Newspaper rack placement avoids exceeding wheelchair user forward- or side-reach requirements.[131] Forward-reach at racks should be no higher than 48 inches (48") for wheelchair users reading newspapers from holders[132] with a 54 inch (54") height side-reach maximum.[133] Holders on rack supports use wooden dowel bindings and center clips to hold newspapers in place. Holders challenge some disabled readers to reach newspaper racks. Rack labels are used on holders requiring sideviewing before selection. Repositioning for sideviewing to select newspapers is difficult for some with disabilities. Labeled holder racks minimize head repositioning.[134] Rack labels may not match titles when newspapers are replaced out of order.

Some patrons are disoriented when newspapers are in disarray and may refuse to further search for needed newsprint information. Shelves and stacked newspaper issues with sections out of order require special librarian attention. In many libraries newspaper reordering is not a high priority. Newspaper spillage is minimized when stacked newspapers have shelf backdrops. Newspaper vandalism is caused when readers remove page contents, tear out advertisements or sections, reducing newspaper utility for subsequent users. Another barrier to library information is thus imposed on patrons with disabilities by others lacking equal information access sensitivity.

Talking Newspapers and Magazines

Among the diverse types of assistive listening systems (ALS)[135] in libraries are talking newspapers.[136] Newspaper recording services are available for low-vision patrons or others experiencing daily, weekly or periodic newspaper access problems.[137] Talking newspaper "readers" are often patrons with low vision, or the "print disabled."[138] Newspaper recording services are a significant library accommodation.

Serial Listing Services

Serial listings catalog the periodical collection and provide bound periodical location information for all. Serial listings are a supplement to patron mental maps. Without serial listings, it would be daunting and exhaustive in most medium-sized periodical collections for patrons to remember how to find specific periodicals. And periodical collections constantly change, necessitating constant patron mental map changes.

Replacing "serial" and "serial listing" during patron orientation with terms such as "magazines" or "newspapers" makes them easier to understand. Library science terminology such as "serials" or "serial listing" is, for many patrons, an unnecessarily difficult terminology barrier.[139] Professional librarian terms used in patron discussions and in library signage should revised to reduce "library terminology overload." All library patrons will quietly appreciate this special library support to improve public relations and library/patron communication.

Multiple serial listing copies throughout the library provide maximum barrier-free serial access for all. Serial listing placement for patrons with disabilities in mind also provides better serial access for others. Serial listings should be carefully placed along accessible service routes for wheelchair users and for other physically challenged.[140] All wheelchair accessible furniture surfaces where serial listings are placed should allow maximum 48-inch (48") height forward-[141] and 54-inch (54") height side-reach.[142]

Serial Listing Migration

Serial listings are placed assuming users will stand, read to search and move on--thereby providing a quick information orientation. Walking aid or leg prostheses users must be seated to effectively read serial printouts, even for short periods. Since serial listing printouts are very portable, they tend to "migrate" away from their original placement. They are often left at nearby seating. Serial listing migration to other sites is a normal patron infosearching activity. Some patrons with disabilities cannot take notes at the serial listing site and must transport the listing closer to the source material sought. While serial listings have been misplaced at many sites within the library, and even some have been removed from the library (without exit control measures), some libraries have resorted to extreme measures. Among these extreme measures are physicaly chaining serial listings to specific sites. The chain, chord or heavy duty wire used limits reading access to the length of the containment, makes serial listings handling more difficult for the mobility-limited and endangers wheelchair users whose equipment may get caught up in the securement. Serial listings should be returned to their original placement for ease of use after disabled patrons read listing content. Seating and furniture at serial listing locations should be strategically placed for ease of seated reading. For patron safety, no other measures should be library-imposed to limit serial listing migration.

Serial Listing Handling

Standard serial listings are thick, bulky computer printouts using fan-fold paper in heavy guage paper or plastic jackets. Wire- or metal-pin binding allows frequent serial listing updates. Errata change sheets are inserted before the entire printout is revised. Dated serial printouts are removed and replaced with updated versions. Until revisions are printed and bound, actual serial listing content may have limited patron utility. Dated serial listings for all patrons are information barriers.

Reading bound computer printout serial listings requires further special consideration for those with disabilities. Bulky wire-bound computer printouts require special handling to avoid bent or dislocated pages and page fallbacks. Leaving serial printouts open and face-down damages fanfold paper bindings and loosens pages. Pages frequently tear out after normal use, causing missing serial information. The more serial listings are used, the sooner they become damaged in this way. Heavy and bulky printouts are easily dropped, causing further damage. Dropping or mishandling printouts may be a common and unavoidable event for anyone with restricted arm movements. "Greenbar" paper bond serial listings are oversized library books and must be treated and handled as other oversized titles.

Computer serial listing printouts on oversized "greenbar" paper may not be readable by low-vision patrons. Plain white bond printouts increase serial listing visibility and makes for easier reading. Periodical location codes should be designed to be highly visible and easily read through column arrangements across the printed page. Columnar arrangement shows serial number, periodical title, bound periodical year-ranges designated by shelf location, and the years periodicals have been microformed. The library should insert a serial listings reading guide on the inside cover of each printout to assist patrons to interpret columnar information as well as show a periodical service area map to assist with locating specific periodicals. An oversized book handling insert may also be added to provide heavy book handling guidelines.

Too much serial listing information is often displayed to be handled effectively by many patrons for each serial entry. Readers are visually distracted by patron-irrelevant information on serial listing printouts. Noncustomized mainframe serial printouts show information in cryptic format. Much serial information display is of use only to librarians. Patron format needs may not be evident in printout formats chosen. Serial listings are "user unfriendly" without format changes that simplify reading and help users find specific shelf or microform media locations. Will serial listing printouts be dictated by librarian or patron needs?

Library Patrons With Disabilities

The Reference Service Area

Personalized help for patrons with disabilities may be provided to make reference the central library barrier-free information access zone.[143] Orientation encourages information retrieval using reference sources. With orientation users locate the reference desk, find the reference librarian, state reference needs, and follow professional recommendations.[144] The reference worker may accompany users[145] or respect the preference of some disabled individuals to do independent infosearching.[146]

Librarians answer questions, help all patrons think through search strategies, and give directions to requested information. Experienced library workers wait while patrons read and think before assisting further. Reasonable library accommodation may, and often is, most successful when subtle.[147] Reference help for patrons with disabilities does not include preemptive librarian judgments about patron information needs. There are many ways librarians can be sensitized to information stakeholders with disabilities.

For some disabled patrons, reference resource selection, gaining information and obtaining reference answers may be an unplanned or random process.[148] For example, patrons with learning disabilities may continue to randomly search for information in inappropriate reference sources or locations for information following orientation. Some may continue unsuccessful searches without asking for further reference help.[149] Others require reorientation or full library support while infosearching.[150] It is the patron's obligation during library orientation to identify him or herself as having a disability.[151] Librarians are not responsible for accommodating those who refuse to identify their library-relevant disabilities during or following orientation.[152] Adapted reference orientation also is an ADA-defined patron free choice.[153]

Patron Reference Skill

Coming to the library with a clear personal information need is a great help in removing any information barriers and an effective guide to getting reference help. Interpreting information by applying critical thinking and problem solving is a successful search requirement. Yet reference collection independence may not indicate patron reference skills.[154] Reference workers may not be able to communicate with some patrons with disabilities.[155] Some librarians provide irrelevant information based on personal emotions or misconceptions about disabled-patron information access needs, not on the basis of patron information requests.[156] Librarians may not listen to specific queries or may fail to understand user reference needs if that patron is disabled, in the opinion of the librarian.[157] When these librarian-dictated events occur, then disabled-patron dependence on librarian help is maintained.[158] Librarians as gatekeepers can themselves be barriers to information stakeholders with disabilities. Proactive librarians do not anticipate special patron reference needs but patiently wait and respond to specifically requested information. No librarian does the patron's own thinking or supplements fundamental research skill development beyond the stated reference needs of the user. Librarians otherwise limit patrons with disabilities by overhelping.

Coming to the library with a clear personal information need is a great help in removing any information barriers and an effective guide to getting reference help.

Library Service Areas

Reference Format Alternatives

Information in print, radio, film and video formats must apply to the patron's own information needs. People select current titles, wait for new orders or returned titles, or use interlibrary loan. Information is personally valued when it is appropriate to patron self-defined needs. People compare and contrast personal information found by reference workers or interpret library information independently. Collections are patron-selected and patron-judged for accuracy, completeness, bias, prejudice and stereotypes without librarian input, unless help is requested to validate the information selected. Patrons may have disabilities only in the library context that would dictate alternative media format access needs.[159] Librarians are sensitive to disabled-patron format requirements. Gunde (1991) reminds us that the Americans with Disabilities Act requires:

> ...both publicly funded and private libraries [as]... public accommodations must provide services and equipment necessary for readers with disabilities to benefit from the library's reference materials, which usually are not available in accessible formats from any source. This can be done through making staff available to read material to patrons, the acquisition of reading machines and text-magnification systems, or through other means depending on the needs of the patron (page 100).

Patrons driven by format dependency must select personally-appropriate sources or modify reference questions before effective information gain.[160] Interpreting information in accessible formats is an absolute right for the disabled, as it is for all patrons.[161] Successful patrons have widely varying competency levels for doing basic library research.[162]

Patrons with speech disabilities experience difficulty making information needs known and may avoid interacting with librarians.[163] Research questions are not well-formulated or expressed.[164] Reasonable accommodation including auxiliary aids and services[165] ensures that communication between reference workers and patrons with disabilities of speech or language is as effective as communication between librarians and others.[166] But facilitating communication between librarian and patron still places the responsibility on the patron for infosearching content as stated by the patron. With reference service, many patron questions can be answered for information gain.[167]

Other Reference Accommodation

Help comes with subject or specific media item search consultation, guidance to media subject areas, or direction to specific titles. Librarians retrieve and handle specific titles or patrons retrieve titles themselves.[168] People are helped to negotiate stack, periodical, paperback, vertical file, study carrel and audiovisual storage aisles. Patrons are oriented to read audiovisual, vertical file or periodical end- and front-shelf guides or shelf-identifiers and guides are read for them.[169] Patron support includes using newspaper holders, finding fiction and nonfiction paperpacks, and using paperback title waiting lists. Reference directs patrons to audiovisual study or computer carrels, or to find and initiate appropriate use of listening areas, listening rooms, or reading tables. Reference workers guide patrons to return titles to book trucks and to avoid reshelving. Help does not have to be "state-of-the-art" but is enough to enable patrons with disabilities to successfully interact with librarians during library searches.[170]

People are helped to negotiate stack, periodical, paperback, vertical file, study carrel and audiovisual storage aisles. Patrons are oriented to read audiovisual, vertical file or periodical end- and front-shelf guides or shelf-identifiers and guides are read for them.

Walking Aid Users In Reference

Reference services for leg braces or artificial leg users, or for cane, crutch or walker users, are accommodated based on their stated, not implied, physical challenges.[171] Reasonable accommodation includes shelf reach and handling print or nonprint titles. Completing searches and finding primary and secondary sources or doing more than a superficial search is difficult for persons using walking aids who cannot reach all needed shelves without help. Walking aid users may have no difficulty taking research notes or writing research outlines and bibliographies to produce information but only after that information has been physically accessed. Seated reach to titles or help from the librarian is generally required. Prolonged standing access to reference sources is not recommended for walking aid users. Standing reach above shoulder level is not likely without dropping titles. Circulation and checkouts for walking aid users require assistance to carry and process titles.

Librarians need not acquiesce to unnecessary disabled-patron demands.[172] Some who cannot carry media themselves effectively use shoulder- or walker-mounted backpacks. Policy should include authorization to use backpacks in the library as needed. Backpack use in libraries without magnetic title exit security for patron personal effects control is often restricted or backpack inspections may be required before departure.[173] Walking-aid users are helped by securing print and audiovisual media from shelving or storage areas and moving media to circulation for charging titles and backpack placement.

The Learning Disabled In Reference

Individuals with learning disabilities (LD) may require help for appropriate reference service.[174] The LD require specific reasonable library accommodation:

> ...a learning disabled student may have had so many bad experiences with teachers, librarians and peers who mistook LD problems as symptoms of laziness or stupidity and refused help that the student may be afraid to come up to a librarian at all...Be...available to LD students on an as-needed or appointment basis (Power, 1989, page 215).

Reference and Patrons With Developmental Disabilities

Adults with mental retardation or developmental disabilities (DD) may need personalized help to select materials that develop concepts in logical sequence, have no distracting parts and provide much concept repetition to be understood.[175] These cognitively disabled patrons may need help selecting quality titles reflecting their stated or directly implied information needs. Their selected titles may not be appropriate from the librarian's viewpoint, but title selection is an absolute patron right.[176]

Reference services may be in greatest DD demand in late afternoon, night, or early morning hours around work and transportation schedules.[177] Caretakers may be reticent to bring DD persons to the library because they mistakenly believe attendants will be held responsible for library fines.[178]

Cagle (1983) advises planning reference services specifically for the developmentally disabled:

> Planning reference services for the developmentally disabled population, service-providing agencies, advocacy groups, advisory councils, regional, state and local agencies, and policy and budgetary level decision makers in a time of fiscal constraints for libraries is a challenge which will continue to confront library administrators... Reference librarians "who are the first-line information officers for the general public," should join other concerned human service providers in identifying needs and providing appropriate services (Page 266).

Library Service Areas

151

Reference for the Blind

The blind are at a serious disadvantage when seeking reference service.[179] These reasonable accommodations are provided for patrons with visual impairments:

> Qualified readers, taped texts, audio recordings, Brailled materials, large print materials, or other effective methods of making visually delivered materials available to individuals with visual impairments (ADA Handbook, III-79).

Tactile learning using Braille-based library technology gives access to reference print information.[180] The reference collection can include Braille books, Braille dictionaries, Braille signage,[181] Braille documents, even tactile letter information in elevators and on Brailled library guides.[182] For the blind, text-to-speech (Kurzweil Reading Machine)[183] or Braille technology (Optacon[184] and Viewscan[185]) are important library technology accommodation options. Because much information is visual, the blind may experience many infosearching problems. The blind are often referred to as the "print disabled."[186]

Paper Braille Copier (PBC) technology permits PBC-equipped remote patrons producing paper Braille print media to send and receive Braille via modem-equipped library computers. The Cranner Modified Perkins Brailler[187] (Maryland Computer Services, Inc.) prints computer keyboard input to conventional paper Braille. Hard copy Braille is produced at the patron keyboard or sent over modem to similarly equipped libraries. This technology permits conventional cassette audiotape storage media and retrieval, as does electronic Braille.

While hearing, the blind cannot see the written word or view library audiovisual information conventionally. Hearing may be the primary learning channel for patrons with visual disabilities although tactile information is a very close second. Listening services, using videotape or audiocassette players, are important information sources. Auditory information such as "talking books," "talking newspapers" and "talking magazines" provide patrons supplemental information.[188] Synthesized speech devices translating printed text into computer-speech are useful if library reference services are appropriately equipped.[189]

Reference and the Hearing Impaired

Hearing reference librarians can be contacted who are competent in American Sign Language (ASL). But the ASL competent librarian may not be a reference worker. And most hearing impaired patrons do not use ASL to communicate with others. Because reference work is often telephone-intensive, reference by telephone may be the only critical link possible with patrons with hearing impairment when face-to-face communication does not meet their reference needs. Without a patron volume control telephone or hearing aid compatible telephone intermediary, some patrons with hearing impairment are not effective infosearchers in the library.[190] Volume control-equipped, or adaptive telephones, are identified by map and library signage depicting a telephone handset with radiating sound waves.[191] The hearing impaired are reassured reference help with library adaptive telephones that enable both inbound or outbound calls. Libraries with adaptive telephones can be used within the library, and between library service areas, for patrons with hearing impairment. They can more easily contact librarians in all library service areas, not face-to-face, but by amplified speech using the library internal telephone system. Adaptive telephones on the patron side should be linked to librarian phones. Adaptive telephones shown on library maps and in library telephone directory listings should be close to, or in the reference area, since reference workers often are patron direct service providers.[192] Peer helpers or qualified interpreters associated with the hearing disabled assist patrons to express reference needs.[193] Kruger (1984) suggests:

> The hearing impaired patron is often the "invisible patron," since communication is the main barrier to that individual. Library staff must be able to communicate with the deaf

Library Patrons With Disabilities

patron in sign language. Telecaption devices and telecommunication devices are aids that help the hearing impaired, and these should be in the reference area of the library so that the patron can obtain reference service by telephone at least. Also visual aids, such as slide-tape orientation programs, should have captions as well as recorded sound (page 9).

The Americans with Disabilities Act also describes:

> Qualified interpreters, notetakers, computer-aided transcription services, written materials, telephone handset amplifiers, assistive listening devices, assitive listening systems, telephones compatible with hearing aids, closed caption decoders, open and closed captioning, telecommunications devices for deaf persons (TDD's), videotext displays, or other effective methods of making aurally delivered materials available to individuals with hearing impairments (ADA Handbook, III-78).

Special Collections

Special collections have been recommended <u>for</u> patrons with disabilities.[194] Displays about a disabling condition or collections separated from the main collection have also been suggested.[195] Professionals must carefully consider the implications of special collections specifically for disabled patrons in the library context. The issues are complex. The <u>ADA Handbook</u> (1991) does not clearly address or recommend reasonable accommodation alternatives:

> In choosing among available methods for meeting the requirements of this section, a public entity [library] shall give priority to those methods that offer services, programs and activities to qualified individuals with disabilities in the most integrated setting appropriate (ADA Handbook, II-59).

Establishing special collections appears not to offer services in the most integrated library setting. Special collections are by definition segregated collections. Another test may determine whether special collections specifically for the disabled provide "...services, programs, or activities readily acessible to and usable by individuals with disabilities" (ADA Handbook, II-58). While special collections by design may be relatively more accessible and usable by disabled patrons, such collections are created based on the assumed need of categories of disabilities, not specifically for individuals with disabilities. This categorical approach is invalid. Special collections may further isolate disabled patrons, and not at the same time better inform them. Special collections for the disabled draw attention to patron differences rather than to their similarities with the nondisabled.

Hodges (1989) addressed the special collection interfiling issue:

> In all libraries, there is a discussion at one time or another on special collections versus interfiled materials. The entire collection should be made available with assistance provided by library staff. Setting up a special area for [disabled] patrons, staff, and parents [of the disabled] will limit their selection. To incorporate the idea of mainstreaming at the library, materials added should be cataloged and shelved in their normal place (page 467).

Special collections established and based on assumptions concerning disabled patron information needs are examples of librarian stereotypical thinking. Librarians are cautioned in the ADA not to build services for patrons with disabilities based on myths.[196] And for librarians to think that any disabled individual will think, act or infosearch like all others with that same disability is wrong. Special collections inherently afford disparate treatment on the basis of disabilities and are ADA-prohibited.[197]

Special collections <u>about</u> disabilities that are intended for general public access may not be valid either. Special collection creation assumes permanence in the overall collection, requiring the public interested in disability topics to go to the special collection, thereby limiting entire collection infosearches. Intensive searches on disability topics quickly exhaust local collections and extend the infosearching to regional, statewide, national or international collections. Temporary disability information library displays have greater general public impact, generating topical searches, further reading interest, greater disability awareness, and possibly increased public sensitivity to patrons with disabilities. Since the display is temporary, the disability focus is on relevant information and not on any assumption that the disabled individuals would desire to read or "exhult" in their own disability.

Collection Diversity

Evaluating diverse reader needs is an ongoing librarian concern. Acquisitions may not show a balance in the collection without consideration of format diversity, collection currency, duplicate titles to cover special needs user demand, formats and reading levels that span reading, viewing, listening and comprehension levels. Titles that span the spectrum of related issues and points of view, and titles of current interest to readers with disabilities all must be considered together.[198] Format diversity is a common library reader characteristic. The disabled patron may have specific format requirements.[199] Readers with disabilities require current information in appropriate and accessible formats.[200] Multiple copies of popular titles cover reader demand. Titles that represent a wide reading, viewing, listening and comprehension level spectrum accommodate the diverse patron group libraries often serve. Sources balancing all viewpoints surrounding information issues are also an important accommodation, particularly to those readers with pressing personal issues associated with their disabilities.[201] Popular titles maintain reader interest and do not restrict the disabled from an active reading life.[202] Collections must represent format and content diversity.

Responsible Book Handling

Patrons with disabilities, like the general public, may regularly engage in improper book handling.[203] The physically challenged routinely drop, bend book spines backward, tear or bend pages while paging through, or engage in other book mishandling.[204] Some handle titles improperly due to other associated physical challenges. For example, manual wheelchair users must have clean hands when contacting library print media--but wheelchair wheels are dirty and gloves for better wheel grip become soiled under normal use. Soiled gloves must be removed before handling library books. Proper book handling in the stacks, while moving titles to reading areas, to circulation and to use over normal loan periods, reduces print media wear and damage. All patrons can properly handle library titles or be assisted to do so. People may not gently turn title pages at corners or avoid tearing pages when browsing.[205] Holding books without spine damage, book cover damage and avoiding open book stacking is difficult for some with mobility or upper body strength limitations. Patrons using arm prostheses frequently damage book covers and pages even while demonstrating special book handling care.[206] Some individuals may need repeated orientation to establish proper title handling, avoiding book damage beyond normal use. Individual orientation to properly handle titles is a requirement for many with disabilities as it is for the general library public.[207] Book handling is based on individual patron book handling experience and history, not on speculation, stereotypes and generalizations about the disabled.[208] Special collections may receive greater title mishandling--not because those titles are designed for disabed access but because some disabled may compete among themselves to read titles meeting their needs.

Patrons with disabilities, like the general public, may regularly engage in improper book handling.

Library Patrons With Disabilities

Paging through titles is also difficult or results in page damage. Prosthetic arm users may use computer-based information more readily than print media avoiding title damage altogether. Title damage from dropping, scratching, denting or unintentional misuse is library monitored. Unintentional resource misuse reduces title access for others. All patrons have the right to access library information. None have the right to vandalize library titles.[209]

Illustrated bookmarks distributed throughout the library encourage proper book handling and show how to avoid improper book handling practices. But illustrations cannot effectively describe all the diversity in patrons and their book handling problems to be overcome. Caring for library titles requires supervision and careful librarian modelling. When librarians properly handle titles--then patrons will likely do the same. Some with disabilities, no matter how careful they are handling titles, still damage them without librarian accommodation.

Dictionary Service Areas

Dictionaries are typically located and displayed in reference areas and adjacent to reading tables for convenient use. Orientation includes dictionary stand access, turning dictionary pages and using thumb indents when provided. Disabled patrons acquire the "dictionary habit" after successful dictionary orientation. Orientation includes proper dictionary care while reading or notetaking. The print disabled experience major barriers at the reference dictionary.[210] Reference accommodations include page turners[211] or qualified readers or interpreters for dictionary information access.[212]

Dictionaries are sometimes difficult to negotiate for the physically challenged. Hand, arm or finger prosthesis users experience difficulties using oversized dictionaries or when securing or moving shelved dictionaries to reading areas. Dictionary damage results when some are unable to turn through pages, tear pages during use, or let large sections fall back onto folded pages. Oversized dictionary negotiation requires tight-grasping or wrist-twisting beyond some physically challenged capability to access pages or thumb indents.[213] Corner page-notching leads to accelerated dictionary wear. Pictograms should caution patrons not to take notes directly on dictionary surfaces and to avoid writing on or marking dictionaries.[214] Quicker dictionary replacement cycles can result from patron mishandling and from legitimate infosearching wear and tear. Dictionary replacement may be driven more by the evolution of the English language than by any normal wear and tear to provide word reference information.

Dictionary Stands

Patrons using hand magnifiers often attempt to move dictionary stands closer for easier reading.[215] Dictionary stands are considered ADA-accessible when surface levels are 28 (28") to 34 inches (34") above floor level.[216] Stands for dictionaries are typically 22 inches (22") wide, 16 inches (16") deep and 44 inches (44") high for adolescents or adults. Wheelchair users at seated reading levels cannot read dictionaries on stands displayed 34 inches (34") or higher but can view and handle dictionaries displayed at 28 inches (28"). Dictionary stands often do not provide adequate patron forward-reach from a wheelchair.[217] Side-reach[218] is better negotiated when dictionaries are on stands or tabletop displays. File cabinets with dictionary stands on top are usually beyond patron forward- or side-reach requirements from a wheelchair.[219] Moving dictionary stands should be discouraged and alternative library service provided. Columnar-mounted dictionary stands are inherently unstable and should be replaced by stands or tables with four-sided bases.

Revolving dictionary bases pose unique problems for the physically challenged. Once movement is initiated, dictionary momentum must also be cancelled. Bases wide enough to accommodate dictionaries must remain stable while patrons adjust to any open- or closed-book position.

Encyclopedia Service Areas

General and special purpose reference encyclopedias must be fully accessible since the unskilled begin and end infosearches using only encyclopedias. Full barrier-free access includes identifying encyclopedia scope and sequence, selecting appropriate encyclopedias, and locating and interpreting information found. Some choose to copy verbatim from encyclopedias while others treat them as one of many worthwhile sources. Reference librarians counsel the young to use single source encyclopedias as a last resort.[220]

Encyclopedic collections are typically shelved and displayed in reference and adjacent to reading tables. Orientation includes finding the reference area and the encyclopedia collection. Patrons are oriented to use specific oversized, shelved encyclopedias after recognizing alphabetical title series arrangement. Proper orientation for title care while reading or notetaking also requires effective oversized encyclopedia handling skill. People lacking upper body strength have difficulty managing if encyclopedias are oversized. Wheelchair users at seated viewing levels reach forward for encyclopedias displayed on shelves 48 inches (48") or higher or below 15 inches (15").[221] Encyclopedias displayed on portable stands may not give forward reach from a wheelchair without interfering with rollup to stands. Wheelchair users cannot side-reach for encyclopedias displayed on shelves at 54 inches (54") or higher or below 9 inches (9").[222] Wheelchair user side-reach can be maintained when stand displays or encyclopedia collections on reference shelves are within these high- and low-reach ranges. Handling oversized encyclopedias, using alphabetical shelving and specific information retrieval after consulting encyclopedia indexes is part of the process. As with oversized books, encyclopedia damage results when patrons are unable to turn through pages, tear pages during use, or let large sections fall back onto folded pages. Note-taking on encyclopedia surfaces marks page surfaces. How to avoid marking page surfaces by note-taking is illustrated using area pictograms.[223] Page-turning equipment may be an effective solution.[224]

Atlases and Map Service Areas

Finding oversized atlases and flat maps requires locating map file cabinets or asking librarians for direct access at special map displays. Non-circulating atlases and flat maps shelved and displayed in reference are also provided at reading tables in or near reference stack aisles. When not displayed on atlas stands or on walls, flat maps are stored in special map file cabinets. Viewers are instructed to manage wide, deep pullout shelves during inspection, or map removal. Even with great care, large flat maps can be damaged during handling. People must learn to avoid bending, folding or damaging pages and check for turned page layering and alignment. Laminated maps prevent fingerprint damage or tearing during handling. But lamination increases viewing map surface glare or reflectivity.[225] Laminated maps are slippery during handling. Atlases with tab markers enable quick paging to map sections but may be difficult to manage for arm, hand or finger prosthesis users.[226] Heavy, oversized titles are often dropped when carried by hand.

General and special purpose reference encyclopedias must be fully accessible since the unskilled begin and end infosearches using only encyclopedias. Full barrier-free access includes identifying encyclopedia scope and sequence, selecting appropriate encyclopedias, and locating and interpreting information found.

Special Atlas or Map File Cabinets

Viewer accessible atlas or map file cabinet storage is considered modern oversized title display technology. File cabinet storage does not permit effective atlas- or map-viewing or page- turning unless these oversized titles are first removed. Map area ventilation drafts also disturb some maps not held down flat, further damaging them.

Large open spaces are required to turn atlas pages or position maps for viewing. These file cabinets provide spacious flat viewing areas on top. File cabinet top-viewing surfaces are considered work surfaces. There patrons manipulate oversized atlases or maps where flat surface viewing height is 10 inches (10") below average elbow height for standing users. Wheelchair users' work surfaces are at 26 (26") to 32 inches (32") above the floor.[227] Most map file cabinet storage units that have top-viewing surfaces above 32 inches (32") above floor surface may not be wheelchair accessible. For a wheelchair user, seated work surface is 26 (26") to 32 inches (32") above the floor.[228]

Atlases and maps in storage units can be lifted to the cabinet top for easier viewing. Careful lifting is required. Atlas and map handling shown on pictograms assures patron and media safety. Lifting oversized atlases or flat maps to a cabinet top is a physically demanding task when titles frequently exceed 5 pounds deadweight.[229] OSHA lifting requirements are met by employees but do not require patrons to observe these same safe lifting procedures. This deadweight book lifting may be beyond the capability of persons using wheelchairs and others with upper-body mobility limitations. Pictograms in the file cabinet storage area may guide patrons away from using cabinet tops while map reading and toward better, safer viewing alternatives.[230]

Map file cabinets equipped with large pull-out shelves extend further toward the viewer than many other library files or shelves. Extended map file cabinet shelving left open blocks working aisles and service routes.[231] Clearance for low vision users is a temporary threat to walking or head room safety.[232]

Users should be cautioned against pulling map shelves to the full-open position by area pictogram warnings.[233] Full extension causes the unsecured map file cabinet to become unstable. Map shelving moves off track guides, and the cabinet tips forward, causing personal injury. Map file cabinets should be secured to the floor to avoid tipping. Moving oversized atlases or flat maps to reading tables requires patron balance, upper body strength and determination. Librarians help patrons with disabilities remove maps or atlases and carry them to the reading area after help is requested. Maps should be reshelved or returned to original map file cabinet locations by library workers, not by patrons.

Floor-mounted atlas stands for adults must be 30 inches (30") wide, 27 inches (27") deep and 44 inches (44") high with slanted tops for displaying opened atlases. Youth atlas stands should be no more than 30 inches (30") wide, 27 inches (27") deep and 26 inches (26") high. Wheelchair users lack forward-reach for page turning or viewing[234] when atlases are displayed on stands higher than 48 inches (48") above floor surfaces or require patron side-reach above 54 inches (54").[235] Floor-mounted atlas stands may not provide enough knee clearance for wheelchair users. Stands also must meet wheelchair forward- and side-reach

> **Users should be cautioned against pulling map shelves to the full-open position by area pictogram warnings. Full extension causes the unsecured map file cabinet to become unstable. Map shelving moves off track guides, and the cabinet tips forward, causing personal injury.**

requirements.[236] Floor-mounted atlas stands are unstable for walker or crutch users who must balance by leaning on them while standing. Pictograms should warn against leaning against floor-mounted atlas stands.[237] Table-mounted stands must have 27-inch (27″) height, 30-inch (30″) width and 19-inch (19″) depth knee clearances for wheelchair users.

Library Wall-Displayed Maps

Wall-displayed map placement height is dependent upon the size of the map that when centered would be at typical patron eye level. Map details and the size of the print or other map characters may require lowered wall-displayed map placement for effective patron reading and viewing. Wall-displayed map surfaces, when laminated, are not damaged when patrons touch the map. Laminated or surface-protected maps can be lowered further to accomodate viewers using wheelchairs. Wall-displayed maps are considered the most viewable for people who can walk to vertical map surfaces or roll up in wheelchairs for close map inspection. However, wall-map displays with furniture, shelves or other objects in the foreground prohibit viewers from moving to the map for closer inspection. The severely nearsighted may be required to move close to recognize wall map characters or features.[238]

Wall-displayed maps are considered the most viewable for people who can walk to vertical map surfaces or roll up in wheelchairs for close map inspection.

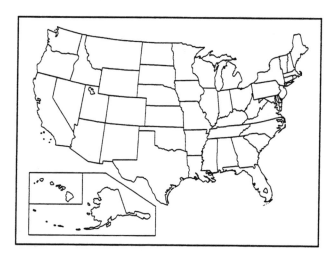

Vertical Files

Orientation enables people to retrieve needed information from vertical files by locating the file area, finding specific file shelves and folders, and reading content independently. Readers use vertical file-end and front-shelf guides as well as folder labels independently or with librarian help. File shelf guides should be clearly visible on vertical files with high-contrast lettering and dark characters on a light background or light characters on a dark background.[239] After the vertical file area has been located, end- and front-shelf guides must be read or an exhaustive file collection search mounted. Users find vertical file content by using alphabetized folder labels. Specific vertical file folders are located by reading labels and handling folder content. People who are library-oriented demonstrate vertical file care.

A unique mission for vertical files may be to offer single- point-of- access disability- related information.

Vertical files are user-ready topical searches. A unique mission for vertical files may be to offer single- point-of-access disability-related information. There are hundreds of disability interest and support groups who distribute information in brochure, pamphlet, flyer, handout, newsletter and other non-book formats. Single point of access in the vertical file provides comprehensive infosearching support. The volume of incoming solicited and unsolicited information arriving at any library from diverse disability information groups must be managed effectively to be patron accessible. This information forms a natural information database and the basis for library ADA-coordinator service and consultation. Local, regional and nationwide disability information sources arrive in libraries in paper format. To convert print data to full-text database access that provides locally relevant information is a slow process. Until this text print to electronic access conversion occurs, the vertical file disability special collection helps direct access to disability-related information.

Vertical File Handling

Vertical file help may often be requested by the disabled.[240] Vertical files are typically legal-sized with frames for hanging folders and tab labels alphabetically arranged. For successful use, tab and folder visibility is required. Users should avoid pulling out file drawers to their full extended position. Pictograms should illustrate avoiding overextended drawers.[241] Cabinets become unstable and tip forward when fully extended and not secured against tipping or when fully extended file shelving often moves off track guides. Vertical files must be positioned to permit more than one user at a time. Files should be clustered together facing outward to provide ample floor space.[242] Instruction for vertical file use should restrict readers from moving file information beyond designated areas. Photocopy services should provide designated vertical file return shelves, containers or procedures. Patrons are shown vertical file special content handling and returns to include refolding pamphlets after reading or resequencing folder contents for the next user. Pictures require resequencing. Maps require refolding for the next user. File content can be patron rearranged without significant information loss for the next user. Holding transparencies by edge-mounting rather than finger contact-with-acetate is suggested. Some posters require tight rerolling and return to oversized vertical file cabinets or special vertical file cylinder, map, and poster storage. Oversized art imposes unique folding or handling requirements to be carefully returned to vertical files as originally stored. Continuous handling unavoidably damages oversized art in vertical files. This special-care handling may be beyond the capability of some physically challenged patrons. Legal or oversized files provide more convenient pamphlet, clipping, picture, folded map and transparency access but not a particularly convenient presentation. Large storage cabinets with shallow drawers, useful for storing large art prints, maps, posters and oversized art are often located in vertical files as a variant to conventional vertical file cabinets.

Library Service Areas

Wheelchair User Vertical File Access

Vertical file media poses major access problems when shelves are positioned above seated person eye-level and files require reach to other extended shelf levels. Inaccessible vertical files are those when a high forward-reach over file shelf front becomes a viewing obstruction or when extended forward-reach is required by users from wheelchairs.[243] Files above wheelchair user eye-level at 54 inches (54") or higher have limited utility.[244] Vertical files below 9 inches (9") above floor level offers limited wheelchair side- or down-reach. Vertical refiling is not recommended policy for everyone. File baskets or book carts can be used by the patron to return vertical files before library workers refile. But library worker file replacement must be frequent, to allow others to do new vertical file searches unimpeded by earlier infosearches.

Vertical File Users with Limb Protheses

Patrons with arm, hand or finger protheses may experience difficulty at vertical files. Opening vertical file drawers, removing file folders, paging through contents, handling flat paper content, even picking up a dropped paper from tables or the floor is difficult. Handling flat maps or unfolding and refolding papers, charts, illustrations, posters, pictures, photographs, pamphlets, and clippings are difficult and may cause media damage. Vertical file materials cause handling difficulties for those with upper body, hand, arm or finger challenges. File contents falling from folders can be avoided when closed-end folders are used. Contents spill easily from open-ended file folders during handling. File handling barriers include the requirement to use both hands, employing tight vertical file folder grasping while removing files, grasping contents during carrying to avoid contents spilling from folder ends, and wrist-twisting to lay file contents on flat reading surfaces.[245]

File handling barriers include the requirement to use both hands, employing tight vertical file folder grasping while removing files, grasping contents during carrying to avoid contents spilling from folder ends, and wrist-twisting to lay file contents on flat reading surfaces.

Vertical File Patrons Using Walking Aids

Vertical file positioning enables patrons with leg prostheses to readily access file shelving, folders and information located at mid-level. Their independent access to high- or ground-level files is problematic. Vertical files at difficult- to-reach locations are retrieved by librarians. Vertical files requiring patron standing for long periods are not recommended. Walking aid users at vertical files may require reaching file shelving, folders and information from a seated position to avoid prolonged standing. While standing at vertical files is required temporarily, walking aid users should be provided seating there as well. Pictures, pamphlets, clippings and maps may be difficult to handle, carry or use unless library help is forthcoming.

The Stacks

Librarians must consider what, in addition to personalized adaptive orientation, the library can do for patrons with disabilities to make the stacks a working, barrier-free information service area. Reference workers orient visitors to use stacks, enabling effective and safe title retrieval.[246] Stack orientation includes locating and reading stack-end and shelving guides before retrieving titles. Without readable stack-end and shelving guides, the diligent infosearcher with disabilities must tour the stacks one aisle and one shelf per aisle at a time. This "touring phenomenon" among some patrons makes the stacks a cumbersome information gain site and at the same time a barrier-rich information access zone. Libraries without readable stack guides reduce disabled patrons to this low information access level.

Library Patrons With Disabilities

Stack Browsing

While stack browsing is an inefficient and time-consuming search process, it is regularly done by many patrons. Included in that group are some patrons with disabilities. Some browse stacks without specific title or subject search strategies. Browsing cannot be limited to prevent frequently blocked aisles. Ambulatory patrons or patrons using wheelchairs find no stack shelving space to place a title to read, requiring that they stand while reading. Even they are considered stack browsers. The term "stack browsers" is not operationally defined. Anyone who lingers in aisles to read for prolonged periods might be considered a stack browser. Walking-aid users browse using book step seating but ordinarily cannot be seated on aisle floors without help from others to stand up. These conditions fail to assure barrier-free movement in stack aisles. There are minimal patron mobility problems in stack aisles when only one stack browser occupies an aisle and no one else needs to move through or join the other browser. When multiple browsers are present and the aisle user mix includes patrons with disabilities, someone will not be able to access the titles they need. Librarian attention assures barrier-free movement within stacks for all, in single or multiple aisle-user settings. Stack aisles are an equal access service area but do not provide equal access under all possible conditions without librarian intervention.

Stack Arrangement

Stacks are often located near periodicals. Stack layout determines information access for patrons with disabilities while others may search while not considering stack configuration or experiencing barrier movement. Stack access varies greatly for disabled persons.[247] Free-standing double-faced stacks placed in rows of four to six sections allow firm, loaded stack securement that prevents mobility-limited patrons who fall against stacks, spill media and injure themselves. Single-faced shelving units placed around outside library walls allow greater floor space for wheelchair movement and better stack aisle traffic flow.[248] Stack placement allowing occupants to be viewed along aisles reduces supervision problems. Not all libraries will be retrofitted to make patron stack visibility their highest priority. Libraries serving children and youth are more likely to select stack occupant visibility configuration when patron supervision is paramount. Patrons not seen except from stack ends may not be helped by librarians otherwise ready to assist.

Stack End-Guides

With card catalog information in hand, people locate shelves to search for specific subjects, authors and titles.[249] Libraries provide diverse stack collection access including fiction, nonfiction or special titles using the Library of Congress (LC) or the older Dewey Decimal system. Stack users recognize the LC system as the modern standard print and nonprint classification system. People are helped to find specific print collections in the stacks when they request help. End-guides lead patrons to specific stack aisles for specific title searches. Brochures show maps to help patrons with disabilities find stack locations.[250] Persons with mobility limitations may need librarian or peer accompaniment for stack use.[251]

Stack aisles are an equal access service area but do not provide equal access under all possible conditions without librarian intervention.

Library Service Areas

Stack Aisles

Stacks are among the least accessible library service areas. To make stack aisles barrier-free is a challenge that requires effective library planning, patron stack aisle orientation and continuing supervision. Many barriers are associated with stack aisles and title access there.[252] Stacks must be well-lighted for aisle users.[253] But adequate stack lighting for one may not meet another's lighting search requirements. Few libraries provide rheostat lighting controls to modify aisle lighting according to individual reader requests.

Stack Shelving

Adjustable and movable stack shelving used in place of built-in-place shelving enhances collection management, title display and increased title access. Special open-stack shelving gives maximum title visibility for videotapes, compact disks, records, audiocassettes, large print and talking books.[254] Open-stack shelving also provides shelf look-through for next-aisle patron observation. For optimal title viewing and selection, picture and reference books or special interest displays are created with counter-height stacks. Counter-height stacks give maximum librarian stack user visibility and supervision.[255] Stack barriers cause some stack occupants not to access library stack information. When stacks do not allow effective patron access, library workarounds must be implemented.

Book Steps

People step up and reach highly-placed titles using book steps that provide vertical barrier-free stack access. Persons with balance or mobility limitations should not use book steps. Instead they should request help to retrieve highly-placed titles.[256] Many stack titles are beyond maximum 48-inch (48″) reach height limitations applied to other library information displays.[257] A very few dangerously climb stack shelving to retrieve highly-placed titles, ignoring book steps. Book steps are provided in aisles to redirect shelf climbers. In stack aisles book steps are frequently used as reading seats. This aisle-seating blocks others from stack access. Mobile patrons safely reach highly-placed titles using book steps. But the physically challenged lose balance when stretching upward to reach titles using book step support. Book steps with gripping action on floor surfaces limit this slipping danger. Heavy book step construction meets OSHA safety requirements but makes them often difficult to reposition and use. A warning label should be attached to each book step warning against patrons lifting them. Book steps do not address low-shelf titles accessed only by patrons bending or kneeling. Book steps are moved by patrons when low-shelf visibility is blocked. Vertical barrier-free title access is provided by book steps on upper, but not on lower, stack shelves. Stack aisle access, shelf and book reach are consistent wheelchair-user problems which must be addressed by library policy and librarian assistance. Wheechair users temporarily and necessarily block library service areas, walkways, and stack aisles.[258] Stack aisles are physically limiting when used by more than one wheelchair at a time or by a wheelchair and another aisle user. Again the stack aisle access for all is reduced when the aisle user mix includes a person with wheelchair.

Oversized Books

Many oversized books exist in the library including dictionaries, encyclopedias, art texts and large print collections as well as picture, historical narrative, art collections, science books, maps, and atlases. Oversized books are typically located in or near reference. Some may be noncirculating. Oversized books frequently require--but do not routinely include--user safe handling instructions. Orientation for oversized book use includes locating titles, reading oversized book notation at lowest accessible stack shelf locations, in temporary displays, or in reference. Placement of oversized books is possible in upper shelf stacks since stack shelf height is unrestricted.[259] Oversized books falling from high shelf placement can be dangerous. Reshelving is not recommended since books may be mishelved and thereby less available to future users. Oversized books are safely located only in the stacks at lower shelves for easier and safer patron reach.

Library Patrons With Disabilities

Oversized books require stacking orientation, with oversized books at the bottom and others arranged by increasing size to the top. For carrying, stacked oversized books slip out midstack and spill when not carefully stacked by progressive size. Handling or carrying oversized and overweight books to reading or study areas can get out of control. Oversized book handling requires tight grasping of book surfaces, twisting the wrist for balance while carrying, and strength to manage the overall task. This may be beyond some physically challenged users' capabilities.[260] Access may require help for patrons in wheelchairs whose forward-reach to the lowest shelf is not safely done below 15 inches (15") above the floor surface[261] or whose side-reach is not safely done below 9 inches (9").[262] Being unable to reach downward from the wheelchair seated position restricts patron oversized book access. Wheelchair viewing height is below 48 inches (48") for forward-viewing[263] and 54 inches (54") for side-viewing.[264] Above this level oversized books cannot be safely reached or title spines viewed. Lower shelves housing oversized books are the least accessible areas to those with mobility limitations when reaching, lifting or carrying heavy titles.[265]

People also learn to judge potential oversized book handling problems by book weight. Some oversized books are large, relatively light-weight, yet have dimensions that make handling them cumbersome. Other oversized books are heavier than 5 pounds. Overweight books present major challenges for patrons with severe disabilities unable to lift books over 5 pounds deadweight.[266] The Occupational Safety and Health Administration (OSHA) requires heavy lifting precautions for library workers--but not for library patrons. Heavy library books (overweight) with unusually large dimensions (oversized) are difficult to handle for many disabled.[267]

Moving overweight/oversized books to reading areas requires help if user requested.[268] Bringing these books to circulation for checkout and library exit may also be a reasonable request made of librarians by patrons with mobility limitations.[269] Libraries may wisely add OSHA heavy lifting precaution signage that can be viewed by patrons with disabilities before they attempt heavy book lifting themselves. Library acquisition staff should weigh books to determine if each exceeds 5 pounds deadweight or are oversized to make

Library Service Areas

them difficult for patrons to lift, carry or handle. For each of these titles, a library insert can be secured to the inside cover page that illustrates book lifting precautions, safe book handling, and how to avoid dropping oversized or heavy books to avoid personal injury and book damage. Library signage at all oversized book locations should similarly illustrate book handling precautions that can be read by patrons before they attempt lifting and before patrons can open the book to read the cautionary insert. Titles, once located, may not be reachable:

> In order to locate and retrieve a book or books from shelves or stacks the ambulant person usually faces the shelves and obtains the book from a frontal stance. A semiambulant person, dependent on a walking aid for balance, must use one hand to brace the body and retain the aid while retrieving a book with the other. If the patient wishes to scan through it he or she must either lay it on the shelf or flip through it using one hand or, if no convenient space is available, carry the material to another surface. A person in crutches finds this difficult. One crutch must be propped against the shelves, body braced against the crutch or shelving; when the book or other material is obtained it must be carried, clutched along with the crutches, to a table or clear surface (Phinney, 1977, 232).

Book Packs

When wheelchair users move, oversized books held on the lap do not remain secure. Oversized books must be carefully managed by wheelchairs users who typically rely on book bags or packs attached to the rear of the chair. Book pack placement to the side interferes with wheel grip and chair balance when packs are heavily loaded. Rear-placed book-pack wheelchair users have difficulty removing oversized books and with limited arm movements or low stamina have serious difficulty using oversized books without help.[270]

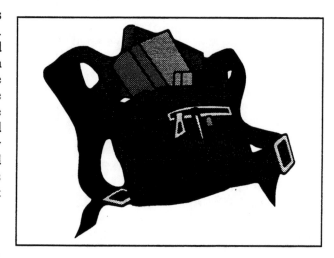

Wheelchair Stack Users

Some wheelchair users self-restrict narrow stack aisle use since they know that high- or low-stack shelving cannot be independently reached without help. They instead request librarian help to find titles. A common library scenario is for the librarian to retrieve titles in stack aisles while the patron with wheelchair observes at the end of the aisle. This scenario does not describe effective and personal roll-up stack aisle access. This process must not evolve to formal library policy which would constitute disparate treatment and violate ADA principles of barrier-free stack information access as a public service.[271] Any librarian-imposed informal wheelchair stack aisle-use restrictions must be initiated by the patron with wheelchair, not the librarian. Temporary aisle use restrictions are self-imposed access conditions between mutually agreeing occupants.

Low-Vision Patrons in the Stacks

Any library stack system must be identifiable both by reading signage and by touch. Persons with low vision do not locate titles without Braille and tactile stack system identifiers.[272] Neither the Dewey Decimal nor Library of Congress systems are useful without Braille or tactile indicators. Many blind or low-vision patrons do not read Braille. Sighted patrons can also read the effective stack system identifiers by touch if

Library Patrons With Disabilities

they care to do so. Tactile stack system signage helps everyone. Braille helps only those who can read Braille. Stack end guides must be Brailled and tactilely marked to give access to people with low vision.[273] End-guide characters are sized to be read at normal viewing distance by most users.[274] Auxiliary end guides must be added with raised and Brailled characters or stack area pictograms.[275] High contrast, light-on-dark or dark-on-light characters should only be used.[276] Consistent end-guide signage using these high contrast characters should be presented throughout the stacks.[277] Nonprint collections of interest to low-vision patrons include films, videotapes, microforms, computer software, slides, audiocassettes, audio reel-to-reel tapes, maps and globes. But these formats are not typically stack-housed and instead are available in special audiovisual collections. Nonprint collections may not have the same effective storage system identifiers as the library stacks. This demands that patrons with disabilities learn two or more stack identifier systems in order to access all the library information they require.[278] Nonprint titles without tactile, Braille or recorded stack guides are of limited use.[279] Using periodicals, Braille book collections, or talking books is problematic without Brailled directions, shelf and specific title identification. Recorded stack guides logically link patrons who can use only recorded library information to recorded stack guides that avoid requiring the patron to "read." Book steps, sitting aisle readers and other conditions restrict user stack and title access.[280] The visually limited trip over book steps or sitting aisle readers unless brightly painted for high visibility.[281]

The Talking Book Collection

The talking book collection provides an alternative way for some patrons with disabilities to "read" by listening. Talking book library collections provide recorded audio reading services to persons with low vision.[282] Magazines, newspapers and other print media are recorded by publishers, libraries, volunteer readers and other audiocassette distribution sources.[283] Audiocassettes are distributed by mail or mobile van, or are available for library pickup. Patron equipment requirements include a home audiocassette player with earphones, amplification control and access to the United States Postal Service delivery system or library mobile van delivery. Physical library access may be necessary since library policy often prohibits returning talking books to exterior book returns. Personal talking book returns to circulation may be required.

Stack Users with Limb Prostheses

The average leg-braced or artificial leg-equipped patron walks narrow stack aisles without difficulty.[284] High-shelf locations pose problems when stepping up is required. Some libraries provide library stands, ladders or book steps. Library stands allow maximum shelf reach height by providing steps and a wider base. But library stands without rails at steps and on the platform are unsafe. Ladders are not safe for general patron use and may be restricted only to librarians. The most dangerous ladder use is not facing the steps when using the treads. Pictograms on the ladder should prohibit this activity for all. Poor balance among stack users with leg prostheses when attempting to reach high-shelf locations requires them to ask for librarian or personal attendant help. Patrons who have poor balance also have great difficulty bending, kneeling and pulling up after independent reaching for lowest shelf locations. Title retrieval and aisle movement difficulties require others to help when patron requested.[285] Middle-level shelf locations cause fewer reach problems since those locations may not challenge patron balance when reaching. Some patrons with limb prostheses will lose balance when reading library titles. Patrons with balance impairment cannot be librarian-ignored. They must be comprehensively helped during their library visits. Without librarian attention, patrons who fall and injure themselves also disrupt others from the infosearching process and increase library liability.

The average leg-braced or artificial leg-equipped patron walks narrow stack aisles without difficulty. High-shelf locations pose problems when stepping up is required.

With difficulty, arm prosthesis users can complete print searches in the stacks. Primary and secondary source access may be limited due to book handling problems. Taking research notes on paper or note cards is their formidable challenge. Patrons using alternative laptops for word processing or portable manual or electric typewriters may require direct librarian attention. Recording research notes on audiocassette is a viable note-taking support alternative but reviewing tapes using audio playback disturbs other area patrons. Audiocassette controls and tape operation may require librarian intervention for effective note-taking by patrons with arm prosthesis. Patrons may be required to move to designated library listening areas when playing back recorded notes and when their equipment lacks earphone access to reduce stack noise pollution.

Stack Use by the Cognitively Disabled

People with cognitive impairments may not independently locate print media without help. Without user understanding, each patron library visit exemplifies random infosearching behaviors without probable success. The learning disabled and other at-risk patrons may engage in dysfunctional library and stack search strategies.[286] Stack titles found more by accident than by intentional searches may be their normal infosearching process. Some become confused, loiter in stacks or roam all stack aisles.[287]

Stack-Use Policy

Stack use policy or a policy that is built on a presumption concerning patrons with disabilities must be carefully reviewed.[288] Few professionals would argue that disabled patrons should be restricted from the stacks or from stack aisle access. But the net effect of librarian support may be to further restrict them. Some suggest that librarians clear the aisle of other patrons and personally assist the disabled during aisle searches before resuming unsupervised aisle service to others. Limiting stack aisles to one occupant at a time discriminates against the disabled and is prevented by the Americans with Disabilities Act (ADA).[289] Limiting stack aisle access to any class of patrons or to those without disabilities is also discriminatory. Only when stacks are restricted for all patrons is the library avoiding discrimination. But what library could function without patron stack access? Library staff would be doubled when aisle runners retrieve titles only on patron request. Stacks should be barrier-free access zones without any user occupancy limits imposed by librarians or library policy. The disabled have no automatic privileged status to receive library help unless and until information access is prohibited by library policy.[290] When policy creates de facto disabled disparate treatment, then the situation must be evaluated and disparate treatment avoided.[291]

> **Stack use policy or a policy that is built on a presumption concerning patrons with disabilities must be carefully reviewed.**

Nonprint or Audiovisual Title Service Areas

Persons with reading disabilities often find nonprint or audiovisual (AV) titles that do not require reading to enjoy, but still require reading to access. Direct librarian title reading support is required before viewing and listening can begin. Nonprint infosearching requires understanding AV formats. AV collection orientation should include helping patrons to read end- and front-shelf guides as well as finding specific AV titles. AV access also requires using library AV display equipment. Patrons must learn how to operate reading equipment for each nonprint format needed if playback will be done in the library. User orientation to safely and independently use AV equipment is a librarian responsibility. Well-oriented users independently find specific film, video or audiotape, compact disk, or record titles while often using AV labeling systems that do not conform to other print title shelving systems. Each AV title search may require separate patron orientation unless the library has adopted AV collection identifiers. Some may be unable to read AV checkout procedural guides.

Some patrons with disabilities may require supervision when they are at actual risk during equipment use.[292] Librarians become preemptive and intervene while AV equipment is being used by new equipment operators, or when personal or equipment safety becomes an issue. But being a disabled patron does not automatically confer this need for library accommodation. When AV equipment has doors, shelves or equipment half ajar, jutting out into pedestrian areas, the librarian must also intervene and correct the situation. Unprotected sharp edges are dangerous for visually-impaired patrons using the "trailing" method to identify equipment controls or positioning. Equipment that has been repositioned from conventional placement through normal use requires the visually limited to reorient for safe equipment operation. Orientation clues become confusing when equipment conditions have changed.

Help is needed for audiovisual reaching, title selection and reading titles placed within high or low shelves.[293] Patrons with disabilities should be encouraged to handle titles carefully and appropriately. Backstops added to all open AV shelving avoids titles sliding to the shelf behind. Open shelving alone or AV open shelving without backstops should be avoided. Reading devices and personal readers are appropriate auxiliary aids and services that, where necessary, permit an disabled individual to participate in, or benefit from, library services.[294] Some require and ask for help to move AV titles to circulation.

Patron AV title availability is critical, whether provided from restricted storage areas limited to library worker retrieval or in open storage area public access. AV storage systems are selected after cataloging methods, circulation policies, intershelving philosophies and available library space interactions are all carefully considered. AV storage arrangement should assure fully accessible service routes with minimum clear width[295] and passing space.[296] Audiovisual aisle restrictions singling out the disabled are discriminatory.[297] Restrictions for AV use should be avoided since they may be based on presumptions as to what, in the library, a class of individuals with disabilities can or cannot do.[298] AV use restrictions must apply to all to be equitable.

Utility Book Trucks

Utility book trucks permit pulling titles and title reshelving for library workers. Any book truck without casters or not readily movable is of limited library utility. Book trucks temporarily block stack aisles or library routes during reshelving.[299] Free stack access for patrons with disabilities may already be limited. Restricted stack access occurs when improperly positioned book trucks remain in stack aisles. Book trucks not positioned at stack ends should be restricted to those currently in use by library workers. Book truck placement should also not block stack end-guide visibility or extend stack-end guide viewing distance. End-guide signage should be positioned to be readable above the average loaded book truck height for visibility. High book trucks that would, if placed at any stack-end, block stack-end signage viewing should be placed in nonpublic use areas and used only with a library stack worker present. All book trucks can be temporarily stored in nonpublic use areas. Book trucks could be used by the patron to move oversized titles from stacks, reading or study areas and on to circulation. People with upper body strength limitations or those who use walking aids are cautioned not to reshelve or carry oversized books without help and may require using book trucks when other workable alternatives are not available. Book truck users who are disabled move them to circulation and possibly even outside the library. Book truck movements may have to be supervised and the trucks retrieved from the library parking lot.

Free stack access for patrons with disabilities may already be limited. Restricted stack access occurs when improperly positioned book trucks remain in stack aisles.

Overloaded book trucks are unstable during movement, cornering or abrupt stops. Overloaded trucks are not accessible when viewing and sorting through titles not yet reshelved. Instructions and illustrations on book trucks should caution users not to move, lean on or use the trucks as makeshift step-ladders for stack shelf reach. Guide signage on book trucks should comply with uniform signage viewer distance, character height and other reading requirements.[300] Unsupervised book trucks are not patron safe. Unauthorized patron overloaded book truck movement is dangerous.

Circulation Services

Personalized help for patrons with disabilities provides circulation as a library barrier-free approach zone. Circulation is the library virtual information clearinghouse. Circulation encourages information gain for all while providing maximum internal access to the collection and external title circulation among patron members. Service area personnel orient people to the method of borrowing circulating titles while following prescribed charging and circulation procedures. Patrons locate the circulation desk, interact with circulation personnel, sign out noncirculating titles from reserve, and charge intended titles using established manual or electronic charging procedures. Manual charging procedures may differ from electronic charges and be reflected in different orientation content and emphasis. Disabled patrons, like others, may require repeated orientation to establish effective title return habits.[301] Part of circulation orientation is understanding that some titles may be subject to immediate or short-term recall and other titles will not be renewable. Patrons are oriented to return titles in the same condition as received with allowance for normal use. ADA-required and patron-requested orientation must be specific to individuals on a personal basis rather than on the basis of any disability service category.[302] Librarians should avoid anticipating disabled patron categorical needs for circulation services without a legitimate local circulation needs study.[303] Even with local circulation needs studied, disabled individuals vary greatly in their circulation service needs. Professionals orient themselves to physically or cognitively challenged individuals, not groups, to determine appropriate patron circulation help.[304] To determine circulation orientation content, librarians interact with each disabled patron and analyze circulation services actually requested and provided. Library orientation policy or content does not impose burdens on patrons with disabilities that are not also placed on all other patrons.[305]

The Circulation Desk

Circulation desks and charging lanes are often crowded areas. Libraries assure circulation desk access for all since all entering patrons must, at a minimum, pass the circulation desk on library exit.[306] [307] Circulation desks should have a maximum surface counter height of no more than 36 inches (36″).[308] Consulting with patrons with disabilities about circulation desk-specific help may be necessary.[309] Specific circulation desk help can be identified while considering disabled-patron preferences.[310] Ability to return or renew titles routinely without help or supervision is assumed. For example, patrons with leg prostheses or leg braces moving several titles to circulation for checkout may require library support. Professionals help with circulation and checkouts, carrying and processing patron titles for those who cannot carry titles themselves. Leg brace users are helped, on their request, to secure print and audiovisual titles from shelves or storage and to move them to circulation. Charging lanes are library walkways and part of wheelchair user accessible service routes linking library public routes.[311] Charging lanes offer barrier-free movement to entrances or exits and lead to interior library service access.[312] All traffic control or book security gates leading to exits should be wheelchair accessible or provide alternate, immediately accessible routes.[313] Where revolving doors or turnstiles are an integral part of the circulation exit, accessible gates adjacent to the turnstile or revolving door should be provided.[314]

Library Patrons With Disabilities

Access To Returned Titles Before Reshelving

Book trucks provide acces to returned titles before reshelving. For title return patrons are oriented to use book trucks. They are directed to book truck locations at stack ends and throughout the library. But recognizing book trucks does not mean that patrons will use them for title returns. Titles are typically left in the library, where they can be read if not checked out. Many titles are found at reading tables.

Titles in study carrels are more difficult to retrieve and reshelve because they are easily overlooked by library workers. Patrons are advised not to reshelve titles in the stacks. Patron stack reshelving may be mishelving, requiring routine librarian shelf and title reordering. Titles yet to be correctly sequenced on shelves are mishelved and may not be located by infosearchers. Returning titles not checked out at circulation to book trucks is the ideal library goal. But patrons often have another goal in mind when they leave the title in the library and do not use book truck returns.

If anyone must abandon titles, then the librarian-preferred action is for titles to be left at reading tables or on book trucks to facilitate quick retrieval and reshelving. Patrons are oriented to avoid abandoning titles in stack aisle floors, since stack aisles must remain user accessible.[315] Patrons with disabilities are oriented to use a more effective library title return system than abandonment, as are all patrons who fail to properly return titles that remain within the library.[316] They regard abandoning titles as personally absolving them from responsible returns or do not understand the concept of abandoned titles within the library until they accompany the librarian on an exhaustive search, and find someone else has abandoned their title.

Patrons with disabilities are oriented to use a more effective library title return system than abandonment, as are all patrons who fail to properly return titles that remain within the library.

Title Search Requests

Readers are helped to find titles when notshelved or when misshelved. Patrons and librarians first check temporary shelving for titles or for mishelving. If no resolution exists then circulation personnel check title, call number and author data to confirm that all duplicate copies are already checked out. If charged to another the borrower circulation places a HOLD on that title. Circulation then recalls the title. The reader is personally notified by phone and/or mail by circulation workers when the title is available. Title delivery for disabled patrons may include location delivery, perhaps outside the library, and convenient to the patron with disabilities.[317] For some disabled individuals, title searching and delivery to an accessible site is a bureaucratic nightmare. Search requests are an unfortunate byproduct of lost titles and cause considerable information access delay. Posing verbal title search requests is a challenge for the learning disabled; for example.[318] Titles not available, not charged out, and not at their appropriate shelf locations, or housed in temporary shelving, can be traced if cataloged in the collection. Verbal or written title requests drive circulation search efforts. Circulation workers inquire if titles are in bindery shipments, on other floors, misallocated to other libraries, stolen, lost or damaged, in faculty studies or mishelved. If found, the title is held at circulation, the patron notified, allowing patron pickup and conventional title charging. If not found within a specified time period, an automatic interlibrary loan request is placed to borrow from another library. But borrowing from another library is dependent on local library membership in a library network that shares collection resources. Many patron complaints originate from mishelved titles and requests for title searching and delivery to an accessible site. All this technical effort may not be patron appreciated, understood or used.

Interlibrary Loans

Titles not currently held in the local collection can be acquired through Interlibrary Loan (ILL). Automatic interlibary loan processing after unsuccessful internal searches may be restricted to patrons authorized for this extended circulation service. ILL access restrictions must be met by all patrons before services are provided. Lending libraries set rules and restrictions for ILL titles, including the loan period, renewal options, and costs. Under no circumstances, however, is access to ILL titles witheld for patrons on the basis of their disabilities. To do so would impose burdens on those disabled patrons not placed on others.[319] There can be no librarian-based presumption about what is best for disabled patrons suggesting automatic ILL processing following unsuccessful internal library title searches.[320] Any informal or unilateral librarian decision not to pursue ILL searches or remote title acquisition from ILL member libraries is a clear violation of equal information access for patrons with disabilities. Interlibrary loan title access should not restrict service on the basis of patron disabilities, but on the basis of actual title location and the willingness of other ILL members to share their collection titles.

The ILL process is frequently misunderstood. Patrons with disabilities may require explanations for the need to use Interlibrary Loan to avoid infosearching failures. Frequent reader retreat from further infosearching effort occurs at this service stage. All patrons using ILL service are consulted and preapprove costs. Fee-based ILL service cannot be provided without charge for disabled patrons when all others must pay reasonable fees. Where ILL costs are defined by other lenders, no surcharge to cover interlibrary loan services can be placed on the disabled that is not equally placed on all patrons using the service.[321] Interlibrary loan forms require librarian completion and submission for eventual title delivery. Library workers relying on patron user form completion with minimal professional help greatly reduces ILL use. The local library ILL professional contacts the reader for fee-based pickup when the title is received.

International Interlending

While it is not possible to provide every title or source in a format wanted or needed by a diverse public, given the reader timeframe and when format needs continue, appropriate format title delivery is possible using interlibrary loan or international interlending.[322] But the disabled patron, like all others, must expect to pay additional costs. Voice phone, FAX, telex, or courier international interlending requests are all expensive, compared to postage costs, between nations. Book rate shipment timeframes alone exhaust international lending periods. All available lending options may be slowed by customs authorities or slow exchange rates even for prepaid requests. Lending foreign library loan periods may be exceeded by an international lending request, making lending libraries reluctant to forward their titles.[323] The special format needs of patrons with disabilities are theoretically, but not practically, served through international interlending. Disabled-patron format dependency drives interlibrary and international interlibrary loan needs. Visually-impaired readers with special format requirements may need the local library to secure print resources that, for them, are available only through international interlending.[324]

Title Returns

Title return orientation within the library requires patron awareness of library hours, knowing dates and times when titles are due, title return restrictions, physical access to return equipment and actual title return performance. Users are oriented for the special handling required for audiovisual media and book returns during or after library hours. All are oriented to return titles without help and to accept personal responsibility as a condition for checking out titles. But unassisted returns may not be possible for some disabled patrons without other library adjustments. If patrons with disabilities cannot be oriented to responsibly return titles, librarians accept parents, legal guardians, or conservators who are responsible. The library must also fully account for disabled-patron title return challenges as a reasonable accommodation. Library acceptance of others returning titles does not remove personal responsibility for patrons to have their titles returned. Skill levels and patron responsibility for returning titles is recognized by librarians and patron skill development is systematically encouraged.

Direct personal user return to circulation during regular business hours is required for any library equipment loans, computer hardware, software, realia, display returns, and special reserve circulating collections within the library. Library policy may require direct video or audiocassette returns. Since many patrons with disabilities may already be accustomed to commercial video rental returns, this return process may be a familiar one. Arrangements can be made between local video rental stores and the library to exchange misreturned titles. Direct returns are typically permitted only at circulation desks using regular title check-in procedures. Direct return conditions are often confusing to disabled patrons.

Patrons with disabilities may not distinguish title format-specific return requirements. Blind or visually impaired patrons have difficulty locating librarians to accept direct title returns. The cognitively disabled may be confused about the proper procedure for returning different media formats unless all formats are accepted by the library in the same manner.

If patrons cannot view, read or understand return restrictions, they may not be able to comply. While ignorance is no excuse before the law, libraries may not be so constrained in their enforcement of title return policy. ADA-allowed permissive orientation and reasonable accommodation includes any special policies, handling or tolerance for title returns made for, or on behalf of, disabled individuals. When special return provisions are made for individuals with disabilities, or when specific title return procedures for a class of disabled individuals are library-designated, the library does not incur additional ADA-defined obligation to any other patrons.[325] In this instance, the ADA allows for unequal information access on the basis of disabilities in patrons.

All are oriented to return titles without help and to accept personal responsibility as a condition for checking out titles. But unassisted returns may not be possible for some disabled patrons without other library adjustments.

Library Service Areas

Patron Title Return Histories

Librarians verify checkout behaviors when readers establish return histories. Readers observe return time limits. For patrons with cognitive disabilities, time limitations may not guide actual returns. Library workers guide the cognitively disabled to return titles appropriately shaping behavior over extended periods before full return compliance can be expected.[326] Patrons with disabilities, like others, learn to return overnight titles to the circulation desk or exterior book returns within time limits and to distinguish between overnight and regular circulating title returns. For noncirculating titles, readers must return material to the circulation desk within time limits before leaving and avoid abandoning titles within the library. Returning titles to the circulation desk before leaving is self-correcting when unauthorized title exit or overdue attempts are made. For each circulation process, continuous library monitoring and orientation may be needed.[327]

Library Fines, Charges and Title Replacement

Readers should be oriented to library fines, lost title replacement charges, and grace periods. Some have argued that special handling and waiving fines, charges or grace periods are a necessary component of a sensitive staff to meet the needs of the disabled.[328] Others have suggested that helpers may be reticent to permit patrons with disabilities to charge titles for which helpers or personal attendants may be personally responsible.[329] Classifying library fine policy, title replacement charges and grace periods must not be on the basis of disabilities.[330] The disabled should be subject to the same policies as nondisabled patrons holding library passes:

> ...[the ADA provides that] requiring presentation of a driver's license as the sole means of identification for purposes of paying a library fine by check would violate this section in situations where individuals with severe vision impairments or developmental disabilities or epilepsy are ineligible to receive a driver's license, and the use of an alternative means of identification, such as another photo ID or credit card, is feasible (Miller, 1992, page 8).

Title Charging Before Exit

Self-charging is the preferred independent library service for patrons with disabilities who understand charging procedures and who verify they are leaving with intended titles. Younger patrons, or the cognitively impaired, may require librarian intervention and followup if they do not understand charging procedures or when they regularly exit with unintended titles that are quickly returned. Some patrons with disabilities may charge unintended titles to appear socially normal or to be recognized as "regular" or "mainstream" library patrons. Only patron behavior clearly indicating this would assist librarians to infer this internal patron mental state. Librarians cannot confirm, but can only infer, that this attitude really exists in individual disabled patrons. Circulation staff routinely check titles with all patrons during charging by reading aloud each title. Librarians can cooperatively determine whether an item meets younger patron individual needs and expectations. Yet each patron has the right to check out any library title.

Circulation provides help in hand-charging procedures. Manual charging may be done with the librarian writing entries into a logbook system or using an electronic wand to read the International Bar Code (IBC) book markings. The wand must point to the IBC markings to register title information. Independent charging using the wand may be difficult for some with upper limb mobility limitations, the cognitively impaired, the hearing impaired, or others lacking specific wand orientation. Librarians charge titles for patrons with disabilities who do not handle the wand appropriately. If patrons express a desire to learn how to use hand wands, then inappropriate but incremental improvements in wand handling can be expected. Library independence is encouraged in patrons and is a necessary part of overall patron infosearching skill.

Some electronic devices use laser technology to read embedded title markers and automatically charge titles. A single sweep of the inside title cover registers the charge automatically and requires different patron handling than wand use. An audible "beep" confirms that the title is charged. Opening the inside title cover to register the title is less physically challenging for patrons than using a wand. Librarians assisting patrons to charge titles using wands or laser devices on request is another important element in disabled patron library independence and personal information gain. Automated charging systems that do not require the patron to open the title cover are the preferred accessibility service standard.

Circulation desks equipped with computer monitor, keyboard and related equipment must not distract or reduce librarians from immediate patron service or cause excessive patron waits. The computer equipment should in fact accelerate checkout. Automated checkout system monitors have a swivel base for patron and librarian co-viewing while verifying intended titles. Co-viewing intended titles on the monitor is particularly appropriate for patrons with hearing impairment. Patrons with disabilities comply with library circulation procedures or face the same natural consequences as all other patrons. Patron loan status is determined at checkout and any problems identified and resolved then.

Noncirculating titles are equipped with embedded title markers that alert librarians to title status and provide a setting for patron advisement regarding circulation policy. Patrons are provided a natural "safety net" through automated circulation technology to prevent them from unintentionally leaving the library with noncirculating titles or titles not yet charged. This safety net also helps identify titles already charged but not patron returned.

Exit From Circulation

Circulation follow-up includes determining reader title selection satisfaction, alternate title access, and acquisition of titles not on the shelf through on-search status, electronic access, or interlibrary loan. A major concern is a circulation librarian determination if user-charged titles have met the disabled person's information needs. Short of charged titles meeting personal needs, did the patron engage in successful infosearches? Does successful infosearching include the need for other title searches or further access to Interlibrary Loan? Did the reader access alternative library electronic information to meet personal information needs? Must the patron remotely access the library for further information follow-up? How can the circulation librarian help?

Circulation desks are often used by patrons to assemble title collections and ready themselves for library exit. They load titles into knapsacks, book bags at the rear of wheelchairs, or briefcases, and rearrange titles for carrying comfort while exiting the library door. Mobility-limited patrons make various adjustments to prepare for exit with borrowed and personally-valued library information after successful infosearching. Book bags or backpacks enable some wheelchair users to leave the library without checking out titles, since librarians can override the security system during library egress.

> A major concern is a circulation librarian determination if user-charged titles have the disabled person's information needs.

Library Service Areas

Summary

Library service suggests librarians help patrons with disabilities in many ways, some obvious and some subtle. Librarians assess patron mobility and information access skills and evaluate the physical library layout for possible information and architectural barriers. Numerous barriers may be found from a careful overall library physical plant and collection assessment. Barrier-free service area criteria are provided in this chapter to complete a building and library access self-assessment, from parking lot to a wide array of internal library services. Specific service area standards were provided for stacks, periodical shelving, card catalog, circulation desk, reference, vertical files, study and computer carrels, reading tables, listening areas and book returns. Patron service area access includes search skills, physical and service access and accommodating librarians.

End Notes:

1. Goltz, Eileen. (1991). The provision of services to students with special needs in Canadian academic libraries. Canadian Library Journal, 48(4), 265.

2. Phinney, Eleanor. (1977). The librarian and the patient. Chicago, IL: American Library Association.

3. Neville, Ann & Kupersmith, John. (1991). Online access for visually impaired students. Database, 14,102: "Until recently such students have had to rely on human "readers" (Fellow sighted students, either volunteer or paid, who read textbooks and other assigned material aloud) to serve as intermediaries in using card catalogs and printed indexes. There are several drawbacks to doing library research through an intermediary. The reader may well not know how to choose and use appropriate search strategies and sources, and the visually impaired student will not be able to provide guidance."

4. ADAAG. Appendix B. Americans with Disability Accessibility Guidelines. In, U.S. Department of Justice. (1991). Americans with Disabilities Act Handbook. Washington, DC: U.S. Government Printing Office. Pages 4.30.3 & A4.30.2.

5. Allegri, Francesca. (1984). On the other side of the reference desk: The patron with a physical disability. Medical Reference Services Quarterly, 3(3), 73-74.

6. Ibid, Neville & Kupersmith, 103. See also, Goltz, 266.

7. Power, M.T., Rundlett, Carol & David, Myra. (1989). New challenges in helping students uncover information: The learning disabled student. The Bookmark, 47(11), 214. See also, Malinconico, S. Michael. (1989). Technologies and barriers to information access. In Effective access to information. Trezza, A.F. (Ed.). Boston: G.K. Hall. Page 132: "Traditional bibliographic access tools-card catalogs, printed indexes, and so forth although inefficient, cumbersome, and unresponsive in some cases, can, at least, be used by anyone; this may not be so for the newer electronic technologies. As electronic tools replace traditional ones, barriers will be lowered by many, but for others, newer, perhaps more formidable barriers will be erected."

8. Ibid, Goltz, 266.

9. Ibid, ADAAG, 8.4: Minimum clear aisle space at card catalogs and magazine displays shall comply with Fig.55." (Figure 55 indicates a 36 inch minimum card catalog aisle space minimum.)

10. Ibid, ADAAG, 8.4: "Maximum reach height shall comply with 4.2, with a height of 48 in (1220 mm) preferred irrespective of approach allowed." See also, ADAAG, 4.2.5.

11. Ibid, ADAAG, 4.2.6 & 8.4.

12. Smale, Rebecca. (1992). Australian university library services for visually impaired students: Results of a survey. The Australian Library Journal, 41, 203.

13. Ibid, Allegri, 74: "...having a low, rather than a tall, table, at the card catalog, with room for wheelchairs as well as chairs, would be less tiring for all patrons, as well as facilitate access by those with mobility impairments. Lowering the card catalog...will allow more disabled patrons to use these with minimal or no assistance."

14. ADA Handbook. U.S. Department of Justice. (1991). Americans with Disabilities Act Handbook. Washington, DC: U.S. Government Printing Office. Pages II-39 & III-51.

15. Ibid, Smale, 203: "The catalog facilities of most university libraries did not allow independent use by visually impaired students...students stated that their use of the catalogs was dependent on assistance, but did not specify details..."

16. Ibid, ADAAG, 4.30.4 & A4.30.4.

17. Ibid, Smale, 203: "A recurrent complaint involved crammed drawers which prevented the use of hand-held magnifiers to read the cards. These problems were apparently not widely recognized by reference staff who provided very little routine supplementary assistance with catalog searching, despite the acknowledgement voiced by most library respondents that their catalogs could not presently be used directly by visually impaired patrons and that assistance was therefore necessary..."

18. Ibid, ADA Handbook, I-63.

19. Ibid, Pinion, 27: "Public library staffs are very positive about helping individuals find what they want in a library, and if there is a disability they will (usually) go out of their way to help. However, it is increasingly being acknowledged that many disabled people (whatever the disability) wish to retain their independence as far as they can. This is understandable. A sensitive librarian will respect this, giving the necessary help as unobtrusively as possible."

20. Ibid, ADA Handbook, I-79.

21. Ibid, ADA Handbook, II-39 & III-51.

22. Ibid, ADA Handbook, II-42 & III-71.

23. Pack, Nancy C. & Foos, Donald D. (1992). Planning for compliance with the Americans with Disabilities Act. Public Libraries, 31, 228.

24. Thiele, Paul E. (1984). New technologies for the blindreading community. Canadian Library Journal, 41, 138.

25. Willoughby, Edith L. (1983). Library services in a school for the blind. Catholic Library World, 54, 120-121..

26. Edwards, Sandra. (1989). Computer technology and the physically disabled. Online Computer Library Center Micro, 5, 22-23.

27. Ibid, Edwards, 22: "Unfortunately, the same technology that offers so much power is sometimes an effective barrier to access to information in the library. As more libraries install online catalogs and close their card catalogs, users with physical and visual disabilites (as well as the rest of us) are often confronted with the need to type inquiries and press chordlike key combinations, usually while standing."

28. Roatch, Mary A. (1992). High tech and library access for people with disabilities. Public Libraries, 31, 97: "Library computer access is more effective when the library users assist in the decision making process of what access technology works best for them. As electronic print becomes a common denominator in libraries and information centers, we will see more and more machines and devices taking the places of shelves of library books. This use of electronic print in place of inkprint on paper will make libraries more and more accessible, especially for people whose disabilities made it difficult in the past for them to read the printed page... It is the responsibility of librarians and library managers to be aware of the many ways high tech can be used in their libraries for both the library users who are not disabled and the library users who have disabilities."

29. Ibid, Goltz, 266.

30. Mularski, Carol. (1987). Academic library service to deafstudents: Survey and recommendations. Reference Quarterly, 26, 478.

31. Ibid, Neville & Kupersmith, 104.

32. Powell, Faye. (1990). A library center for disabled students. College & Research Libraries News, 51, 418-420.

33. Ibid, ADAAG, 4.30.1 & A4.30.1

34. Ibid, ADAAG, 4.30.5 & A4.30.5 See also, Foster, Terry & Lindell, Linda. (1991). Libraries and the Americans with Disabilities Act. Texas Libraries, 52, 61.

35. Ibid, ADAAG, 4.30.1 & A4.30.1.

36. Ibid, Allegri, 73.

37. Ibid, Mularski, 481.

38. Ibid, <u>ADA Handbook</u>, II-59.

39. Ibid, <u>ADA Handbook</u>, II-14: "The Department...emphasizes that, although the definition would include "state of the art" devices, public entities [libraries] are not required to use the newest or most advanced technologies as long as the auxiliary aid or service that is selected affords effective communication."

40. Ibid, <u>ADAAG</u>, 8.2, 4.2 & 4.32.

41. Ibid, <u>ADA Handook</u>, I-77.

42. Ibid, <u>ADAAG</u>, 4.32.2.

43. Ibid, Smale, 208.

44. Ibid, <u>ADAAG</u>, 4.2.5.

45. Ibid, <u>ADAAG</u>, 4.2.6.

46. Ibid, <u>ADAAG</u>, 8.2.

47. Ibid, <u>ADAAG</u> 4.2.

48. Ibid, <u>ADAAG</u>, 4.3.2(3).

49. Ibid, Edwards, 22.

50. Ibid, <u>ADA Handbook</u>, I-77.

51. Ibid, Goltz, 265-266: "With regard to seating, most libraries indicated that special seating was not necessary, but four did provide special study carrels, tables, and terminals at the correct height to accommodate wheelchairs."

52. Ibid, <u>ADA Handook</u>, I-62: "Consider the preference of the individual to be accommodated and implement the accommodation that is most appropriate."

53. Roberts, Melissa Locke. (1985). Welcoming disabled readers to a new world of information. <u>Texas Libraries</u>, <u>46</u>, 55.

54. O'Donnell, Ruth. (1992b). Adapting print for improved access, Part 2. <u>Library Journal</u>, November 1, 60.

55. Lisson, Paul. (1987). Large print placebo. <u>Canadian Library Journal</u>, <u>44</u>, 5.

56. Ibid, Willoughby, 120.

57. Ibid, Smale, 203.

58. Ibid, Neville & Kupersmith, 104.

59. O'Donnell, Ruth. (1992a). Adapting print for improved access. <u>Library Journal</u>, October 1, 68-69.

60. Ibid, Foster & Lindell, 62.

61. Ibid, Neville & Kupersmith, 103.

62. Medrinos, Roxanne Baxter. (1992). CD-ROM and at-risk students. <u>School Library Journal</u>, <u>38</u>, 29-31.

63. Ibid, Allegri, 71: "Unavoidably, the reference librarian will experience a situation where a person with an "invisible" or minimal disability will be seeking help." See also, Summit, Leon. (1983). Counting the invisible. <u>School Library Journal</u>, <u>29</u>, 5.

64. Ibid, Power, 213: "Neither a casual look nor an intense look at an individual reveals specific learning disabilities. Librarians should not and cannot have the responsibility of recognizing the learning disabled student..."

65. Ibid, <u>ADA Handbook</u>, I-61 & 67.

66. Ibid, <u>ADA Handbook</u>, II-39 & III-51.

67. Ibid, Power, 214.

68. Walling, Linda Lucas. (1992). Granting each equal access. <u>School Library Media Quarterly</u>, <u>20</u>, 217.

69. Ibid, <u>ADAAG</u>, 4.32.3.

70. Ibid, Smale, 210.

71. Ibid, <u>ADA Handbook</u>, II-89 to 92.

72. Ibid, Pinion, 28: "It is important, though not essential, that a disadvantaged person knows the name of the local librarian on his or her first visit to the library. A personal contact can overcome many barriers and a thinking librarian can also plan ahead to make the service more accessible to the visually handicapped user."

73. Ibid, <u>ADAAG</u>, 8.5. "Shelf height in stack areas is unrestricted."

74. Ibid, <u>ADAAG</u>, A4.2.3.

75. Ibid, <u>ADAAG</u>, 4.30.5.

76. Irwin, Marilyn. (1992). Library media specialist: Information specialist for students with disabilities. Indiana Media Journal, 14(1), 15: "Students with disabilities, like all students, need to be able to evaluate materials to determine appropriateness for their personal or academic needs. Advising students how to maximize the available resources and utilize quality materials will ease access to information and increase the potential for appropriate lifelong information seeking behavior."

77. Ibid, ADAAG, 4.30.1 & A4.30.1.

78. Ibid, Smale, 208.

79. Ibid, ADAAG, 4.30.5.

80. Ibid, ADAAG, 4.30.4 & A4.30.4.

81. Kruger, Kathleen Joyce. (1984). Library service to disabled citizens: Guidelines to sources and issues. Technicalities, 4, 9.

82. Ibid, Goltz, 264.

83. Gunde, Michael. (1991). Working with the Americans with Disabilities Act. Library Journal, 116(21), 100.

84. Havens, Shirley E. (1987). Large print in focus. Library Journal, 112, 32-34.

85. Kuhlenschmidt, E., Swan, K. & Scholes, J. (1992). Ms. K, there's a tiger in the computer. Indiana Media Journal, 14(1), 6-10.

86. Ibid, Smale, 210.

87. Ibid, ADAAG, A4.3.1.

88. Ibid, ADAGG, 8.2: "At least 5 percent or a minimum of one of each element of fixed seating, tables, or study carrels shall comply with 4.2 and 4.32." See also, ADAAG, 4.2 & 4.32.

89. Ibid, ADAAG, 4.3.2(3): "At least one accessible route shall connect accessible building or facility entrances with all accessible spaces and elements and with all accessible dwelling units within the building or facility."

90. Ibid, ADAAG, 4.3.3 & 4.3.4.

91. Ibid, ADAAG, A4.2.4.

92. Ibid, ADAAG, A4.2.3: "This space is usually satisfactory for turning around, but many people will not be able to turn without repeated tries and bumping into surrounding objects."

93. Ibid, ADAAG, 4.32.

94. Ibid, ADAAG, 4.3.3.

95. Ibid, ADAAG, 4.3.4.

96. Ibid, ADAAG, 4.2.4.1.

97. Ibid, ADAAG, 4.2.4.1.

98. Ibid, ADAAG, 4.5.

99. Ibid, ADAAG, 4.33.3.

100. Ibid, ADAAG, 4.30.7(1).

101. Ibid, ADAAG, 8.5.

102. Ibid, ADAAG, 8.2: "At least 5 percent or a minimum of one of each element of fixed seating, tables or study carrels shall comply with 4.2 and 4.32."

103. Ibid, ADAAG, 4.2.5 & 4.2.6.

104. Ibid, Smale, 200-201: "...students listed the provision of a particular service which was not mentioned by the corresponding library [survey] respondent, or alternatively, students were unaware of services which the library respondent claimed was available...staff as well as students have an imperfect knowledge of their libraries' services, and that some services and resources are only brought to students' notice through personal discovery, rather than through fully informed reiteration by library staff and effective promotion of all available services."

105. Ibid, ADAAG, 4.2.4.1. "Clear floor or ground space for wheelchairs may be part of the knee space required under some objects."

106. Ibid, ADAAG, 4.32.4.

107. Ibid, ADA Handbook, II-65. See also ADAAG, 4.3.2(3).

108. Ibid, ADAAG, 4.30.6.

Library Service Areas

109. Ibid, ADAAG, 8.2.

110. Ibid, ADAAG, 4.2.5.

111. Ibid, ADAAG, 4.2.6.

112. Ibid, ADA Handbook, II-53.

113. Ibid, Lisson, 5.

114. Ibid, Lisson, 5.

115. Ibid, Lisson, 5.

116. Ibid, O'Donnell, 60.

117. International Business Machines. National Support Center for Persons with Disabilities. (1991). Resource Guide for persons with mobility impairments. Atlanta, GA: IBM. Various pages.

118. Ibid, ADAAG, 4.32.4.

119. Ibid, ADAAG, 4.32.1.

120. Ibid, ADAAG, 4.32.4.

121. Ibid, ADAAG, 4.3.2.

122. Ibid, ADAAG, 4.30.5.

123. Ibid, Lisson, 6.

124. U.S. Department of Labor. Occupational Safety and Health Administration. (1991). Working safety with video display terminals. Washington, DC: U.S. Government Printing Office. Pages 2-4.

125. Ibid, OSHA, 5-9.

126. Ibid, Pinion, 26.

127. Quarterly newsletter from the National Council on Disability, 800 Independence Ave., S.W., Suite 814, Washington, DC 20591--(202) 267-3846 (Voice) or (202) 267-3232 (TDD). See also, the quarterly newsletter from the Clearinghouse on Disability Information Office of Special Education and Rehabilitation Services, U.S. Department of Education, Switzer Bldg., Rm. 3132, Washington, DC 20202-2524--(202) 732-1241 or (202) 732-1723 (Voice/TDD); A bi-monthly news magazine from the AMERICAN COUNCIL OF THE BLIND, 1155 15th St., N.W., Suite 720, Washington, DC 20005--(202) 467-5081 or (800) 424-8666 (3:00-5:30 PM EST); A quarterly newsletter from the NATIONAL CENTER FOR LEARNING DISABILITIES, 99 Park Ave., New York, New York 10016--(212) 687-7211 or (212) 370-0837 (Fax).

128. Ibid, Foster, & Lindell, 61.

129. Ibid, ADAAG, A4.30.5.

130. Ibid, ADAAG, A4.30.2. See also, Lisson, 5.

131. Ibid, ADAAG, 4.2.5 & 4.2.6.

132. Ibid, ADAAG, 4.2.5.

133. Ibid, ADAAG, 4.2.6.

134. Ibid, ADAAG, A4.30.1: "Many people with disabilities have limitations in movement of their heads and reduced peripheral vision. Thus, signage positioned perpendicular to the path of travel is easiest for them to notice. People can generally distinguish signage within an angle of 30 degrees to either side of the centerlines of their faces without moving their heads."

135. Ibid, ADAAG, 4.33.7: "Assistive listening systems (ALS) are intended to augment standard public address and audio systems by providing signals which can be received directly by persons with special receivers or their own hearing aids."

136. Ibid, Pinion, 26-28.

137. Purdue, Bill. (1984). Talking newspapers and magazines. Audiovisual Librarian, 10, 82-85.

138. Ibid, Roberts, 55.

139. Irwin, Marilyn. (1992). Library Media Specialist as teacher for students who are disabled. Indiana Media Journal, 14, 12.

140. Ibid, ADAAG, 4.3.2(1).

141. Ibid, ADAAG, 4.2.5.

142. Ibid, ADAAG, 4.2.6.

143. Lane, Elizabeth & Lane, James. (1982). Reference materials for the disabled. <u>Reference Services Review</u>, <u>10</u>, 73: "Because of limited experience with library services and resources, the disabled library user may be unaware of and reluctant to use reference services."

144. Temsky, R. Marlene. (1982). Some suggestions for public library service to disabled persons. <u>Bay State Librarian</u>, <u>71</u>, 9: "The key to successful service to the disabled remains awareness: know who is out there; know what their needs might be; know what resources, human and material, are available. Keep cooperation between the library and the disabled community a lively process. Whereas some people may need to be met more than halfway because of physical or psychological limitations, it is encumbent upon any library user to make his/her wishes as clear as possible."

145. Ibid, <u>ADA Handbook</u>, I-63.

146. Ibid, <u>ADA Handbook</u>, II-39 & III-51.

147. Ibid, <u>ADA Handbook</u>, I-63. See also, Pinion, 27.

148. Ibid, Power, 213.

149. Ibid, Power, 215.

150. Ibid, Power, 214: "Learning disabled students may also have long-term memory problems that require the librarian to reinstruct the learning disabled student in the use of equipment or materials several times."

151. Ibid, <u>ADA Handbook</u>, I-61 & 67.

152. Ibid, <u>ADA Handbook</u>, I-67.

153. Ibid, <u>ADA Handbook</u>, II-38.

154. Ibid, Allegri, 68-69: "Many individuals, in an effort to achieve as much independence as possible, may decline help at the onset but be willing to accept it later if they have been unsuccessful. Be willing to allow this approach and be attentive to both verbal and nonverbal cues which indicate help is needed."

155. Ibid, Kruger, 8-9.

156. Ibid, Allegri, 72.

157. Ibid, Kruger, 8-9: "Equipment and information should not be considered the end goals of service to disabled patrons. Library staffs have a responsibility to provide service with a positive attitude, with the understanding that members of the disabled population are motivated to live independently, as contributors to society rather than as a group maintained by society. As disabled people become more assertive of their civil rights, active support of their needs must become part of the service philosophy of all types of libraries."

158. Ibid, Malinconico, 132.

159. Freese, Michele & Cohen, Susan F. (1986). Awareness project for library service for the hearing impaired. <u>Illinois Libraries</u>, <u>68</u>(1), 552.

160. Ibid, Havens, 32-33.

161. Cagle, R. Brantley. (1983). Reference service to the developmentally disabled: Normalization of access. <u>Catholic Library World</u>, <u>54</u>, 268. See also, <u>Information 2000: Library and Information Services for the 21st Century. A summary report of the 1991 White House Conference on Library and Information Services</u>. (1991). Washington, DC: U.S. Government Printing Office. Page 19: "Ensure that all library and information service users have access to all forms and formats of information and library materials. Page 34: "All barriers to library and information services should be eliminated to achieve full and complete access, as set forth in the Americans with Disabilities Act of 1990. Federal funds should be made available to assure compliance and to provide incentives for making existing library facilities accessible to persons with disabilities."

162. Weingand, Darlene E. (1990). The invisible client: Meeting the needs of persons with learning disabilities. In <u>The Reference Librarian</u>. New York: Haworth Press. Page 79.

163. Ibid, Foster & Lindell, 61:"Keep pencil and paper within reach to ease communication with people who have impaired speech or hearing."

164. Ibid, Power, 214: "When an individual approaches a librarian and indicates that she or he is learning disabled, what information is that person communicating?"

165. Ibid, O'Donnell, 54: "Making listening devices available at information, circulation, and reference desks allows people to effectively use the library."

Library Service Areas

166. Ibid, <u>ADA Handbook</u>, III-78: "...appropriate auxiliary aids and services be furnished to ensure that communication with persons with disabilities is as effective as communication with others."

167. Needham, William & Jahoda, Gerald. (1983). <u>Improving library service to physically disabled persons</u>. Littleton, CO: Libraries Unlimited. Pages 36-37.

168. Ibid, Power, 213.

169. Ibid, Needham & Jahoda, 83.

170. Ibid, <u>ADA Handbook</u>, II-14 & III-78: "The most advanced technology is not required so long as effective communication is ensured."

171. Ibid, <u>ADA Handbook</u>, I-61 & 67.

172. Ibid, Allegri, 69: "Disabled persons recommend that librarians not accede to excessive and unnecessary demands and not let persons making such demands prejudice the librarian against other disabled persons...Some patrons may have difficulty reaching or reading titles on low or high shelves or carrying materials-particularly heavy items."

173. Ibid, <u>ADAAG</u>, 8.3: "Any traffic control or book security gates shall comply with 4.13." See also, <u>ADAAG</u>, 4.13.

174. Ibid, Power, 213.

175. Editor. (1983). California LSCA project to mainstream mentally impaired. <u>Library Journal</u>, <u>108</u>, 340.

176. Ibid, <u>Information 2000</u>, 57.

177. Ibid, California LSCA Project, 340.

178. Ibid, California LSCA Project, 340.

179. Ibid, Smale, 204: "Most university courses require students to undertake individual research and reading, and difficulties associated with using standard print can seriously disadvantage visually impaired students."

180. Ibid, Goltz, 265-266.

181. Ibid, <u>ADAAG</u>, 4.30.4 & A4.30.4.

182. Ibid, Goltz, 266.

183. Kazlauskas, Diane W., Weaver, Sharon T. & Jones, William R. (1987). Kurzweil reading machine: A study of usage patterns. <u>Journal of Academic Librarianship</u>, <u>12</u>(6), 356-358.

184. OPTACON II by TeleSensory, P.O. Box 7455, Mountain View, CA 94039-7455 (800) 227-8418 or (415) 960-0920.

185. Cotter, Eithne & McCarty, Emily. (1983). Technology for the handicapped: Kurzweil and Viewscan. <u>Library Hi Tech</u>, <u>1</u>, 63-67.

186. Ibid, Roberts, 55.

187. Ruconich, S.K., Ashcroft, S.C. & Young, M.F. (1986). Making microcomputers accessible to blind persons. <u>Journal of Special Education Technology</u>, 7(1), 37-46.

188. Ibid, Purdue, 82-85.

189. Carter, Robert & Jackson, Kathy. (1992). Speech synthesizer and screen reading software make CD-ROM databases accessible to visually impaired users. <u>CD-ROM Professional</u>, <u>5</u>, 129-131.

190. Ibid, Lane, 75: "The use of the telephone provides the quickest access for a disabled person to the reference librarian and the collection. A telephone, which already exists at most reference desks, is not an added, but a standard aid for reference work."

191. Ibid, <u>ADAAG</u>, 4.30.7(2).

192. Ibid, Kruger, 9: "Telecaption devices and telecommunication devices are aids that help the hearing impaired, and these should be in the reference area of the library so that the patron can obtain reference service by telephone at least."

193. Ibid, <u>ADA Handbook</u>, III-78.

194. Ibid, Allegri, 68: "Know the library's collections and services in terms of the special needs of disabled patrons."

195. Ibid, California LSCA project, 340: "Materials for these special [developmentally disabled] patrons were placed in a special collection to make it easy for them to browse. There is no stigma attached to this special collection, because it is located near other popular adult special collections..."

196. Ibid, <u>ADA Handbook</u>, I-36/36. See also, II-37.

197. Ibid, <u>ADA Handbook</u>, I-77.

198. American Library Association. (1988). <u>Information power: Guidelines for school library media programs.</u> Chicago: American Library Association. Page 78.

199. Ibid, Needham & Jahoda, 36.

200. Ibid, Needham & Jahoda, 38.

201. Ibid, Temsky, 5.

202. Ibid, Temsky, 7-8.

203. Ibid, Irwin, 15.

204. Ibid, Havens, 34.

205. Green, Gill. (1991). It's nice in here, init miss? How a special school reorganized its library. <u>The School Librarian, 39</u>, 51.

206. Ibid, Havens, 34.

207. Irwin, Marilyn. (1992). Library media specialist: Information specialist for students with disabilities. <u>Indiana Media Journal, 14</u>(1), 15.

208. Ibid, <u>ADA Handbook</u>, II-42.

209. Ibid, Pack & Foos, 227: "Disability awareness sessions, which address attitudes toward patrons with disabilities, especially in larger library systems that might employ law enforce-ment officers, such as library guards, may be necessary for library staff members without experience in serving patrons with disabilities, even if library policies are designed to enforce nondiscrimination activities toward library patrons with disabilities."

210. Ibid, Foster, 62.

211. Ibid, Kruger, 9.

212. Ibid, <u>ADA Handbook</u>, II-13 & 28.

213. Ibid, <u>ADAAG</u>, 4.13.9.

214. Ibid, <u>ADAAG</u>, 4.30.4 & A4.30.4.

215. Ibid, Lisson, 5.

216. Ibid, <u>ADAAG</u>, 4.32.4: "The tops of accessible tables and counters shall be from 28 in to 34 in (710 mm to 865 mm)above the finish floor or ground."

217. Ibid, <u>ADAAG</u>, 4.2.5.

218. Ibid, <u>ADAAG</u>, 4.2.6.

219. Ibid, <u>ADAAG</u>, 4.2.5 & 4.2.6.

220. Ibid, Kuhlenschmidt, 9.

221. Ibid, <u>ADAAG</u>, 4.2.5.

222. Ibid, <u>ADAAG</u>, 4.2.6.

223. Ibid, <u>ADAAG</u>, 4.30.4 & A4.30.4.

224. Ibid, <u>ADA Handbook</u>, I-41.

225. Ibid, <u>ADAAG</u>, 4.30.5.

226. Ibid, <u>ADAAG</u>, 4.27.4.

227. Ibid, <u>ADAAG</u>, A4.32.4.

228. Ibid, <u>ADAAG</u>, 4.32.4.

229. Ibid, <u>ADAAG</u>, A4.13.11.

230. Ibid, <u>ADAAG</u>, 4.30.4 & A4.30.4.

231. Ibid, <u>ADAAG</u>, 4.3.1.

232. Ibid, <u>ADAAG</u>, 4.4.2.

233. Ibid, <u>ADAAG</u>, 4.30.4 & A4.30.4.

234. Ibid, <u>ADAAG</u>, 4.2.5.

235. Ibid, <u>ADAAG</u>, 4.2.6.

236. Ibid, <u>ADAAG</u>, 4.2.5 & 4.2.6.

237. Ibid, <u>ADAAG</u>, 4.30.4 & A4.30.4.

238. Ibid, <u>ADAAG</u>, A4.30.2. See also, Lisson, 5.

239. Ibid, <u>ADAAG</u>, 4.30.5.

240. Ibid, <u>ADA Handbook</u>, II-44.

241. Ibid, <u>ADAAG</u>, 4.30.4 & A4.30.4.

242. Ibid, <u>ADAAG</u>, 4.3.3.

243. Ibid, <u>ADAAG</u>, 4.2.6.

244. Ibid, <u>ADAAG</u>, 4.2.6.

245. Ibid, <u>ADAAG</u>, 4.27.4.

246. Ibid, <u>ADAAG</u>, 8.1.

247. Hagemeyer, Alice. (1982). Library service and outreach programs for the deaf. <u>Wyoming Library Roundup</u>, <u>38</u>(2), 17: "The library world also has a responsibility to help by providing information. Be part of the solution, not the problem...Demonstrate a commitment to serve everyone and treat each person as an individual!"

248. Ibid, Phinney, 225: "Floor space should be as uncluttered as possible. It is desirable to locate as much shelving for both books and periodicals as possible along the walls of the reading area with plenty of space between the shelves and any chairs or tables."

249. Ibid, Phinney, 229: "In order to obtain a particular book or look up a reference without help, the individual must be able to read and record information from the card or book catalog, go to the source indicated, read both call number and title, retrieve the book from the shelf, perhaps open it and scan it, take it to a table and read the material or carry it to the circulation desk, go through the required procedures for borrowing materials, and carry them away---an easily learned, relatively simple procedure for the normal ambulant person without visual limitations. Not so simple a task for the...physically handicapped!"

250. Robinson, Joan & Henry, Margaret. (1982). Serving the disabled borrower. <u>Ontario Library Review</u>, <u>66</u>, 16: "To inform library patrons and members of the community about the library, a brochure summarizing access and services of particular interest to disabled patrons was compiled... Designators were used to indicate whether public buildings were accessible."

251. Ibid, Goltz, 267.

252. Ibid, Irwin, 11: "An environment that is physically accessible not only allows students the ability to obtain their own materials, it provides evidence that students with disabilities are welcome in the library media center."

253. Shaw, Alison. (1986). Better services for the visually handicapped. <u>Library Association Record</u>, <u>88</u>, 85.

254. Ibid, Havens, 34: "Even such a simple device as labeling the large print shelves with a sign in large print proves attention getting. Many [large print] collections are prominently displayed near the main entrance of the library, across from the reference desk, or in other high-visibility areas."

255. Ibid, Goltz, 266.

256. Ibid, Goltz, 267.

257. Ibid, <u>ADAAG</u>, 8.4: "Maximum reach height shall comply with 4.2 with a height of 48 in (1220 mm) preferred irrespective of approach allowed."

258. Ibid, <u>ADAAG</u>, A4.2.1.

259. Ibid, <u>ADAAG</u>, 8.5.

260. Ibid, <u>ADAAG</u>, 4.27.4.

261. Ibid, <u>ADAAG</u>, 4.2.5.

262. Ibid, <u>ADAAG</u>, 4.2.6.

263. Ibid, <u>ADAAG</u>, 4.2.5.

264. Ibid, <u>ADAAG</u>, 4.2.6.

265. Ibid, <u>ADAAG</u>, A4.13.11.

266. Ibid, <u>ADAAG</u>, A4.13.11.

267. Ibid, <u>ADAAG</u>, A4.13.11.

268. Ibid, <u>ADAAG</u>, 8.2.

269. Ibid, <u>ADAAG</u>, 8.3.

270. Ibid, <u>ADAAG</u>, A4.8.2.

271. Ibid, <u>ADA Handbook</u>, I-77. See also, Smale, 199: "It is generally recognized that persons with physical disabilities hav the same aspirations, interests, talents and skills as the majority of the community. No longer is it acceptable to deny access and opportunity of education to people purely on the grounds of physical disability."

272. Ibid, <u>ADAAG</u>, 4.30.4 & A4.30.4.

273. Ibid, <u>ADAAG</u>, 4.30.4.

274. Ibid, <u>ADAAG</u>, 4.30.3.

275. Ibid, <u>ADAAG</u>, 4.30.4 & A4.30.4.

276. Ibid, <u>ADAAG</u>, 4.30.5.

277. Ibid, Foster & Lindell, 61.

278. Ibid, Havens, 34. See also, Phinney, 241: "In order to locate reading material in the library, wheelchair users must be able to read shelf labels, book titles, call numbers on the spines of books, etc., from the confines of a seated position. Legible, easily seen labels will not only facilitate use of the library services for the chairbound but will be an aid to all library users."

279. Gregg, Alison. (1992). On her blindness: Reflections on the use of spoken word cassettes from the public library. <u>The Australian Library Journal</u>, <u>41</u>(1), 129-132.

280. Ibid, Irwin, 11: "Access may be as simple as making sure the aisles are clear of obstacles such as step stools and book carts."

281. Ibid, Phinney, 299.

282. Beatty, Susan & Maguire, Wesla. (1985). Service to handicapped people. <u>Canadian Library Journal</u>, <u>42</u>, 11.

283. Ibid, Allegri, 74; Ibid, Goltz, 264; Ibid, Lane, 76.

284. Ibid, <u>ADAAG</u>, A4.2.1(3).

285. Ibid, Gunde, 100: "Fundamental to this process is the realization that you cannot meet the needs of people without actually asking them what they want."

286. Ibid, Medrinos, 30.

287. Ibid, Power, 214.

288. Ibid, <u>ADA Handbook</u>, I-53.

289. Ibid, <u>ADA Handbook</u>, I-77.

290. Ibid, Irwin, 15: "[While this does not mean that special policies should be developed that provide extra privileges for students with disabilities, it does mean that restrictions should not be placed on use of materials based on the disability of the student."

291. Ibid, Gunde, 99: "Essentially, library services must be provided in a manner that allows each eligible user with a disability to equally benefit from the local library. Because the needs of each individual with a disability differ and the range of disabilities is infinite, it is not possible to categorically state which specific actions a library will need to take. This is why the ADA's regulations are guidelines for make ADA decisions and not an exhaustive catalog of all possible required accomodations or modifications."

292. Ibid, <u>ADA Handbook</u>, II-42.

293. Ibid, <u>ADAAG</u>, 4.2.5 & 4.2.6.

294. Ibid, <u>ADA Handbook</u>, II-68.

295. Ibid, <u>ADAAG</u>, 4.3.3.

296. Ibid, <u>ADAAG</u>, 4.3.4.

297. Ibid, <u>ADA Handbook</u>, I-12/13.

298. Ibid, <u>ADA Handbook</u>, II-37.

299. Ibid, <u>ADAAG</u>, 43.2(3).

300. Ibid, <u>ADAAG</u>, 4.30.6.

301. Hirsch, E.B. (1984). Homebound and senior citizen service at the Allard K. Lowenstein Public Library. <u>The Bookmark</u>, <u>42</u>, 99.

302. Ibid, <u>ADA Handbook</u>, I-53.

Library Service Areas

303. Wigmore, Hilary & Morris, Deirdre. (1988). Opening doors to disabled people: Improving services for the disabled library user. Library Association Record, 90(3), 155: "The need for people with disabilities to use libraries in the 'normal' way rather than have special services which increase their isolation, raised questions of transport. Some people would be helped by being driven to and from the library, others by having their materials delivered after they had made a selection at the library...We have become more aware in the context of this work [the library survey] how necessary it is to respond to what people want, and not just to do what we think they want."

304. Ibid, Needham & Jahoda, 35 & 37.

305. Ibid, ADA Handbook, II-42.

306. Ibid, ADAAG, 8.3.

307. Ibid, ADA Handbook, I-56. See also Information 2000, 18 & 49.

308. Ibid, ADAAG, 7.2(1). See specifically, ADAAG, 8.3: Check-out areas. At least one lane at each check-out area shall comply with 7.2(1)."

309. Ibid, Needham & Jahoda, 37.

310. Ibid, ADA Handbook, I-62: "(4) consider the preference of the individual to be accomodated and select and implement the accomodation that is most appropriate for both the [library] and the [patron]."

311. Ibid, ADAAG, 4.3.2.(3). See also, ADA Handbook, III-74: "...check-out aisles must ensure that an adequate number of accessible check-out aisles is kept open during [library] hours, or must otherwise modify its policies and practices, in order to ensure that an equivalent level of convenient service is provided to individuals with disabilities as it provided to others. For example, if only one check-out aisle is accessible, and it is generally used for express service, one way of providing equivalent service is to allow persons with mobility impairments to make all of their [title charges] at that aisle."

312. Ibid, ADAAG, 4.3.2.(4).

313. Ibid, ADAAG, 4.13.1 & 4.13.2.

314. Ibid, ADAAG, 4.13.2.

315. Ibid, ADAAG, 8.5.

316. Ibid, Hirsch, 100.

317. Ibid, Goltz, 267.

318. Ibid, Power, 215.

319. Ibid, ADA Handbook, I-42.

320. Ibid, ADA Handbook, I-53.

321. Ibid, Information 2000, 36.

322. Ibid, Information 2000, 9.

323. Ibid, Information 2000, 10.

324. Cornish, Graham P. (1991). The philosophy behind international interlending and its implications for the visually handicapped. Interlending and Document Supply, 19(1), 8.

325. Miller, Richard T. (1992). The Americans with Disabilities Act: Library facility and program access under Titles II and III. Ohio Libraries, 5,, 9: "...the regulations note that public entites may provide special benefits, beyond those required by the nondiscrimination requirement of this part, that are limited to individuals with disabilities or a particular class of individuals with disabilities, without incurring additional obligations to persons with disabilities or to other classes of individuals with disabilities."

326. Wesson, Caren L. & Keefe, Margaret. (1989). Teaching library skills to special education students. School Library Media Quarterly, 17(2), 73.

327. Ibid, Weingand, 85.

328. Ibid, Weingand, 85.

329. Ibid, California LSCA project, 339-340.

330. Ibid, ADA Handbook, I-53.

Suggested Reading:

Beatty, Susan & Maguire, Wesla. (1985). Service to handicapped people. Canadian Library Journal, 42, 11-15.

Cagle, R. Brantley. (1983). Reference service to the developmentally disabled: Normalization of access. Catholic Library World, 54, 266-270.

Carter, Robert & Jackson, Kathy. (1992). Speech synthesizer and screen reading software make CD-ROM databases accessible to visually impaired users. CD-ROM Professional, 5, 129-131.

Edwards, Sandra. (1989). Computer technology and the physically disabled. Online Computer Library Center Micro, 5, 22-23.

Foster, Terry & Lindell, Linda. (1991). Libraries and the Americans with Disabilities Act. Texas Libraries, 52, 59-63.

Gregg, Alison. (1992). On her blindness: Reflections on the use of spoken word cassettes from the public library. Australian Library Journal, 41, 129-132.

Gunde, Michael. (1991). Working with the Americans with Disabilities Act. Library Journal, 116(21), 99-100.

International Business Machines. National Support Center for Persons with Disabilities. (1991). Resource Guide for persons with mobility impairments. Atlanta, GA: IBM.

International Business Machines. National Support Center for Persons with Disabilities. (1991). Resource Guide for persons with vision impairments. Atlanta, GA: IBM.

Lane, Elizabeth & Lane, James. (1982). Reference materials for the disabled. Reference Services Review, 10, 73-76.

Malinconico, S. Michael. (1989). Technologies and barriers to information access. In Effective access to information. Trezza, A.F. (Ed.). Boston: G.K. Hall. Pages 123-137.

Miller, Richard T. (1992). The Americans with Disabilities Act: Library facility and program access under Titles II and III. Ohio Libraries, 5, 8-11.

Mularski, Carol. (1987). Academic library service to deaf students: Survey and recommendations. Reference Quarterly, 26, 477-486.

Needham, William & Jahoda, Gerald. (1983). Improving library service to physically disabled persons. Littleton, CO: Libraries Unlimited.

Neville, Ann & Kupersmith, John. (1991). Online access for visually impaired students. Database, 14, 102-104.

Pack, Nancy C. & Foos, Donald D. (1992). Planning for compliance with the Americans with Disabilities Act. Public Libraries, 31, 225-228.

Phinney, Eleanor. (1977). The librarian and the patient. Chicago, IL: American Library Association.

Library Service Areas

Powell, Faye. (1990). A library center for disabled students. College & Research Libraries News, 51, 418-420.

Purdue, Bill. (1984). Talking newspapers and magazines. Audiovisual Librarian, 10, 82-85.

Roatch, Mary A. (1992). High tech and library access for people with disabilities. Public Libraries, 31, 88-98.

Ruconich, S.K., Ashcroft, S.C. & Young, M.F. (1986). Making microcomputers accessible to blind persons. Journal of Special Education Technology, 7(1), 37-46.

Shaw, Alison. (1986). Better services for the visually handicapped. Library Association Record, 88(2), 85.

Temsky, R. Marlene. (1982). Some suggestions for public library service to disabled persons. Bay State Librarian, 71, 4-10.

Walling, Linda Lucas. (1992). Granting each equal access. School Library Media Quarterly, 20, 216-222.

Wesson, Caren L. & Keefe, Margaret. (1989). Teaching library skills to special education students. School Library Media Quarterly, 17(2), 71-77.

Wigmore, Hilary & Morris, Deirdre. (1988). Opening doors to disabled people: Improving services for the disabled library user. Library Association Record, 90(3), 153-156.

Library Patrons With Disabilities

Chapter Five

Library Equipment Support

Facilitating Patron Library Equipment Access

Patrons may or may not have disabilities or be physically or cognitively challenged in any way that relates to their library equipment access or use. Disability type or severity may provide virtually no library physical or cognitive challenges for some. Some can operate library equipment on their own to gain information. These patrons have no equipment-related disabilities in the library context. Others with the same disability or severity of disability condition are greatly challenged by equipment in the library. These other patrons have library context disabilities. Librarians must accommodate patrons with library context disabilities particularly when they need equipment support. But that equipment accommodation should be fully under patron control. Each patron should be provided the maximum possible equipment independence.

Librarians should not assume that information needs of patrons with disabilities are different from other library patrons. Librarians already understand that gaining information often requires library equipment use. Patrons may not share that same understanding. Patron equipment use to gain information may not be independent or appropriate equipment use. By disability category, and when specific disabilities are known about each patron, some librarians regard a "standard equipment orientation" as the most likely approach to meet that patron's information or equipment support requests. Some librarians impose a standard equipment orientation on disabled patrons who do not request specific information or equipment support. Perhaps patrons do not want to participate in, for example, "library activities for the developmentally disabled," or "library equipment orientation for the learning disabled." Standard equipment orientation is a form of information equipment co-dependency between the librarian and physically or cognitively challenged patrons.

Information Equipment Co-Dependency

Information equipment co-dependency forces librarians into patterned, unresponsive, and unhelpful standard equipment orientation for all patrons including those with disabilities. And the patron is assumed to cooperate in the librarian's "sincere and professional efforts to help disabled patrons." Instead librarians must listen when patrons express their equipment accommodation needs and related infosearching strategies. And librarians must accommodate patrons appropriately. Professionals should intervene only when patron safety is genuinely at-risk at library equipment. Patrons have the obligation to state their accommodation needs and not permit ongoing librarian presumptions as to what those infosearching or equipment accommodation needs are. Patrons should be provided the least intrusive equipment support needed for infosearching success.

Supported Infosearching Using Library Equipment

There are four guiding principles for patron-supported infosearching using library equipment that counteract any tendency for librarians to foster or maintain information equipment co-dependency. These guiding principles for supported infosearching, using library equipment, permit the professional librarian to "take the lead" counteracting any challenged patron who fosters co-dependency in librarians or in themselves. The guiding principles, adopted from Szymanski, (1994)[1] are:

Librarians must accommodate patrons with library context disabilities particularly when they need library equipment support. Patrons should be provided the least intrusive equipment support needed for infosearching success.

Library Patrons With Disabilities

1. Equipment Accommodation Under Patron Control

Equipment accommodation should be librarian designed to be maximally under patron with disabilities control. Valid equipment support suggests that the patron is in control of receiving librarian support strategies, not the librarian for providing or imposing those support strategies.

2. Maximum Possible Patron Equipment Independence

Equipment accommodation should be designed by the librarian to facilitate the most patron independence or interdependence with autonomy. Independent supported infosearching using library equipment suggests maximum patron equipment independence to be the operative library goal. Equipment independence suggests that the patron with disabilities can appropriately operate equipment to infosearch with as much personal control as others have without disabilities. With other disabled patrons less able, interdependence with autonomy at library equipment suggests minimal librarian support and maximal patron autonomy in using library equipment to infosearch. Patron interdependence with autonomy and effective supported equipment operation may be with the librarian, a personal attendant, or both. This patron interdependence suggests a "hands off until absolutely needed" approach at equipment by the librarian.

3. Least Intrusive Patron Equipment Support

The least intrusive patron equipment support that is still patron effective should be used. Least instrusive suggests that minimal patron equipment support or orientation be provided, not standard equipment orientation. Patrons who are physically or cognitively challenged have the right to fail, and perhaps the need to initially fail at library equipment, before least instrusive equipment support is provided. When outright or partial patron failure with library equipment occurs then the least intrusive equipment support is provided by the librarian.

4. Natural Equipment Accommodation

The most natural equipment accommodation provided by the librarian for the patron with disabilities is in the library service area where equipment support and supported infosearching occur. Natural library equipment accommodation is the same for disabled patrons as it is for patrons not disabled in conventional library service areas and at equipment sites. Equipment accommodation prevents librarians from finding secluded library sites away from public view where "equipment can be operated by challenged patrons." If any equipment site is used by the nondisabled, that same site must also be used by the disabled. Just as patrons with disabilities can be assisted in meeting information needs, professionals can identify numerous equipment barriers to resolve any special patron equipment support needs. Personal library equipment barriers are transformed into natural patron equipment support events by effective librarians. By resolving equipment barriers for disabled patrons in the library service area where they naturally occur, they are better served.

Equipment accommodation should be librarian designed to be maximally under patron with disabilities control.

Library Equipment Support

Evaluating Patron Library Equipment Use

Patrons with disabilities who must use library equipment are evaluated for their operational skill. That necessary skill evaluation occurs only when equipment access is patron-requested. Equipment skill evaluation will not make them use library equipment or be successful infosearchers. Neither does evaluation presume to anticipate disabled patron needs. Equipment skill evaluation only follows specific requests made by any disabled or nondisabled patron to be helped to operate equipment.

A reactive librarian response to patrons with disabilities equipment orientation requests is appropriate. Proactive equipment orientation, in this instance, would discriminate against patrons solely because of their disabilities, since librarians do not demand equipment skill evaluation for everyone entering the library or requesting to use library equipment.[2] Each patron, with or without disabilities, must ask for professional evaluation of their equipment operational skill before they can be assisted with that equipment to find their own information. When the disabled request equipment skill evaluation those results provide specific orientation strategies. Equipment support for the disabled is provided in much the same way as it is provided to others in the most natural accommodation setting where the equipment is located and by means of the least intrusive orientation support that leads to maximum possible patron equipment independence.

Patron behavior toward equipment determines equipment support strategies since accommodation is under patron control. Librarians may safely assume that all patrons with disabilities are sufficiently skilled and mature to operate equipment independently unless their behavior indicates otherwise, or if they ask for help. Professionals do not dictate information needs or interests. Neither do librarians frame for patrons what their role must be as an "information stakeholder." Each patron self-defines their information stakeholder role and identifies their own information needs. Previous successful experiences using library equipment and confidence gained when reusing familiar equipment directly affects orientation content. The most natural orientation setting is the library service area equipment site. All patrons should move confidently to library equipment and use it to gain personal information. To do so, they must be able to access all library service areas. Previous equipment failure and the lack of confidence using equipment also directly affects orientation content. And equipment orientation content should be the least intrusive equipment support possible that can be provided. The risk of failure at using library equipment or of taking library risks in general is a self-chosen right.[3] Librarians do not obtrusively intervene for patrons with disabilities and their library equipment use. Professionals ascertain patron willingness to obtain information independently or to ask for reasonable library support. Without a patron request, no equipment support is provided.[4] Equipment support levels are selected by the patron, not the librarian.

Patron Attitude Toward Equipment

Patron attitude toward library equipment use may not be immediately recognizable until situations arise when information cannot be gained without using that equipment. Equipment avoidance and the resulting loss of information access is a clear indicator of negative patron equipment attitude. But patron attitude regarding library equipment use is difficult to measure. Dependence on equipment to infosearch and lack of orientation to use that equipment makes infosearchers dependent on librarians. The disabled are more likely to need equipment support from the librarian than equipment supervision.

Appropriate equipment setup must be done by the librarian. Equipment requires setup before patron use, including video, audiocassette, record, compact disk, filmstrip, slide, opaque, overhead and film projectors. Librarian setup is done for all patrons without reference to patron disabilities. Some equipment requires individuals to control settings and make adjustments that preempt patron independent equipment use.

Library Patrons With Disabilities

Patron Novice Equipment User Syndrome

Novice operators or patrons with disabilities may defer asking for librarian orientation, subsequently misusing library equipment. This may be more an indicator of problems in the relationship between patron and librarian than between patron and library equipment. Patron attitude toward the librarian during equipment orientation may cause resistance to whatever orientation is provided. Patrons with disabilities, or others, do not have to "like" the librarian. But they must, as patrons, demonstrate effective and appropriate equipment use. Damaging equipment through misuse is learned both by observing others misuse, and misusing equipment through trial-and-error. Orientation must address how patrons as equipment operators can avoid library equipment misuse. Disability status does not automatically confer novice or unskilled library equipment user status. But some disabled patrons can be inexperienced library equipment users, like some members of the general library public. For the library patron majority, equipment skills remain largely unknown to the librarian until each patron operates equipment.[5] Librarians may falsely assume that patrons with disabilities, by virtue of their disabilities alone, are novice users of library equipment, even initially incompetent. Professionals may falsely assume that an automatic ground-up orientation will be needed, with a lot of stops for drill- and-practice along the way. Librarians may set an orientation level below actual patron skill levels. Slow-paced orientation may comfort the librarian, but not the disabled patron. Equipment orientation level and pace must be set by the patron.

Hand-Holding Syndrome

Hand-holding provides constant and continuous library equipment supervision but eliminates the opportunity to independently infosearch using equipment. Professional librarians sometimes falsely assume that if a patron is disabled, then library equipment hand-holding is needed. Hand-holding masks particular problems that individual patrons experience and their equipment expertise. It also stifles any patron opportunity to develop true equipment independence. Novice patrons with disabilities will never become library independent through librarian hand-holding. This syndrome must be replaced with professional "arms-length distancing" or nonintrusive equipment support to allow patrons the opportunity to reasonably succeed or fail and then be helped without continuous equipment operation monitoring. The nonintrusive approach is another way of describing librarians allowing the patron to dictate librarian equipment support levels.

Patrons Orienting Librarians for Equipment Use

There are instances where patrons orient the librarian for supporting them to use personal assistive devices (PADs). Some with disabilities may prefer to bring personal auxiliary aids and services to the library rather than relying on library equipment support. Equipment at the library often does not represent state-of-the-art personal accommodation comparable with that brought in by the disabled patron.[6] Libraries may be "technology laggards" in their acquisition of adaptive, augmentive or assistive information technology.[7] Not every librarian is expected to have the same specialized skills, acquired by extensive personal assistive device use, that patrons have. In this instance, and for information gain, patrons with disabilities are the equipment experts. Patrons are frequently the "technology experts," entering the library for "accommodation." Librarians may require training by that patron before being able to further accommodate the expert patron with disabilities. The question arises: "Who accommodates who?" Professional librarians consider that any "training" provided by a disabled technologically-expert patron will also help the librarian better accommodate others using similar specialized library-owned technology. Patron accommodation to help librarians learn about personal assistive devices (PADs) is not ADA-required. Nor can librarians demand that disabled patrons bring in or use their own personal assistive devices when not already library-provided.[8] Both librarian and patron must agree to link library equipment with PADs.

Library Equipment Support

Librarian Equipment Skill

Librarians can assist with patron equipment-use anxiety. But librarians must not themselves be anxious toward equipment use--particularly when their anxiety influences patron equipment support. Librarians differ in personal confidence and skill at using library equipment just as patrons differ. The best person to orient patrons is the librarian who is expert at operating library equipment if other disabled patron operators cannot be found to assist their peers. Few librarians can assert that they are expert at all library equipment, either for themselves and for their patrons. Library equipment expertise takes on a new meaning and a new challenge when personal assistive devices (PADs) are brought to the library. Professional librarians can only assert that they remain ready, willing, and able to learn new equipment challenges and help all patrons better use the equipment for which they request librarian support.

True librarian equipment expertise has two dimensions: the librarian must be an expert library equipment user as well as an expert in helping users with disabilities operate library equipment.

Are librarians themselves similarly skilled operating all library equipment? Librarian operating skill on diverse library equipment types combined with multiple patron equipment orientation, reorientation and supervision needs is a professional challenge. Equipment availability, patron needs and personal assistive devices (PADs) brought into the library should also be operationally mastered by the librarian. With acquired and demonstrated skills, librarians better support patrons with disabilities when they ask. If librarians do not master this diverse equipment array, including PADs brought to the library, they must learn-by-doing with the patron. But patrons with disabilities must inform librarians if there is a need for equipment orientation both on library equipment and on their personal assistive devices.

True librarian equipment expertise has two dimensions: the librarian must be an expert library equipment user as well as an expert in helping users with disabilities operate library equipment. Librarians themselves range from novice-to-expert in equipment user skill. Personality differences among librarians suggest that some are equipment-use experts and yet fail to be equally expert in helping patrons with disabilities. Other librarians have people-helping expertise but lack full library equipment skills. Equipment skills based on extensive use may isolate librarians from common operational novice-user mistakes. Expert librarians are often removed from the novice user's viewpoint.[9]

Supported Equipment Intervention

After disabled patron equipment skills improve, some will require continuing equipment support. After equipment misuse supported equipment intervention must be provided. Some patrons may continue to misuse or damage equipment. Then it is the librarian's necessary right to intervene and to limit or refuse further patron equipment access. No one has the right to wilfully damage library equipment. Anyone unintentionally damaging library equipment is responsible for repair or replacement. Continuing misuse reflects more on patron-librarian attitudes toward each other. Rarely do humans hold particular, negative attitudes toward specific library equipment types. Instead, they hold attitudes toward the information they need and cannot get without equipment access. Or they have an attitude toward their needing help from the librarian. These conditions describe mutual communication problems and the need to establish mutual respect. Sometimes librarians cannot find this common ground with some patrons because of a patron choice, not the professional's choice. The alternative is no library equipment access for patrons with disabilities.

Equitable Library Equipment Access

Conventional orientation helps patrons with disabilities understand how to operate library equipment safely and effectively. Reasonable accommodation leading to equitable library equipment access is defined by the Americans with Disabilities Act (ADA). The ADA suggests library equipment be made accessible for patrons with physical or cognitive challenges on an equitable basis as provided to other patrons. Equal access to library equipment also gives equal information access. Not all libraries can provide equal conventional equipment access. When conventional equipment access does not meet the needs of disabled patrons, library assistive devices or other specialized equipment augmentation will. Conventional, specialized, or state-of-the-art equipment is not a library end but a patron means to collection information.

The library cannot impose equipment burdens on individuals with library context disabilities that are not also placed on others.[10] Libraries must not, through policy implementation, omit equipment services,[11] or provide disparate equipment accommodation solely on the basis of patron disabilities.[12] Individuals with library context disabilities have diverse library needs, as do other patrons. Librarians determine individual reasonable accommodation collaboratively with each patron. What do library disabled patrons need for equipment use and information access? Ask them.

> **The library cannot impose equipment burdens on individuals with library context disabilities that are not also placed on others.**

Grateful Disabled Syndrome

Librarians may hold a false assumption that patrons with disabilities should be grateful for any equipment accommodation offered. But they would not expect equal gratitude for any assistance given to nondisabled patrons. For them, challenged patrons are "so different" that they should be grateful for any help provided. Another expectation is that patrons with disabilities will be fully satisfied with the professional support they receive and will not complain. Gratefulness is not exhibited by patron complaints to library supervisors. Gratefulness is being quiet and accepting "what you get." The grateful disabled syndrome is a harmful condition that should be corrected and never repeated among librarians who wish to orient patrons with disabilities as individuals. And some of "those people" may not be grateful.

Library Equipment Signage

Part of independent library equipment use is signage that directs patrons with disabilities to specific equipment sites. Equipment signage may not be accessible to all, particularly to those with library context disabilities.[13] Signage often directs patrons to library service areas but does not show specific equipment locations.[14] Patrons expect equipment to be located in logical service areas based on their previous library experience. Nonstandard library equipment placement requires initial library service area orientation and effective directional signage. If equipment cannot be easily found, or if moved since the last library visit, patron access is limited. Well-planned equipment placement reduces patron reliance on library signage to find equipment. Library equipment "in-place" is at patron-expected equipment locations. Few libraries have studied patron expectations for equipment placement to learn what those expectations are. Consistent placement keeps library equipment relocation to a minimum. Effective equipment placement and directional signage helps patrons and librarians jointly determine optimal equipment use.

Library Equipment Support

Librarian Assumptions About Patron Equipment Access

Patron equipment access, orientation and use may not be needed every library visit. Each time patrons with disabilities request equipment use, several accommodation assumptions are tested. When assumptions are verified, reasonable library support becomes evident. This author fundamentally assumes that when the need for librarian accommodation is evident, librarians will support disabled patrons. Yet neither this author nor professional librarians can assure that when appropriate accommodation is provided, each patron will accept that accommodation. It is an individual patron choice, and their ultimate right, to accept or refuse library accommodation.

Many faulty assumptions and curious myths exist concerning library equipment use by patrons with disabilities or patrons with special information needs. Not all libraries provide major types of library equipment for general public use. Though "state-of-the-art" equipment exists, libraries are not required to acquire the most modern technology. Conventional library equipment works well for a patron majority. As long as equipment affords effective communication or information access, state-of-the art technology for the disabled is not needed.[15] Library policy should not impose burdens on patrons with disabilities that are not placed on others.[16] Library equipment services must be based on actual accommodation need, not on speculation, stereotypes and generalizations about disabled individuals or patrons with special information needs.[17] Allegri (1984) provides a list of faulty assumptions that may be held by some librarians concerning patrons with disabilities:

> Assuming that disabled persons are incompetent... Assuming that the disabled patron's information needs are different from everyone else's; Assuming that once one knows how one physically disabled person thinks and acts, one knows how all persons with that particular disability think and act; Assuming that helping disabled persons will be a wonderful and fulfilling experience and that the disabled person will be grateful for the help; Assuming that a mental disability automatically accompanies a physical disability, particularly where communicative disorders or lack of verbal skills are involved; Assuming that persons with hearing impairments (including deafness) cannot speak or make sounds; Endowing the disabled with superhuman sensory capacities which have helped them compensate for their disabilities, e.g., super acute hearing accompanying visual impairments...Assuming that a person's disability is the primary aspect of his/her life, overriding all other concerns; Assuming that library patrons with physical disabilities demand an inordinate amount of assistance or "hand holding" (Pages 67-68).

Fundamental differences exist between librarian assumptions concerning the disabled and their actual information and library equipment support needs. Patrons may not need to use library equipment when they can independently infosearch with success. The librarian must challenge the validity of each equipment/disability myth and any underlying assumptions concerning any patron with disabilities. It is necessary to challenge assumptions to eliminate equipment myths concerning disabled users. Every person entering the library is unique and has a unique set of equipment access needs. Some have virtually no need for library equipment but must bring in and use their own personal assistive devices. Disabilities alone do not dictate patrons' need for library equipment. But for specific types of information gain, some library equipment must be used. Invalid assumptions concerning library equipment use or need by the disabled may be an integral part of librarian professional service style, attitudes or expectations. Librarian assumptions about the equipment skills of disabled patrons must be challenged to find personalized service that works for each patron. Valid patron observations identify equally valid patron equipment support needs. All people who visit the library benefit from librarians who challenge their assumptions and personally observe or interview patrons to identify individual patron equipment needs. Equipment support strategies also emerge when the librarian interviews the patron and watches attempted patron information access problems using library or personal assistive devices.

Library Patrons With Disabilities

Equipment Format Access Equity: The Information Window

Some patrons with disabilities do not have accessibility across all library-available information formats.[18] Patrons are "information-format disabled" when information format, rather than equipment use, limits their library information window. A limited information window in the library is as real a "disability" as patrons with library context physical or cognitive challenges. Information in specific alternate formats may be the only information window accessible to some patrons with disabilities. Professionals extend patron equipment orientation to alternate information formats to accommodate their diverse format needs.[19] Format alternatives requiring conventional equipment support include compact disk, audiocassette and videocassete, photocopier or microform information. The disabled find some needed information formats are not directly accessible without specialized library equipment or personal assistive devices (PADs).[20] Personal assistive devices brought to the library can be combined with library equipment that increases their information window.

Can library information be accessed in a variety of formats with equal patron success? When several information formats are available, the patron with library context disabilities has the right to choose between formats. The patron has the opportunity to make information format preferences known to the librarian, to be in control of the information window. When patron preferences are known the librarian should gear those responses to maximum independent infosearching with the least librarian support required for success. As novice users with disabilities increase in skill and format accessibility, some may continue to have limited format access.[21] With increased equipment skill and experience patron access to library information also increases. But with more types of library equipment used, patron reliance on equipment support also increases. Patron and librarian together determine mutually acceptable levels of equipment support after the patron has selected information format and asked for equipment help. Patrons receive no support when they do not inform librarians of their accommodation needs.[22] Librarians do not force accommodation on anyone.

When patron preferences are known the librarian should gear those responses to maximum independent infosearching with the least librarian support required for success.

Auxiliary Equipment Aids and Services

Specialized equipment orientation adapts library equipment to help patrons with disabilities access the right information. Any information accessed that does not meet disabled-patron needs is the wrong information. Librarians must assure patrons access to preferred (right) information when using library equipment. Specialized equipment orientation may involve other patron auxiliary aids and services or state-of-the-art equipment, such as:

> Qualified interpreters, notetakers, transcription services, written materials, telephone handset amplifiers, assistive listening devices, assistive listening systems, telephones compatible with hearing aids, closed caption decoders, open and closed captioning, telecommunication devices for the deaf (TDDs),[23] videotext displays, or other effective methods of making aurally delivered materials available to individuals with hearing impairments...Qualified readers, taped texts, audio recordings, Brailled materials, large print materials, or other effective methods of making visually delivered materials available to individuals with visual impairments" (ADA Handbook II-13 & 14).

Library Equipment Support

Note that the ADA includes personal attendants, interpreters and other human services that help gain special access to library information. Not all auxiliary aids and services are provided only by conventional or specialized library equipment. Some are very people-intensive.

Libraries may provide other auxiliary aids including electronic Braille,[24] paper Braille copiers,[25] Braille printers (such as Versabraille),[26] reading machines and scanners (such as the Kurzweil Reading Machine),[27] synthesized speech devices,[28] screen enlarged print (such as Vista),[29] talking book playback machines,[30] Braille embossers,[31] Braille converted keyboards,[32] voice activation or recognition of computers,[33] adaptive (single) switches,[34] hand-held magnification devices,[35] closed circuit magnification devices,[36] page turners,[37] and closed-captioned videocassettes.[38] The ADA suggests:

> It is not possible to provide an exhaustive list, and an attempt to do so would omit the new [library auxiliary aid and service] devices that will become available with emerging technology (ADA Handbook, II-13).

Personal Assistive Devices and Library Equipment Links

Personal assistive equipment brought to the library can be linked with specialized library equipment to facilitate disabled patron information gain. Specialized equipment access is provided on an individual basis where it is most useful to challenged patrons in study or computer carrels. Study carrels house much of the library equipment that may be appropriate to patrons with disabilities. These include electronic page-turners, closed-circuit magnification devices, reading machines that read print aloud, tape recorders and players equipped with earphones, and large print typewriters.[39] Special equipment use distracts others unless done at a study carrel. Only the disabled reader can best decide if study carrels are preferred. Many disabled find a mix of library and personal auxiliary equipment works best. But the library conventional equipment and the disabled patron auxiliary aids must link before that mix can yield individually appropriate information access. Without library equipment support or personal auxiliary aid equipment brought in, patrons who are physically or cognitively challenged may not effectively enter and participate in the Information Age. Some who lack personal auxiliary equipment must rely entirely on library equipment. Librarians who succeed in providing effective equipment support and personal auxiliary aid mix greatly facilitate equal collection access.[40] Roatch (1992) suggests:

Personal assistive equipment brought to the library can be linked with specialized library equipment to facilitate disabled patron information gain.

> Libraries will need to reevaluate their resources because one of the mandates of this act [ADA] is that libraries must furnish auxiliary aids and services necessary to afford an individual with a disability an equal opportunity to participate in and enjoy the benefits of a service, program, or activity conducted by a public entity (Page 96).

Equipment Linkage Teams

When librarians lack personal assistive device (PAD) skill on equipment brought in, each disabled patron and librarian can form an equipment linkage team. Both learn together how to operate patron-owned PADs not yet mastered by patron or librarian. PAD/library equipment support links are sometimes complex. The solution may require calling original equipment manufacturer (OEM) customer support. Unless customer support OEMs provide a toll-free (1-800) number the call is a long distance charge to the library. Libraries may not have the budget for such immediate and direct patron equipment support.

Library Patrons With Disabilities

Customers (patron and librarian) are both in a stressful situation because of their steep learning curves to master exotic equipment linkages. For the OEM customer support calls are everyday events. Yet for the novice patron or librarian operator, those equipment linkages are difficult, frustrating, even frightening. The same calm, logical approach librarians would provide patrons with disabilities experiencing infosearching access problems in the library, and the resulting successful infosearching gains made by the patron, are paralleled by the equipment linkage team and the OEM customer support person on the other end of the telephone line.

A library equipment linkage team can expect not only immediate customer support by phone to the library, but a followup call. Followup measures may also include OEM-initiated patron home, school or workplace or library onsite troubleshooting when online solutions are not found. Even equipment linkage team reconstructions in the library--with the OEM customer support representative--help find solutions. The OEM may bring new, or adapted, replacement PADs to the patron, to the librarian or to both. Specialized library equipment adjustments, equipment system upgrading, or equipment replacement can be done at the library, often while equipment linkage teams watch. OEMs and their customer support personnel do not know how their equipment works or fails to work without understanding customer support requests or patron and librarian complaints. OEMs support library linkage teams just as librarians support patrons with disabilities--one patron at a time. Equipment adjustments, upgrading or replacements drive further OEM operational guide modifications. When complaints or requests for onsite customer support occur, OEMs may also respond by rewriting and updating equipment guides.

Library Equipment Support Plans

Local community disability surveys often do not identify individual patron equipment accommodation needs or situations in which specific access or accommodation is required. Disability surveys describe only general needs of patrons with disabilities, or by category of disability. "Head counts" of each major disability type within local library service areas are meaningless because they do not yield individual patron service needs. Individuals must describe their own special equipment access needs to the librarian during each visit and for each type of library information desired. It is on this individual patron situational basis, in this library context, that libraries should plan how to meet disabled patron equipment support needs.

Valid library accommodation or support plans for local disabled patron groups and individuals with disabilities who are regularly served by the local library evolve into an overall and systematic library support plan. Local library equipment support plans can suggest specific changes in overall equipment services that would bear on: (1) Library equipment placement and uniform accessible signage changes; (2) Equipment types that accommodate both individuals with disabilities and the local library general public; (3) Specialized local library equipment that serves more than one local patron with disabilities and serves other disabled patrons who have common equipment or infosearching access problems; (4) Numbers of conventional library equipment types as they are repositioned to better serve the library general public and how repositioning existing library equipment would deter patron-to-patron equipment conflicts and competition; (5) Conventional or specialized library equipment and how that equipment links to personal assistive devices (PADs) brought in by the disabled patron; (6) Any other specialized library equipment that provides information access to disabled patrons as it also would be accessible by the library general public; and the (7) Design and provision of local adapted library equipment guides that can be used by everyone, especially by patrons with disabilities.

Equipment changes make patrons with disabilities and others more likely to damage equipment than any need for librarian supervision. Equipment changes, changes in operational guide steps, or patron skill changes each dictate the need for patron reorientation and renewed librarian support. Replaced equipment with operational steps may require patron reorientation when those new steps are not user-transparent.

Library Equipment Support

When library equipment is replaced, it becomes unfamiliar. Changes in manufacturer-imposed operational steps require disabled reorientation for disabled patrons.[41] Some patrons with disabilities, like others, are inflexible when asked to change library equipment-use habits. They repeat old mistakes and continue to be dysfunctional equipment users.[42] Library equipment use patterns are difficult for patrons to initially learn. Equipment use patterns are equally difficult for patrons to change. Unlearning bad equipment habits is more difficult than replacing them with good habits during effective equipment orientation.

Librarians should evaluate equipment from a patron viewpoint before new equipment models and technology are purchased. Newly purchased state-of-the-art library technology lacks equally important state-of-the-art, disabled-patron user-friendliness. State-of-the-art user-friendliness claims are usually made with patrons who fit the traditional library patron equipment-user role. Patrons with disabilities may not fit the conventional equipment user role. Many patron equipment challenges go unnoticed by librarians. Patrons silently fail, then quietly refuse to return to library equipment that, for them, is clearly not user-friendly. Equipment user-friendliness varies for patrons with library context disabilities. User-friendly for one may not be user-friendly for another. The best test for hidden patron equipment challenges comes from patrons with disabilities who field-test the equipment before library purchase. It is imperative that librarians invite disabled patrons to use new equipment being considered for purchase before the final purchase decision. Patron new equipment tryouts are most valuable before purchase to assure ADA-compliance as well as to assure patron user-friendliness. A major component of the purchase decision is the extent to which OEM customer support is available and responsive.

Libraries acquire augmentive, assistive or adaptive technology not based on equipment advertisements, but to meet a need for disabled patron requirements already identified. Professional journals promote advanced library technology purchase. Library costs for emerging technology acquisition are prohibitive unless based on careful individual disabled patron planning at the local level. Libraries are not ADA-required to purchase adaptive equipment. Only when groups of patrons with disabilities consistently need adaptive library equipment is there any valid reason for additional library equipment purchases. When that equipment is purchased it must be thoughtfully positioned in specific library service areas to maximize patron accessibility. Disabled patron input is essential for appropriate new equipment placement.

Competition for Library Equipment

High-demand equipment such as CD-ROM, audiocassette and videocassette players brings those with disabilities and others into conflict or competition over library equipment.[43] Equipment conflict or competition magnifies equipment skill challenges and librarian support needs for disabled patrons. Anyone under conflict or competition with others may not perform as well as when no conflict or competition exists. Librarian intervention may be required between patrons at high-demand library equipment. Inappropriate high-demand equipment use may not be noticeable until damage, accelerated repair cycles, or reduced equipment lifetime indicates patron competition and misuse.

> RULE OF THUMB: The most frequently used library equipment is placed at the most
> highly visible library service areas. Library equipment use there can be monitored and
> patron conflicts or competition minimized.

Only when the disabled take their equipment support requests to the librarian or when they complain about equipment being "dominated" by others is competition between disabled and nondisabled most evident. Competition can be minimized when equitable equipment use contraints are imposed on all library patrons.

Library Patrons With Disabilities

Equipment-Use Time Limits

Part of disabled patron equipment support is the establishment of clear equipment-use time limits. Time constraints and lack of focused library equipment use create hostility between patrons. High-demand equipment requires clearly stated patron-use time limits to avoid or minimize conflicts. Lack of a patron time limit or not monitoring equipment use intervals represents poor library planning and patron service. Stated and enforced patron equipment access time limits are not one and the same. Even library signage stating high-demand equipment time limits may be ignored. Equipment use time limits that are not librarian monitored or consistently applied engender both patron-patron and patron-librarian conflicts. While equipment may operate at the same speed for everyone, patrons do not operate library equipment controls or make infosearching judgments at similar rates. Some may be noticeably slower using library equipment than others, adding to possible patron-to-patron tension and conflicts. For information to be relevant, librarians must reasonably assure "quick" patron information access. "Slow" patron information access may be provided, but that slow information access by the disabled patron can just as readily be ignored, refused or rejected. State-of-the-art information technology may have made us all "information impatient." Our information needs now seem always immediate and pressing. Reorienting patrons to appropriate equipment access, posting time limit signage, informing them about equipment use time limits, and resolving their conflicts are necessary library equipment support elements.

High-demand equipment requires clearly stated patron-use time limits to avoid or minimize conflicts.

Low-Demand Library Equipment

Modern libraries emphasize high-technology information access and equipment use. Libraries may, in some sense, de-emphasize low-demand library equipment. High-technology library equipment use, however, is done by relatively low-technology human beings. Nor should access to low-demand or conventional library equipment technology suggest this equipment is less than satisfactory. People are in a sense "low-technology" beings who do not read as fast as high-technology, state-of-the-art library equipment can present information. Humans are all "low tek" beings in a relatively "high tek" world. And all must learn to live with information technology equipment in the library without competition or conflicts as a natural part of the infosearching process.

Low-demand library equipment lends itself to patron conflicts when patrons with disabilities compete with each other for equipment access. The general library public does not usually demand equal access to low demand equipment. Low-demand library equipment can be very much in high-demand among a sufficiently large group of disabled patron users. "Low-demand equipment" may be a more meaningful term for the general public, but not necessarily for the disabled whose access to specific equipment is critical for their information gain.

Reel-to-reel tape players, slide projectors and viewers, sound filmstrip and film projectors, and opaque and overhead projectors are low-demand

While state-of-the-art library technology provides wider information access, infosearching remains more a thought-intensive, than an equipment-intensive, process.

Library Equipment Support

equipment for the library general public but not necessarily for patrons with disabilities. Special low-demand equipment access may be continuously required for some disabled patrons. Older reel-to-reel tape player technology may be the only equipment accommodation available for low-vision patrons[44] using National Lending Service tape media. While the NLS provides specialized tape playback equipment directly to disabled individuals, that equipment may fail at home. In this situation, the NLS user visits the library and uses library-based NLS-formatted playback equipment until the NLS replaces the home equipment.

Slide projectors and viewers, and opaque and overhead projectors magnify images for low-vision patrons. Without magnification there is no library print reading for them. Low-demand equipment does not equate to unimportant library equipment. For information access that cannot be obtained any other way by disabled patrons, low-demand equipment is unique, important and essential. For librarians, some "low-demand library equipment" is high-priority equipment to be supported for disabled patron access.

Equipment Requiring Complex Operational Steps

Some library equipment requires complex operational steps. Patrons experience demands from the simplest television monitor viewing to complex equipment controls such as multistep coin-operated copiers. Examples of complex library equipment include photocopiers and microform equipment. While state-of-the-art library technology provides wider information access, infosearching remains more a thought-intensive, than an equipment-intensive, process. Patrons search in thought-intensive ways while overcoming physical and cognitive challenges. Library equipment does not have to be state-of-the-art to be helpful. Patron infosearching skill is the key.

Photocopier Access

All patrons are provided full copier access and photocopying privileges within library policy and procedural restrictions. Copier access allows copying, and reduction or enlargement from originals within equipment size parameters. Equipment capability permits patrons to copy portions of large items, reduce large items to copy size specifications and enlarge original copy to copier limits. Independent equipment operation requires knowledge and successful photocopier control settings for minimal copy success. Equipment control access, and interpreting control options and settings make successful copying possible. Control settings either default to preset copying parameters or are patron-specified. Novice operators may not know they must view presettings to change to desired copying parameters. They may make copies to the previous operator's specifications. Library policy often makes patrons, including those with disabilities, responsible for all copies made. When library photocopy equipment malfunctions produce unsatisfactory copies, copy costs are reimbursed or credited to the patron. When photocopier presettings result in multiple unwanted copies, librarians overseeing equipment operation, at minimum, supervise desired copies redone to patron satisfaction. Supervised successful recopying is a right of all library patrons. Librarians refusing recopying access to patrons based on their disability status is untenable. Repeated recopying is a real librarian frustration but it is a patron fundamental right to gain information access. The patron is also paying for recopying as personally needed. Librarian "time" is a paid public service.

Photocopiers should be located within circulation view where coin and bill change or copier passes can be obtained from the librarian. Feeding bill-changers with paper money face-up and positioned appropriately requires bill denomination visual recognition along with bill and change handling skill. The blind, for example, accommodate themselves by carefully folding paper money by denominations before billfold placement and can skillfully recognize by touch loose change received. Personalized patron coin return,

Library Patrons With Disabilities

change-making or refund support should be provided to the sighted, just as it is provided to patrons with low vision or the blind. Discrimination toward patrons with disabilities for photocopy access is ADA-prohibited.[45] Library policy that requires special handling or equipment support based on any patron category of disability is prohibited.[46] Individuals needing librarian-supported infosearching using library equipment are helped as individuals, not soley as disabled individuals. Library policy specifically avoids disparate treatment between patrons with disabilities and others at the copier or any other publicly accessible library equipment.[47] Some patrons are unable to make change or

budget copying costs within personal resources. Some may have only high-demand copying needs for short durations. Access to, and understanding the privileges of, limits copy card use. Successful photocopying may require librarian nonintrusive support.

Unauthorized Photocopying

Librarians prohibit patron unauthorized copying of copyright restricted material.[48] Patrons with disabilities, even with the most obvious or severe disabling conditions, have no more legal basis to violate copyright restrictions at the photocopier than any other users. Coin-operated photocopiers offer library copyright and intellectual property protection. The disabled, solely by virtue of their disabilities, are not exempt from those issues. All titles from the library collection can and probably will be copied unless physical access to the copier is restricted and consistent copier supervision provided for all patrons.[49]

Photocopier orientation should include copyright restrictions that apply to all library patrons. Library signage at photocopiers providing copyright notice may not be accessible for some patrons with library context disabilities.[50] Copyright pictograms[51] should illustrate patron copyright guidelines using highly visible graphics. Highlighted, bold type or large print copyright notices facilitate reading notice content. Yet librarians observe some patrons who ignore copyright restrictions as well as library signage and repeatedly attempt illegal copies.

Low-Vision Patron Photocopier Use

Patrons with low vision have difficulty reading library photocopier signage including the controls that direct correct register placement of media to be copied. Successful photocopying requires them to closely approach the register to check media positioning before copying. Positioning materials on the register also may require exaggerated body positions at the machine, compared to those required by the normally sighted.

Librarians prohibit patron unauthorized copying of copyright restricted material. Patrons with disabilities, even with the most obvious or severe disabling conditions, have no more legal basis to violate copyright restrictions at the photocopier than any other users.

Library Equipment Support

Librarians must be willing to adjust copy contrast settings beyond personal reading comfort when helping patrons who are print disabled. Or the patron can experiment with contrast control settings independently to maximize copy readability. Librarian orientation and continued photocopier support is provided only on patron request. There are many library equipment solutions that apply to the print disabled who may use the photocopier to modify print for visual engagement.

Patrons with low vision can use special library photocopiers that produce raised-relief or Braille, when they are available.[52] Many have limited access to, or the need for, conventional library photocopier hardcopy. Low-vision patrons may experiment with copy enlargement and contrast enhancements to make library print accessible. Light/dark photocopier controls may not move contrast to their standard reading level requirements. Library photocopier controls often include 125 to 150% enlargement, with 100% being an exact image-size duplication. After repeated enlargements, hard copy reading quality deteriorates. Low-vision patrons may not be able to visually engage even the best quality copies made after these modifications have been done. Other routes to print information must be found.

Wheelchair Users At The Photocopier

Wheelchair users may need help with library maps[53] to find photocopy equipment that is sited along wheelchair-accessible service routes.[54] Librarians may need to provide photocopying assistance or help in handling media at the copier.[55] Coin vending machines or bill changers placed on walls above eye level may not be accessible to wheelchair users since they require feeding money denominations correctly positioned for machine recognition and change service.[56] Coin-operated photocopier access is not an accommodation without coin service. Failure to provide coin service is a library photocopier access barrier in it's own right.

Electric wheelchair patrons with arm, hand or finger movement limitations have more difficulty photopying. Manual wheelchair users may also lack arm, hand and finger strength and coordination to operate controls successfully.[57] Photocopier controls may not be visible from a wheelchair-seated position. Table-top photocopiers should be lowered to provide access.[58] Among several library photocopiers, one at minimum should permit wheelchair accessibility. That accessible photocopier should be within full librarian view for emergency assistance.

Operating photocopier controls, handling and positioning media on the register and retrieving copies from the tray may require wheelchair repositioning. Wheelchair users have difficultly reaching and extending forward to photocopiers from the seated position.[59] Persons with wheelchairs frequently position themselves to the right or left, and access photocopy equipment from the side, while maintaining balance during copying. Free-standing library floor copier models provide access when positioned with surfaces between 28 (28") and 34 inches (34").[60] Library copiers mounted on tables permit wheelchair roll-up and roll-under accommodation.[61] Wheelchair users without roll-under access for copying require specific library equipment support.

Well-planned library equipment instructions are clearly visible, with pictograms showing copy platform positions.[62] Positioning media requires reading skill and orientation for copier register placement. Some photocopiers require careful register placement for effective whole-page copies of face-down media. But that required placement is not easily seen from a seated position. Horizontal or vertical page placement instructions on the photocopier register are not easily read from the sitting position. Wheelchair users must locate a desired page for copying while reading during register placement from a reversed or sideview position. All operators carefully position pages in full-face view before copying. They avoid leaving hands or fingers on the register. Register covers are placed in the "down" position for safe copying to avoid operator eye damage. Wheelchair users cannot move away from lighted copying events as quickly as others. They also must reposition, sometimes with difficulty, to manually pull printouts from the tray. People using wheelchairs may tire more quickly during photocopying or other complex library equipment use.[63]

Library Patrons With Disabilities

Walking Aid Users At The Photocopier

Librarians assume patrons will stand while photocopying. Many disabled cannot stand for prolonged periods during photocopying.[64] Library policy requiring standing photocopy operation should be reviewed and accommodations made for patrons who cannot stand for prolonged periods. For minimal success, photocopying also requires upper body strength and balance, as well as arm, hand and finger control in addition to standing access. Patrons using canes, crutches or walkers may have some difficulty operating library copiers, including coin-deposit, copy feature selection and adjustments, positioning copies correctly, and removing duplicates and original media. Balance, coordination and sustained effort are required for standing while operating photocopiers, since most library models are floor-standing with copy registers 30 inches (30") high. Leg prostheses users may have prolonged copying difficulty unless unless done while seated. Repeated media adjustments and user movements are required. Leg or arm prosthesis users require help in accessing the photocopier, handling media, reaching from a sitting position to operate controls and moving pages during copying.

> **Librarians assume patrons will stand while photocopying. Many disabled cannot stand for prolonged periods during photocopying.**

Microform Equipment Access

Much collection information exists that can only be read using library equipment. A comprehensive library analysis reveals what percentage of the local collection is machine-accessible only. The balance of the collection can be assumed to be directly patron-readable without library equipment. This library collection percentage figure predicts the emphasis librarians must place on library equipment support needed by patrons with disabilities. Equipment-dependent library information also predicts additional purchase requirements and helps determine best placement of specialized library reading equipment for use, in part, by disabled patrons. This is a direct library equipment support decision on behalf of challenged patrons.

Microform equipment access for patrons with disabilities is insufficient support to give them information gain. Alternative format periodicals require patron decision-making to find available information in hard copy or on microform. Barrier-free access to library microform information must be assured. Microformed periodicals require access to storage and independent or supervised microform reader equipment support. Microform equipment located near periodicals minimize patron movement between reference-based periodical indexing and periodical titles stored only on microform. Microform operation assumes equipment orientation when patrons are inexperienced or request support.[65] All novice patrons require directions to microform reader/copiers, help interpreting maps or accompaniment to find microform equipment and media. When display equipment is located, disabled patrons read manufacturer or ADAPTED USER GUIDES or interpret library or manufacturer graphic signage showing equipment operation to use microforms. They may require supervision to read and interpret microform operational signage.

Coin-operated microform reader/copiers require multistep operation and are complex. Reader/copiers are patron-negotiated to satisfy coin-copy requirements. The cost of unintended copies may not be reimbursed. Bad microform copies due to machine malfunction present a judgment problem to many who may not be sure whether the fault was theirs or a library equipment malfunction. They must interact with librarians to retrieve lost coins and make change from paper money. Librarians provide easy patron access to correct coin-operated equipment or support patrons requesting cost adjustments. Professionals are calm and helpful to patrons who, at this library service level, may be highly frustrated. Personalized patron coin-return, change-making or refunds are a service provided to all. Refunds provided only to patrons with disabilities is disparate treatment based on disabilities as cited in ADA requirements.[66]

Some patrons with disabilities require both initial and ongoing equipment support. Microform equipment display stands or tables, readers and copiers are accessible to all by placement on sturdy display tables or stands no more than 32 inches (32") in height, with equipment positioned toward the table front for stability during use.

Microform Wheelchair User Access

Microform information provides a large alternative information source in addition to electronic- or print-based information available in the library to patrons with disabilities. The standard for accessibility for microform access is measured by the library providing inforeach to wheelchair users. Wheelchair users require roll-up and roll-under sitting access during microform reader/copier operation.[67] Librarians may be required to help with reading library maps to find microform media locations along wheelchair accessible service routes.[68] They also provide help accessing media from storage areas, handling fiche card holders and film reels. Reaching shelved microform media above or below seated eye-level is difficult for wheelchair users. People in wheelchairs also find it difficult to reach and extend forward from the seated position to operate microform equipment controls.[69] They frequently position themselves to the right or left to access display equipment from the side while maintaining body balance.[70] Some experience problems gaining sufficient reach for library equipment operation and microform viewing at comfortable reading levels. Microform focus controls may not be adjusted for wheelchair-seated patron users. Both manual and electric wheelchair users have more difficulty operating microform equipment if they have associated arm, hand or finger movement limitations. They may also physically and/or mentally tire more quickly during microform use than while reading print or electronic media.

Wheelchair roll-up access to library equipment is not the major issue of patrons using a wheelchair. Their concern, rather, is for information access in the library.

Locating the desired frame requires reading skill and microform orientation. The desired display frame must be located while reading rapidly moving visual information and may be disorienting to many, causing eye fatigue and taxing concentration. Fiche print presentations may not always be level or focused across each page. Viewing, skimming or reading pages requires more reading effort. Horizontal fiche page arrangement or fiche placement guides etched into metal fiche holders are not easily read from a wheelchair seated position. Those without a fiche "mental map" must be willing to experiment with fiche movement to find desired pages. Microfilm placement avoids out-of-focus page display but requires the operator to carefully position each page in full-screen view before reading or copying. Full-screen viewing may not be possible for wheelchair users without further body repositioning. Some may be unable to assume any position that provides full-screen viewing at the seated level.

Wheelchair user library equipment access is an oversimplified standard for library services provided to all patrons with other disabilities. All equipment types made "wheelchair accessible" in the library is a worthy goal, even an ADA-influenced mandate, but conceptually limited in scope. To provide all library equipment with wheelchair access is not ADA-mandated. The ADA requires library equipment access equity. This means that all types of library equipment have at least one specific piece of each equipment type that is wheelchair accessible. It does not mean that all library equipment needs to be wheelchair accessible. That is the important difference, but a continuing library myth. Wheelchair accessible library equipment does not assure equal or equitable equipment access to other disabled patrons. Library equipment support must be different based on disability differences in people. Retrofitting all library equipment accessible to the public is not ADA-required. Making all library equipment wheelchair accessible makes that equipment more accessible equally to the general public. Designating specific equipment types as wheelchair accessible should have been completed since Section 504 of the 1973 Vocational Rehabilitation Act for all libraries receiving federal assistance.[71] Since July 26, 1992 and under the requirements of the Americans with Disabilities Act all libraries must have formulated a plan for wheelchair accessibility.[72] Now libraries have to fully comply, while earlier federal requirements may have been circumvented.

Wheelchair roll-up access to library equipment is not the major issue of patrons using a wheelchair. Their concern, rather, is for information access in the library. Users with electric or manual wheelchairs require extensive equipment support in libraries where wheelchair roll-up access to equipment is nonexistent or nominal access provided only with librarian intervention. Those libraries that provide patron-with-wheelchair access to many equipment types lessen the need for librarian support beyond immediate access issues. But equipment accessible to patrons with wheelchairs must ultimately make library information fully accessible. Without information access, library equipment that is accessible does not meet their needs. The question is more information access for wheelchair users, not wheelchair access.

Low-Vision Patron Microform Access

Microforms, unreadable without equipment intervention, may help low-vision patrons better access library information. An historical argument among librarians was that repurposing print collections to microform would reduce collection maintenance and expense. Another argument suggested that microforms would provide cheap and easy access to all. The "access to all" has often precluded library patrons with low vision or the blind. Patrons with low vision self-determine whether microform magnified and focused images are visually accessible and may only occasionally request librarian microform orientation and sustained equipment support. The totally blind may have good reason to access or "read" microform information using personal attendants. Microform original source information can be transferred to paper copy by microform reader/copiers, then read page-by-page into electronic page readers that are audible to the blind.[73]

Persons with low vision have difficulty reading library microform signage and equipment control labels. They have particular difficulty with equipment bright/dim controls that do not move brightness to their personal standard reading level. Microform reader/copiers provide extra copy magnification. But enlarged output quality limits reading utility.[74] Librarians adjust contrast and focus settings or equipment controls well beyond their own reading requirements when helping the partially sighted. The setting adjustments are not determined by the librarian, but adjusted for the low-vision patron's reading comfort. The next microform reader may find equipment controls well out of focus, requiring further readjustment.

Current library microform equipment represents older technology without provision for effective information format changes using computer technology. Significant library microform technology upgrading to interface with computer text readers, speech synthesizers, augmented (oversized or large print) computer printouts remains to be done. Microfiche screen area-magnified displays are now available. Persons with low vision are left with two options: use library microform access as library-provided or avoid microform-based information altogether. Since many libraries have moved collections from original print to microform, many with low vision must wait for the slower access by borrowing original source print media. When print titles arrive persons with low vision can then directly read from printed original pages using hand magnifiers[75] or large area magnification Fresnel sheets.[76] People with low vision must bring personal magnification equipment to use at microform displays if successful reading requires such augmentation.

Successful microform reading requires those with low vision to closely approach the screen or equipment controls. Body positioning for sustained close-range reading at microform displays appears exaggerated when compared to the reading positions of normally-sighted patrons.[77] Microform reading requires repositioning for comfort or taking "visual breaks" away from screen displays. Persons with low vision have a significantly slower reading rate than others using microforms.[78] They require more frequent rest periods. Since the number of microform reader/copiers is usually limited, patron equipment conflicts may occur.

Library Equipment Support

Telecommunication Devices For The Deaf (TDDs)

An example of low-demand library equipment is access by patrons with disabilities to Telecommunication Devices for the Deaf (TDDs). Library equipment access must include TDDs.[79] A single TDD in the library may place several hearing-impaired or deaf patrons in direct conflict for TDD access. TDD use patterns during regular library hours, as with other low-demand equipment for specialized disabled use, may indicate that libraries should have multiple TDDs available. Low-demand TDD equipment becomes high-demand equipment when local libraries have an active deaf community demanding access to the same single library TDD. Where increased competition occurs, patron access time limits on using specialized equipment can be reasonably imposed and should be equitably enforced. Locating specialized equipment in special or separate library service rooms has been suggested.[80] But housing TDDs in special rooms does not meet the natural library setting guiding principle for library equipment service to all disabled patrons.

Library study carrels or special designated library rooms or areas may house telecommunication devices for the deaf (TDDs) for private communication using a dedicated telephone line.[81] TDDs are locked at study carrels for authorized use only and to avoid nuisance long distance charges. The ADA encourages libraries to specifically provide TDD access for deaf and hearing interactions as a public service standard.[82] All federal agencies are now required to do so. Teletype (TTY) equipment for the deaf or TDDs can connect off-site patrons and library telephones, using TDD communications equipment at both ends. Television screen messages are TDD keyboard-displayed for library or patron operation. Placing a TDD telephone call requires either party to dial the number, turn on the TDD and place the receiver in an acoustic coupler, allowing voice-grade telephone signals to be sent and received by TDDs. Telephones receiving TDD calls must be flasher-equipped. Incoming TDD calls are accepted by picking up the phone receiver, turning the TDD on, and placing the receiver in an acoustic coupler. TDD receivers read incoming messages at the screen and interact with the other TDD party through the keyboard. All TDD equipment is standard and intercompatible.

There must be no presumption that TDD users must be deaf or hearing impaired. It often occurs that hearing TDD users, including other patrons and librarians, must communicate with those who require TDD-level interactions and format. Local conditions may dictate that the only accessible TDD is the one located in the library. When this occurs, TDD use can be extensive both for calling in and calling out from the library. This leads to further TDD access competition that soon comes into high-demand.

Captioned Video Playback

Deaf or hearing impaired patrons profit from access to library closed- or open-captioned video collections using specialized library playback equipment, or utilizing that same equipment in their homes.[83] The hearing impaired experience difficulty gaining information with conventional VCR and VHS videotape auditory playback systems. At least one VCR amplification device and earphone output with patron volume control should be library-accessible to the hearing impaired. Easily readable and understood library signs and handouts enable patrons to independently use VCR playback and handle VHS tapes that are also closed-captioned. The deaf or hearing impaired need access to specialized and conventional library equipment sometimes used in unconventional ways to meet their unique or personal information needs. In no sense are they limited only to library-based visually-oriented information.

The deaf or hearing impaired need access to specialized and conventional library equipment sometimes used in unconventional ways to meet their unique or personal information needs.

Library Patrons With Disabilities

Hearing-Impaired Access to Audio Equipment

The hearing impaired have a broad spectrum of library information interests to be met. They may require equal and integrated library equipment support, like other members of the general public.[84] Being deaf or hearing impaired does not inhibit or restrict the need for information but may restrict library equipment types that effectively support information access. The deaf often bring personal auxiliary aids and services during library visits.[85]

Patrons with hearing impairment may experience initial difficulty using library audiocassettes, videotape, record, and compact disk players, as well as other audio playback equipment where audio amplification is required beyond a hearing person's comfort level. Audio equipment may be adjusted to levels that disturb nearby hearing patrons. Equipment volume controls at maximum output distort sounds and may still not achieve their minimal hearing requirements. Public address systems, for example, are inappropriate or ineffective since volume adjustments for the hearing impaired would clearly disrupt hearing patrons. Using earphones sometimes avoids that disruption. The hearing impaired also require assistive listening devices during library assemblies.[86] They sometimes create considerable noise and distraction during their library occupancy.

When library listening skills associated with equipment operation are required, hearing disabilities limit patron infosearching independence. Although patron verbal responses to the librarian are required, each may fail to successfully communicate with the other at library equipment. Librarians support the deaf or hearing impaired by effectively communicating during equipment use orientation or reorientation.[87]

Low-Vision Computer Technology Users

Low-vision users require adaptations to optimize viewing or reading computer monitor displays. Contrast, brightness control and magnified screen-area viewing may be necessary.[88] Home keys are more easily recognized on computer keyboards by touch for thos with low vision than reading from computer monitor screens. Large print software enables low-vision patrons to read from computer monitor screens.[89] Persons with low vision require computer literacy skills assessment for library support needs. Such assessment, library equipment reconfiguration, specialized service and other library support is driven by specific patron requests.[90] No library equipment support is imposed on patrons with low vision who do not request them.[91]

CD-ROM Players

Compact Disk-Read Only Memory (CD-ROM) player access is an example of a library natural setting where patron equipment orientation takes place. CD-ROM players give access to reference databases which are an important library information source. External or internal optical laser disk drives provide massive database access on library microcomputers.[92] CD-ROM facilitates viewing, selecting and printing out patron-defined information. Yet with all state-of-the-art infosearching technology benefits, some patrons with disabilities do not accept the CD-ROM infosearching alternative. Because some information can only be accessed by CD-ROM, each CD-ROM must be made fully wheelchair accessible.[93] CD-ROM library systems provide separate information access windows for all patrons. Since most CD-ROMs are dedicated to one information database, and are not duplicated across the library, dedicated CD-ROM access for all patrons with disabilities is ADA-required. Titles available to libraries may not be accessible to all state-of-the-art library computers with CD-ROM. Format incompatability currently reduces the number of industry-controlled CD-ROM titles accessible by a single library computer that is CD-ROM player equipped.[94] This requires libraries to dedicate computers to groups of compatible CD-ROM media or to one dedicated CD-ROM title service. Public and academic libraries often provide banks of dedicated CD-ROM-specific computers.

Library Equipment Support

Persons with low vision are often described as the "print disabled." Patrons with low vision require special adaptations to access CD-ROM, database-dedicated computers. CD-ROM may be the only viable library technology alternative for low-vision patrons providing access to entire print reference collections. Computer technology is a critical information and library equipment access barrier for patrons with low vision. Onscreen displays may not be interpretable without devices translating printed text to computer-synthesized speech. But there remains many problems with text screen translators that limit patron prolonged or effective use.

CD-ROM access for the disabled is complex since use of this technology requires an interface between patron and the library computer. Because of the human/machine interface complexity, CD-ROM may be low-demand until challenged patrons become familiarized, oriented, and comfortable with this technology. Librarians may point proudly to the bank of library CD-ROM dedicated computers during group library orientations. Yet individual access to each CD-ROM dedicated computer, and the massive inherent database often requires extensive personal equipment support. All library innovations have a human price in orientation, effort, and ease of use to gain library information.

Preparation for CD-ROM format use is done during librarian startup. No patron CD-ROM media handling is expected or required. Patrons do not have to "platter swap" CD-ROM media sources to access information on the same library computer. CD-ROM-dedicated computers should be repositioned throughout the library to facilitate CD-ROM format access for all. CD-ROM database access begins with keyboard entry after librarians power up CD-ROM- dedicated microcomputers and associated peripheral equipment, including impact or laser printers. CD-ROM databases are accessed by using a keyboard or repositioning and clicking a mouse while viewing monitor displays.[95] Following librarian or publisher embedded prompts, patrons access user-friendly CD-ROM databases with onscreen menus. Most patrons with disabilities can independently access CD-ROM keyboards, make menu selections, display information on screen, make printouts, and exit programs. Printouts are taken with the patron after being torn off from fan-fold paper or hand-collated on plain paper stock. User-friendliness varies significantly for disabled patrons between the various CD-ROM media providers. There are many inherent CD-ROM information access challenges with this library equipment.

Synthesized Speech Devices

Library computers with synthesized speech translate blind operator keyboard entry, screen output[96] or printed text-to-speech.[97] Synthesized speech technology requires library computers configured for the blind.[98] The sighted may find computer synthesized speech distracting. Librarians can gear computer equipment to allow all library patrons to elect to hear it or switch off the computer-generated speech.

Reading Machines

Reading machines such as OPTACON(tm) use an array of 144 electrically activated pins to translate printed symbols into raised, vibrating print that is readable by touch.[99] OPTACON(tm) equipment requires users to scan single lines of print with a small, hand-held camera that produces a tactile-screen image. Tactile output is readable as visual symbols. The touch output pattern read by the library patron moving the scanner produces a tactile counterpart of visible symbols, letters and numbers, not Braille symbols. Reading machine output is one-way local library site communication, where patrons receive tactile information that may not be sent by computer, telephone or other conventional means. Reading machine output is not recordable in other mediums for later patron reference. The process must be repeated for each reading event. Patrons can read print-based collections using this technology. OPTACON(tm) use requies extensive patron training.[100] Study carrels are the focal point for disabled access to other library equipment and patron-owned auxiliary equipment brought in. Synthesized speech using library Information Through Speech (Maryland Computer Services) reading equipment requires scanning single print lines with a small hand-held camera. The Xerox

Library Patrons With Disabilities

Corporation has developed a table-mounted scanner that reads aloud entire pages of text. Equipment converts print materials into synthetic speech output. No storage or synthesized speech retrieval is available once equipment produces speech unless the user brings personal recording equipment for long-term audio information storage.

Synthesized speech approaches but is not natural human speech. Recognizing and gaining information from this auditory output may require user adaptation and training. Since methods like Kurzweil[101] require the user to operate a small hand-held camera, anyone needing this library equipment support must also be able to closely control the camera unless table-mounted scanners are available. Patrons with upper-body mobility limitations find camera use difficult. Kurzweil technology provides effective library equipment support for some patrons with vision disabilities. But Kurzweil technology is expensive.

User-Friendly Library Equipment

Many patrons regard library equipment with no sense of familiarity or comfort. They avoid equipment use whenever possible and, to gain information, use library equipment only as a last resort. Some use equipment without remembering previously demonstrated skills. Library equipment varies greatly in user-friendliness.[102] User-friendly equipment has complex controls that are made obvious to the user at every operational step. Equipment control mistakes and complex operational procedures are thereby minimized. Instructions on how to recover from common equipment mistakes are shown near user-friendly equipment using library signage. The term "user-friendly" originated from computer technology and the frustrations novice users often experienced while accessing computer hardware, software and operational manuals. A computer system said to be user-friendly is one where during operation, multistep controls are made obvious to the user. The net effect makes equipment easy to use. For some with disabilities, library equipment is not considered user-friendly. And non-user-friendly equipment reduces the effectiveness of patron's library infosearching when using that equipment is required and there are no other equipment or information access alternatives.

Study carrels are the focal point for disabled access to other library equipment and patron-owned auxiliary equipment brought in.

Computer control steps are "user-transparent" when patrons understand specific operational steps, user activities and judgments. Operating computer controls that are user transparent are said to be "intuitive" controls. Equipment operational guides developed through librarian accommodation are both user-friendly and user-transparent. User-friendly equipment controls differ with library equipment type. Manufacturers sometimes exaggerate user-friendliness or user transparency for operators in their claims to librarians during sales promotions. Some claims assure that particular equipment brands, models or versions minimize library patron-support requirements. Others assure that the patron can easily utilize the specific equipment type during the infosearching process. More relevant to the equipment support needs of patrons with disabilities is their requirement that library equipment must be both ADA-compliant and user-friendly.

Computer equipment that does not "lock-up" when the wrong control setting is pushed is said to be "error-trapped." Error-trapping accommodates common patron equipment and computer mistakes. Error-trapped controls prevent patrons from having to retreat from errors by leaving the equipment, turning it off, or seeking immediate librarian support.

Library Equipment User Guides

Patrons with disabilities should be provided clear interpretive user guides showing library equipment operational steps. Operational manuals are not user-friendly unless they are translated into clearly indicated operational steps. Operational steps should be easily readable and in full view near that equipment. Common user mistakes to avoid should be shown in operational guide content. Multistep library equipment operational sequences may not be understandable to many patrons.[103] Few library equipment guides are prepared with disabled patrons in mind.[104]

To support library purchase, manufacturers provide "user-friendly" equipment guides. Claims assure librarians that particular equipment brands, models or versions minimize patron support requirements. Promotional literature suggests or implies guarantees for successful library patron operation under "normal use." The "normal use" condition is vague. "Normal use" may not apply to patrons with disabilities. They may be unable to use equipment in conventional ways without personalized adaptation and librarian accommodation. Shall "normal use" guide reading and equipment operation be required of disabled patrons without input from them after trying out that equipment? Do manufacturer guides do the job for all library patrons--even the physically or cognitively challenged?

Original equipment manufacturer (OEM) user equipment guides may not provide sufficiently detailed, meaningful, or simplified, accessible information.[105] OEM guide content should adhere to basic instructional design principles for effective use by patrons with disabilities and the general library public.[106] Guide steps should be shown in clear or usable formats from the patron, not librarian perspective. OEM guides should use pictograms to reduce reading requirements and help assure successful equipment operation.[107]

Original equipment manufacturer (OEM) user equipment guides may not provide sufficiently detailed, meaningful, or simplified, accessible information.

Operational sequences are often assumed by the librarian but are not clearly indicated to the patron. OEM guides may not show steps in literal operational sequence. Steps branch to accomplish a variety of library user activities, requiring unstated or unexpected user judgments at each decision point.[108] Decision points may not be clearly shown or recognizable to disabled patrons. Critical decision points should be not just implied, but explicitly stated. Unclear OEM guide content makes patrons with disabilities librarian-dependent.

Successful adapted library equipment guides have clear and explicit steps that avoid complex patron decisions. Complex patron decision-making should be information driven, not driven by equipment operational steps. Librarians construct effective and accessible equipment operational guides after observing use problems by the disabled. Both patron and librarian interact over time to create optimal adaptive equipment guides. Remembering previous operational steps is sometimes implicitly required for library equipment success. Alternate operational steps have unclear implications for patron-expected results. Unexpected equipment results require further patron-librarian interaction. Alternate steps may not be comprehensible to users with disabilities. The disabled patron must build and modify a working mental map of library equipment to operate it successfully. Guides help build and maintain these equipment operation mental maps.

Library Patrons With Disabilities

Updating Equipment User Guides

Changes in existing library equipment and new equipment upgrades must be reflected in user guides to reduce their need for equipment orientation and supervision. Patrons with disabilities vary in their ability to consistently perform at equipment over time. Some do not maintain consistent equipment performance levels or skill. Disabled patrons may need the same upgraded orientation, reorientation and ongoing librarian equipment support. Most patrons do not require librarian hand-holding. When they need equipment support, they ask librarians for updated equipment user guides.

Manufacturers may claim "ADA compliant" as an essential product feature without real ADA-compliance documentation. Other manufacturers do not specifically refer to ADA requirements at all. The patron with disabilities, as a real user of new equipment rather than an equally real avoider of it, may be left out of the loop in the library decision to purchase newer equipment. The United States Congress or any federal agency currently maintains a policy of not endorsing any equipment manufacturer over any other manufacturer. The principle of caveat emptor (let the buyer beware) applies here.

Adapted User Guides

Adapted user guides are librarian-edited, "personalized" or "library-specific" OEM user guide versions. Without library adaptation, OEM guides may be informative only to professional librarians, not to patrons with library context disabilities. Adapted user guide design requires extensive library editing to give patrons multiple access points into the guide. Edited guides provide a complete library equipment orientation document across all conventional, adaptive and augmentative equipment available in the library. Guides are assembled with all separate OEM guides under one cover. These edited and adapted equipment guides accommodate diverse patron needs and include all local library equipment. Guides are placed in three-ring bound notebooks with laminated pages and a content securement system to allow easy page removal and replacement as content changes are made. They can also be taken with the patron to each library equipment site. Information in the guide should match equipment signage, directions and operational steps. The patron thus receives two sources of consistent information to operate library equipment: one from the adapted guide and the other from on-site library equipment signage. Edited guides are designed for the patron, not for the librarian or the manufacturer, and should exclude library worker maintenance and repair steps. Equipment maintenance and repair is a library, not a patron, responsibility.

OEM drawings or illustrations are designed for professional librarian use. These visual graphics may not be designed or presented for direct patron access. Graphics in the adapted user guide should be embedded in parallel text when describing equipment operational steps. If text operational steps are required, they are illustrated with embedded pictograms. Edited guide steps should provide operational access to nonliterate or non-English language users. OEM graphics are not ready for patron presentation without further librarian editing. Librarian-adapted graphics provide a complete, fully illustrated, step-by-step equipment guide to the equipment being described. When completed, adapted user guides provide complete library equipment pictorial.guidance without requiring the patron to read.

Adapted user guides are librarian-edited, "personalized" or "library-specific" OEM user guide versions.

Library Equipment Support

Adapted user guides become patron self-orientation manuals for library equipment operation. Patrons refer to the adapted user guide or take it with them during library equipment use. Returning user guides before library exit permits others' use. At any one time, and on request, several locally adapted guides should be available for all library patrons. This is a significant library accommodation for patrons with disabilities and the general library public. Embedded exit control identifiers should be added to guides to control unauthorized guide removal from the library.

Copyright law may be violated when library user guides are adapted unless original equipment manufacturers (OEM) give permission to modify guide content. Not all OEM guides are copyrighted, implying librarian permission to adapt guide content to local conditions and patron special needs. Altered OEM guides should be approved by the manufacturer or OEM-validated for effective equipment use represented in the newly adapted way. Adapting guide content and obtaining its approval alerts OEMs of the need to change conventional guide content. Without OEM approval, copyrighted conventional guide content cannot be adapted to local conditions or for patrons with disabilities. Part of the library decision to purchase should be a careful review of OEM policy permitting local library adapted user guide changes.

Operational steps should be rearranged from left-to-right and top-to-bottom to establish conventional reading, viewing or operational order. General information gain is best done from page upper-left to bottom-right. Instructional design principles suggest that conventional reading patterns better assist patrons to absorb and utilize new information. New information must be presented on the page where it is patron-expected. OEMs present equipment guides in multiple language formats. Formats often include parallel translations of English, German, French, Spanish or Japanese. Librarians should edit conventional multi-language guide content leaving English-only instruction. In adapted guides, steps in English are further edited for simple and direct patron use. Simply worded English directions are the industry standard for adapted guides. English-only adapted user guide content is supplemented by graphics or pictograms also accommodate non-English language users.

User Guide Text Readability

OEM guide text is not often simplified to accommodate readability levels for patrons with reading disabilities. Existing guide text far exceeds the reading difficulty standards regularly maintained even by newspapers. Librarians must reword OEM guide text to fourth-grade readability. This adapted guide standard, below newspaper reading difficulty level, allows for maximum patron numbers to read equipment operational controls. Librarians also substitute technical terms for easily recognized control symbol ICONS embedded in simplified text steps.[109] Overall sentence length used to describe operational steps is reduced. The barest essential sentences use the fewest words and employ the simplest vocabulary. Professional library jargon should be avoided as well as OEM technical terms since those terms require high levels of reading ability in library patrons and library terms imply advanced equipment orientation as a prerequisite to successful equipment operation.

Librarians embed "STEP NO. 1, 2, 3" features to match adapted user guide illustrations. Text steps on pictograms are linked with arrows to library equipment controls. Arrows are sequenced where possible showing pictogrms or illustrations from upper-left to lower-right, progressing clockwise around the equipment. These steps match with equipment operational control sequences as well as parallel steps decribed in the adapted user guide text. The reader thereby gains parallel step instructions--one from text and the other from graphics. Original OEM text guide font size should also be increased as needed to LARGE PRINT STANDARD FONTS or larger, for effective guide display. Original OEM drawings can be enlarged by photocopy without significant picture, illustration or text quality loss.[110] Bold, italicized or UPPER-CASE words are embedded in adapted user guide text, in addition to pictograms. Re-emphasized TERMS illustrated on pictograms and on library equipment controls, displays or operational guides focus patron attention.

Library Patrons With Disabilities

Adapted user tab guides showing equipment content illustrations help people quickly find specific library equipment references. Color-coded tab guides can direct patrons to matching color-coded equipment in library service areas. (See Chapter Four for related library service color-coded route trails.) All OEM changes, equipment removal or replacement must be reflected in constantly updated tab guides and guide content.

Alternative Equipment User Guides

Various year equipment models from the same manufacturer are often on the library floor at the same time. In conventional guides, OEMs resist comparing their older models with newer equipment. Yet libraries are free to purchase and place a variety of similar equipment made by different manufacturers or by the same manufacturer. Local library user guides can show side-by-side operational step comparisons with simpler make-model-year library equipment alternatives.

Avoiding User Guide Bias

Operational steps related to individuals with disabilities are often ignored in conventional library user OEM guides. While OEM guides illustrate library equipment operational steps, they do not show the physically challenged accomplishing those equipment operational steps. Illustrations showing patrons with visible or obvious library context disability successfully operating equipment should be used throughout adapted library equipment user guides. Adaptations subtly illustrate competency in patrons with disabilities and impact nondisabled readers or the general public to rethink library equipment access for all. The guide's emphasis should not be on characteristics of disabled patrons, but on equipment operational characteristics accessible to everyone. This is an important difference in contextual disabled patron representations and is significant for the dignity and acceptance of disabled patrons.

Adapted User Guides For All: Gender and Disability Bias

OEM guides generally use gender-specific professional models that do not represent a balance of equipment-user typical male and female characteristics. OEM guide gender bias distracts from essential operational steps when only attractive adult females are shown. Adapted user guides should show gender-neutral models or a balance of male and female patrons, as well as patrons with visible or obvious disabilities, at OEM controls. The overall impact of such an adapted user guide is to provide all library patrons with successful equipment operator role models. Since library patrons with disabilities may not fit the traditional library patron role or appearance, adapted user guides can make an important difference in public disabled individual acceptance. Patrons with library context disabilities shown at library equipment controls should not be restricted to persons with wheelchairs. Better adapted guides balance the representation of people with other visible disabilities. Wheelchair users do not fully illustrate how equipment access can be accomplished by patrons with diverse library context disabilities. People with canes, braces, crutches, walkers, long canes, and service animals should be shown in favorable library equipment-use contexts. Librarians build in an inherent adapted user guide bias when adapted guide illustrations are limited only to adaptive, assistive or augmentive library equipment. The general public does not understand that many disabled individuals do not have obvious or observable disabilities in the library.

Disability-Neutral Adapted Equipment User Guides

Specialized equipment intended primarily for use by disabled patrons implies adapted user guides should contain only that specialized library equipment. Guides must instead include conventional library equipment use by all individuals with library context disabilities. While separate sections of adapted user guides show specialized library equipment access and operation for disability-specific patron use, they should not be presented first. "Disability-neutral" library equipment tabs and content should be alphabetically presented

Library Equipment Support

in adapted library guides. Librarians must demonstrate care when any message to patrons with disabilities implies that only disabled patrons will be using that library equipment. Some patrons with physical or cognitive challenges will reject library equipment use for that reason alone, considering that librarians implicitly or explicitly focus on patron <u>disabilities</u>, rather than their equipment <u>abilities</u>. This distinction may not be clear to individuals without disabilities or to librarians. But it is a significant distinction about which many with disabilities are highly sensitive. User guides frequently assume user illustrations for right-handed operators when some have right-hand only prostheses, missing limbs, or who are left-handed. A general acceptance of left-handed patrons with or without disabilities can thereby be library-implied and patron-accepted. User guides often have no OEM illustrations showing alternative disabled operator strategies or accommodation. The overall nonverbal, subconscious and OEM user-guide message for the disabled: "Do Not Attempt to Use This Equipment Without Help." User guide content provides an implied dependence on librarians for equipment accommodation.

User guides often have no OEM illustrations showing disabled operator strategies or accommodation.

User Guide Disclaimers

OEM guide content is not intended for public use but for professional librarian operation, repair or maintenance. OEMs assume librarians will fully orient users with disabilities through equipment demonstration or that their equipment operation will demonstrate itself. Librarians do not rely on OEM guide content to provide the sole means of patron library equipment self-orientation. Some disabled patrons are unable to orient themselves on library equipment without further librarian accommodation.

OEM disclaimers help influence librarians to develop local adapted user guides. Once local guides are developed, OEMs may implement user guide modifications more sensitive to patrons with physical or cognitive challenges. OEMs may wish to adopt effective local adapted user guide content for general, market-wide distribution. Professional librarians determine on specific equipment or model basis whether OEM user guides should be reinterpreted in local adapted guides. The necessity of meeting local needs with library-specific adapted user guides is a strong argument to obtain OEM permission to alter copyrighted material. Since no distribution to other libraries, resale or profit from adapted guides is intended, and guide adaptations and content are for solely educational purposes, copyright permission usually can be obtained. Copyright permits adapted user guides as genuinely educational, not commercial, products.

User Guides or Librarian Orientation

Patron orientation is librarian- and time-intensive to meet local library-disabled needs. Time and effort required to create adapted guides must be balanced against library resources to provide effective individualized equipment support. Each library must balance local needs with accommodation requirements for all patrons. Local community surveys and assessment of patron equipment-use patterns may reveal the need for adapted user guide creation, content and implementation.

Summary

This chapter addressed patron equipment support issues in the context of librarian myths and assumptions. Librarians support people with disabilities just as they support all individual library patron needs. They assess patron mobility and equipment access and operation skills, and judge whether library equipment is safely and appropriately used. They evaluate patron-accessible equipment for possible barriers. Removal of library equipment barriers was discussed.

End Notes:

1. Szymanski, Edna Mora. (1994) Transition: Life-span and life-space considerations for empowerment. Exceptional Children, 60(5), 402-410.

2. ADA Handbook. U.S. Department of Justice. (1991). Americans with Disabilities Act Handbook. Washington, DC: U.S. Government Printing Office. Page I-77.

3. Cagle, R. Brantley. (1983). Reference service to the developmentally disabled: Normalization of access. Catholic Library World, 54, 267.

4. Ibid, ADA Handbook, I-63.

5. Ibid, ADA Handbook, I-61 & 67.

6. Ibid, ADA Handbook, II-14.

7. Rogers, Everett. (1983). Diffusion of innovation. Third Edition. New York: The Free Press.

8. Ibid, ADA Handbook, II-53: "This part does not require a public entity to provide to individuals with disabilities personal devices, such as wheelchairs; individually prescribed devices, such as prescription eyeglasses or hearing aids; readers for personal use or study; or services of a personal nature including assistance in eating, toileting, or dressing."

9. Vertelney, Laurie, Arent, Michael and Lieberman, Henry. (1990). Two disciplines in search of an interface: Reflections on a design problem. In, The art of human-computer interface design. Laurel, Brenda (Ed.) Menlo Park, CA: Addison Wesley. Page 53.

10. Ibid, ADA Handbook, II-42.

11. Ibid, ADA Handbook, II-39.

12. Ibid, ADA Handbook, II-77.

13. Goltz, Eileen. (1991). The provision of services to students with special needs in Canadian academic libraries. Canadian Library Journal, 48(4), 266. See also Irwin, Irwin, Marilyn. (1992). Library Media Specialist as teacher for students who are disabled. Indiana Media Journal, 14, 11; and Miller, Richard T. (1992). The Americans with Disabilities Act: Library facility and program access under Titles II and III. Ohio Libraries, 5, 10-11; and Temsky, R. Marlene. (1982). Some suggestions for public library service to disabled persons. Bay State Librarian, 71,5.

14. ADAAG. Appendix B. Americans with Disability Accessibility Guidelines. In, U.S. Department of Justice. (1991). Americans with Disabilities Act Handbook. Washington, DC: U.S. Government Printing Office. Page A4.30.4.

15. Ibid, ADA Handbook, II-14.

16. Ibid, ADA Handbook, II-42.

17. Ibid, ADA Handbook, II-42.

18. Havens, Shirley E. (1987). Large print in focus. Library Journal, 112, 32-33.

19. Foster, Terry & Lindell, Linda. (1991). Libraries and the Americans with Disabilities Act. Texas Libraries, 52, 61-62.

20. Ibid, ADA Handbook, II-59.

21. Ibid, Havens, 32-33.

22. Ibid, ADA Handbook, I-62(3).

23. Ibid, ADA Handbook II-69 & 70.

24. Roatch, Mary A. (1992). High tech and library access for people with disabilities. Public Libraries, 31, 89.

25. Ibid, Roatch, 90.

26. Ibid, Irwin, 12. See also, Versabraille II+, Telesensory, 455 North Bernardo Avenue, P.O. Box 7455, Mountain View, CA 94039-7455. (800) 227-8418 or (415) 960-0920.

27. Jahoda, Gerald & Johnson, Elizabeth A. (1987). The use of the Kurzweil reading machine in academic libraries. Journal of Academic Librarianship, 13(2), 99.

28. Neville, Ann & Kupersmith, John. (1991). Online access for visually impaired students. Database, 14, 103.

29. Ibid, Roatch, 89. See also, Vista, by TeleSensory, Mountain View, CA.

Library Equipment Support

30. Kuhlenschmidt, Eden, Swan, Kim & Scholes, Jan. (1992). Ms. K, there's a tiger in the computer. <u>Indiana Media Journal</u>, <u>14</u>, 8.

31. O'Donnell, Ruth. (1992). Adapting print for improved access. Part 2. <u>Library Journal</u>, November 1, 1992, 61.

32. Ibid, O'Donnell, Part 2, 60.

33. Kurzweil, Raymond. (1992). The futurecast: The end of handicaps, part 2. <u>Library Journal</u>, 66-67.

34. Haynes, Douglas E. (1989). The switch library: New service in rehabilitation librarianship. <u>Bulletin of the Medical Library Association</u>, <u>77</u>, 15.

35. Ibid, Foster & Lindell, 61.

36. Ibid, Foster & Lindell, 62.

37. Ibid, <u>ADA Handbook</u>, II-41.

38. Gunde, Michael. (1991). Working with the Americans with Disabilities Act. <u>Library Journal</u>, <u>116</u>(21), 99-100.

39. Ibid, Foster & Lindell, 61.

40. Ibid, <u>ADA Handbook</u>, II-41 & 42.

41. Ibid, Neville & Kupersmith, 103. See also, Power, M.T., Rundlett, Carol & David, Myra. (1989). New challenges in helping students uncover information: The learning disabled student. <u>The Bookmark</u>, <u>47</u>(11), 214.

42. Ibid, Neville & Kupersmith, 103. See also, Power, 214 and Rogers (1983).

43. Walling, Linda Lucas. (1992). Granting each equal access. <u>School Library Media Quarterly</u>, <u>20</u>, 217.

44. Lisson, Paul. (1987). Large print placebo. <u>Canadian Library Journal</u>, <u>44</u>, 5. "More than 80 percent of all people considered legally blind have usable vision. They are not blind; they have low vision."

45. Ibid, <u>ADA Handbook</u>, I-77.

46. Ibid, <u>ADA Handbook</u>, I-77.

47. Ibid, <u>ADA Handbook</u>, I-77.

48. Thiele, Paul E. (1984). New technologies for the blind reading community. <u>Canadian Library Journal</u>, <u>41</u>, 132. See also American Library Association. (1988). <u>Information power: Guidelines for school library media programs</u>. Chicago: American Library Association. Pages 5-6.

49. Allegri, Francesca. (1984). On the other side of the reference desk: The patron with a physical disability. <u>Medical Reference Services Quarterly</u>, <u>3</u>(3), 73.

50. Ibid, <u>ADAAG</u>, 4.30.1 to 4.30.6.

51. Ibid, <u>ADAAG</u>, 4.30.4.

52. Editor. (1983). Photocopier produces raised-relief Braille copies. <u>Industrial Research & Development</u>, 25, 65-66.

53. Ibid, <u>ADAAG</u>, A4.30.4.

54. Ibid, <u>ADA Handbook</u>, II-65. See also, <u>ADAAG</u>, 4.3.2(3) and 4.6.2. See also, Mannheim, Peter. (1992). The Americans with Disabilities Act: The legal implications. In, Foos, Donald D. & Pack, Nancy C. (Eds.). (1992). <u>How libraries must comply with the Americans with Disabilities Act (ADA)</u>. Phoenix, AZ: Oryx. Page 106.

55. Ibid, Allegri, 73. See also, Goltz, 267.

56. Ibid, Allegri, 74.

57. Ibid, <u>ADAAG</u>, 4.27.4.

58. Ibid, Allegri, 74. See also, Goltz, 267.

59. Ibid, <u>ADAAG</u>, 4.2.5.

60. Ibid, <u>ADAAG</u>, 4.32.4.

61. Ibid, <u>ADAAG</u>, 4.32.3.

62. Ibid, <u>ADAAG</u>, 4.30.4 & A4.30.4.

63. Ibid, <u>ADAAG</u>, A4.3.1.

64. Ibid, <u>ADAAG</u>, A4.3.1.

65. Ibid, <u>ADA Handbook</u>, I-63.

66. Ibid, <u>ADA Handbook</u>, I-77.

67. Ibid, <u>ADAAG</u>, 4.2.4.1.

68. Ibid, <u>ADA Handbook</u>, II-65 & <u>ADAAG</u>, 4.3.2(3).

69. Ibid, <u>ADAAG</u>, 4.2.5.

70. Ibid, <u>ADAAG</u>, 4.2.6.

71. Public Law 93-112, 87 Stat. 394 (29 U.S.C. 794), as amended.

72. Ibid, Gunde, 99-100.

73. Optacon II-Telesensory, 455 North Bernardo Ave., P.O. Box 7455, Mountain View, CA 94039-7455. (800) 227-8418 or (415) 960-0920.

74. Ibid, Goltz, 265.

75. Ibid, Foster & Lindell, 61.

76. Major, Jean A. (1982). The visually impaired reader in the academic library. In, <u>Library services for the handicapped adult</u>. Thomas, J.L. & Thomas, C.H. (Eds.). Phoenix, AZ: Oryx Press. Pages 39-48.

77. Ibid, Lisson, 5.

78. Kirtley, D.D. (1975). <u>The psychology of blindness.</u> Chicago, IL: Nelson-Hall.

79. Ibid, <u>ADA Handbook</u>, II-13.

80. Ibid, Allegri, 74.

81. Ibid, <u>ADA Handbook</u>, II-73.

82. Ibid, <u>ADA Handbook</u>, II-71 to 73.

83. Freese, Michele & Cohen, Susan F. (1986). Awareness project for library service for the hearing impaired. <u>Illinois Libraries, 68</u>, 552.

84. Day, John Michael. (1992). Guidelines for library services to deaf people: Development and interpretation. <u>IFLA Journal, 18</u>, 33: "...it is imperative that the same level of service available to the general constituency of the library be equally available to clientele who are deaf."

85. Ibid, <u>ADA Handbook</u>, II-53.

86. Ibid, <u>ADAAG</u>, A4.30.7. See also <u>ADAAG</u>, Table A2. Summary of Assistive Listening Devices.

87. Hagemeyer, Alice. (1982). Library service and outreach programs for the deaf. <u>Wyoming Library Roundup, 38</u>(2), 15-21.

88. MagniWORD, General Business Machines Corp., 5819 Uplander Way, Culver City, CA 90230. (800) 228-3349 or (213) 216-9955.

89. Large Print DOS (LP-DOS). Optelec US Inc., P.O. Box 796, Westford, MA 01886. (800) 828-1056 or (617) 789-5321.

90. Ibid, <u>ADA Handbook</u>, I-61 & 67.

91. Ibid, <u>ADA Handbook</u>, II-39 & III-51.

92. Medrinos, Roxanne Baxter. (1992). CD-ROM and at-risk students. <u>School Library Journal, 38</u>, 30.

93. Ibid, <u>ADAAG</u>, 4.32.3.

94. The CD-ROM industry is currently underway to establish an international and industry-standard CD-ROM format interchangeability. To date, full CD-ROM interchangeability has not been library implemented.

95. Computer mouse operation, viewing screens and other patron specific library relevant disability characteristics is beyond the scope of this book. Consult the ergonomic computer design for individuals with disabilities and man/machine interface literature.

96. Ibid, O'Donnell, 68-69.

97. Ibid, O'Donnell, 68-69.

98. Ibid, O'Donnell, Part 2, 60-61.

99. OPTACON II, Telesensory, Inc., 455 North Bernardo Ave., P.O. Box 7455, Mountain View, CA 94039-7455. (800) 227-8418 or (415) 960-0920.

100. Bekiares, Susan E. (1984). Technology for the Handicapped: Selection and evaluation of aids and devices for the visually impaired. <u>Library Hi Tech, 5</u>(2), 60.

101. Kurzweil Personal Reader, Kurzweil Computer Products, 185 Albany Street, Cambridge, MA 02139 (800) 343-0311 or (617) 864-4700.

Library Equipment Support

102. Rheingold, Howard. (1990). An interview with Don Norman. In The art of human-computer interface design. Laurel, Brenda (Ed.) Menlo Park, CA: Addison Wesley. Page 10: "Users...are often fearful. Fear is an important element in every novice computer user's first attempts to use a new machine or new software: fear of destroying data, fear of hurting the machine, fear of seeming stupid in comparison to other users, or even to the machine itself."

103. Howell, Richard. (1989). Some issues related to technological intervention with disabled learners: Cues for instructional designers. Ohio Media Spectrum, 41, 50-53.

104. Ibid, Howell, 51.

105. Ibid, ADAAG, A4.30.4.

106. Dick, Walter & Carey, Lou. (1990). The systematic design of instruction. Third Edition. Glenview, Illinois: Scott Foresman.

107. Ibid, ADAAG, 4.30.4 & A.4.30.4.

108. Oren, Tim, Salomon, Gitta, Kreitman, Kristee & Don, Abbe. (1990). Guides: Characterizing the interface. In, The art of human-computer interface design. Laurel, Brenda (Ed.). Reading, MA: Addison Wesley. Pages 367-381.

109. Gengle, Dean. (1984). The netweaver's sourcebook: A guide to micro networking and communications. Menlo Park, CA: Addison-Wesley. 20: "ICON: An image, representation, or symbol that stands for something else, usually something physical in the real world."

110. Ibid, Goltz, 265.

Suggested Reading:

Dick, Walter & Carey, Lou. (1990). The systematic design of instruction. Third Edition. Glenview, Illinois: Scott Foresman.

Gengle, Dean. (1984). The netweaver's sourcebook: A guide to micro networking and communications. Menlo Park, CA: Addison-Wesley.

Haynes, Douglas E. (1989). The switch library: New service in rehabilitation librarianship. Bulletin of the Medical Library Association, 77, 15-18.

Howell, Richard. (1989). Some issues related to technological intervention with disabled learners: Cues for instructional designers. Ohio Media Spectrum, 41, 50-53.

Jahoda, Gerald & Johnson, Elizabeth A. (1987). The use of the Kurzweil reading machine in academic libraries. Journal of Academic Librarianship, 13(2), 99-103.

Kuhlenschmidt, Eden, Swan, Kim & Scholes, Jan. (1992). Ms. K, there's a tiger in the computer. Indiana Media Journal, 14, 6-10.

Kurzweil, Raymond. (1992). The futurecast: The end of handicaps, part 1. Library Journal, 69-70.

Kurzweil, Raymond. (1992). The futurecast: The end of handicaps, part 2. Library Journal, 66-67.

Lisson, Paul. (1987). Large print placebo. Canadian Library Journal, 44, 5-6.

Library Patrons With Disabilities

Chapter Six

Remote Library
Patron Support

Library Outreach
or
Patron Inforeach

Library patrons with disabilities have the right to self-select the information they need from remote locations rather than from within the library itself.[1] Remote library access alternatives exist because of the library's electronic information service. Remote patron access is a relatively new library service that allows library electronic information gain. External library barriers, part of the library trek for many patrons with disabilities, may be more easily overcome when using library/patron electronic information links. Remote library technology (RLT) dictates how disabled patrons, or the general public, remotely access electronic library information.

Remote Library Technology

Remote library technology means transmission of library information between the library and geographically dispersed individuals and groups.[2] The extent to which a library serves remote patrons and the community of remote patrons with disabilities is defined as "inforeach."[3] But inforeach has many levels of interaction and electronic information exchange between remote patrons, some with disabilities, and librarians:

> [Library patrons]...who receive instruction at remote sites, whether for physical or geographic reasons, must have access to information and materials through electronic transmissions, interlibrary loans, mobile collections, and other circulation procedures (American Library Association, 1986, page 31).

Remote-Context Patron Disabilities

All libraries serving the public must be accessible to remote patrons with library context disabilities.[4] Equal (remote, face-to-face or outreach) access for all disabled has been guaranteed by Federal law (Vocational Rehabilitation Act of 1973, Section 504; Americans with Disabilities Act of 1990, Public Law 101-336) for every public school, library, and public building. Every disabled person has the right to fully access their own library's electronic-based information.[5] If electronic information is within inforeach of any, it must be accessible to all.

Disabled patrons struggling to overcome library architectural or service barrers may meet entirely new challenges and have to find new solutions when remotely accessing library electronic information. The "information access style" for disabled patrons changes when they interact with librarians over distance using RLTs. How disabled patrons have learned to interact face-to-face with librarians may be quite different from how they will learn to interact over the network. RLT proficiency demands thoughtful decision-making for remote patron infosearching success. Patron RLT proficiency can be acquired through effective library orientation by librarians who are themselves skilled RLT users.

Library patrons with disabilities have the right to self-select the information they need from remote locations rather than from within the library itself. Remote library technology (RLT) dictates how disabled patrons, or the general public, remotely access electronic library information.

Library Patrons With Disabilities

Patron RLT Inforeach Ethics

Some assume that disabled patrons should have remote access privileges over and above the remote access rights and privileges of others. Special disabled access is based on the presumption that patrons cannot and do not already effectively use RLTs from their remote site. Special access assumes that special remote users have clearly defined needs beyond other remote patrons' needs. Those clearly defined special needs argue for special access privileges. But without special access needs, disabled patron access should not exceed the remote access rights and privileges of others. There is an increased probability of ultimate infosearching failure unless library access privileges are extended to remote patrons with disabilities. Special access privileges are highly time-constrained. Each access is limited for specific durations to meet remote patron infosearching needs. If special access time is unused or misused, it is summarily library-withdrawn. A remote patron history of repeated or continued special access misuse limits further special access privileges.

Librarians expedite remote patron infosearching and expressly avoid excessive cost, time and effort. Some libraries have provided reduced-rate library electronic access services. Others share costs with the patron within the library electronic access budget. Libraries share library-only access privileges with outside library network providers and thereby make a larger information base indirectly patron-accessible. Libraries provide extra librarian support to individual special search requests. Each of these strategies has implications for overall library service. Each strategy has a library budgetary impact. Available librarian outreach time is a limited library human resource.

Some assume that disabled patrons should have remote access privileges over and above the remote access rights and privileges of others.

Libraries go to extraordinary lengths to assist remote patrons with disabilities in their continued successful inforeach. One of the central methods of assistance is to provide special remote access privileges justified by patron need. Special remote patron library access privileges are not in themselves special. The people helped are special or unique in their remote information access needs. Patron RLT inforeach rights are balanced by RLT inforeach responsibilities. Ethical RLT use must be assured to continue effective and appropriate library services. RLT ethical use suggests learning to use a system without causing harm to others.[6] Nineteen principles have been identified concerning RLT user ethics.[7] When does a new technology evolve into a "patron right" to access that new technology?

Inforeach Gates

Some RLT users with library context disabilities cannot make the physical library trek. They must choose among acceptable RLT options provided by library gatekeepers. Personal and library RLTs must also link for effective library information access. When personal and RLT barriers fail to link, the patron is not just physically remote from the library building but also "information remote." Any library that presents insurmountable RLT access barriers is technologically isolated from the remote disabled. The conditions by which patrons remotely access libraries are different from where they inforeach. These site conditions are inforeach gates. Patron inforeach location dictates if, when, and how all types of RLTs can be used. The home has fewer inforeach restrictions than the school or the workplace. Home inforeach requires the patron to be an eligible RLT user and have access from home to the linking technology. The school imposes greater inforeach restrictions because of the patron's student status as well as the need for school-based RLT linking technology. The workplace has the greatest restrictions and is a more imposing inforeach gatekeeper for the remote patron. Patron home, school or workplace site barriers can conflict with library site barriers to make RLT use problematic or impossible. In some instances, the inforeach gate is closed and locked.

Library Outreach or Patron Inforeach

People with library context disabilities use RLTs to infosearch because they lack parking lot, loading zone, or library building access, cannot directly access media or use library equipment. Others, with physical access assured, may prefer to remotely access libraries. Patrons with physical or cognitive challenges have the right to choose among inreach, outreach or physical library access options:[8]

> Major barriers between students and resources include: imposing age or grade level restrictions on the use of resources, limiting the use of interlibrary loan and access to electronic information, charging fees for information in specific formats, requiring permissions from parents or teachers, establishing restricted shelves or closed collections, and labeling. Policies, procedures and rules related to the use of resources and services support free and open access to information (American Library Association. 1986. Information Power: Guidelines for School Library Media Programs, 141-142).

Librarians may assume that electronic information access will also provide increased patron with disabilities information access.[9] This may not be true for them and their specialized electronic information access needs:[10]

> ...it is insufficient to speak of barriers to access to a library's holdings, but rather we need to consider barriers to the satisfaction of a user's information needs, independent of the resources of any particular library. This at once expands the possibilities for satisfying a user's needs and makes the problem of gaining access to specific materials more complex (page 124)... The introduction of complex, new systems into libraries will have many unanticipated consequences. For example, the relative complexity of these facilities may create... 'librarian-dependence' (i.e., undue reliance upon 'professionals' as information intermediaries). This will doubtless do much to enhance the status of librarians, but may also contribute to feelings of inadequacy among users and potential users reinforcing and raising barriers to library use. Sophisticated information access tools lower barriers for those who learn to use them, but raise new barriers for those who have difficulty learning to do so. Traditional bibliographic access tools--card catalogs, printed indexes, and so forth although inefficient, cumbersome, and unresponsive in some cases, can, at least, be used by anyone; this may not be so for the newer electronic technologies. As electronic tools replace traditional ones, barriers will be lowered by many, but for others, newer, perhaps more formidable barriers will be erected (Malinconico, 1989, page 132).

Librarians As RLT Gatekeepers

The librarian gatekeeper role changes to a facilitator of remote patron access as barriers of place are removed. Technology barriers impose other "gates" to the global information network. Technology, now more than ever, is in remote disabled patron hands. Dispersed patron contact with local libraries is expanding. It may be unrealistic to guarantee equal access to RLTs until many libraries resolve local remote patron RLT access issues. It is even more difficult to assure equal patron access to RLTs if those patrons have diverse disabilty-related information needs. Librarians may lack appropriate RLT training to serve remote patrons even in a passive, automatic, machine-link mode. Librarians carefully translate and interpret information to remote patrons, using RLT technologies. Competent professionals, as RLT gatekeepers, effectively control the library's "willingness" to serve patrons remotely. Library RLT barriers may be the result of librarian resistance to using RLT links with remote patrons.

Patrons with physical or cognitive challenges have the right to choose among inreach, outreach or physical library access options.

Remote Disabled Patrons As RLT Gatekeepers

Many remote patrons with disabilities have their own RLTs at home, or gain RLT access from school- or workplace-based sites.[11] These patrons become their own information gatekeepers. The librarian's gatekeeper role rapidly changes when the traditional role of remote patron as information stakeholder is changed to patron RLT gatekeeper. RLT competency enables effective remote access to the librarian and the local collection. RLTs, particularly those requiring computers and modems, have been called "freedom machines." They provide alternative communication formats for disabled patrons who are unable to speak, or word processing options for those not able to hold pencil to paper.[12] Those homebound and physically disabled who have personal RLT access are ideal remote library outreach users.[13] But they must personally choose to use RLTs. Disabled individuals of all ages lacking access to appropriate information require library RLT access. Public and private libraries should expand outreach services to isolated clients through RLTs and avoid relying solely on print media or mobile van information delivery.[14]

Many remote patrons with disabilities have their own RLTs at home, or gain RLT access from school- or workplace-based sites.

Remote Patron Information Overload

Patrons become information empowered when they become effective information networkers.[15] Other remote patrons with disabilities experience RLT information overload and may go into information retreat because of that overload. Information overload results when information cannot be patron-controlled.[16] Patron information control and handling requires finding or receiving delivered information at the most useful time. Useful incoming information from the librarian must be in the right patron-receivable format as well as compatible with remote patron personal technology. Librarians must review service delivery for "just in time" information delivery. Patrons balance their conflicting roles as students and infosearchers or workers and infosearchers with the newly interactive library environment, with incoming library information and librarians ready to personally interact at a distance. Personal and information privacy is of utmost concern to many RLT users at each of their respective sites. Physical distance between patron and library no longer becomes a significant factor. Patrons must switch to a defensive information gatekeeper role for remote library inforeach when librarians take the initiative to contact them at home, school or the workplace. Personal calls to school or the workplace are already controlled by others. How can librarian calls to these locations be made accessible to the patron? Remote patrons with disabilities begin to consider what for them is information overloading (Infoglut), information irrelevant (Infotrash) or usable information (Infowealth)[17] to use Gengle's (1984) "netweaver" terminology.

Library Outreach

Library outreach means information exchange in which patron and librarian are physically separated.[18] After conventional telephone reference, mobile van delivery, and the U.S. Postal Service, remote patron access to librarian and collection relies on other technology. Facsimile (FAX), computer/modem, microwave satellite, cable and other outreach RLTs bring patrons directly to the collection. Remote patrons require RLTs for effective library inquiry or to be connected to librarians. Technology outreach must be mastered by librarians who link with remote library patrons. Outreach RLTs provided through library outreach may not be used or understood by remote patrons with disabilities. Learning RLTs may be frustrating to the disabled just as it may be also frustrating to other patrons. The steep learning curves required by new RLT technologies do not attract many disabled to the RLT library information opportunity. Remote patrons with disabilities are the "library outreach underclass" when they need librarian help and cannot get it.

Library Outreach or Patron Inforeach

Some librarians maintain the conventional library remote patron gatekeeper role. As barriers of place (the library building) are removed for remote patrons, it becomes possible to consider librarians as regional or national resources, rather than local information providers. Some librarians with extraordinary RLT skill and remote patron orientation expertise may be in regional, statewide or national demand over the RLT network. And this may radically change the expert librarians local patron service mandate.

Current and cost-effective conventional library technology capable of supporting remote patrons far exceeds effective patron use.[19] There is a lack of established library policy and procedures that facilitate patron workarounds using RLTs. Librarians are unfamiliar with patron-owned RLT links already existing at home, school or worksite. Local library community surveys must establish the patron RLT technology capability already in place. Local librarians will never know the extent to which local information can be shared remotely. They do not know who may elect to link with the library, using their own destination site RLT capability. As with many technology owners, some elect not to use their technology. Average patron informational needs have changed rapidly over time. Remote patrons with disabilities come to have expanded library information needs. Patrons with disabilities may not think in terms of remotely connecting to libraries using conventional technology. They may envision the need to get library information only by making the local library trek.

Multiple library barriers within and outside the immediate library building affecting patrons with disabilities have already been identified in earlier chapters. Among patrons who experience library barriers, some cannot or will not physically access collections.[20] Some refuse to connect with the library remotely, thereby eliminating library access save through the United States Postal Service or delivery and pickup of materials by library workers. This personal delivery service for remote patrons unable/unwilling to link with the library electronically, or make the library trek, is the lowest technology format for remotely gaining library information.

Among these personal delivery services is the National Lending Service for the Blind and Physically Handicapped of the Library of Congress (NLS). The NLS offers a variety of no-cost services for the visually impaired, physically challenged, learning disabled and mentally retarded or developmentally disabled.[21] This includes free U.S. Postal Service delivery to and from the patron's home and extensive format-specific titles.[22] But home service may be painfully slow and limited titles in nationwide high-demand. These services require special access to secure media. NLS materials may require local library equipment support if individuals do not have personal auxiliary aids available at home when information access is needed. NLS formats include extensive talking books, nonprint and print title collections, with priority direct service to qualifying readers of need. Local librarians may suggest this supplementary service to disabled readers who qualify. Remote patron contacts made by local librarians initiate NLS service, leaving the local librarian out of the loop beyond initial referral. Qualified patrons connect directly with NLS to be served. Yet the patron mode of contacting NLS may be through local library RLT use. Significant delays in receiving appropriate Brailled media formats or lack of Brailled reading material for NLS delivery limit every eligible disabled person. Perhaps the local librarian can act as ombudsman to assist in reducing NLS service delays to remote patrons in the local library service area.

Local Mobile Van Delivery

Mobile van information delivery cannot be accomplished effectively without patrons borrowing appropriate information formats available in the local collection. Limited library collections are deliverable by mobile van but may not meet patron with disabilities information needs. Local mobile van delivery does not stop remote patron inforeach to the local collection, or require use of the U.S. Postal Service, a much slower process. Yet for some, the library trek is not possible or practical. For others, it is not safe.

Library Patrons With Disabilities

Librarians cannot assume that increased RLT use and growing technology available in the local library will reduce the need for mobile van delivery services. Even conventional mobile van or bookmobile service can be altered by RLTs: "In Whitman County, Washington a bookmobile equipped with a packet radio offers mobile access to the central library's online card catalog" (Office of Technology Assessment, 1990, 228). There are other possible changes in mobile van service roles including: Remote patron RLT personal equipment consultation, support or repair by the van librarian; bookmobile return to the library of patron-owned RLT equipment requiring manufacturer repair or replacement; and bringing RLT equipment from the library directly to the remote patron. Libraries may make personal RLT loans to remote patrons. Will libraries start offering "remote RLT customer support" with a library pass? These RLT delivery issues are further complicated by remote disabled patron information needs.

Patrons Not Free To Enter The Library

Dispersed patrons include the homebound disabled, persons in short-term hospital stays, the incarcerated, and the adult disabled at workplace destinations needing library information. Short or long-term incarcerated learners are eligible for K-12 special education funding and for distance special education services provided by the library.[23] Correctional educators have become service leaders in providing instruction via RLTs to remote incarcerated or confined learners, using library resources.[24]

Among patrons not free to enter the library are remote patrons with health problems that underly their disabilities in major life activities including reading and library use. Patron health problems are diverse and complex. Many have direct impact on patron dispersion from librarians and from the library collection. Remote patrons with contagious disease electronically access library information without risk to anyone. Others are recovering from temporary diseases or experiencing temporary movement or mobility limitations forcing them to rely on RLTs rather than make the library trek. Individuals with health problems may transition later from RLT use to renew their library treks. Some will prefer

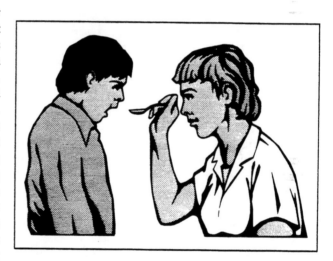

to continue using RLTs and voluntarily not make the library trek after recovery. Such RLTs as telecopying (FAX) and instructional television (ITV) viewing at remote sites are appropriate for them. What current local library links have been established with hospitals, nursing homes, group homes, and residential service centers? How many libraries have linked with the technologically advanced physician and direct health care provider community who can facilitate remote infosearching by patrons with health problems?

Patron Transit Isolation From The Library

Transit isolation includes community geographical and patron isolation from libraries or because of long-term bad weather making travel to the library hazardous. Isolated patrons, who otherwise would personally visit the library, no longer can use many direct library services. The same conditions that isolate patrons from the library also isolate librarians from providing library outreach to the remote. RLTs overcome patron transit isolation through patron remote inforeach. Temporary library isolation may also result from transit strikes, inaccessible roads, or patron expulsion or exclusion from transit service. In all instances, the remote must have their own RLT-compatible electronic equipment and telephone connections with the library to overcome patron transit or library isolation.

Library Outreach or Patron Inforeach

Remote Patron Telephone Service

No phone access at the patron site reduces or stops library/ patron interaction using selected private phone-line dependent RLTs including audio-conferencing, bulletin boards (BBS), telecopying (FAX), electronic mail, electronic Braille, telephone amplification and telephone communication devices for the deaf (TDDs). Voice telephone library access may also have the effect of isolating patrons with disabilities from others. A warm librarian voice, even on the telephone, helps considerably. But electronic information exchange may be "cold," impersonal and cryptic.

Telephone conversations ostensibly reduce patron local collection information barriers. Infosearches become more guided and effective. We may assume that the library and a patron majority both have telephones to interconnect. Almost all public schools have public access telephone service accessible to some of the school library's remote patrons. Remote patrons with disabilities use electronic passwords and library telephone numbers as access alternatives to making the physical library trek. Library voice telephone service inreach automatically defaults to data links when remote patrons using FAX or computer modem equipment produce an audible phone line carrier signal. Automatic switching to library FAX or computer modem is done uneventfully. The patron is then automatically and electronically linked for information gain.

Portable or cellular phone service and equipment links remote patrons to the library's electronic information. Portables or cellulars must be further linked with laptop personal computers to access electronic information. Portable or cellular connect time service is expensive. While this technology is feasible, it may not be economically practical for remote patrons with disabilities.

Remote patron unlisted telephone numbers have the same effect as no remote patron telephone. Unlisted patron phone numbers control for patron-initiated library RLT use but prevent librarians from reconnecting later. But with Call-Back(tm) capability, remote patron phone numbers within the same area code can be obtained requiring librarians to further protect remote patron anonymity. Library telephone service makes the patron with disabilities invisible to the librarian and instead focuses conversations on the patron's specific information requests. If telephone access interconnects patron to library computer, patron anonymity is further enhanced, unlike face-to-face patron interaction with librarians. Patrons then become free to access information within or remotely as they choose without violating their infosearching privacy.

Remote users via telephone-linked computer and modem have library-imposed restrictions. Calling the librarian avoids physical library access barriers and they can obtain information without library passes. Patrons beyond library service areas are not authorized to use library services. Libraries may institute Caller-ID(tm) tracking devices to avoid unauthorized remote patron users. Call-back capability is also greatly enhanced with unintentional remote/librarian disconnects using Caller-ID(tm).

Remote patron telephones in rural or remote areas may be limited to party lines. Many rural telephones provide unreliable service, are subject to uncontrolled interruptions and lack signal-carrier quality. There are other technical remote access problems that limit rural telephone electronic links with the library. With these limitations, the remote patron with disabilities has no effective telephone service for RLT links but can still interact with the librarian by voice phone. But voice phone interactions alone significantly reduce RLT electronic information access.

Library Public Access Telephones

In the United States over 8,000 public libraries, 3,000 college and university libraries, 88,000 elementary and secondary school libraries, 2,700 federal libraries and 11,000 private and other special libraries have public access telephone numbers.[25] A General Accounting Office 1988 survey of depository libraries indicated 337 of 403 had microcomputers with modems and online access.[26] Many provide patron electronic

Library Patrons With Disabilities

access to librarian help. Fewer libraries provide access via computer and modem to interconnect patrons with similar library computers. A broad spectrum of library/patron telephone (voice) and computer/modem (data) communication is possible:

> Today, a telephone subscriber can have touch-tone service, custom-calling services, measured service, wide-area calling, speed-dialing, cellular service, and any number of other features. A bibliographic search can be done in the card catalog--the old fashioned way--or via one of several different computer databases, containing either citations only or full copy. A text message can be sent via paper mail, electronic mail, facsimile, or overnight courier. In short, the range of communication options is much wider (Office of Technology Assessment, 1990, 233).

Various telephone configurations require careful planning for general library patron accessibility. Telephone booths generally cannot be used by the mobility limited. Standing telephone use is difficult for many with mobility limitations or who use walking aids. Telephone booth use may be impossible for patrons using walking aids who must manage the aid and the confined space of the booth at the same time. Cord length from telephone to handset should be at least 29 inches (29").[27] Seated telephone areas offer general access but may cause users with walking aids to interfere with others if telephones are face-to-face, in close proximity, or at kiosks. Consultation with the local telephone service representative assures effective library planning to meet the needs of a diverse disabled community. Patrons with disabilities should be consulted regarding their library phone support needs. Public accessible telephones should be provided in the host building, if not within the library itself.[28] External or internal public telephones provide communication service with the outside world. Patron access to telephones is an essential library service. Telephone bases, enclosures, and fixed seats do not impede approach by people using wheelchairs.[29] Clear floor and ground space allows forward or parallel wheelchair user approach. Public telephones should provide dial, push button and coin slot height at no higher than 48 inches (48") for easy forward[30] or side reach from a wheelchair.[31] In dial-tone first systems, calls are operator-assisted without requiring physically challenged patrons to insert coins.[32] Without dial-tone first systems, the disabled may not be able to expedite coin calls without librarian help. If this condition exists, policy should allow patrons to use library telephones for outgoing local calls. Supervision may be needed to assure that no long distance calls are made from library phones, even for patrons with disabilities. There is no implied permission or library policy for the disabled to be underwritten by the library for long distance calls.

Public accessible telephones should be provided in the host building, if not within the library itself.

The deaf exchange information using Telecommunications Devices for the Deaf (TDD). TDD is a form of RLT communications technology linking the deaf patrons with other deaf or hearing patrons. No TDD at the library stops the deaf remote from accessing hearing librarians unless TDD/Voice relay service is provided through a local telephone company operator. The deaf do not directly interact with the hearing librarian without the hearing telephone operator as intermediary. And each member must respond one at a time to communicate effectively. At least one telephone should have volume controls for hearing-impaired users.[33] Text telephone service (Telecommunication Devices for the Deaf/TDDs) for the hearing impaired are best provided in special service areas with full librarian support.[34] The nearby publicly accessible TDD for patrons with hearing disabilities may be within the library only.

Corporate America and both state and federal governments list 1-800 toll-free numbers (Wide Area Telephone Service) to greatly facilitate access by remote patrons with disabilities.[35] They also routinely provide FAX and TDD access numbers. PHONEFICHE(tm) at libraries provides microform-based telephone numbers for the entire nation. There are other CD-ROM technology-based titles in the library that can be purchased by remote patrons to access the entire national private telephone or business listing.

Multiple service-area telephone books should be accessible in reference but are often not available at public telephones outside the library. Directories at public phones, where there is no librarian supervision, are often missing or damaged. Pencils and writing pads enable all to record numbers at library telephone locations but not at outside telephones. Updated directories in good condition should be positioned at in-library telephones to accommodate wheelchair users.[36] Outside-library telephones are often not maintained, repaired or provided with telephone directory service.

Remote Patrons Without Computer Equipment

No computer system--or one without a modem at the remote patron site--is a major patron RLT access barrier. No computer access at the patron site precludes library/patron interaction through bulletin boards (BBS), electronic mail, electronic Braille and many other RLTs. Remote disabled patrons who are students, however, have access to more than 6,000 modems that can communicate with external libraries, using computers at 88,000 elementary and secondary school libraries.[37] No home or workplace site-based computer can be overcome by remote patrons with disabilities who have access to school- or workplace-based computer-modem equipment. Yet constraints of the school or workplace may limit remote patron library access for anything other than school- or work-related infosearching.

Satellite-Ready Remote Patron Homes

Library supervised satellite downlinks provide receiving, recording and copyright-authorized temporary telecourse video storage for scheduled rebroadcasting. Even satellite pointing and selection is a complex skill for the disabled remote. Satellite dishes with preset memory-pointing technology resolve this recurrent access problem. Manually satellite operated dish-pointing may be beyond disabled patron capability. Enter the high technology-skilled, mobile van librarian to adjust patron school, home or workplace satellite equipment (a new nontraditional librarian RLT role). When satellite dishes are pointed from the remote patron destination site, satellite-based information is opened to the disabled remote.

Satellite or Cable-Ready Workplaces

RLT links are possible because of cable-ready workplaces that link disabled workers with library-based instructional or public-use television. There are many circumstances under which workers become remote with disabilities who may need to access library-based electronic information. Since library-based electronic information can be obtained through cable-based links with remote patrons, cable-ready workplaces are important conduits for remote patron-librarian information exchange.

Library Patrons With Disabilities

Satellite or Cable-Ready Schools

Remote patrons without satellite links cannot access public instructional television (ITV), or captioned video (CC), or noncable or nonlocal remote television program RLTs. Cable connections exist in more than 20,000 schools and 17 million households in the United States.[38] Enormous potential exists for household and school RLT links with the library. But they are rarely used for remote infosearching. Television channels are reserved by the Federal Communications Commission (FCC) for instructional or public-use television that can be accessed by library patrons with disabilities.[39] Cable-ready schools interconnect more remote student patrons than adults to the library collection. Schools and librarians are authorized to downlink broadcast programming, record programs and replay them for specified periods for local or remote RLT patron viewing. Cable-ready postsecondary schools connect more remote adult students to the library than other adults can link using home- or workplace-based interconnections. In many cases, school access to cable programming is provided through the school library or media centers and not routed directly to separate classrooms. This condition can be overcome by resourceful patrons with no home or workplace cable service who obtain library information through school-based RLTs. Over 86 percent of the elementary and secondary schools in the United States have at least one VHS format VCR; over 50 percent have two or more.[40] This suggests that adult remote patrons have fewer opportunities than student patrons for remote library outreach through videotape technology, viewing broadcast programs or using cable-fed multi-media from the library. Some remote patrons have no access to television monitors or videotape equipment.

Satellite or Cable-Ready Libraries

Cable-ready workplaces, homes and schools must also link with cable-ready libraries for RLT electronic information gain. Library-generated cable programs are of limited use to patrons without program recording/playback capability. Broadcast program off-line videotaping under other circumstances may violate copyright law. Remote patrons with disabilities engage in further copyright violation by downloading library software collections--including multimedia software from cable-ready libraries. Federal Communication Commission (FCC) service access is guaranteed to the local cable provider with the license conditional or the provision of local public program access to libraries and other public entities.[41] Few libraries have elected to use their local cable channel access rights to serve their remote library patrons. This RLT format remains to be fully implemented, even with libraries that have large remote patron constituencies. The deaf or hearing impaired remote need to remotely access library-captioned programs either through mobile van delivery, U.S. Postal Service or library cable access. Replays on local cable service originating from libraries require captioned support to address remote caption-user needs.[42] On alternate schedules, closed- or open-captioned signals originally broadcast are relayed to the library without modification. Few libraries have the economic resources or personnel to caption programs not originally captioned at the production or distribution source.

Library Audio-Conferencing

Library audio-conferencing (AC) may be necessary for one or more remote patrons with disabilities and their local librarian helpers. Remote patrons are voice-linked on telephones to librarians if patrons have the minimal hearing, concentration and visualization skills required to use audio-conferencing. AC requires RLT two-way electronic voice communication between librarian and remote patrons using a common carrier telephone link and a library telephone receiver. A speaker-equipped telephone at all remote sites is often used with groups. Each conferee uses a personal phone at home, school or at the workplace. AC can include multiple users at multiple sites but only one patron at a time can speak during audio-conferencing. Overspeaking creates unmangeable AC line noise. This equipment also requires minimal librarian and remote orientation for reasonable disabled patron success. The hearing impaired require AC autodial speaker phones with built-in amplification controls and earphones. Audio-conferencing equipment requires background noise control for the hearing impaired and concentration by the hearing conferee. Audio-conferencing etiquette is demonstrated by remote interacting parties who learn to: (1) Acknowledge operator-assisted conference beginning and termination steps; (2) Identify who is online at initial conference; (3) State name before any message is offered to other conference listeners; (4) Control local background noise that accumulates across users, giving a general telephone line hearing degradation; (5) Direct messages to specific conference members by name; or (6) State clearly that each message is for all listeners to respond.

Interactive Television From The Local Library

Interactive television (ITV) broadcasting provides library-based two-way RLT[2] information between library and remote patrons. ITV can be used in conjunction with library-based audio-conferencing to interact with a large group of remote patrons.[43] This technology allows either immediate or delayed interaction between librarian and patron and can be sourced at the library and conveyed via community cable television service. Patron-required ITV equipment includes a television set with specific access codes and an instructional broadcast schedule. Book reading circles, for example, come to have a new meaning when done with remote viewers and listeners using ITV. Libraries without a community ITV survey do not know the many remote patrons who would use ITV technology if available or how many disabled patrons would use ITV over all other remote technology. Some remote patrons with disabilities who have no other options except the library trek would consider ITV effective personal information gain. But how many are out there and would those patrons justify the added ITV service expense?

Library Instructional Television Fixed Service

Instructional television fixed service (ITFS) is a line-of-sight television broadcast reception RLT system permitting two-way audio and video interactive communication, limited to a 20-mile reception radius from the library. A station rebroadcasting system gives further signal reach but still provides a geographically limited patron broadcast receiving area. ITFS is a form of instructional television (ITV) technology that can be library-based for remote patron RLT outreach. ITFS equipment required by patron users includes a television set with specific access codes and an instructional broadcast schedule. This technology, when limited to cable feed, reaches a geographically limited

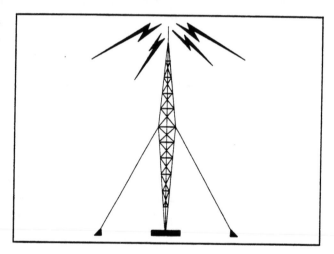

area when not further rebroadcast. Local or cable-channel signal reception is limited to patrons with disabilities using a specialized ITFS downconverter linked to the patron's television set. Not every disabled person can afford cable service, much less ITFS service add-ons. Does the local library community survey determine ITFS over ITV users?

Local Library Telecourses

Library telecourses are television programs broadcast on very high frequency (VHF) or ultra high frequency (UHF) channels available for scheduled patron viewing. Telecourses represent another RLT outreach format. Workable receiving antenna, television monitor, cable service (CATV) or pointable satellite dish equipment (SATV) is required. Two-way interaction is not possible between telecourse patron and librarian, but can be generally limited to patron telephone call-ins. Any call-in telephone interaction initiated by the patron with disabilities also brings to bear patron telephone-related disabilities. Effective patron telephone-connected auxiliary aid use may also be required. Telephone conversations at remote sites may mean long distance charges for the patron. Local and long distance telephone service boundaries are not always contiguous with library service area boundaries.

Telecourses are limited in the local library collection. Library loans, leases or outright telecourse purchases are very expensive information sources with limited local patron audiences. Telecourses may provide narrow-focus topics of little interest to the wider disabled patron viewing public. There are many telecourses that can be downlinked to the local library and rebroadcast to the local disabled patron community which may be of direct interest to them. Many postsecondary schools rely on essential course delivery via distance education. With each distance education course there is a direct implication for local library information support. But that local library support may not also require remote patrons to make the library trek. There is a virtual national shopping list of distance education telecourses that apply to the disabled (American Sign Language, Speechreading, Braille Technology, Adaptive Workplace Equipment Management, TDD Technology, and Assistive Computer Technology).

Blind or Low-Vision Remote Patrons

Electronic Braille (EBB) technology permits both patrons and librarians to send and receive Braille-based print information. Using an audiocassette tape memory storage media, up to 400 pages of equivalent paper Braille can be stored, saved and shared with others at EBB equipment locations. Versabraille[44] (a product produced by Tele Sensory Systems, Inc.) is such a Braille-based remote interactive machine. EBB technology requires Braille machines, modem-equipped computers and cassette tape recorder/players at distant sites and at the library. Various electronic Braille machine manufacturers do not share compatible media formats during audiocassette tape exchanges requiring patrons to dedicate machine use to one manufacturer or another.

> ...the inherent flexibility of manipulating information electronically effectively compensates for users whose disabilities impede their ability to handle standard print documents or review them visually, or both...[for persons with limitations of sight] When information is reviewed and manipulated electronically, the limitations associated with the mechanical aspects of reading, writing, handling, and distributing of printed information are effectively removed...Documents can be readily converted into accessible forms such as large print, Braille, or audio tape, in contrast to the limited availability of such alternatives in the past...Electronic messaging and Voice Mail provide a "disability transparent" means for a blind user to send and receive information efficiently and independently (General Services Administration, 1989, page 3).

For remote low-vision patrons certain personal computer adaptations facilitate linking their homes, schools or workplaces with the library:

> Glare Protection Screen--Minimizes visual fatigue associated with glare on the monitor; Large Monitor (19"-25")--Increases character size in proportion to monitor dimensions; Magnifying Screen—Reduces glare and enlarges characters to approximately double their original size; [and] Large Character Display--Provides large character display capability (hardware or software) that increases character size approximately 2-15 times in a manner that is transparent to the applications program (General Services Administration, 1989, page 5).

The blind or visually impaired not yet mobility proficient in the library, the host building, or on campus, or not yet safely accessing transit service require remote RLTs to access information. Blind RLT users can effectively use audio-conferencing or instructional television. Remote blind patrons also mix other RLTs such as electronic Braille and talking books.[45] Low-vision patrons using RLTs require magnification, high-contrast or contrast-control technology for electronic bulletin board use.[46] They can use all RLTs for the blind listed by the General Services Administration above, as well as telecopying (FAX) RLTs where electronic FAX files can be further manipulated to enhance patron visual engagement. The blind may not profitably use electronic mail, teletype links and telephone communication devices (TDDs) which are designed for users with other disabilities. Yet no one can effectively predict when these technologies will be accessible remotely to the blind or persons with low vision.[47] RLT opens up communication links so quickly that each innovation is difficult to track by even the most diligent and technologically proficient librarian.

Remote Patrons With Mobility Impairments

Functional activities of daily living dictate for patrons with disabilities how, when and why they need RLTs. Technology designed to facilitate or teach daily living skills is useful for those who need special support. After training, this technology provides support for daily living. Functional daily living includes technology-assisted interactions or communication with others in face-to-face situations or at-a-distance, using RLTs.

Remote patrons unable to use a computer keyboard because of visual, auditory, physical or perceptual disabilities may not be able to use bulletin boards (BBS), electronic mail, electronic Braille (EBB), teletype links (TTY) and telephone communication devices for the deaf (TDDs). The following solutions are suggested for patrons with specific keyboard disabilities.

> Electronic manipulation of information can be significantly more efficient and effective than more traditional means for an individual with limited dexterity. For some, it may be the only means [of remote access]. The mechanical problems of accessing a filing cabinet, handwriting...or turning the pages of a book are eliminated; Keyboard enhancement capabilities (macros, word prediction) can significantly boost [library connectivity] by reducing the number of keystrokes required to generate text; Electronic mail is also an effective communication medium for users with physical limitations of mobility or speech, or both (General Services Administration, 1989, page 3 & 4).

Modified Computer Keyboards

The remote patron's computer keyboard is one communication option as a telecommunication device usable for remote library linkage. Typical systems provide a portable or laptop computer with printer output (frequently a tape printer for hard copy). The patron makes keyboard entries that are speech synthesized as whole words are typed. If the speech synthesized quality is sufficient and connected to an audio link with the distant librarian, it is possible for the librarian to hear computer output equivalent to a remote patron's responses. With this technology librarians can expect to pick up the phone and hear the keyboard user at the other end initiate speech-synthesized infosearching requests. Such systems usually lack the capability for patron review or repeating of words or phrases before the signal is sent to the distant librarian. Building words from letters is a time-consuming process. Without whole-word recognition software, it taxes patrons to remember words just sent to the librarian when they cannot see or hear sentence structure repeated. The patron is also forced to remember answers to distant librarian questions during this message exchange process. Patrons must phrase questions or answers before sending. This latter problem is often termed "technology overload" and is a major factor in remote patron and RLT use success or failure.

Library Patrons With Disabilities

Certain modified computer keyboard technologies have applications for remote patrons with output disabilities and their librarians. Modified keyboards have fewer operable keys for patron keyboard input. Some keyboards are equipped with recognition software that makes certain keys inoperable to allow only selected key use for patron-generated messages. Single keystrokes may represent whole words. This accelerates remote patron output to, or communication with, the librarian. Yet that technology requires a disabled patron "mental map" to know and remember what keys represent what words in orchestrating keyboard responses to the librarian. This technology assumes that the remote patron can receive information and process it but has difficulty outputting information understandable to the librarian at another distant library computer monitor. Single keystrokes for whole word output assumes further that patrons can meaningfully read from the computer screen to understand messages to and from the librarian.

This technology assumes that the remote patron can receive information and process it but has difficulty outputting information understandable to the librarian at another distant library computer monitor.

Eye-Controlled Computer Keyboards

Remote library patrons with output disabilities use their gaze, directed to eye-controlled devices, for computer keyboard input that sends screen messages to distant librarians. The remote output disabled patron selects areas on eye-controlled devices much like the numbers, letter or word overlays on communication boards. Selecting an area will input to the patron's computer keyboard that number, letter or word to produce synthesized speech or text via e-mail then readable by the distant librarian with compatible computer or voice telephone equipment. Communication is slow, cumbersome and requires concentration both from the producer (the patron) and the receiver (the librarian). The output disabled have less difficulty receiving or interpreting librarian messages (input) than they do when generating messages to be sent to the librarian. The librarian can in turn generate keyboard messages at conventional speed to be read onscreen by the remote patron.

Distance Pointing and Keyboarding Aids

The remote library output disabled may require pointing or typing to initiate or maintain communication with distant librarians. Headsticks, mouthsticks, hand splints, lightbeam pointers and other devices facilitate pointing to objects or pressing keys. Pointing and typing aids used or keys pressed at computer keyboards relay messages to library computers. Remote library patrons are evaluated to determine their ability to sustain communication with the library. Various library or remote patron technologies exist that work but may not work effectively in the remote environment to serve patrons with output limitations or communication disabilities. This same remote user with output disabilities is assumed to have no difficulty receiving librarian messages. But the output disabled will be unable, or will have great difficulty, initiating or responding to librarian messages without assistive technology.

Head-, Mouth- and Light-Pointing Devices

Remote patrons communicate via head, mouth or light pointing devices by outputting very slowly, with distant librarians listening to patron-initiated synthesized speech on library telephones. Patrons who are slow in responding to library messages are very limited in their vocabulary output using these devices. Pointer technology is workable for some remote patrons who require the largest electronic- or software-generated vocabulary and phrase lists possible, along with a spell-checking option that ensures patron-controlled message modifiability. Patron messages are then routed to library computer screens for immediate librarian

Library Outreach or Patron Inforeach

reponse. Pointers are usually used in conjunction with computer keyboards, screen displays or other electronic devices that produce whole word outputs as synthesized speech when activated by a single switch or as text that can be read by the distant librarian at the library computer. But whole word production by pointing to individual letters is a slow, cumbersome communication process between patron and distant librarian.

Head-pointing devices use the chin or forehead as a remote library patron point of reference. These output devices do not interrupt the user's field of vision at the patron computer keyboard during communication efforts with the distant librarian. Some audible feedback to the patron is provided when pointing selections are made while messages are being sent. Head-pointing devices are generally used in conjunction with single-stroke keyboard technology to facilitate patron messaging at their computer. Mouth-pointing devices provide a mouthpiece gripped by the teeth, leaving the tongue free for pointing. These remote patron output devices do not interrupt the user's field of vision during communication effort just as head-pointing devices. Audible feedback to the remote patron is also provided, while sending messages. Again, single-stroke keyboard technology is used to facilitate patron messaging. Light-pointing devices controlled by the head or mouth project light beams to light-sensitive receivers such as disabled patron communication boards that in turn generate synthesized speech output carried by voice phone to the distant librarian or generate text sent via computer and e-mail to the library.

Single-Switch Controls

Single-switch control technology provides an entire family of devices enabling not only remote output disabled patron environmental control but also providing them the ability to communicate with the library using RLTs. Any electrical device controlled by an off/on switch is activated or turned off using a single-switch operated by a disabled patron. Since many RLTs require more than simple on/off response, only some RLTs are workable for physically challenged patrons to connect remotely to their librarians. Overlays can be used as a part of communication boards or as computer touchscreens using visible overlays. Communication board technology (CBT) can be adapted for remote patrons with output disabilities to facilitate communication with the distant librarian. The remote output disabled process information well but cannot speak or write to indicate library infosearching sophistication. CBT must interface with RLTs to facilitate distance communication between parties. CBT user sound output must be understandable to the librarian. Synthesized speech produced by some CBTs is difficult for librarians to understand at a distance without patron gestures or facial references. Newer CBT technology permits digital encoding of human, not synthesized, voice vocabulary using other persons voice recordings. This digital CBT output allows excellent voice quality and auditory recognition by the librarian. CBT digital technology, however, is dependent on remote patron computer random access memory (RAM) or storage media limitations. And the stored vocabulary must be as large as possible for the technology to allow effective remote patron infosearching.

Remote patron technology dictates compatible library and patron RLT links. Voice, keyboarding or visual signal interface is exchanged via RLT between distant librarian and patron without retranslation or reformatting required by the patron's CBT. It is assumed that remote patrons using distance CBT receive and process information well, but have difficulty outputting information understandable to the librarian.

Single-switch control technology provides an entire family of devices enabling not only remote output disabled patron environmental control but also providing them the ability to communicate with the library using RLTs.

Overlays representing various words, numbers, alphabet characters or other basic needs applications are pointed to, using single-switch technology. Movement of these device indicators communicates for the nonverbal patron within a narrow range of options provided by each overlay. Overlays are designed to show the most frequently used words or numbers that permit the remote disabled patron to react to, or initiate, communication with the distant librarian. Orientation is limited to yes/no, or other specific, narrow-range responses that overlays dictate. To be effective, overlays must contain terms for infosearching. While many single-switch communication board overlays exist, few are adapted to the remote disabled who require a sophisticated infosearching vocabulary for minimal library information gain.

Overlay use with single-switch devices is meaningful face-to-face communication by the disabled patron to the librarian while both are in the library and when synthesized speech is patron-generated that can be heard by librarian and patron alike. Pointing to pictures, words or numbers using the single-switch activates speech synthesizer sound production by the remote patron that can also be heard by the librarian via library telephone.

Single-switch devices used to communicate with librarians at a distance and overlays used to activate specific infosearching responses enable the remote patron with output disabilities to evolve a relatively sophisticated communication system with the librarian. The essential basis for single-switch use in remote disabled patron communication is that of infosearching decision-making, with questions framed by the librarian in fairly simplistic formats such as "yes/no," "more/less," and "keep going." Any of these simple patron output responses can carefully guide librarians who give clear verbal instruction and choices to the remote listener through infosearching steps in the library. This is not easy for the librarian or for the remote patron with output disabilities. But infosearching in this way can be done. As remote patrons with disabilities develop skill using single-switch devices and overlays, communication with the librarian becomes more sophisticated and remote infosearches become more effective. From the librarian's perspective, infosearching instructions, choices and options must be carefully task-analyzed to guide the remote patron through the infosearching and decision-making maze. Library science has evolved over the years certain infosearching strategies, particularly in reference, that could apply in this remote patron support situation. Strategies reduced to a flowchart with yes/no options at every decision point received from the remote patron would quickly lead the remote patron to desired information. Without this infosearching systems flowchart each librarian would be required to recreate the decision process each time it was used. Single-switch devices can be replaced with dual- or multiple-switch devices, according to remote patron output capability to manipulate switches and to communicate infosearching needs to the librarian over distance.

Single-Switch Overlay Scanners

Single-switch scanners repeatedly move across an overlay and stop, when remote library patron-activated, on an infosearching response desired. This is communicated by synthesized speech to the librarian. When scanners produce speech output to the telephone, librarians do not require matching or on-site library equipment to meet patron information needs. Multiple input selectors provide one-switch selection connected to multiple single-switch devices. While only one single-switch can be activated at a time, these selectors provide a patron choice between various single-switch devices and between multiple overlays, scanners and communication options. Most single-switch technology can be upgraded to dual- or multiple-switch controls, based on distant patron need and sophistication for output while remotely infosearching. Two or more switches activate overlays or scanners for a quicker remote patron response to the distant librarian. Clockwise or counterclockwise, forward or backward scanning or pointing devices enable the disabled patron to reach the option selected and manipulate dual or multiple-switch controls for communicating their infosearching options to the library. The end result of single-switch overlay scanners is a somewhat more sophisticated range of synthesized speech vocabulary output to express disabled patron output decisions and selections to be met by the librarian in accessing the library collection. This considerable upstepping of communication speech and verbal message complexity can be heard and responded to by the librarian via voice telephone. With single-switch overlays, even the most output-disabled remote library patron can communicate and respond to librarians. A whole new area of librarian training is needed to effectively and professionally respond to remote disabled patron overlay users. Remote patron messages to the librarian tend to be cryptic, disjointed sentences or thoughts, requiring careful extrapolation and analysis for a meaningful response. With orientation and better understanding of disabled patron individual information needs, patterns or infosearching habits, professional librarians can respond to relevant, specific, patron-designated information requests.

Initiating communication between parties represents the beginning skill level for remote library patrons. Maintaining communication is a necessary remote library linkage prerequisite. Communication between patron and librarian can take place via speech, gestures, or pointing. Remote patron communication is a major functional daily living activity and adaptive keyboard writing is a communication form. Adaptive keyboards permit communication between librarian and remote patrons with output disabilities. Communication between remote patron and librarian frequently requires computer technology and supportive software. Such software should:

> ...provide anticipatory or predictive routines which improve the efficiency of letter and word selection by ranking selections according to their frequency of use by the particular user. Once the user begins spelling a word, the [technology should] offer the user those words most likely to be chosen, and organize the [subsequent output according to those word responses that are user selected] (Brandenburg & Vanderheiden, 1987, page 71).

Anticipatory Spelling Software

Anticipatory spelling software provides remote patrons with both standard and phonetic spelling. Since many remote library patrons are more proficient in one or the other spelling technique, spelling software emphasizes word acquisition from the user and de-emphasizes correct spelling. Correct spelling, or spell-checkers that stop the user during output to correct spelling errors, inhibit remote patron attempts to communicate with the distant librarian. Abbreviation expansion software routines spell out user abbreviations in full word representations. When messages can be remote patron-formed with anticipatory spelling software, they can then be forwarded via computer to the librarian. The librarian in turn receives a clearly worded, complete remote patron infosearching request.

Repeat Key Software

Communication software also provides shortcut patron inputs such as "repeat key" input for duplicate responses during distance communication. In addition, each communication technology is individualized for remote patron personal use and not limited only to specific use during remote library contacts. Repeat key software also helps remote patrons build text-based requests to be sent via computer to the librarian.

Speech-Impaired Remote Patrons

Remote speech-impaired patrons are communication supported by synthesized speech devices. When Kurzweil, more than two decades ago, determined 1,100 English pronunciation and syntax rules and combined this with 1,600 rule exceptions, effective synthesized speech was born. Speech synthesizers help remote patrons communicate initial needs in the immediate environment, to interact with face-to-face or distant significant others, and to maintain communication between patron and librarian. Speech synthesized production quality to emulate the human voice is a central requirement for successful and sustained library links. Remote patrons with output disabilities deserve no less.

Speech synthesized voice output is matched with visual on-screen patron word production. Synthesized voice output supports patron letter, phoneme, word or phrase output entered at the keyboard. Voice output software delay permits whole-word speech rather than single-letter sound production, a feature which should dramatically increase the intelligibility of patron speech for the librarian listening on the library telephone. Software programs provide inflection control to emphasize contextual speech meaning.

Peripheral devices are often a necessary adjunct to communication technologies used by the remote patron with output disabilities when engaging in interaction with the librarian. Peripheral device adaptability and patron interface is the library service standard that assures a seamless technology web to facilitate patron face-to-face or at-a-distance communication with librarians. Peripherals are often not compatible with each other. They require a consistently demanding user-effort to interface or link which frequently exceeds patron capability. Peripheral interface problems also lead to frequent repair, adjustment and technical problems well beyond capability and responsibility of remote patrons with disabilities. Interface with peripheral devices and RLTs combine to help patrons communicate at a distance to, and with, librarians.

Speech synthesis and communications technology for the remote patron with output disabilities moves the novice user to higher library technology access and infosearching levels. Where software and communications technology provides few options, that same technology also provides "room to grow." When this patron window of growth opportunity is restricted to existing library technology, any increased patron sophistication requires additional library technology. The best speech synthesis technology provides menu expansion capability as patrons become more sophisticated, their vocabulary increases, and their skill at communicating with distant librarians improves. Remote library patrons with disabilities may require speech aid to initially communicate infosearching needs and to continue to interact with face-to-face or distant librarians. Two major RLT speech aid categories are artificial larynges and speech amplifiers.

Artificial Larynges

Artificial larynges are speaking aids for individuals who have lost larynx use. These devices are pressed against the person's throat. The user forms words with the mouth in normal fashion while the device produces electronic vibrations that roughly simulate the human voice. Other devices for those with missing or insufficient vocal tone production electronically generate voiced words through a tube in the mouth that uses the tongue and lips. Some devices provide for a male or female voice or offer tone quality control, raising the tone when asking questions or adding emphasis. Artificial larynx use initiates distance interactions but does not maintain communication over time due to two major factors: patron exhaustion while using this technology and the distant librarian's difficulty in interpreting remote patron speech. While signal systems evolve between remote patrons with laryngal disability and the librarian, an information flow over a distance may not take place or be sustained during remote library communication levels. Patron-to-librarian telephone conversations tend to be short to produce effective patron library information gain.

Speech Amplifiers

Speech amplifiers are various electronic devices usually applied to telephones or microphones that amplify the patron's voice during communication. Outgoing patron speech amplification is provided to the librarian via voice telephone. Volume-adjustable personal telephone handsets amplify the user's voice up to 30 percent. Portable amplifiers carried by the patron amplify speech through a small unidirectional microphone. Speech amplifiers enable patrons to both initiate and maintain sustained library distance interactions with their librarian. But two major factors tend to limit the utility of this RLT: the patron using this technology does not speak clearly with amplification and the distant librarian may not be able to interpret remote patron speech. RLT etiquette and style evolves between remote patrons with speech disability and the librarian. When both parties make personal voice communication adjustments a normal information flow over a distance takes place to sustain remote library links.

Remote Communication Aids

Various electric or electronic devices initiate disabled patron communication for face-to-face librarian interaction or remote infosearching responses at a distance. Patron environmental control is the primary requirement of these aids before library distance interaction takes place. Environmental control for patron comfort requires device availability at all times, even during RLT use. Prerequisite training and patron competency to use these aids determines patron/librarian interaction. These various devices, connected during RLT linkage, control the various RLT equipment ordinarily under patron control. The primary purpose of remote communication aids is to initiate and maintain communication between distant patron with disabilities and librarian.

Remote Writing Aids

Initiating and maintaining electronic communication or writing between remote patrons with disabilities and librarians comprises two different communication levels. Patron output is produced by speech synthesis, tape printout, device screen display, or computer screen display. The output is converted from computer screen display to electronic bulletin board communication between computers to reach the librarian. The librarian responds by conventional keyboard entry or voice phone statements.

Various electric or electronic devices initiate disabled patron communication for face-to-face librarian interaction or remote infosearching responses at a distance.

RLT[1]s: One-Way Remote Library Technology

The simplest conventional inforeach is RLT[1] or a one-way exchange between library and remote patron. RLT[1] can also mean one-way information exchange between remote patron and library electronic information databases without librarian interaction. Patrons with disabilities already use RLT[1]s at home, school or work. Now they are ready to use technology to remotely infosearch libraries just as they already file Internal Revenue Service tax forms electronically,[48] bank, shop, vote and do many other daily activities by telephone, computer/modem, keyboard or mouse, and FAX. Ride-sharing for patrons with physical or cognitive challenges is today routinely done by phone, matching disabled riders with drivers and appropriate transit service. Thousands of people, including disabled individuals, call in to recorded weather conditions for mobility or are linked with health monitors and warning devices remotely. Why not remotely contact the librarian for information? Patrons with disabilities may be "information challenged" and require RLTs to access their library remotely. If RLT links are already in place in the home, workplace or at school, patrons with disabilities can also use these RLT links to access electronic library information. For example, FAX is so common among workplaces that many remote disabled patrons use FAX RLT[1] technology to gain library information using one-way communication with the library. Want to request your reference librarians' support remotely? Then modem or FAX them using your RLT[1] and expect another return FAX response from that librarian. Are reference, circulation, reserve, administration, special services and other library service area personnel ready to respond to technology-skilled remote patrons by phone, computer modem, or by FAX? The tradition is already well-established to provide telephone links between but not from each library service area using RLTs. Computer links with FAX RLTs exchange capability between remote patrons and each library service area are now also common information exchange formats. Can professional librarians expect only one-way electronic information requests from remote patrons without verbal interaction with them? RLT[1]s are highly impersonal. RLT[1]s lack the human touch or the human voice. There is a one-way interchange limitation RLTs require to move information between remote patron and librarian. Both respond back to one another several times before the information is successfully exchanged. And when there is a mistake made by either party, one-way RLT exchanges increase to correct each previous error causing remote patron to retreat from further librarian remote contact.

Library Patrons With Disabilities

RLT^2s: Two-Way Interactivity

RLT^2 inforeach state-of the-art-technology allows two-way or interactive communication between remote patron and the library for electronic information gain. Each can talk back to the other. RLT^2 is interactive communication by electronic means. Librarians can confirm with remote patrons their electronic library information needs. Remote patrons can change their mind midstream, during online infosearching, or from librarian verbal feedback that may redirect them to more appropriate electronic library information sources. RLT^2s provide the "human touch," if even at a distance. RLT^2s provide online patron interactive communication with librarians and library databases, compared to simpler RLT^1 one-way patron remote access to electronic library information. Because of the problems associated with the introduction of RLT^1s in library service areas and in remote patron homes, schools and workplaces, much of RLT^1 use has decreased after the initial "excitement" has worn off. Now both librarians and remote patrons expect interactivity with the other using RLT^2s and, at a minimum, the ability to interrupt messages with voice-phone contact between parties which corrects for RLT^1 errors in message content and improves effective information exchange.

RLT^3s: Networking Libraries

RLT^3 is library technology remotely shared or networked between libraries accessed remotely by patrons using RLT^2s. Distant collections also can be accessed by the RLT^3 competent librarian, to meet patron information needs face-to-face in the library. The librarian remains a gatekeeper for remote patron RLT^3-networked technology access. A progressively bigger window of electronic information opportunity is provided remote RLT users. Regularly planned RLT^1 one-way use between librarian and patrons or spontaneous links called on by either party now make information exchange possible. RLT^2 scheduling is the patron's responsibility when infosearch needs require two-way access. Either party can read their electronic mail and respond as soon as they understand message implications. The library need not initiate RLT^2 patron links but must respond to RLT^2 users whenever queried. Library audiences expand greatly when remote patrons can go online at any time to access library information. While determining remote disabled patron requirements will be difficult, libraries must prepare for significant RLT^2 service expansion.[49] There will be many more RLT^1 and RLT^2 users with disabilities moving to RLT^3 sophistication and eventually joining the library network virtual community using RLTs. RLT^3s use essentially the same RLT^2 technology applied to a much more widely accessible information database. Librarians also gain a bigger information window to access electronic information from outside their own library. And so do their remote patrons using RLTs. When libraries network with each other, RLT^3s enable the most advanced information exchange available. When libraries network, RLT^3s interconnect librarians, libraries and their remote patrons to global information. Inforeach becomes as far-reaching as all member libraries who network together. RLT^3 use is a virtual passport to global information.

RLT^4s: The Virtual Community

With all the RLT^3 inforeach capability for electronic information access among network member libraries, remote patrons can only access electronic information in limited voice or data formats with citation, abstract or full-text information. They are information borrowers, users or infosearchers, not infoproducers or infoactualizers. It is only when RLT^4, the information superhighway (also termed the National Information Infrastructure), comes online and people interconnect can they then become both information stakeholders and gatekeepers.[50] The RLT^4 information superhighway provides full networking with people and human information. They become members of the virtual community, even though remote and with disabilities. But infosearching must become alive using electronic information. To become alive, information must be actively shared, compared, contrasted, rejected, accepted and modified. Alive information leads to full networking with people and information. It leads to virtual community membership for remote patrons with disabilities. See Figure 6-1.

Library Outreach or Patron Inforeach

RLT[4]	Information Superhighway (National Information Infrastructure)	Full Networking with People and Information
RLT[3]	Three-Way Technology Links	Libraries Network/ Library Outreach/ & Patron Inreach
RLT[2]	Two-Way Technology Links Between Patron/Librarian	Library Outreach/ & Patron Inreach
RLT[1]	One-Way Technology Links Between Patron/Librarian	Library Outreach/ & Patron Inreach

Figure 6-1. Remote Library Technology Types

Remote patrons using technology gain in informational sophistication and evolve from infosearchers to infoproducers. Some evolve further to infoactualizers. In this natural RLT[4] growth process, remote library patrons join the virtual community:

> Virtual communities, supported by electronic networks, create the opportunity for providing new sources of contact and interaction among people, widening their circle of friends and making it easier to connect with others like themselves. Like the "communities of interest" supported by the postal system and the telephone, virtual communities comprise groups of geographically dispersed people, united by a common interest or purpose and supported by computer communication such as bulletin boards, conferences, and electronic mail (Rheingold, 1987).

Ongoing RLT[4] evaluation yields better library responses to remote patrons with disabilities who inforeach as they become increasingly computer literate and technologically proficient. As virtual community members, remote patrons and librarian collaborators provide RLT[4] change guidelines based on user need. RLT[4] impact assessment on remote patrons is a shared responsiblity between library and the patron. Consultation with remote patrons is the key to fostering functional remote library links and meeting virtual community patron support requirements. Ask what the remote with disabilities need and why.[51] Remote special user library information needs may closely resemble the needs of most other remote users.[52] And remote disabled patrons share many common infosearching needs:

There will be many more RLT[1] and RLT[2] users with disabilities moving to RLT[3] sophistication and eventually joining the library network virtual community using RLT[4]s.

> Accommodation in the broadest sense, therefore, refers to the application of ergonomic principles to maximize the capabilities of all [remote] users...The comprehensive needs assessment required to determine the appropriate accommodation for individuals with disabilities may also be used to determine optimal interface for all end users" (General Services Administration, 1989, page 2).

Library Patrons With Disabilities

Library Network Overload and Access Equity

Overload and equity access problems occur when local librarians provide network electronic information access to remote patrons. Network restrictions become critical for the disabled who wish to access electronic information when infosearching libraries who also network their information to other library members. Library membership in networks, consortia, resource sharing cooperatives, or interlibrary loan agreements significantly affects RLT[4]-based electronic information access.[53] Libraries across resource-sharing networks become more specialized information repositories unique to network memberships.[54] Other libraries may then dictate the conditions for local library information access. By so doing, other libraries in the network also indirectly dictate remote disabled patron access. Remote patron access to library networks must be assured and equitable to access granted the general remote library public without regard to patron disability status. Because equal opportunity to participate in life now depends on equal access to information, networking equity in basic library services must be assured for all, including the disabled.[55] Networking equity or equal access policy for any library patrons, including those with disabilities, has yet to be determined. Networks currently offer first-come, first-served access. Historically, disabled patrons may have not have been placed on first-access status for library services or for networked library services.

Disabled patron network access is virtually defined by library patron access policy.[56] That library policy must also apply to RLT[1]-, RLT[2]-, and RLT[3]-level remote patron access needs. Libraries must also eventually evolve policies governing their participation on the RLT[4] information superhighway. Electronic worldwide access has been called the MATRIX[57] and provides RLT[4]-level access to the information superhighway. Congress has not yet resolved supporting legislation but libraries will be an integral part of this developing national and international-access service. There may also be repeated traffic jams on the information superhighway as it evolves. Blocked information (RLT) routes will directly affect remote disabled patrons. Orienting the disabled for information superhighway negotiation is required. Library networks may be only theoretically, not practically, accessible to patrons with disabilities and instead limited to library staff.

RLT[1]s and RLT[2]s promote the opportunity for patrons with disabilities to link with local librarians and electronic information collections, or databases.[58] Local libraries with these technologies have never been so "open for business" as now. They can outreach a much wider patron clientele now than before RLTs were available to remote patrons. But librarian openess or outreach using RLTs is a radical change in the traditional librarian service role. That library openess using RLTs may eventually reduce remote infosearching opportunities for remote patrons with disabilities due to library network overload. Patrons with disabilities in other libraries may collectively demand more of the entire library network when information needed is not locally held or accessible only through remote library networks or interlibrary loan.[59] Any patron knows this library network access "overload" or bottleneck when failing, after repeated attempts, to link with local library electronic databases that are also linked to larger library networks. Network overload is partially relieved when libraries add multiplexors to their telephone lines, providing multiple, simultaneous network user phone access. Without multiplexors, libraries limit network electronic access to one remote patron at a time because they provide single patron-accessible online phone access to the network. But multiplexors giving multple patron library access must be answered by multiple librarians and multiple library electronic access points at all library service areas.

Do more remote patrons with disabilities inforeach library collections remotely than disabled patrons who make the library trek? This may be a clear future trend in library service. Librarians periodically assess library RLT changes and access problems for those invisible and remote or distant disabled patrons to improve patron library inforeach. Remote patrons are "invisible" when they never physically enter the library. Many remote patrons with disabilities are also "invisible" to local librarians.

Disability Support Networks

Among the multiple, remote library context access problems that patrons with disabilities may face, there are many sources for network support to resolve their electronic information access needs. For the first time in our history, community disability support groups can merge together with other community disability support groups, using electronic networking.[60] An emerging national electronic support network specializes in each of many disability types. Since each remote patron with disabilities is already remote from other patrons with disabilities and they are already communicating electronically over the network, they begin to solve electronic access problems of other remote disabled patrons at a geometric rate. That geometric growth and electronic access problem-solving rate approaches the electronic communication rate of others without disabilities. Disabilities in electronic network participants becomes irrelevant. Disabled patrons begin to achieve, one networking patron at a time--with local technology from the home, the school or the workplace--electronic information access parity. Each local remote library patron with disabilities receives network support to resolve individual remote electronic information access problems one patron at a time.

Inforeach Destroys Infoprivacy

Many technological options exist to link remote patrons with librarians for collection inforeach. It is no longer necessary for patron and librarian to see each other since RLT use does not require local face-to-face interaction. It is possible for local librarians to be "inforeached" by RLTs anywhere, any time, through call-forwarding, pagers, cellular telephones and laptop computers.[61] Local librarian high-profile, state-of-the-art technology accessibility by patrons anywhere/anytime may have the effect of denying both patrons and professionals: "...over who they communicate with, when, and under what circumstances; at the same time, they deprive others of the ability to escape gracefully from unwanted communication or to benefit from anonymity in their communication" (Office of Technology Assessment, 1990, 227).

From the professional viewpoint, librarians deserve the right to screen remote patron inforeach calls, if for no other reason than to match the right librarian or service specialist with patron information needs. Library telephone answering machines, even e-mail addresses, give the librarian time to think, analyze information needs and requests, and respond appropriately to remote patron needs. Different inforeach technology allows different times for individuals to interact. Some technologies provide no time delay, while others provide time for librarians to consider a careful remote patron response. Face-to-face patron library equipment and infosearching support forces librarians to assist at times "on-the-fly" and may suggest rushed, inadequate or insincere responses. With remote patrons, a deeper librarian infosearch can often be done. But librarians must balance their conflicting roles in the new, and interactive, library environment. Other role changes are also occuring there. The librarian is becoming a computer or technology-based operator, facilitating remote patron infosearching. The traditional face-to-face, librarian-with-patron role has changed. Remote patrons, including those with disabilities, are rapidly becoming technologically capable of being "in your ear."

Remote patrons using RLTs have an immediate response expectation that may be even more demanding than face-to-face library interaction. From the remote patron viewpoint, librarians or RLT incoming information has to be "controlled" at home, school or the workplace. Patrons cannot always read whenever library information arrives via RLTs. Information may need to be stored, saved, and handled or read later when personally convenient. Remote patrons thus become "INFOHANDLERS."

Library Patrons With Disabilities

Remote Open or Closed Libraries

Remote patron infosearching is a significantly different alternative means to library information access when compared to patrons making the library trek and interacting face-to-face with librarians. Patrons "inforeach" to library information and librarians "outreach" to remote patrons using RLTs among other means. Library "openness" is the ease with which member remote patrons can access the library.[62] Library remote barriers "close" remote patron access. Remote information barriers are library barriers that are real but not in the direct building access sense, or even in the library/patron face-to-face service sense. They are closed because library electronic barriers restrict remote patron with disabilities electronic information access. Skilled librarians find alternative means to disabled patron information ends.[63] But any local library has a limited collection and few librarians there to help. And there are inherent technological limitations to each type of RLT used.

RLT^2s available to local libraries are rapidly expanding local collection access by redefining what a "local collection" is.[64] Local libraries have an unprecedented opportunity to link with other libraries and expand the "local" collection access for face-to-face or remote patrons using RLT^2s.[65] Local collections no longer restrict remote patron access to "library" information alone, since that "library" information may not be part of the local collection. Local libraries downsize core collections by relying more on patron electronic access, leaving specialized collections accessible to patrons with disabilities only through larger network-member libraries.[66] One of the profound effects on local library collection size will be core collection downsizing driven by library network membership in the information superhighway, with remote patron RLT^3 access locally provided. The greater the remote access activity the more likely local libraries will downsize their collections to reallocate budget and human resources to RLTs.

Librarians As Remote Information Technologists

Many remote information access alternatives are library-designed procedural workarounds for patrons with disabilities. Individualized patron help to use RLTs is an excellent library service standard and within ADA-defined "reasonable accommodation" strategies. Individual RLT access permits maximum patron independence with minimal library intervention if there are no missing RLT links. Librarians are information technologists for remote patrons.

People vary significantly in their information skill development and library support needs. Patrons with disabilities may have significant library-based individual information access problems due to disabilities or to lack of skill or knowledge of how to obtain library-based information. A librarian's highest priority is to orient patrons to overall library services, including RLT access. Remote patron with disabilities RLT orientation requires significant library worker and resource reallocation. Librarians become the equivalent of telephone customer support provided by the software and other industries. Professional familiarity with direct library systems is not enough. Librarians must learn RLTs to use the library remotely themselves. Following skill developed as remote infosearchers, professional librarians become better able to support other RLT users. The term "user-friendly libraries" adds a new professional service dimension when remote patrons are served. But patrons may be reluctant to ask the librarian for help.

There are three sources of RLT customer support expertise. Librarians themselves begin rapidly to require customer support or consultation expertise when faced with the challenge of meeting local disabled patron electronic information requirements. Consultation and expertise also comes from remote patrons themselves who are skilled, experienced and capable of suggesting strategies to help other remote disabled patrons. Community disability support networks or their national support network members can respond to local librarian support requests for specific electronic information access problem of patrons with physical or cognitive challenges. Each of these electronic access problems can be resolved, in most instances, by library workarounds and by effective RLT planning.

Library Outreach or Patron Inforeach

Remote Library Technology Planning

Accommodating remote patrons using RLTs requires library planning before RLT^2 (two-way interactive) communication can occur on library patron demand. RLT^2 interaction between librarian and patron includes voice telephone conversations, electronic mail or computer bulletin board messages. Interaction using RLT^2 enables either librarian- or patron-initiated dialogue. Each expects quick, if not immediate, response from the other to maintain the same time interval response between remote patron and librarian that would be expected during face-to-face library responses. RLT^2 use-planning may include providing the remote patron with standing-search criteria services to provide subject information, updates, new developments as information databases grow in size, sophistication and useful patron applications. When those information databases are accessed via library-to-library interactive networking, RLT^3s are used. Libraries have direct RLT^2 or RLT^3 access to more than 3,169 databases, 1,494 database producers and 486 online services. Theoretically, so do library patrons. In practice, however, many databases are not directly accessible to remote patrons through local libraries. Instead, database access is provided directly to the professional librarian who must further translate information to the remote patron by conventional means, without RLTs.

RLT resource planning and purchasing dictates RLT availability, first to the librarian, then to the remote patron. Broader planning and purchasing issues must be resolved surround library interactions with remote patron RLT users. Some libraries avoid planning when surveys or interview results suggest the need to purchase RLTs. Libraries that plan ahead stay ahead of increasing patron library information demand from remote sites. Good planning includes resource management, effective current resource assessment and RLT resource timeline projections. When purchasing to meet remote patron demand "just in time" occurs, then libraries avoid repeated RLT crises. Remote library technology planning opens the information gates to all remote infosearchers.

RLT Missing Links

Remote disabled patron RLT^1 or RLT^2 use is format specific. Limited library formats restrict remote patron RLT^1 or RLT^2 use. Library collections are further limited by available RLT^3 links within patron format requirements. For example, library RLT^1 includes facsimile (FAX) services. Facsimile (FAX) exchange between librarian and remote patrons provides print information access. When library FAX is available and the remote have no FAX service, no FAX RLT^1 exchange takes place. There is a FAX RLT missing link. When other remote patrons have FAX and the library has none, inforeach is effectively halted. Across all available RLTs, many missing links can be identified. Many missing links are missing because of limited RLT availability in the local library.

Library and remote patron RLT^1 links that exist must also be shared. RLT^1 links account for restricted format patron inforeach requirements. Library outreach from the local collection must include compatible format and equipment. For example, patron equipment requires a personal FAX machine and a working telephone connection at patron site and a compatible library FAX machine with a telephone link. A sufficiently high quality telephone line connection must be maintained to carry out FAX RLT^1 transfer. Librarians reformat print information to single-sheet format, using library photocopy equipment, before FAXing needed information to the remote disabled. No one RLT-level link with librarians and local collections is best for all situations, applications or patrons.[67]

No one RLT-level link with librarians and local collections is best for all situations, applications or patrons.

Library Patrons With Disabilities

Other missing links occur when library RLT[1] capability is mismatched with remote patron personal RLT[2] two-way capability. When library RLTs do not match remote technologically sophisticated users, then remote patrons are the "technology haves" and libraries the "technology have-nots."[68] RLT[1] and RLT[2] conflicts on and off-site are complex and must be overcome. RLT availability alone does not assure remote patron options. Remote patrons must also have navigational skills through their own RLT technology:

> For example, if a library stops updating its paper card catalog (as the Library of Congress did in 1986), should literacy include the ability to perform an online keyword search?...Or the ability to know when not to use an online system? (Office of Technology Assessment, 1990, page 231).

Remote Library Technology Workarounds

Both remote patron and librarian can switch to other RLTs for electronic information access. While the infosearching opportunity window between each RLT type becomes progressively larger how does a larger window help each disabled patron? More expert librarians, disability experts, disability support group members and technology experts can be found who can electronically interact with the each other to find workarounds. Librarians as remote information technologists are the central point of the workaround process. Remote patrons with disabilities, like disabled patrons in the library, have specific information format requirements.[69] We all do. We either prefer print over nonprint library information or we choose microfiche over microform, or audiocassette-based information over still-picture information, or videocassette-based information over a good book. It is an individual information format choice so long as the library provides those format alternatives. In libraries unable to provide format alternatives the infosearcher must choose from available formats. And it is an electronically "forced" choice. Many conventional RLT system configurations do not support remote patrons with disabilities. Without RLT workarounds at both patron and library site, no RLT-based interaction occurs.

Circulation and reference services have experienced considerable growth in providing patron electronic information access within the library that can be further applied to remote patrons. Libraries struggle to move from triple-format in-house information service to remote patron triple-format interactive service. Larger university collections or federal depository libraries have moved from dual format (hard copy and microfiche) to triple format (hard copy, microform and electronic technology).[70] Yet triple-format libraries may not have commensurate RLT disabled patron access capability. Each format isolates patrons with physical or cognitive challenges without RLT service access to that site-specific library information format and requires them to make a library trek to get the information or have it delivered using conventional library outreach.

Triple-format libraries provide hard copy and microform services but must maintain outreach service to remote patrons with disabilities. Those libraries providing remote electronic access create a significantly less expensive and more responsive link between their collections and remote disabled patrons using RLTs over just hard copy, print and microform technology delivered by conventional outreach means. Triple-format access alone is not enough for remote patron infosearchers. Triple-format access must also provide interactive communication between librarian and the remote infosearcher.

For remote patrons with disabilities to access hard copy from local libraries, library worker photocopying service must be combined with mail or FAX service to reach patrons at a distance. This is time consuming and labor-intensive for libraries and expensive both for librarians and remote disabled patrons. While within "physical reach," it may be beyond disabled patron "economic reach" without library outreach resource reallocation or other funding support. Remote disabled patron community surveys should address the issue of photocopying and hard copy transfer technology affordability as well as the need for remote library photocopy delivery services without FAX. Hard copy transfer from microform format engages the library

Library Outreach or Patron Inforeach 245

in the same labor- and time-intensive process described above for hard photocopy transfer. Microform selection, transfer to hard copy, and U.S. Postal Service or FAX delivery is expensive for libraries and for receiving patrons. It is also slow information gain at remote disabled patron sites, since information that is useful must also be timely as well as in appropriate format. FAX copies received may have degraded quality compared to photocopies mailed or mobile van delivered and be relatively less useful for patrons who must further modify print information at their remote site. Triple-format libraries providing microform service to remote patrons also have the responsibility to transfer the wanted material from microform to hard copy and then make that hard copy electronically accessible via library RLTs. With each new transfer step in the library, more expense is added that will eventually be borne by the disabled patron end user. And there are multiple links and multiple workarounds between remote patron and librarian for electronic library information. If the remote technology does not link with the library information other information formats must be substituted:

> ...with digitalization all of the media become translatable to each other-computer bits migrate merrily-and they escape from their traditional means of transmission. A movie, phone call, letter, or magazine article may be sent digitally via phone line, coaxial cable, fiber optic cable, microwave satellite, the broadcast air, or a physical storage medium such as tape or disk. If that's not revolution enough, with digitalization the context becomes totally plastic-any message, sound, or image may be edited from anything into anything else (Brand, 1988, 19).

When librarians and the remote disabled combine skills and technology they create "workarounds" to facilitate information access.

When librarians and the remote disabled combine skills and technology they create "workarounds" to facilitate information access.[71] Workarounds include RLT access alternatives for patrons who experience conventional library access, information barrier or format problems. Workarounds employ RLTs to help disabled patrons access the collection from a distance:

> When the internal [library] holdings do not meet all [patron] needs, [librarians] are responsible for making arrangements to secure materials from other sources. Provision must also be made for [patrons] who need specific pieces of equipment in order to obtain information; such equipment includes Braille writers, adapted electronic and telephone equipment, enlarged print devices and other specialized tools... [Patrons] in remote sites may require specialized access and delivery systems to assure that they, too, have equal access to learning resources. Rotating collections, interlibrary loan, online databases, satellite television, and radio broadcast, and computer delivery systems are examples of ways to address the information resource needs of such [patrons] (American Library Association, 1988, page 73).

Workarounds accommodate patrons with functional visual, learning or mobility-relevant disabilities to flexibly support them. No single accommodation would be optimal for all individuals in every disability category or with differing severities of the same disabling condition.[72] RLTs can be used in unconventional ways adding patron inforeach or library outreach options.[73] Both parties can initiate or respond to the other after an initial voice telephone or face-to-face contact using RLTs such as call-forwarding, call-waiting, Voice Mail, paging systems, cellular phones, audioconferencing, or answering services. RLTs include bulletin boards (BBS), telecopying (FAX), electronic mail (e-mail), electronic Braille, teletype links (TTY), telephone amplification and telecommunication devices for the deaf (TDDs), satellite links, audiocassette players, or captioned equipment on patron television monitors.

Library Patrons With Disabilities

Library Electronic Mail

Electronic mail (e-mail) provides patron and librarian computer two-way (RLT^2) or three-way (RLT^3) interaction. One-to-one e-mail (RLT^2) connects patron and librarian, allowing messages to be exchanged through an electronic mailbox. One-to-many e-mail (RLT^2) is a mailing list utility providing the same message to many patrons who are connected electronically. Many-to-many e-mail (RLT^3) connects large groups of patrons and librarians to each other. Many-to-many e-mail is true computer conferencing called a bulletin board system.[74] E-mail service extended beyond local library service areas becomes RLT^3 or three-way library/patron/library networking system technology. Distant libraries and librarians can interact with local patrons or local librarians on many-to-many e-mail library systems. Librarians or patrons log-on e-mail and reserve messages to anyone with electronic addresses. Private access messages are stored in e-mail. Online group library discussions can occur with anyone currently online. But those discussions are not private. Posted e-mail increases patron privacy. The librarian overcomes privacy issues and assists patrons to obtain information via posted e-mail. E-mail effectiveness suggests users learn to avoid unproductive conferences or messages not relating to personal information needs. Patrons should learn to skillfully scan messages to find information of interest. They also should learn how to avoid "junk" messages.[75] The librarian who is an e-mail systems operator maintains the system, removes old messages, and controls or monitors new messages. This is a nontraditional RLT librarian role as remote patron information gatekeeper. Some would suggest that e-mail system operators act as message censors. For librarians to assume a new nontraditional role as censor of any information, even electronic-based information, raises professional ethical concerns.

> **For librarians to assume a new nontraditional role as censor of any information, even electronic-based information, raises professional ethical concerns.**

E-Mail Software File Support

E-mail between librarian and remote disabled patrons is a workable RLT^2 or RLT^3 technology medium for distance communication.[76] [77] Computer e-mail networking facilitates feedback between librarians and member remote patrons.[78] That information feedback is the essence of librarian orientation for remote library patrons with disabilities. The remote disabled may require additional support beyond reading their library e-mail files. They gain that additional support by storing the messages as files on their personal computers and/or having the librarian store those files on library diskettes for personal patron access. Since many messages are lengthy and reoccur over a period of several days, this file support is often necessary to orient patrons for information gain. Diskette file storage is long term information storage that can be later patron retrieved.

E-Mail Hard Copy Support

Computer networking is augmented by hard copy printouts at library and patron sites. Equipment required for printouts includes a modem-equipped computer with a working modem, e-mail software and a dot matrix or laser printer. E-mail gives the remote patron access to other off-line hard copy access technology. Various print-to-speech RLT transfers exist. Remote patrons can use optical character readers, synthesized speech, electronic Braille readers and Braille translators from e-mail sourced hard copy. E-mail sourced hard copy conversion to other formats is complex and requires compatible equipment and operator skill to accomplish the task before e-mail information can be readable.

Library Outreach or Patron Inforeach

Librarian-Only or Dual-Access Bulletin Boards

Library policy must carefully distinguish between librarian-only bulletin board and remote patron/librarian dual access. Dual "public access" BBSs, or BBSs accessible to both librarian and remote patrons, are numerous. But some "public access" BBSs may not be appropriate library service to remote patrons with disabilities. Some professional or restricted library access BBSs are not intended for remote patron use. These restricted or librarian-only BBSs are offline to remote patrons from library service access but online and accessible directly by the remote patron. There is considerable discussion in library circles concerning the lack of any quality control over information available to all on public access BBS.

DEAFNET integrates commercial telecommunications with the TDD network for library and patron RLT[3] access.[79] SPECIALNET links special educators, students, parents and other professionals with common needs. Library membership in the SOURCE[80] or Compuserve[81] or similar bulletin board service provides print-based telecommunication services including telewriting, telecopying (FAX) and electronic mail (e-mail) or computer-assisted conferencing. Comprehensive lists exist that provide disabled access to the information superhighway using bulletin boards.[82] All these specialized BBSs provide information access to the remote patron with disabilities and a viable interactive library link.

Where patron-accessible BBSs are also used by local librarians to interact, great care should be demonstrated to form library-originated messages fully understandable to patrons. Librarians may not be accustomed to BBS messaging to remote disabled patrons. It is a significant responsibility for librarians to compose messages on BBS to a patron audience in the tens of thousands who can read and respond. Massive patron response may beyond local librarian ability to cope. Message content must be local, with patron-only implications. When distant remote patrons beyond the library service area read local messages, they can assume services are personally available. Patron confusion reigns when local librarians do not carefully word library BBS messages. The remote patron must also leave clear BBS messages to librarians for effective response. The entire gamut of remote patrons with writing (output) disabilities may apply when they frame questions on the BBS to their librarian. Patrons with reading disabilities may have difficulty reading BBS messages without librarian help at a distance. The librarian as distant tutor is another nontraditional librarian role assumed with disabled patrons. Patron library accessible BBS misuse has been reported.[83] Policy must allow access restrictions or access termination for remote patrons with disabilities and others who abuse library BBS privileges, without distinction for disability status.

RLT Economic Access Pressures

Patron electronic information and RLT access using library resources also places on the patron the economic burden of having RLTs available at home, school or workplace.[84] Remote patrons with disabilities already purchase and use RLTs but do not view the simple telephone and other household or workplace technology as providing them remote library information access. Other remote patrons will remain remote from RLT as members of the nationwide, poverty-bound, technology underclass. These economic and access issues must be resolved to give true ADA-guaranteed equal information access. Librarians must also make their information remotely accessible to patrons without, or at nominal, cost. Library remote access via online computer and modem also has library imposed use restrictions. Patrons who abuse those restrictions may be terminated from remote library access. Patron identifier passwords required for logon or to check out library information can be lost or stolen and then library-rescinded. Remote patron logon to library bulletin boards for electronic mail or data file exchange requires use of password-accessible library files. Passwords are required for logon just as patrons must present passes for physical library title checkout. Patrons with identification receive library services. Without passwords they do not. Electronic passwords thus replace patron library cards. Once discovered, passwords can be misused without the knowledge, consent or control of the remote·patron. Password abuse is an integral part of the computer and electronic piracy issues confronting all computer users today.[85]

Summary

Electronic information cannot reach the remote patron without effective library links to that remote patron. At the remote disabled patron site, those missing technology links must be overcome or workarounds found. Remote site barriers include patron transit or physical isolation, no telephone, no computer or modem, computer keyboard access problems, unavailable patron-appropriate information formats, or no patron television, cable, satellite or VCR equipment. The remote may lack satellite links, audiocassette players, or closed captioned (CC) decoders on television monitors. When patron resources are limited, remote library access is not a viable alternative. When individuals own or use RLTs, librarians help them effectively connect to collections and information anywhere on earth. "The remote" comes to have an entirely new meaning in library science.

Some RLT users are not eligible to access the local collection or use electronic links to the local library. Librarians must understand the implications of the greatly expanded window of opportunity opened when libraries go online for remote patron use or misuse. Four levels of remote users exist of which only two provide effective RLT links with library information. Library outreach service areas are blurred when RLTs transcend traditional geographic or service boundaries. RLTs are changing library service outreach boundaries, which have traditionally been defined by location and by institution. RLT^3 technology moves to a new level of remote patron-to-local librarian and collection interaction. RLT^3 permits patrons well outside local library service areas, even across the globe, to access local collections. RLT^3 local collection access policy issues are complex. It is difficult for librarians to establish any board of director control to determine resource allocation across this wider vista of expensive remote information-gain options. For example, RLT^3 accessible library resources can be exhausted, overburdened by RLT^3-capable patrons who are not part of local library service areas. What if a "patron" in Sri Lanka is the heaviest user of local RLT^3 technology? Does this very remote patron prevent patrons in the local service area from easily connecting with the collection or with the librarian? Do librarians know who their RLT users are? Remote patrons with disabilities use remote library technology (RLT) to maintain patron and library interaction. Library planning and RLT provision should assure interactive communication for sustained periods between remote infosearchers and their library. Interactive communication via RLT enables librarian and/or patron to initiate information dialogue and expect immediate response from their counterpart.

End Notes:

1. U.S. Congress, Office of Technology Assessment. (1990). Critical Connections: Communication for the Future. Washington, DC: U.S. Government Printing Office. Page 56: "The technologies used for self-expression, human intercourse, and recording of knowledge are in unprecedented flux. A panoply of electronic devices puts at everyone's hand capacities far beyond anything that the printing press could offer. Machines that think, that bring great libraries into anybody's study, that allow discourse among persons a half-world apart, are expanders of human culture. They allow people to do anything that could be done with communication tools of the past, and many more things too."
2. Adapted from Wagner, Ellen D. (1988). Instructional design and development: Contingency management for distance education. Paper presented to the American Symposium on Research in Distance Education, July 24-27, 1988. Page 12.
3. Ibid, Critical Connections, 44.
4. ADA Handbook. U.S. Department of Justice. (1991). Americans with Disabilities Act Handbook. Washington, DC: U.S. Government Printing Office. Page II-70.
5. Information 2000: Library and Information Services for the 21st Century. A summary report of the 1991 White House Conference on Library and Information Services. (1991). Washington, DC: U.S. Government Printing Office. Page 47.
6. Quarterman, John S. (1990). The MATRIX: Computer networks and conferencing systems worldwide. Burlington, MA: Digital Press. Page 34.

Library Outreach or Patron Inforeach

7. Ibid, Quarterman, 34-37.

8. Wright, Kieth C. (1987). Educating librarians about service to special groups: The emergence of disabled persons into the mainstream. <u>North Carolina Libraries,</u> <u>45</u>, 82: "...librarians should note that information can now be requested and used by persons who cannot see, by those who cannot hear, and by those whose physical conditions previously shut them off from access to any information sources...As libraries turn more and more to online/full text services, information stored in machine-readable form, and access through telecommunications or optical disc, the possibilities for services for disabled persons increase dramatically.

9. Edwards, Sandra. (1989). Computer technology and the physically disabled. <u>Online Computer Library Center Micro,</u> <u>5</u>, 22.

10. Malinconico, S. Michael. (1989). Technologies and barriers to information access. In <u>Effective access to information</u>. Trezza, A.F. (Ed.). Boston: G.K. Hall & Co. Page 132.

11. General Services Administration. (1989). <u>Managing end user computing for users with disabilities</u>. Washington, DC. (ERIC document reproduction service ED 222 726.) Page 2: "Certain add-ons are of particular benefit to users with disabilities; these include speech synthesizers, speech recognition devices, software for screen enlargement, screen review, keystroke control, and other hardware and software items. For users with disabilities, the provision of appropriate add-ons improves access to information resources; in some cases, the add-ons enable an individual to independently complete tasks that previously could not be performed without assistance, due to the disabling condition."

12. U.S. Congress, Office of Technology Assessment. (1988). <u>Power on! New tools for teaching and learning</u>. Washington, DC: U.S. Government Printing Office. Page 14.

13. U.S. Congress, Office of Technology Assessment. (1989). <u>Linking for learning: A new course for education</u>. Washington, DC: U.S. Government Printing Office. 28: "Telecommunications learning opportunities could be extended to other groups of learners who, for a variety of reasons, are educationally disadvantaged or culturally or physically isolated."

14. Wright, Kieth C. & Davie, Judith F. (1989). <u>Library and information services for handicapped individuals</u>. Englewood, CO: Libraries Unlimited.

15. Fitzsimmons, Edward A. (1994). The National Information Infrastructure: An electronic superhighway with promise. <u>Journal of Instructional Delivery Systems,</u> <u>8</u>(1), 4: "Empowerment! We need to create educational environments that allow students to assume the responsibility for their personal learning and development. This makes the student an active participant and the teacher a facilitator, a mentor, a motivator, a navigator helping the student reach positive self-actualization. This isn't something new, it's what all great educators throughout the centuries have worked to do...By the use of skillful questions, facts given at the right time, and resources on demand, the teachers who have made a difference have encouraged their students to think, clarify goals and chart a course of action to reach those goals."

16. Ibid, <u>Critical Connections</u>, 235.

17. Gengle, Dean. (1984). <u>The netweaver's sourcebook: A guide to micro networking and communications</u>. Menlo Park, CA: Addison-Wesley. Page 41-42.

18. Ibid, <u>Linking for Learning</u>, 25.

19. Ibid, <u>General Services Administration</u>, 1.

20. Ibid, Edwards, 22.

21. Library of Congress. (1990). <u>National Library Service for the Blind and Physically Handicapped</u>. Washington, DC: U.S. Government Printing Office.

22. Ibid, <u>National Library Service</u>.

23. Schwartz, G.M. <u>An evaluation model for special education service delivery in state-operated adult and juvenile correctional facilities</u>. Doctoral dissertation. Dissertation Abstracts International: Ann Arbor, Michigan, 50(6), 1629-A. (Order No. DA8921876).

24. Fredrickson, A.A. <u>Teaching incarcerated youths using microcomputer distance education technology: A case study</u>. Doctoral dissertation. Dissertation Abstracts International: Ann Arbor, Michigan, 50(6), 1635-A. (Order no. DA8920896).

25. U.S. Congress, Office of Technology Assessment. (1988). <u>Informing the Nation: Federal information dissemination in an electronic age</u>. Washington, DC: U.S. Government Printing Office. Page 130.

26. Ibid, Informing the Nation, 133.

27. Ibid, ADAAG, 4.31.8.

28. Ibid, ADAAG, 4.31.1.

29. Ibid, ADAAG, 4.31.2.

30. Ibid, ADAAG, 4.2.5.

31. Ibid, ADAAG, 4.2.6.

32. Ibid, ADAAG, A4.31.3.

33. Ibid, ADAAG, 4.31.5.

34. Ibid, ADAAG, A4.31.9.

35. American Telephone and Telegraph. (1993). AT&T toll-free 800 directory: 1993 consumer edition. (2nd Edition). AT&T 800 Information Services: Parsippany, New Jersey.

36. Ibid, ADAAG, 4.31.7.

37. Ibid, Linking for Learning, 33.

38. Ibid, Linking for Learning, 42.

39. U.S. Congress. Public Broadcasting Act of 1967.

40. Quality Educational Data (1986). Video purchasing patterns in schools. Denver, CO.

41. Federal Communications Commission, 1919 M St., N.W., Washington, DC 20554, (202) 632-7260 (Voice) or (202) 632-6999 (TDD).

42. THE CAPTION CENTER, 125 Western Ave., Boston, MA 02134 (617) 492-9225 (Voice/TDD) or (617) 562-0590 (Fax).

43. Johnson, M.K. & Amundsen, C. Distance education: A unique blend of technology and pedagogy to train future special educators. Journal of Special Education Technology, 6(3).

44. Ruconich, S.K., Ashcroft, S.C. & Young, M.F. (1986). Making microcomputers accessible to blind persons. Journal of Special Education Technology, 7(1), 37-46.

45. Ibid, Ruconich.

46. Shell, D.F., Horn, C.A. & Severs, M.A. (1989). Disabled, visually impaired and speech impaired students. Journal of Special Education Technology, 10(1), ??-??.

47. Kurzweil, Raymond. (1992). The futurecast: The end of handicaps, part 1. Library Journal, 69-70. See also, Kurzweil, Raymond. (1992). The futurecast: The end of handicaps, part 2. Library Journal, 66-67.

48. Internal Revenue Service, U.S. Department of the Treasury, 1111 Constitution Ave., N.W., Washington, DC 20224, (202) 566-3292 (Voice) or (800) 829-4059 (TDD), (800) 829-3676 (Publications and Forms).

49. Ibid, Critical Connections, 216: " ...it is necessary to stand back and focus not so much on communication needs per se, but on what people's needs are as individuals, and to ask how communication and the new communication technologies might best fit those needs."

50. Ibid, Fitzsimmons, 4.

51. Ibid, Critical Connections, 212-213.

52. Ibid, General Services Administration, 2.

53. Ibid, Critical Connections, 235.

54. Ibid, Informing the Nation, 132.

55. Ibid, Information 2000, 43.

56. Ibid, Informing the Nation, 316-317.

57. Ibid, Quarterman.

58. Ibid, General Services Administration, 14.

59. Ibid, Critical Connections, 61: "While the proliferation of communication networks makes the communication infrastructure more flexible and response to some users' particular needs, it could serve to limit communication access if it reduces overall system connectivity."

60. Ibid, Critical Connections, 218.

61. Ibid, Critical Connections, 227.

62. Ibid, Critical Connections, 44.

63. ABLEDATA, Adaptive Equipment Center, Newington Children's Hospital, 181 East Cedar St., Newington, CT 06111, (203) 667-5405 (Voice/TDD) or (800) 344-5405 (Voice/TDD).

64. Ibid, Informing the Nation, 57: "The growth of online information industry has been phenomenal. From less than $500 million in annual revenues in 1978, the industry has grown to about $2 billion total revenues in 1986, $3 billion in 1987, and is projected to reach about over $4 billion by 1990."

65. American Library Association. (1986). Commission on freedom and equality of access to information. Chicago, IL: American Library Association. "The new [electronic] technologynot only gives potential users quicker and more convenient access to wider bodies of information, including instantly current information, than can be provided by print alone; it also gives the user a new kind of ability to search through and manipulate the information, and in effect to create new information by the selection, combination, and arrangement of data."

66. Temsky, R. Marlene. (1982). Some suggestions for public library service to disabled persons. Bay State Librarian, 71, 6-7.

67. Adapted from Linking for Learning, 53.

68. Ibid, Critical Connections 232: "Since the 1970s, the debate over the link between socioeconomic status and "access" has intensified, with some claiming that there is an increasing stratification of society based on differential access to communication tools and information sources."

69. Freese, Michele & Cohen, Susan F. (1986). Awareness project for library service for the hearing impaired. Illinois Libraries, 68(1), 552.

70. Ibid, Informing the Nation, 141-142.

71. Ibid, Managing end user, 1: "Consultations with individual users is key to the development of functional performance requirements."

72. Ibid, Managing end user, 15

73. Brand, Stewart. (1988). The media lab: Inventing the future at MIT. New York, NY: Pergamon Press. Page 19: "with digitalization all of the media become translatable to each other-computer bits migrate meriily-and they escape from their traditional means of transmission. A movie, phone call, letter, or magazine article may be sent digitally via phone line, coaxial cable, fiber optic cable, microwave satellite, the broadcast air, or a physical storage medium such as tape or disk. If that's not revolution enough, with digitalization the context becomes totally plastic-any message, sound, or image may be edited from anything into anything else."

74. Ibid, Quarterman, 13-14.

75. Ibid, Quarterman, 29.

76. Cosden, M.A., Michael, M.G., Goldman, S.R., Semmel, D.S. & Semmel, M.I. (1986). Survey of microcomputer access and use by mildly handicapped students in southern California. Journal of Special Education Technology, 7(4), 5-13.

77. Stroble, E.J. Use of electronic mail to facilitate peer group response during the writing process. Doctoral dissertation. Dissertation Abstracts International: Ann Arbor, Michigan, 50(5), 1284-A. (Order no. DA8901250).

78. Woodward, J., Carnine, D., Gersten, R. & Moore, L. (1987). Using computer networking for feedback. Journal of Special Education Technology, 8(4), 28-35.

79. Ibid, Wright & Davie.

80. The Source, P.O. Box 1305, McLean, VA 22102. (800) 336-3366.

81. CompuServe Information System, 5000 Arlington Center Blvd., P.O. Box 20212, Columbus, OH 43220. (614) 457-8650 or (800) 848-8990.

82. Wissick, Cheryl. (1994). On-ramp to the information highway, TAM Newsletter, 9(1), 7-8.

83. Ibid, Quarterman, 34.

84. Ibid. Linking for learning, 33.

85. Ibid, Quarterman, 38-39.

Library Patrons With Disabilities

Subject Index

and References

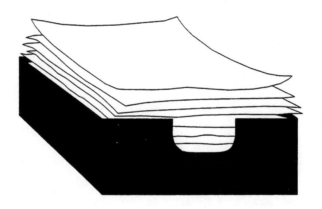

Subject Index:

-A-

Library Patrons With Disabilities

Subject Index and References

Subject Index and References

Library Patrons With Disabilities

-D-

Subject Index and References

Library Patrons With Disabilities

Subject Index and References

-I-

-K-

Library Patrons With Disabilities

Library Patrons With Disabilities

-M-

Library Patrons With Disabilities

Subject Index and References

Library Patrons With Disabilities

Subject Index and References

Library Patrons With Disabilities

Subject Index and References

-S-

Subject Index and References

Library Patrons With Disabilities

Subject Index and References

References:

ADAAG. Appendix B. Americans with Disability Accessibility Guidelines. In, U.S. Department of Justice. (1991). <u>Americans with Disabilities Act Handbook</u>. Washington, DC: U.S. Government Printing Office.

ADA Handbook. U.S. Department of Justice. (1991). <u>Americans with Disabilities Act Handbook</u>. Washington, DC: U.S. Government Printing Office.

Adams, Kathy. (1984). More than meets the eye. <u>CLIC Quarterly</u>, <u>3</u>, 25-28.

Allegri, Francesca. (1984). On the other side of the reference desk: The patron with a physical disability. <u>Medical Reference Services Quarterly</u>, <u>3</u>(3), 65-76.

Alternative Media Corporation. (1979). <u>Telecommunications and services to the developmentally disabled: Needs and opportunities</u> (Working paper WP-3). New York, NY: New York University, School of Art.

American Library Association. (1986). <u>Commission on freedom and equality of access to information</u>. Chicago, IL: American Library Association.

American Library Association. (1988). <u>Information power: Guidelines for school library media programs</u>. Chicago: American Library Association.

American Telephone and Telegraph. (1993). <u>AT&T toll-free 800 directory: 1993 consumer edition. (2nd Edition)</u>. AT&T 800 Information Services: Parsippany, New Jersey.

Barry, A.M.O. & Priestly, L. B. (1980). <u>Coping with inaccessibility: Assisting the wheelchair user</u>. Washington: George Washington University Medical Rehabilitation Research and Training Center.

Beatty, Susan & Maguire, Wesla. (1985). Service to handicapped people. <u>Canadian Library Journal</u>, <u>42</u>, 11-15.

Bekiares, Susan E. (1984). Technology for the Handicapped: Selection and evaluation of aids and devices for the visually impaired. <u>Library Hi Tech</u>, <u>5</u>(2), 57-61.

Blacher, J. (1984). Sequential stages of parental adjustment to the birth of a child with handicaps: Fact or fiction? <u>Mental Retardation</u>, <u>22</u>(2), 551-68.

Brand, Stewart. (1988). <u>The media lab: Inventing the future at MIT</u>. New York, NY: Pergamon Press.

Brandenburg & Vanderheiden (1987). Communication, Control and Computer Access for Disabled and Elderly Individuals. Resource Book 1. (ERIC document reproduction service ED 283 305.)

Braun, Eric. (1994). <u>The INTERNET directory</u>. New York: Ballantine Books.

Cagle, R. Brantley. (1983). Reference service to the developmen-tally disabled: Normalization of access. <u>Catholic Library World</u>, <u>54</u>, 266-270.

Carter, Robert & Jackson, Kathy. (1992). Speech synthesizer and screen reading software make CD-ROM databases accessible to visually impaired users. <u>CD-ROM Professional</u>, <u>5</u>, 129-131.

Cobb, H.B. & Horn, C.J. (1986). Planned change in special education technology. Journal of Special Education Technology, 8(2), 18-27.

Community Childhood Hunger Identification Project. (1991). A survey of childhood hunger in the United States. Washington, DC: Food Research and Action Center.

Cornish, Graham P. (1991). The philosophy behind international interlending and its implications for the visually handicapped. Interlending and Document Supply, 19, 7-10.

Cosden, M.A., Michael, M.G., Goldman, S.R., Semmel, D.S. & Semmel, M.I. (1986). Survey of microcomputer access and use by mildly handicapped students in southern California. Journal of Special Education Technology, 7(4), 5-13.

Cotter, Eithne & McCarty, Emily. (1983). Technology for the handicapped: Kurzweil and VIewscan. Library Hi Tech, 1, 63-67.

Couch, Robert H. (1992). Ramps not steps: A study of accessibility preferences. Journal of Rehabilitation, Winter, 65-69.

Cushman, Ruth-Carol. (1980). The Kurzweil reading machine. Wilson Library Bulletin, 54, 311-315.

Dalton, Phyllis I. (1990). Productivity, not paternalism. Library Personnel News, 4(3), 42-43.

Day, John Michael. (1992). Guidelines for library services to deaf people: Development and interpretation. IFLA Journal, 18, 31-36.

Dequin, Henry C. & Faibisoff, Sylvia G. (1983). The attitudes of public librarians in Illinois toward disabled persons, Illinois Libraries, 65, 231-238.

Developmental Disabilities Assistance and Bill of Rights Act of 1975. Public Law 94-103.

Dick, Walter & Carey, Lou. (1990). The systematic design of instruction. Third Edition. Glenview, Illinois: Scott Foresman.

Editor. (1992). Assistive technology: A student's right. Exceptional Parent, Nov/Dec, 30-32.

Editor. (1993). Berkeley bans bikes on campus pathways. Chronicle of Higher Education, 40(7), A6.

Editor. (1983). California LSCA project to mainstream mentally impaired. Library Journal, 108, 339-340.

Editor. (1988). Library service to hearing impaired people. The Bookmark, 46, 255-256.

Editor. (1989). Library service to the hearing impaired. The Unabashed Librarian, 72, 21-23.

Editor. (1983). Photocopier produces raised-relief Braille copies. Industrial Research & Development, 25, 65-66.

The Education of All Handicapped Children Act, Public Law 94-142.

Edwards, Sandra. (1989). Computer technology and the physically disabled. Online Computer Library Center Micro, 5, 22-23.

Subject Index and References

Ensley, Robert F. (1982). A report on library services for blind and physically handicapped persons in Illinois. Illinois Libraries, 64, 911-916.

Fitzsimmons, Edward A. (1994). The National Information Infrastructure: An electronic superhighway with promise. Journal of Instructional Delivery Systems, 8(1), 4-5.

Foster, Terry & Lindell, Linda. (1991). Libraries and the Americans with Disabilities Act. Texas Libraries, 52, 59-63.

Freiser, W.F.E. (1983). New guidance system for the handicapped. Library Journal, 108(14), 1418.

Freeman, S'Ann & Mabry, Mariana. (1992). The Americans with Disabilities Act (ADA): Library service and the ADA. Public Libraries, 31, 112-114.

Freese, Michele & Cohen, Susan F. (1986). Awareness project for library service for the hearing impaired. Illinois Libraries, 68, 549-622.

Fuller, H. (1981). Access information bulletin: Curb ramps, parking, passenger loading zones and bus stops. Washington: National Center for a Barrier Free Environment.

Gelfand, D.M., Jenson, W.R., & Drew, C.J. (1988). Understanding children's behavior disorders (2nd ed.) New York: Holt, Rinehart & Winston.

General Services Administration. (1989). Managing end user computing for users with disabilities. Washington, DC. (ERIC document reproduction service ED 222 726.)

Gengle, Dean. (1984). The netweaver's sourcebook: A guide to micro networking and communications. Menlo Park, CA: Addison-Wesley.

Gilliland, D. (1989). Library media services to the learning disabled. Unpublished paper. South Dakota Department of Education and Cultural Affairs. Pierre, SD: South Dakota State Library.

Gleadhill, Steve. (1990). Libraries need disability awareness courses. Library Association Record, 92, 213.

Goffman, E. (1975). Characteristics to total institutions. In S. Dinitz, R.R. Dynes & A. C. Clarke (Eds.), Deviance: Studies in definition, management, and treatment. New York: Oxford University Press.

Goltz, Eileen. (1991). The provision of services to students with special needs in Canadian academic libraries. Canadian Library Journal, 48(4), 264-269.

Green, Gill. (1991). It's nice in here, init miss? How a special school reorganized its library. The School Librarian, 39, 51-52.

Gregg, Alison. (1992). On her blindness: Reflections on the use of spoken word cassettes from the public library. Australian Library Journal, 41, 129-132.

Gross, Lois Rubin. (1988). Handicapped children in library programs. Colorado Libraries, 14, 29.

Gunde, Michael. (1991). Working with the Americans with Disabilities Act. Library Journal, 116(21), 99-100.

Library Patrons With Disabilities

Hagemeyer, Alice. (1982). Library service and outreach programs for the deaf. Wyoming Library Roundup, 38(2), 15-21.

Hardman, Michael L., Drew, Clifford J., Egan, Winston & Wolf, Barbara. (1990). Human exceptionality. (3rd Ed.). Boston, MA: Allyn and Bacon.

Harkin, T. (1990). Responses to issues raised about the Americans with Disabilities Act of 1990. Washington, D.C.: United States Senate.

Havens, Shirley E. (1987). Large print in focus. Library Journal, 112, 32-34.

Haynes, Douglas E. (1989). The switch library: New service in rehabilitation librarianship. Bulletin of the Medical Library Association, 77, 15-18.

Heinich, Robert, Molenda, Michael & Russell, James D. (1989). Instructional media and the new technologies of instruction: Third edition. New York: MacMillan.

Heiskell Library. (1992). Heiskell Library for the blind opens in New York City. School Library Journal, 38, 13.

Hill, Everett & Ponder, Purvis. (1976). Orientation and mobility techniques: A guide for the practitioner. New York: American Foundation for the Blind.

Hiltz, S.R. & Turoff, M. (1985). Structuring computer-mediated communication systems to avoid information overload. Communications of the ACM, 28(7), 680-689.

Hirsch, E.B. & Lowenstein, A.K. (1984). Homebound and senior citizen service at the Allard K. Lowenstein Public Library. The Bookmark, 42(11), 99-101.

Hodges, Laura J. (1989). You've got what it takes: Public library services to persons who are mentally retarded. Reference Quarterly, 28(4), 463-469.

Hoehne, Charles W. (1977). Service delivery systems for handicapped individuals. In, U.S. Government. (1977). White House Conference on Handicapped Individuals: Awareness Papers. Washington, DC: U.S. Government Printing Office. Page 391.

Hoffman, Preston. (1992). Covert entry: The backdoor electronic revolution. Wilson Library Bulletin, 35-37.

Homeward Bound V. The Hissom Memorial Center. 1988.

Hopf, P.S. & Raeber, J.A. (1984). Access for the handicapped: The barrier free regulations for design and construction in all 50 states. New York: Van Nostrand Reinhold.

Howard, Cate. (1984). Exceptional children: How do we serve them? North Carolina Libraries, 42, 127-128.

Howell, Richard. (1989). Some issues related to technological intervention with disabled learners: Cues for instructional designers. Ohio Media Spectrum, 41, 50-53.

Howells, Lesley. (1987). Library service to physically handicapped children. In Pacific Rim Conference on Children's Literature. 1987. Melbourne State College. Scarecrow Press. 260-269.

Subject Index and References

International Business Machines. National Support Center for Persons with Disabilities. (1991). Resource Guide for persons with mobility impairments. Atlanta, GA: IBM.

International Business Machines. National Support Center for Persons with Disabilities. (1991). Resource Guide for persons with vision impairments. Atlanta, GA: IBM.

Information 2000: Library and Information Services for the 21st Century. A summary report of the 1991 White House Conference on Library and Information Services. (1991). Washington, DC: U.S. Government Printing Office.

Irwin, Marilyn. (1992). Library Media Specialist as teacher for students who are disabled. Indiana Media Journal. 14, 19-24.

Irwin, Marilyn. (1992). Library media specialist: Information specialist for students with disabilities. Indiana Media Journal, 14(1), 11-15.

Jackson, Kathy. (1992). Vista: The big picture in color. CD-ROM Professional, 5, 124-126.

Jahoda, Gerald & Johnson, Elizabeth A. (1987). The use of the Kurzweil reading machine in academic libraries. Journal of Academic Librarianship, 13(2), 99-103.

Jaschik, Scott. (1994). Colleges and the disabled. Chronicle of Higher Education, 90(33), A38-39.

Johnson, M.K. & Amundsen, C. Distance education: A unique blend of technology and pedagogy to train future special educators. Journal of Special Education Technology, 6(3).

Kazlauskas, Diane W., Weaver, Sharon T. & Jones, William R. (1987). Kurzweil reading machine: A study of usage patterns. Journal of Academic Librarianship, 12(6), 356-358.

Kilburn, Joan. (1983). Changing attitudes. Teaching Exceptional Children, 124-128.

Kirtley, D.D. (1975). The psychology of blindness. Chicago, IL: Nelson-Hall.

Kruger, Kathleen Joyce. (1984). Library service to disabled citizens: Guidelines to sources and issues. Technicalities, 4(9), 8-9.

Kuhlenschmidt, Eden, Swan, Kim & Scholes, Jan. (1992). Ms. K, there's a tiger in the computer. Indiana Media Journal, 14, 6-10.

Kurshan, B. (1990). Educational telecommunications connections for the classroom-Part 1. The Computing Teacher. 17(6), 30-35.

Kurshan, B. (1990b). Educational telecommunications connections for the classroom-Part 2. The Computing Teacher. 17(7), 51-52.

Kurzweil, Raymond. (1992). The futurecast: The end of handicaps, part 1. Library Journal, 69-70.

Kurzweil, Raymond. (1992). The futurecast: The end of handicaps, part 2. Library Journal, 66-67.

Lane, Elizabeth & Lane, James. (1982). Reference materials for the disabled. Reference Services Review, 10, 73-76.

Library Patrons With Disabilities

Laurie, Ty D. (1992). Libraries' duties to accomodate their patrons under the Americans with Disabilities Act. Library Administration & Management, 6, 204-205.

Leatherman, Donald G. (1989). Reaching out to the community. Texas Libraries, 50(2), 61-66.

Lederman, Douglas. (1994). Crime on the campuses. Chronicle of Higher Education, XL(22), A31-41.

Leung, P. (1990). Editor's comments. Journal of Rehabilitation, 56, 5.

Lewis, Christopher. (1992). The Americans with Disabilities Act and Its Effect on Public Libraries. Public Libraries, 31, 25-28.

Lewis, Pauline. (1988). Breaking silence-reaching out to persons who are deaf and hearing impaired. The Bookmark, 46, 252-255.

Library Association. (1990). Libraries need disability awareness courses. Library Association Record, 92, 213.

Library of Congress. (1990). National Library Service for the Blind and Physically Handicapped. Washington, DC: U.S. Government Printing Office.

Library of Congress. (1991). National library service urges standardization at IFLA. Library of Congress Information Bulletin, 50, 369.

Library of Congress. (1983). NLS/BPH produces first voice-indexed dictionary. Library of Congress Information Bulletin, 42, 227-228.

Liner, D.S. (Ed.). (1987). Tactile maps: A listing of maps in the National Library Service for the Blind and Physically Handicapped Collection. Washington, DC: The Library of Congress.

Lisson, Paul. (1987). Large print placebo. Canadian Library Journal, 44, 5-6.

Lucas, Linda. (1983). Education for work with disabled and institutionalized persons. Journal of Education for Librarianship, 23, 207-223.

McCarthy, Robert. (1990). The new library/media center. Electronic Learning, 9(8), 25-28.

McCormick, John A. (1994). Computers and the Americans with Disabilities Act: A Manager's Guide. New York: Windcrest/McGraw-Hill. Pages 216-235.

McCullough, Sheila & Mitchell, Ann. (1988). Disabled Users: How they view and use the public library service. Scottish Libraries, 12, 13.

McDaniel, Julie Ann. (1991). They can't hear us does not mean we can't serve them. Journal of Library Administration, 16(14), 131-141.

Major, Jean A. (1982). The visually impaired reader in the academic library. In, Library services for the handicapped adult. Thomas, J.L. & Thomas, C.H. (Eds.). Phoenix, AZ: Oryx Press. Pages 39-48.

Malinconico, S. Michael. (1989). Technologies and barriers to information access. In Effective access to information. Trezza, A.F. (Ed.). Boston: G.K. Hall. Pages 123-137.

Subject Index and References

Mannheim, Peter. (1992). The Americans with Disabilities Act: The legal implications. In, Foos, Donald D. & Pack, Nancy C. (Eds.). (1992). How libraries must comply with the Americans with Disabilities Act (ADA). Phoenix, AZ: Oryx. Pages 89-111.

Maslow, Abraham. (1943). A theory of motivation. Psychological Bulletin, 50, 370-396.

Matthews, Karen. (1985). Survey of public library services for deaf people. The Bookmark, 43(3), 138-143.

Medrinos, Roxanne Baxter. (1992). CD-ROM and at-risk students. School Library Journal, 38, 29-31

Merker, Hannah. (1992). Deaf patron/ex-librarian rejects board's apology. American Libraries, 201-202.

Midkiff, Ruby B., Towery, Ron & Roark, Susan. (1991). Accomodating learning style needs of academically at-risk students in the library/media center. Ohio Media Spectrum, 43(1), 45-51.

Miller, Richard T. (1992). The Americans with Disabilities Act: Library facility and program access under Titles II and III. Ohio Libraries, 5, 8-11.

Mong, Bonnie. (1986). Special education students can use the library. Indiana Media Journal, 8, 9-10.

Mooney, Carolyn J. (1993). Cultured murmur of academe threatens to be lost in the roar over parking. Chronicle of Higher Education, 39(49), 15-16.

Mularski, Carol. (1987). Academic library service to deaf students: Survey and recommendations. Reference Quarterly, 26, 477-486.

National Commission on Children. (1991). Beyond rhetoric-a new American agenda for children and families: Final report of the National Comission on Children. Washington, DC: U.S. Government Printing Office.

National Endowment for the Arts. (1992). The arts and 504: A handbook for accessible arts programming. Washington, DC: U.S. Government Printing Office.

National Library Service. (1991). National Library Service urges standardization at IFLA. Library of Congress Information Bulletin, 50, 369.

Needham, George M. (1987). Special needs, special resources. Ohio Library Association Bulletin, 57, 26-28.

Needham, William & Jahoda, Gerald. (1983). Improving library service to physically disabled persons. Littleton, CO: Libraries Unlimited.

Neff, Evaline B. Library Programs for the Handicapped. Fiscal year 1987. Office of Educational Research and Improvement. Washington, DC. (ERIC document reproduction service ED 328 278.)

Neville, Ann & Kupersmith, John. (1991). Online access for visually impaired students. Database, 14, 102-104.

New York Library Association. (1992). Guidelines for serving persons with a hearing impairment. Library Trends, 41, 164-172.

Library Patrons With Disabilities

Nicholson, Nowana. (1992). Instructional consulting in the inclusive school: A new role for media specialists. Indiana Media Journal, 14, 1-5.

No Author. (1986). Gallaudet bookmarks spread info on deafness. Library Journal, 111(11), 20

No author. (1985). Hearing aid system for library programs. Library Journal, 110, 24.

O'Donnell, Ruth. (1992). Adapting print for improved access. Library Journal, October 1, 1992, 68-69.

O'Donnell, Ruth. (1992). Adapting print for improved access. Part 2. Library Journal, November 1, 1992, 60-61.

O'Donnell, Ruth. (1992). Breaking down those physical barriers. Library Journal, May 1, 1992, 60-61.

O'Donnell, Ruth. (1992). Electronic aids for the hearing impaired. Library Journal, September 1, 1992, 156-157.

O'Donnell, Ruth. (1992). Helping those with hearing loss. Library Journal, July, 1992, 54-55.

Oertli, David L. (1992). The Americans with Disabilities Act: Nebraska libraries encounter an equal rights bill. Nebraska Library Association Quarterly, 23(2), 9-14.

Oren, Tim, Salomon, Gitta, Kreitman, Kristee & Don, Abbe. (1990). Guides: Characterizing the interface. In, The art of human-computer interface design. Laurel, Brenda (Ed.). Reading, MA: Addison Wesley. Pages 367-381.

Pack, Nancy C. & Foos, Donald D. (1992). Planning for compliance with the Americans with Disabilities Act. Public Libraries, 31, 225-228.

Pendleton, V.E.M. (1988). Libraries and the Americans with Disabilities Act. Ohio Libraries, 4, 28-29.

Phinney, Eleanor. (1977). The librarian and the patient. Chicago, IL: American Library Association.

Pinion, Catherine F. (1990). Audio services for the blind and partially sighted in public libraries. Audiovisual Librarian, 16, 24-28.

Powell, Faye. (1990). A library center for disabled students. College & Research Libraries News, 51, 418-420.

Power, M.T., Rundlett, Carol & David, Myra. (1989). New challenges in helping students uncover information: The learning disabled student. The Bookmark, 47(11), 213-216.

Prevratil, Judy. (1985). Library service to the hard-of-hearing: A workshop report. The Unabashed Librarian, 55, 11.

Prostano, Emanual T. & Prostano, Joyce S. (1987). The school library media center. 4th Ed. Littleton, CO: Libraries Unlimited.

Public Law 93-112, 87 Stat. 394 (29 U.S.C. 794), as amended.

Purdue, Bill. (1984). Talking newspapers and magazines. Audiovisual Librarian, 10, 82-85.

Subject Index and References

Quality Educational Data (1986). <u>Video purchasing patterns in schools</u>. Denver, CO.

Quarterman, John S. (1990). <u>The MATRIX: Computer networks and conferencing systems worldwide</u>. Burlington, MA: Digital Press.

Quay, H.C. (1975). Classification in the treatment of delinquency and antisocial behavior. In N. Hobbs (Ed.), <u>Issues in the classification of children</u>. Vol. 1. San Francisco: Jossey-Bass.

Raffa, M.F. (1985). Removing architectural barriers: The architectural barriers act of 1968. <u>Mental and Physical Disability Law Reporter</u>, <u>9</u>(4), 304-308.

Rheingold, Howard. (1990). An interview with Don Norman. In <u>The art of human-computer interface design</u>. Laurel, Brenda (Ed.) Menlo Park, CA: Addison Wesley. Page 10.

Ritter, Audrey. (1981). The college library serving hearing impaired students. <u>The Bookmark</u>, <u>40</u>, 21.

Roatch, Mary A. (1992). High tech and library access for people with disabilities. <u>Public Libraries</u>, <u>31</u>, 88-98.

Roberts, Melissa Locke. (1985). Welcoming disabled readers to a new world of information. <u>Texas Libraries</u>, <u>46</u>, 54-59.

Robinson, Joan & Henry, Margaret. (1982). Serving the disabled borrower. <u>Ontario Library Review</u>, <u>66</u>, 13-22.

Rogers, Everett. (1983). <u>Diffusion of innovation.</u> Third Edition. New York: The Free Press.

Ruconich, S.K., Ashcroft, S.C. & Young, M.F. (1986). Making microcomputers accessible to blind persons. <u>Journal of Special Education Technology</u>, 7(1), 37-46.

Salter, Charles A. & Salter, Jeffrey L. (1988). <u>On the front lines: Coping with the library's problem patrons</u>. Englewood, CO: Libraries Unlimited.

Sangster, Collette. (1986). Guidelines for library services to hearing-impaired persons. <u>The Bookmark</u>, <u>44</u>, 104-108.

Schell, G.C. (1981). The young handicapped child: A family perspective. <u>Topics in Early Childhood Special Education</u>, <u>1</u>(3), 21-28.

Schwartz, G.M. <u>An evaluation model for special education service delivery in state-operated adult and juvenile correctional facilities</u>. Doctoral dissertation. Dissertation Abstracts International: Ann Arbor,

Shaw, Alison. (1986). Better services for the visually handicapped. <u>Library Association Record</u>, <u>88</u>(2), 85.

Simpson, Jerome D. (1991). The sound of many voices: Library access for the print impaired. <u>School Library Journal</u>, <u>37</u>, 61.

Smale, Rebecca. (1992). Australian university library services for visually impaired students: Results of a survey. <u>The Australian Library Journal</u>, <u>41</u>, 199-212.

Library Patrons With Disabilities

Stroble, E.J. Use of electronic mail to facilitate peer group response during the writing process. Doctoral dissertation. Dissertation Abstracts International: Ann Arbor, Michigan, 50(5), 1284-A. (Order no. DA8901250).

Summit, Leon. (1983). Counting the invisible. School Library Journal, 29, 5.

Szymanski, Edna Mora. (1994) Transition: Life-span and life-space considerations for empowerment. Exceptional Children, 60(5), 402-410.

Temsky, R. Marlene. (1982). Some suggestions for public library service to disabled persons. Bay State Librarian, 71, 4-10.

Thiele, Paul E. (1984). New technologies for the blind reading community. Canadian Library Journal, 41, 131-139.

U.S. Architectural and Transportation Barriers Compliance Board. (1992). Americans with Disabilities Act Accessibility Guidelines Checklist for Buildings and Facilities. Washington, DC: U.S. Government Printing Office.

U.S. Congress, House of Representatives, Select Committee on Children, Youth and Families. No place to call home: Discarded children in America. (1989). Washington, D.C. U.S. Government Printing Office.

U.S. Congress, Office of Technology Assessment. (1990). Critical Connections: Communication for the Future. Washington, DC: U.S. Government Printing Office.

U.S. Congress, Office of Technology Assessment. (1988). Informing the Nation: Federal information dissemination in an electronic age. Washington, DC: U.S. Government Printing Office.

U.S. Congress, Office of Technology Assessment. (1989). Linking for learning: A new course for education. Washington, DC: U.S. Government Printing Office.

U.S. Congress, Office of Technology Assessment. (1988). Power on! New tools for teaching and learning. Washington, DC: U.S. Government Printing Office.

U.S. Congress, Office of Technology Assessment. (1991). Rural America at the crossroads: Networking for the future. Washington, DC: U.S. Government Printing Office.

U. S. Congress. Student Right-to-Know and Campus Security Act of 1990. (Federal Register, October 22, 1993).

U.S. Department of Justice. (1991). Americans with Disabilities Act Handbook. Washington, DC: U.S. Government Printing Office.

U.S. Department of Labor. Occupational Safety and Health Administration. (1991). Working safety with video display terminals. Washington, DC: U.S. Government Printing Office.

U.S. Government. (1977). White House Conference on Handicapped Individuals: Awareness Papers. Washington, DC: U.S. Government Printing Office.

Velleman, Ruth A. (1979). Serving physically disabled people. New York: R.R. Bowker. Page 145.

Subject Index and References

Vertelney, Laurie, Arent, Michael and Lieberman, Henry. (1990). Two disciplines in search of an interface: Reflections on a design problem. In, The art of human-computer interface design. Laurel, Brenda (Ed.) Menlo Park, CA: Addison Wesley. Page 53.

Wagner, Ellen D. (1988). Instructional design and development: Contingency management for distance education. Paper presented to the American Symposium on Research in Distance Education, July 24-27, 1988. Page 12.

Walling, Linda Lucas. (1992). Granting each equal access. School Library Media Quarterly, 20, 216-222.

Weinberg, Belle. (1980). The Kurzweil machine: Half a miracle. American Libraries, 11, 603-604, 627.

Weingand, Darlene E. (1990). The invisible client: Meeting the needs of persons with learning disabilities. In The Reference Librarian. New York: Haworth Press. Pages 77-88.

Wesson, Caren L. & Keefe, Margaret. (1989). Teaching library skills to special education students. School Library Media Quarterly, 17(2), 71-77.

Wigmore, Hilary & Morris, Deirdre. (1988). Opening doors to disabled people: Improving services for the disabled library user. Library Association Record, 90(3), 153-156.

Willoughby, Edith L. (1983). Library services in a school for the blind. Catholic Library World, 54, 120-121.

Wissick, Cheryl. (1994). On-ramp to the information highway, TAM Newsletter, 9(1), 7-8.

Wolfe, Gail E. (1991). Management paper: Management of materials for Indiana youth with visual disabilities. Indiana Media Journal, 13, 18-19.

Wolfensberger, W. (1975). The principle of normalization. In B. Blatt (Ed.), An alternative textbook in special education. Denver, CO: Love Publishing Co.

Wood, K.S. (1971). Terminology and nomenclature. In L.E. Travis (Ed.), Handbook of speech pathology and audiology. New York: Appleton-Century-Crofts.

Wright, Benjamin. (1990). Computer mediated communication and the law. In Quarterman, John S. (1990). The MATRIX: Computer networks and conferencing systems worldwide. Burlington, MA: Digital Press. Pages 637-655.

Wright, Kieth C. (1987). Educating librarians about service to special groups: The emergence of disabled persons into the mainstream. North Carolina Libraries, 45, 79-82.

Wright, Kieth C. & Davie, Judith F. (1989). Library and information services for handicapped individuals. Englewood, CO: Libraries Unlimited.

Yuker, Harold, Block, H.R. & Young, Janet H. (1966) The measurement of attitudes toward disabled persons. Albertson, NY: Human Resources Center.

Zipkowitz, Fay. (1990). "No one wants to see them: Meeting the reference needs of the deinstitutionalized." The Reference Librarian. New York: Hawthorn Press. Pages 53-67.

Library Patrons With Disabilities